JACK & BOBBY

JACK&BOBBY

Leo McKinstry

TED SMART

This edition produced for The Book People Ltd,
Hall Wood Avenue, Haydock, St Helens, WA11 9UL

First published in 2002 by
CollinsWillow
an imprint of HarperCollins*Publishers*
London

1 3 5 7 9 8 6 4 2

A CIP catalogue record for this book is
available from the British Library

ISBN 0 00 767192 X

Set in Minion with Folio Display by
Rowland Phototypesetting Ltd,
Bury St Edmunds, Suffolk

Printed and bound in Great Britain by
William Clowes Limited, Beccles and London

The HarperCollins website address is
www.fireandwater.com

Career appendix by David Reilly

Photographic acknowledgments
Action Images 6cl, 7cl, 8b, 9b, 13t;
Colorsport 1t, 1b, 2, 3, 6b, 15c; **Empics** 4br, 6cr,
8t, 15bl, 16tr, 16bl; **Hulton Archive** 4t, 7t, 8c, 10b, 12t, 13br,
14t; **Mirror Syndication** 7b; **Popperfoto** 4bl, 5t, 5cr, 5cl,
5b, 6t, 9t, 11t, 11c, 12c, 14b, 15t, 15br, 16tl, 16br;
Rex Features 12b, 14c.

To James Perry,
whose devotion to Torquay United should have
resulted in a long spell in Broadmoor

Contents

Acknowledgements

Firstly, I would like to thank the makers of Bacardi Rum and Carlsberg Special lager, without whose constant refreshment this volume would have never been written.

The central theme of this book has been the yawning chasm between Bobby and Jack Charlton, but on one recent issue they have been united: neither of them wanted to co-operate with this biography. They were both perfectly civil when I informed them of my research but said they did not wish to be involved.

Many other people, however, have proved extremely helpful and I wish to place on record my thanks to them. I am grateful to all those footballers who provided me with first-hand testimony about Bobby and Jack as players, including Tony Allen, Stan Anderson, John Aston, Joe Baker, Willie Bell, Warren Bradley, Martin Buchan, Francis Burns, Noel Cantwell, Joe Carolan, Alan Clarke, Ronnie Clayton, Ronnie Cope, John Docherty, Jimmy Dunn, Bryan Douglas, Bobby Forrest, Barry Fry, Freddie Goodwin, Alan Gowling, Ian Greaves, Harry Gregg, David Harvey, Bobby Harrop, Frank Haydock, Johnny Haynes, Doug Holden, Norman Hunter, Reg Hunter, Joe Jordan, Frank Kopel, Brian Labone, Nobby Lawton, Peter Lorrimer, Wilf McGuinness, Sammy McMillan, Bob McNab, Willie Morgan, Albert Nightingale, George O'Brien, Alan Peacock,

Fred Pickering, Ray Pointer, David Sadler, Ian St John, Carlo Sartori, Albert Scanlon, Maurice Setters, Ian Storey-Moore, Derek Temple, Peter Thompson, Tony Waiters, Walter Whitehurst, Wilf Tranter, and Ray Wood. I am also in the debt of the many other professionals who talked to me about the performances of Bobby and Jack as managers: John Aldridge, David Armstrong, Liam Brady, Tony Cascarino, John Craggs, Stan Cummins, Brian Hornsby, David Kelly, Mark Lawrenson, Mick McCarthy, Andy McCulloch, Alan McLoughlin, Ian Mellor, Tony Morley, John Pearson, Mike Pickering, Mark Smith, Ray Treacy, Ray Tunks, and Gary Waddock.

I would particularly like to thank two Irishmen for all the information they gave me. One is John Giles, who, as a former Manchester United and Leeds player and Eire manager, is uniquely placed to analyse the careers of the two brothers. The other is Eamon Dunphy, Ireland's most brilliant and controversial broadcaster, who could not have been more generous with both time and memories of the Charltons.

On the Charltons' background in Ashington, the advice and support of Mike Kirkup, a local historian and contemporary of Bobby and Jack's, was invaluable during my several visits to the north-east. His own books make fascinating reading, especially his superb life of another Ashington football hero Jackie Milburn. I would like to thank those others from Ashington who gave me interviews: Ronnie Cameron, Alan Lavelle, Walter Lavery, Jackie Lothian, Bill Merryweather, Ken Prior, Ron Routledge, Rob Storey, and Bobby Whitehead.

Further insights into various aspects of the careers of Bobby and Jack were provided by Laura Crowther, Steve Double, Brian Glanville, Paul Greengrass, Tom Hedderley, Bill Hodgkiss, Graham Kelly, Alec McGivan, Evan Martin, Mike Newland, Les Olive, Mark Piermann, Chris Robinson, and Maurice Watkins. More assistance came from a large number of commentators, journalists and authors, including Clive Crickmer, Vince Gledhill, Bryan James, Richard Kurt, Lynda Lee-Potter, Martin Lipton, Iain McCartney, Ken Montgomery, Jeff Powell, Brian Scovell, Frank Taylor, Andy

Walsh, Jim White, and the late Kenneth Wolstenholme. I am especially grateful to Michael Crick, the author of the recent magisterial life of Sir Alex Ferguson, for all his advice. The research for this book would not have been possible without the assistance of the following institutions: the BBC archives, BBC Manchester, London Weekend Television, the House of Commons, the libraries of the *Daily Mail*, the *Manchester Evening News*, the *Yorkshire Post*, the *Newcastle Journal*, and Ashington, Newcastle, Sheffield and Manchester reference libraries. John Robinson at Soccer Books Ltd was very helpful in tracking down out of print titles, while David Reilly at the Association of Football Statisticians produced an excellent appendix.

Finally, I would like to thank Michael Doggart and Tom Whiting at CollinsWillow for all their excellent work in overseeing the project so wisely and patiently. As always, a huge debt of gratitude is due to my literary agent, Andrew Lownie, and to my beloved wife Elizabeth and Jack Russell terrier Matthew for all their support and tolerance.

Introduction

The images of that Saturday afternoon in July 1966 have become forever ingrained on our national consciousness: Jack Charlton falling to his knees at the final whistle, his face buried in his hands as if in grateful, exhausted prayer; his brother Bobby crying freely as he climbs up to the Royal Box to collect his World Cup winner's medal. It was a display of emotion that perfectly captured the mood of triumph and relief that swept across the country.

'Nobody can ever take this moment away from us,' said Bobby to his brother as they hugged each other at the end of the match. He was absolutely correct. Whatever else they have achieved in life, the two Charlton brothers will always be best remembered for their part in England's glory of 1966. Indeed, their contrasting roles on the field symbolized the virtues of England's performance during that unique campaign: Jack, the rock of the defence, ungainly but uncompromising, lacking sophistication but never valour, as tough and honest as the mining stock into which he was born; Bobby, the fulcrum of the attack, gliding across the turf like a thoroughbred, destroying opponents with his explosive goals, long-range passes and incisive runs. Never, it seemed, were there two more patriotic footballers, willing, in Churchill's phrase, to give 'blood, toil, tears and sweat' in the national cause.

The bond between the brothers, forged at birth and reinforced by their mutual choice of a career in football, must have seemed unbreakable that day at Wembley. Any belief that they were close to each other can only have been strengthened by a host of other striking parallels about their lives. Both played the game obsessively in their youth and turned out for the same local YMCA side. Both joined major city clubs, Leeds and Manchester United, at exactly the same age, 15, and each won a cabinet-full of domestic honours. In 1965, they became the first brothers this century to play together for England. The links continued after the triumph of 1966. Both retired from First Division football in the same year, after careers of outstanding loyalty – each holds the League appearance record for their club, Jack with 629 for Leeds, Bobby with 606 for Manchester United. Both started in League management in the same 1973/74 season in the Second Division. Later, they both became major figures on the international stage, Jack as a brilliantly successful manager of the Republic of Ireland, Bobby as a roving ambassador for top-class sports bids, such as the campaign to bring the 2006 World Cup to England.

Brought up in a close-knit working-class mining community where the values of respectability were paramount, both have had led lives of restraint and dignity. Given their celebrity status – Jimmy Hill once described Bobby, not unjustly, as 'the most famous Englishman in the world' – it would have been easy for either of them to have fallen into the destructive pattern of heavy drinking, financial chaos and private dissolution that has characterized the lives of too many sporting greats, such as George Best, James Hunt or Denis Compton. Yet there has never been a whiff of scandal about their personal lives, both of them enjoying remarkably strong, happy marriages, as well as becoming millionaires through football and business. As John Giles, of Leeds, Manchester United and Ireland, put it to me: 'I think Bobby and Jack have been great ambassadors for both football and for working-class England, because they have always behaved impeccably throughout their careers, handling fame and fortune in a way that most people could not begin to comprehend. They have never put a foot wrong, never become big-headed or gone astray. There is an underlying decency about them which stems from that background.'

That spirit of honour extended to football, where they were seen by most of their colleagues as hard-working professionals, fiercely competitive by nature, who would never let their side down. 'The great thing about Jack,' says his former Leeds colleague Willie Bell, 'was that he would absolutely never give up. I have seen Jack with blood running down his face and, even then, he would not come off the field. He would never surrender, even when we were down, and that attitude rubbed off on the rest of the team. He was just a great professional.' It is a view echoed by David Harvey, the Leeds and Scotland goalkeeper, who told me: 'It was very reassuring to have Jack in front of me. He was a bit of a Godfather, looking after me really well. He was so commanding, always shouting at the rest of us and organizing the defence like a military policeman. He always played to such a high standard. His consistency was first class, no matter what the occasion.'

Exactly the same views are expressed about Bobby. His team-mate David Sadler says, 'Bobby had a terrific appetite and energy for the game and always worked so hard for the team. He took the knocks, which are part and parcel of football, and just got on with it.' Martin Buchan recalls him as an ideal professional, even at the end of his career: 'He was so utterly dedicated, dedicated to both United and to football. He was a wonderful example to any youngster coming into the game. I remember once, in his last season, he was left out of the team and when he got the news, he did not storm out of the ground, as a lot of other players would have done, but instead put his kit on and did several laps around the pitch, just so he would remain fit. That was the kind of man he was, always working so hard.' It was because of this outlook that both Bobby and Jack fitted easily into Sir Alf Ramsey's England team of the 1960s, where so much emphasis was placed on the work ethic.

Yet, for all such superficial similarities, the really fascinating point about Jack and Bobby is how utterly different they are. Almost every person who knows them says that they are 'chalk and cheese' – so dissimilar that it is hard to believe that they are from the same family. 'The difference between them is enormous,' says Ian Greaves, the former Manchester United player, who went on to be a highly successful manager at Huddersfield, Bolton and Mansfield. 'You would not take them for brothers at all. I remember Jack in his early days at Leeds: loud, ebullient, down to earth and very, very stubborn. All he wanted to do was party and fight. He was so unlike Bobby, who was very quiet, shy, polite.' Joe Carolan, another Manchester United player, agrees: 'Jack is a different kettle of fish altogether from Bobby. Bobby was a gentleman, whereas Jack would kick you straight up in the air. Jack would never shut up on the field, but you hardly ever heard a word out of Bobby.'

This chasm between Bobby and Jack covers every aspect of their lives, from the playing styles to their political outlook. In truth, it is not just that they are different, but that they are almost opposites. On the football field, for instance, Jack was the Roundhead, Bobby the Cavalier. Bobby's entire game was focused on scoring goals, Jack's on stopping them. Bobby's football vocabulary was dominated by words like creative, opening, expansive and flair, whereas Jack's was filled with terms like keeping it tight and closing them down. A 0–0 draw was a triumph for Jack, a disaster for Bobby. Where Bobby was hailed by international critics for his attacking genius, Jack was seen as the epitome of rugged English defending.

In action, Bobby was lithe and fluent, while Jack was angular and hard. Hardly a soul would pay to watch Jack Charlton play; millions did to watch Bobby. Even the most cynical professionals admit that when Bobby was in full flow, there was no more beautiful sight in football. In 1969 *The Times* football correspondent Geoffrey Green wrote this famous description of Bobby's approach: 'It is the explosive facets of his play that will remain in the memory. His thinning, fair hair streaming in the wind, he has moved like a ship in full sail. He always possessed an elemental quality; jinking, changing feet and direction, turning gracefully on the ball, or accelerating through a gap surrendered by a confused enemy.' Contrast that lyricism with the words of Bobby Moore about Jack: 'Some days we would be going out and I'd look at him and wonder how this big giraffe played football. We used to argue black and blue because I wanted to get the ball down and play the game and he wanted to hoof it away to safety.' In the same way, Bobby played far more within the rules of the game. During his long career, he was only booked twice, and both of those were in dubious circumstances when he had not committed any foul but was deemed to have shown dissent. 'He was like a giant who would kick anything. If you were in the way, you went with it. He was hard, really hard,' says Tony Allen of Stoke and England.

Jack and Bobby were from the Milburn footballing clan of Northumberland. But their football reflected the two different sides of this family. So Jack followed in the footsteps of his four uncles, who were all uncompromising defenders with top-class clubs, and his great-grandfather Jack Milburn, who was known to local fans as 'Warhorse'. Bobby took much more after his mother's cousin, the great Newcastle and England striker Jackie Milburn, whose brilliant goals in the 1950s made him perhaps the most loved of all Geordie footballers.

Physically, Jack and Bobby do not look like brothers at all. 'Bobby is handsome, whereas Jack is ugly,' is the rather brutal verdict of former Liverpool winger Peter Thompson. Jack is gangly, 6′ 3″, thin, with a long neck and telescopic legs and 'looks like a cactus', according to Brian Labone, his England rival for the centre-half position. Bobby is much shorter, just 5′ 9″, and, when he was a player, he was built like an athlete. 'When we were in first in the dressing room together,' says Bob McNab of Arsenal and England, 'what really struck me about Bobby was his magnificent physique. We worked out at Arsenal more than at most other clubs, but it really impressed me how strong Bobby was. I could not believe what he looked like. Besides his supreme gifts as a footballer, God gave him a great body to go with it.' In contrast, McNab claims that Jack was 'a big, horrible bugger, not likely to win any fashion competition'.

There is just as big a contrast in their personalities. Jack is explosive, gregarious, self-confident, and voluble. A brilliant after-dinner speaker, he loves an audience and speaking his mind. 'He would argue anything with anyone,' says his wife Pat. Forgetful and disorganised, he cares little about his appearance and became notorious in the football world for his untidiness in both the dressing room and hotels.

Every one of these traits is absent in Bobby. A stickler for punctuality, he is always well groomed. Where Jack does not have a shy bone in his body, shyness is the word that is most frequently used about Bobby. This characteristic is sometimes regarded as aloofness, a charge often labelled at him by some hardcore Manchester United fans of today. In the football fraternity, his occasional reluctance to greet others has caused more offence than his brother's expression of his forthright views. Former United manager Ron Atkinson has even described him as a 'grizzlin' old misery, a dour, very distant individual.' The truth is that Bobby, because of his self-conscious, reserved nature, is wary of strangers and dislikes large public gatherings, much preferring the company of a small circle of trusted friends. Hearing the sound of his own voice is a delight to Jack, an anathema to Bobby.

With his fiery temper and rhinoceros hide, Jack can dish it out and take it much more easily than Bobby, who is sensitive to criticism and cannot ignore a slight. John Giles recalls, 'I would have a blazing row with Jack on Saturday. We would even be grabbing each other by the throat, especially because Jack has a short fuse, and over the weekend I would think about it. On Monday I would come in and say, "Sorry Jack," and he would have genuinely forgotten about it. Bobby would be different. He would take a row to heart, and might not speak for a week afterwards.' Because of his willingness to express his opinions, Jack's career has been littered with public controversies, perhaps most notoriously over his claim, made on television in 1970, that he had 'a little black book' in which he kept the names of his footballing enemies. It turned out to be a joke, for the 'little black book' existed only in Jack's volatile imagination. But the row did him untold damage at the Football

Association, perhaps ensuring that he was never appointed to the England management job he wanted so badly. Bobby, on the other hand, became a standard bearer for the English game, serving as a director of Manchester United and an ambassador for England's World Cup bid in 2006.

Yet the same diplomatic streak meant Bobby was doomed to fail in management when he took over at Preston. Unlike his brother, he did not have the outward strength of personality needed to cope with the endless conflicts of the manager's job. Furthermore, because he was such a gifted footballer, playing by natural instinct, he had never had to analyse the game too deeply. So when it came to tactics and patterns of play, he struggled. But Jack, with far less ability, had long been fascinated by systems, and was a qualified FA coach before he was 30. Unlike Bobby, he had no reluctance about stamping his methods on every team he organized. He knew exactly what he wanted, whether it be at Middlesbrough or Ireland, and he would brook no arguments. 'It was Jack's way or you didn't play,' says David Kelly, who served under Jack with the Republic of Ireland.

The gap between them runs far beyond football. They also have completely different interests, with Jack liking country pursuits such as shooting and Bobby preferring the more suburban activity of golf. Where Jack cultivates the image of the cloth-capped country-man, with a gun in his hands and wellingtons on his feet, Bobby is much more at ease in the director's box, wearing a dapper suit or blazer. Despite the Munich crash, Bobby loves to travel all over the world, whereas Jack is always at his happiest in the fields of his native Northumberland. Bobby is essentially conservative in his outlook, while Jack is a staunch socialist.

This sense of difference goes right back to the brothers' childhood in Ashington. Tellingly, Jack went to secondary school, while Bobby went to grammar school. Again, the separation of pupils along grammar and secondary lines was one of the great fault lines of working class life until the arrival of comprehensive education in the 1960s. Yet, while the gap between Bobby and Jack was undoubtedly

exacerbated by their schooling, they were always travelling on different paths from their early years, since they were such very different
children. Jack was the rebel, Bobby the conformist. Trouble was an
alien word to Bobby. It was Jack's middle name.

And so it remained for the rest of their lives. While on the football
field their careers flourished, the rift between the brothers grew in
private. This mutual antagonism was fuelled not only by the tragedy
of the Munich air crash in 1958, which made Bobby even more
introspective and distant, but also by a long-term feud between their
closest relatives, which tore Jack and Bobby apart and left them
barely on speaking terms.

Given the fascinating contours of the Charltons' tale, it is remarkable that there has never been a comprehensive, joint biography
until now. The only previous book on them was written more than
thirty years ago, in 1971, by the New Zealander Norman Harris.
Though it provides some compelling insights, particularly about
their early lives, it is based entirely on their own testimony and uses
hardly any other sources. The shelf is equally bare when it comes to
separate biographies. Astonishingly, despite the deluge of books on
Manchester United stars – even Dennis Viollet, winner of just two
England caps, was the subject of a 333-page work in 2001 – no-one
has ever attempted to write a life of England's greatest living footballer, Sir Bobby Charlton, while Jack has been rewarded with just
a thin 1994 account from journalist Stan Liversedge. Moreover,
unlike Jack, who penned a bestselling autobiography in 1996, Sir
Bobby has never written his own life story. Since his retirement as a
player, all he has produced is one light book of soccer anecdotes.

It is my hope that, with this joint biography, I will go some way
towards rectifying this strange gap in British football literature.
No-one can dispute the vast contribution the Charltons have made
to the soccer of our islands over the last half century. It is now right
that the story behind that contribution should be told for the first
time.

CHAPTER ONE

The Boys

'If ever I'm feeling a bit uppity, whenever I get on my high horse, I go and take another look at my dear mam's mangle that has pride of place in the dining room of my home. The mangle has the greatest significance. It is the symbol of my beginnings. It serves as the reminder of the days when I learned what life was all about.' These are the words with which Brian Clough, another footballer from a north-eastern family, begins his autobiography, emphasizing how much his mother meant to him.

The mother of the Charlton brothers was an equally dominant figure in their upbringing. Born Cissie (a shortening of Elizabeth) Milburn, she was the classic matriarch: strong, passionate, sociable, and outspoken, as protective of her brood as she was ambitious for them. Her husband, Bob, could hardly have been more different. A coalminer who spent his whole working life underground, he was quiet, dry, undemonstrative, but strong-willed. Indeed, it is striking how, in their personalities, Jack seems to have taken after his mother, and Bobby after his father, though, like Jack, old Bob could be quick-tempered if the mood took him. Walter Lavery, who grew up with Bobby and Jack, recalls: 'You would go round to their house after playing in the park, and old Bob would be sitting by the fire, in his braces, just reading the paper. Cissie would be talking away, asking you all about football and school, while Bob made no contribution at all. It was not that he didn't like his children, but just that he didn't like the fuss.'

What made the influence of Cissie all the more powerful was the fact that football was in her blood. Her great-grandfather and grandfather, both called Jack, had played for top-class local sides in Northumberland, while her own father – yet another Jack but known universally as 'Tanner' Milburn – played in goal for Ashington FC when the club was in the old Third Division North in the 1920s. All four of her brothers played League football as full-backs: Jack, George and Jimmy for Leeds and Stan, the youngest of the quartet, for Chesterfield, then Leicester and Rochdale. Her cousin, 'Wor' Jackie Milburn, the greatest of all the family soccer stars before the arrival of her sons, won 13 England caps and three FA Cup winners' medals as a striker with Newcastle. It is hardly a surprise, then, that Cissie herself should have become a serious football enthusiast, with an understanding of the game that surpassed most male fans. She often said that she wished she had been born a boy. 'For years, I kicked footballs around the parks and back streets of Ashington with a bunch of lads, usually with my skirt tucked into my knickers,' she said in her autobiography. Bobby Whitehead, who played for Newcastle and was another contemporary of Jack and Bobby's, remembers, 'When we played at school or in the park, there would usually be a few dads around. But there was nearly always one woman there, Cissie Charlton, who would be able to shout more loudly than most fathers. And she would travel with the school team on the bus to away games. She was so wrapped up in the game and was very knowledgeable about it.'

Cissie Charlton's fixation with soccer might have been rare in a woman in that era, but just as odd was her husband's total indifference to the sport, given its grip on masculine working-class culture in the north-east. Bob Charlton had absolutely no interest in football. He never went to games with his wife, never played and, in 1966, did not even watch the World Cup semi-final between England and Portugal – regarded by many as his son Bobby's greatest-ever match

– preferring to work his shift down the mine. The two sports he enjoyed were boxing and pigeon fancying. Like many miners used to back-breaking manual labour, he was a good fighter, sometimes holding his own against travelling professionals who earned their living by touring the country and setting up challenges with local men. In fact, Bob won the money to buy Cissie a wedding ring in just such a bout. Later, he would help train boxers in the area, earning the nickname 'Boxer'. Pigeons were his other great interest. 'I remember old Bob sitting, very quiet and still, by his loft on his allotment, where he kept his pigeons. His conversation was always limited. And he had a catapult with him. Suddenly he fired it, straight up the arse of a cat. Pigeon fanciers hate cats,' recalls Ron Routledge, an Ashington local who went on to play League football for Sunderland. But it should not be thought that Bob had any streak of cruelty. He was actually a soft-hearted man, who felt so sorry for the pit ponies that he would regularly bring them treats. Once he even purchased one of them because he could not bear the thought of her being taken to the knacker's yard. He was so devoted to the animal, going out at all hours of the night to see her, that Cissie thought he was having an affair.

Bob's lack of enthusiasm for football was particularly striking in Ashington, because soccer and coalmining were the twin forces that shaped the town. By 1930, it boasted that it was 'the biggest mining village in the world, with more than a third of its 30,000 population employed in the coal industry. And coal had a direct influence on soccer, the chief recreation of the town. The Ashington Colliery Welfare ground had no less than seven pitches, catering for three separate leagues and more than 20 local sides, many of them playing to a high standard. The upkeep of these excellent facilities was maintained by a penny a week off the miners' pay. In addition, all the working men's clubs had their own sides. No wonder, in view of such enthusiasm, Ashington was able to produce a stream of League football professionals, such as Joe Bell of Middlesbrough, Jim Potts, the Leeds goalkeeper, and George Prior of Sheffield Wednesday. Perhaps the most interesting case is that of the great Jimmy Adamson, captain of the Burnley championship-winning side of 1959/60 who, like both Bobby and Jack, was awarded the title of Footballer of the Year. Coincidentally, Adamson grew up in Beatrice Street, where the Charlton brothers also lived – I doubt there is any other terrace in Britain that has produced three Footballers of the Year. The eagerness for football rubbed off on the boys of Ashington, who spent most of their free time kicking a ball around in Hirst Park and then, when darkness descended, continued in the streets, their play illuminated by the overhead lamps. Such games were illegal and could result in heavy fines if the participants were caught, so lookouts were posted at each end of the street to warn of the approach of a police officer. 'Everything in our lives was football-orientated. That's all we were interested in,' says Walter Lavery. 'We were so fanatical that even when the football season was over in the summer, and the council was trying to allow the grass to grow long in Hirst Park, we would still take out a ball, flatten down a patch of grass in one corner of the ground and get a game going.'

Despite the attractions of football, pigeons, boxing and a few pints with mates, it was still a very tough life for the miners of Ashington. The pay was poor, the job insecure, the conditions dangerous. Bob Charlton worked through the 1966 World Cup semi-final not just because of his indifference towards football but also because he was worried about losing a day's pay. In the same way, he never missed a day's work even when seriously injured. Mike Kirkup, an Ashington local historian, a contemporary of Bobby's and himself a former miner, gives this glimpse into the precarious existence faced by miners. 'A miner's cottage was tied to work at the pit. So the colliery owners could always use that as a threat. On one notorious occasion, when 13 men were killed at the Woodhorn colliery in 1916, the notices of eviction went out to the widows within just three months of this disaster. It was a pretty harsh regime.'

The actual work for the miners could hardly have been more unpleasant. Forced to toil in a dirty, dark environment more than 800 feet underground, they were so cramped that they had permanent scabs on their backs from crawling along the tunnels. Little wonder that old Bob Charlton, who started work in the mines the day after he left school at the age of just 14, once took his second son, Bobby, to the colliery and told him, 'I don't want you ever going down there, doing what I've had to do all my life to earn a living.' But Bobby never had any intention of joining his father in the pit. 'I was determined about that, even if I had to travel and seek my fortune elsewhere,' he once said. What had particularly struck Bobby was the physical legacy of the job. 'You can always tell a miner just be looking at his hands. At first glance, you might just think they were dirty, but when you looked more closely, you saw that they were full of scars, the accumulation of hundreds and hundreds of cuts made over the years.' Similarly, Jack Charlton spent just one day underground as a 16-year-old trainee miner before handing in his notice. 'I've seen it, I've done it, I've had enough. I don't know what I'm going to do with the rest of my life, but it won't be that,' he told his colliery manager when he resigned his post.

Nor were there many financial rewards for a miner's family. Bobby recalls his father going out to work every morning and checking the contents of his satchel: 'Bait (sandwiches), bottle (water), lamp, carbide, tabs (cigarettes),' and adding with a grin and a tap of his pockets, 'but nae money.' In contrast to their wealthy status today, Jack and Bobby grew up in a small house without an inside toilet or running water. The brothers, now so distant, had, as small children, to share the same bed because of the lack of space. Though Cissie provided a warm home, there were precious few luxuries. Food that we take for granted today, such as pork and chicken, was a rarity then, as Bobby once recalled. 'It was a great celebration in the street when a pig was killed. Everyone came from all over the place and got their little share of it. I used to ask, "Why can't we just eat it straight away?" But I was told that it had to be hung and salted, otherwise it would not keep.'

In the hardened circumstances of the time, the values of family solidarity were a vital source of support. But that is not to say that the Charltons or the Milburns were paragons of domestic virtue. One of Cissie's grandfathers was a heavy drinker who suffered from mental instability after taking a blow from a policeman's truncheon. When he was in one of his more savage, drunken moods, his wife was forced to flee the family home. Her own father, Tanner Milburn, was a selfish, mean, scheming rogue who would rather spend his money on gambling and alcohol than on his own family. A fly-by-night bookmaker, he also trained athletes, who were used as a means of enhancing his illegal profits. His disloyalty to his family was graphically exposed by his cynical behaviour over a major 110-yard sprint in which his own son Stan, a fine local runner, was one of the two favourites. Instead of backing his son, for whom he acted as a trainer, he struck a deal with the manager of the other favourite, whereby they agreed to share equally the £20 prize money – a vast sum in pre-war Ashington – whichever boy won. After the race, in which Stan came second, Tanner refused to give his son a penny and instead attacked him for his failure to win. Stan was so furious with his father that he threw his sprint shoes in the fire, vowing never to run again.

Cissie and Bob had their own problems. They had married just six months after they first met, at a dance in the Princess Ballroom of Ashington, and had four sons, Jack the oldest, followed by Bobby, Gordon and Tommy. There was a time when they came close to splitting up, since Cissie could find her husband intensely aggravating. 'He embarrassed me, he annoyed me, he argued just for the sake of an argument,' she once wrote, while Bob disliked her boasting and all the attention that she encouraged over her sons. Alan Lavelle, who went to school with the Charltons, recalls that when he was secretary of the Newbiggin working men's club, 'Old Bob used to come in, looking a bit down. I would say, "Bob, what's the matter?" And he'd reply, "I just get sick of everyone asking about wor Bobby. Why can't I just have a drink in peace?"' In an interview with local historian Mike Kirkup, Cissie revealed how close she came to separation: 'There was no such thing as divorce for the likes of us. If you made a mistake in your choice of man, you just stuck it out for the sake of the bairns. Me and Bob were going through a rough patch and I said to him, "I'm leaving you the minute wor Tommy is 15." Come the day of his 15th birthday, Bob says to me, "Well, are you not leaving then?" "No," I told him, "You've mellowed since then."'

Bob and Cissie's first child, Jack, was born on 8 May 1935. Reflecting her obsession with football, one of her first comments to a neighbour about her new son was, 'Eee, the bairn's lovely. And his feet are fine too.' But, as a child, Jack did not just use his feet for football; he also used them to wander endlessly in the countryside around Ashington. The fields, woods and streams of Northumberland became almost a second home to him as he would walk for miles, studying wildlife, trapping small animals with his makeshift snares, and even attempting to catch fish with his bare hands before he bought his first rod. His deep attachment to rural life was formed in those long, childhood journeys. 'I loved that landscape and I love it to this day. I have to go into cities and crowds as part of my job, but I loathe it,' he said in 1994. Bill Merryweather, a childhood friend of Jack's, gave me this memory: 'He always had to be outdoors, picking up anything from mushrooms to fish. Sometimes the two of us would go out poaching at five in the morning. If it went well, we would end up with two or three rabbits. And he's never changed from when he was a little lad. He's still at his happiest when he's out shooting and fishing.'

Jack developed his favourite haunts, such as a local swamp called the Sandy Desert. In winter this was a vast, festering bog. But in summer, when it had dried out, it became a large, dusty hollow, riven with cracks. Used as a rubbish dump, it always attracted a large number of rats and Jack would spend hours shooting at them with his catapult. When he was older and had acquired the right equipment, Jack would regularly spend his nights fishing off the coast at Newbiggin, a seaside village just three miles from Ashington. Jackie Lothian remembers an incident which illustrates both Jack's bravery and his devotion to fishing. 'When we were about 13, Jack would often cycle over to my home at Newbiggin, have a game of cards and some supper, and then go out fishing. One night Jack cast his line, and somehow the hook went right into his thumb. Another lad and I tried to get it out but couldn't, because the sky was pitch black. Then Jack breezily said, "I'll have to go off to hospital, so look after my things." Off he cycled over to Ashington hospital, with the hook still in his thumb. He got it out, had the wound stitched up, and then, that very night, he cycled back and carried on fishing with us.' Jackie Lothian says that they could be far more reckless as children than would be tolerated today. 'I cannot believe the things we used to get up to. As a dare, for instance, we would get on the swings at Hirst Park, and push as hard as we could until we could complete a full circle, right over the top through 360 degrees. We also used to try and catch minnows in Bothal Woods, where there was a big waterfall. I suppose, looking back, it was very dangerous but we just never used to think about it.'

In such a climate, it was inevitable that accidents did happen. Once Jack and his friends were playing a chasing game at the top of an old disused windmill, when one of the boys fell out of a window on the third floor and broke his arm. Another boy broke his leg in a race through a field with Jack, when he tripped over a wire fence and was thrown through the air before landing heavily on his back. Far more serious, though, was the horrific night when Jack returned home covered in blood. Jack explained to his mother that he and his friends had been playing in a railway cutting, placing coins on the line. Tragically one of them had been hit by a train and killed. The rest of the gang had dragged the body to the nearest roadway, where they had just left it. Nothing more happened and the event gradually faded from Jack's memory. Today, such an incident would almost certainly involve the police and social services.

Jack Charlton has always been known as a rebel, an individualist, no great respecter of either authority or convention. And so it was in his childhood. At the age of just two, he caused some embarrassment to his family by wandering out of the house, dressed only in his nappy, to join a passing funeral procession. The sight of Jack, without any trousers, toddling proudly behind the Salvation Army band, has become part of Ashington legend. 'I was forever getting into scrapes,' Jack admits. Once a baker drove from Ashington to Gosforth and, when he arrived, he was surprised to find young Jack stowed away in the back of his van. On another occasion, he stole a cauliflower from a neighbour's back garden. Then he had the cheek to walk round to the front and try and sell it back to him. 'As a schoolboy, like most of us, he was a bit of a rascal, stealing from orchards, pinching vegetables. He was a real Jack the lad,' says Bobby Whitehead.

'From the time he could walk, Jack was full of devilment. I would often say to myself, "God give me strength." He was a livewire,' wrote Cissie in her autobiography. The spirit of rebellion applied in the classroom as well as the countryside. Jackie Lothian recalls: 'He was certainly not frightened of anyone at school. The teachers were on top of you all the time and there was no answering back – except from Jack, of course. He was a likeable lad, but he would put you in your place if he didn't like what you said. He could have been more successful at school if he had put his mind to it, and I remember he was interested in history, especially the local history of the area. But he did not really care about bookwork; he wanted to be away in the fields all the time.' One of Jack's school reports stated: 'Jack would do better at school if he kept his mind on his work instead of looking out the window all the time.'

Jack was in trouble for much more than daydreaming one day, after he shot another pupil, Bernadette Reed. With typical impetuosity, Jack had taken it into his mind to bring his father's rifle – used for game shooting – into school. Having fired the gun towards a nearby church, he then watched as the bullet hit a fence and ricocheted into the face of the unfortunate young Bernadette, who suffered a grazed eye. Jack was given a severe reprimand by his headmaster and was then frogmarched by Cissie to apologize to Bernadette's father. Yet there was a surprising response at the Reed household.

'This is the lad who shot your daughter,' said Cissie when she and Jack turned up on the Reeds' doorstep.

'So you're interested in guns, son?'

'Well, er, yes,' said Jack.

'So am I. Come inside and I'll show you what I've got.'

Predictably, the man who became a tough defender with Leeds was also a good boxer in his youth, winning both official bouts in the school gym and unofficial ones in the schoolyard. In a *Daily Telegraph* interview in 1994, he recalled: 'I was the best fighter in the street for my age and there was a lad from the next street who was the best fighter in his. We called him "Skinny" Harmer. When I went to school at five, he was in the same class as me and I thought a fight was imminent. But we never, ever fought. We avoided each other in case we got beat.' In another echo of the adult Jack Charlton, who made a fortune in his shrewd handling of money, particularly during his spell as Ireland manager, the young Jack had a host of money-making schemes. These included: a paper round organized like a military operation; deliveries for a nearby grocery store; and the collection – from local collieries – of unused timber, which he then chopped up and sold for firewood.

But perhaps the most interesting parallel with today is that, as young brothers, Bobby and Jack did not get on with each other. Some of their contemporaries claim that this was because of the age difference between them. Bobby Charlton was born on 10 October 1937, two-and-a-half years after Jack's arrival. 'When you're young, the gap in years tends to count much more,' says Walter Lavery, 'so Bobby and Jack did not really mix much. They had different pursuits and different friends.' Bobby also takes this view. 'Though it appears now we are the same age, he's actually a good deal older than me, so we just did not spend a lot of time together when we were growing up,' he said in 1968.

The reality, however, was down more to a clash of temperaments. Jack was the adventurer, ever eager to plough his own furrow, while Bobby was far keener to stay at home reading or playing football. Jack knew that his younger brother never shared his interest in the countryside, so he hated to bring Bobby along on his wanderings – and he only did so at the instruction of his mother. What particularly annoyed him was when the infant Bobby messed himself or demanded to be taken home when he grew bored or tired. As Cissie wrote, 'Jack wanted to be off on his own, not nurse-maiding someone who was regarded as the family's fair-haired favourite. If I still insisted and made Jack take Bobby with him, he often gave Bobby a swift clout before they got very far and that usually sent him running home in tears, while Jack went on his own sweet way himself.'

With his usual diplomacy, Bobby has claimed that he enjoyed these trips, speaking fondly of his bike rides into the woods to go bird-nesting with Jack or the times they went to the 'lovely coast' of Newbiggin to pick up coal that had been washed ashore from the mines which ran under the sea. But he has also admitted: 'Like most elder brothers, Jack regarded me as a pest when we were kids, especially when I'd plead to go with him to pick potatoes or on fishing trips. "He's not coming," Jack would say defiantly. "You take him," my mother would reply. From then on it would be nothing but moans, and there are people who will suggest that he's never stopped moaning. He never tried to conceal his darker moods and once his mind was made up, nothing would alter it.' Jack's memory is similar: 'Bobby was more of a mother's boy. He was never a bloke to get out into the country and he still isn't. I took him fishing a couple of times but he was no good. I had to keep changing worms for him. He'd wave to me from 100 yards down the river, and I'd have to trudge all the way back and change the bait, because he just hadn't got a clue.' On another occasion, Bobby and Jack were playing in separate matches at the Hirst Miners' Welfare ground. Towards the final whistle of his game, Jack was penalized for committing a foul in his own box. Bobby got to hear of the incident, and when Jack arrived home, Bobby teased him about it. 'Fancy giving away a penalty like that,' said Bobby, sitting on the edge of a chair in the living room. Without breaking his stride, Jack gave Bobby an almighty smack on the back of his head, sending his younger brother crashing to the ground. 'Jack got thumped for that, but it wasn't about to change him,' recalled Bobby.

For all his sense of independence, there is no doubt that Jack deeply resented the apparent bias of his mother towards Bobby. 'She never said she was proud of me,' admitted Jack in 1996. 'I was driven to try and please her. Sometimes, I would go down to the dog track and spend hours hunting through mountains of rubbish, searching for old glasses they'd thrown out. When I found some that were not too badly chipped, I'd clean them and take them home as presents for her. She would always thank me, but I suspect she then threw them away. I always knew that I was not her favourite.'

Unlike the outgoing, noisy Jack, Bobby was very shy as a child, so shy that when strangers came to the house he would hide behind his mother or run upstairs to the bedroom. Rob Storey, who grew up with them both, told me: 'Jack wouldn't stand for anything. You couldn't put much on him. I don't mean that he had an aggressive nature but if someone confronted him, he could certainly look after himself. On the other hand Bobby was much more serious, more withdrawn than Jack. He would keep himself to himself, whereas Jack would just say what he thought. In that respect, they were total opposites. Jack always seemed to be striving for what he wanted, whereas things seemed to come more easily for Bobby. Jack was a determined lad, much more determined than Bobby seemed to be.' They were also physically very different, even when they were children. In a BBC radio interview in 1989, Cissie Charlton said: 'When Jack was born, his granny would take him around the town to let everyone see how long he was. He was tall even when he was born. Bobby was stumpy, thickset, different altogether. They were two different people.'

Bobby was more concerned about his appearance than Jack, sometimes even wearing a tie at home, something Jack would never willingly have done. Jackie Lothian recalls: 'Bobby was smart, polite, diplomatic; he knew how to address people properly. He was always very tidy, unlike Jack who was a scruffy bairn.' Bobby hated being in trouble whether at school or with his parents. When he called his brothers for tea, they thought it amusing to run away, which prompted him to anger. 'Why do you always have to be so stubborn?' he would ask of them. He was never in playground fights with other boys, though, like both Jack and his father, he was an excellent boxer, once winning a youth competition staged in his neighbourhood.

Yet Bobby did have his playful side. He could do good impersonations, and sometimes surprised his brothers by covering himself in a sheet and pretending to be a ghost, a spectacle that became known in the Charlton household as 'wor kid's mad half-hour'. Using a pair of his father's rolled up socks, he played football in the sitting room with his brother. With his greater height, Jack would usually win the aerial contest, though Bobby was almost unbeatable on the floor. 'Once he'd put it on the ground he'd murder me. Murder me! That's why I like to see the ball in the air to this day,' says Jack. Bobby was never bashful at these moments. While he was kicking the socks around, he would take his mother's iron and use the plug as a fake microphone to provide a running commentary on the match, putting himself in the role of the great soccer stars of the time: 'Mortensen knocks it out to Stanley Matthews. Matthews goes down the line, crosses and it's there by Lawton. A magnificent goal,' would be a typical passage of play in the Charlton home.

Like many reserved boys, Bobby loved to retreat into his own fantasy world of cartoon heroes and exotic fables. He adored films such as *Ali Baba* and *Robin Hood*, while he explained in a radio interview in 2001 that his favourite comic character was 'Morgan the Mighty, a great big, strong, blond Englishman trapped on an island. The real baddies used to send in opponents for him to fight. And the theme of the story was how he ended up being the greatest fighter in the world.' It does not take a great leap of imagination to see how Bobby, a strong, fair-haired young Englishman, might aspire to such a role.

Football was undoubtedly the greatest form of escape for Bobby, not just from the smoky drabness of Ashington, but also from a future life trapped underground. To a much greater extent than his elder brother, he fell in love with the game in his childhood. 'From his earliest age, he was football mad,' said his mother. When his uncles visited Ashington on a Sunday, they took Bobby out in the street or down to the beach at Newbiggin to show off his skills. Then they came home and discussed League football. 'I listened to them talking about the matches they had played on Saturday and I heard with awe names like Frank Swift and Wilf Mannion. Particularly at that age – and I was only six – there was an unforgettable magic about it. I suppose it was then that the seed was sown in my mind that I would never be anything else but a footballer, if I was good enough,' Bobby wrote in 1967 in his book *Forward for England*.

Bobby loved everything about football. He spent hours reading his soccer books, his favourite being *Stanley Matthews' Football Album*. He pored over results in the back of newspapers, developing such an affection for the sports pages that he decided, if he did not make it as a footballer, he would become a football journalist, 'that would be the next best thing, because journalists got into matches for free,' he said. He always had some sort of ball at his feet. If he went to the cinema, he would bring a ball with him and kick it along the gutter. Similarly, he would take one if his mother sent him on an errand to the shops. Through his fascination with soccer, he formed a powerful bond with his grandfather, old 'Tanner' Milburn. Though Tanner was a hard, stubborn man, distrusted by many within the family, he doted on Bobby, recognizing the boy's exceptional ability. In return, young Bobby idolized Tanner.

On many evenings during the war, the two of them went down to the local park, where Tanner still held training sessions for sprinters. Bobby got a rubdown just like the adults, his grandfather telling him, 'You'll never be fast unless your muscles are loose.' Bobby then raced against the professionals in the 110 yards, having been given a 70-yard start. If Bobby won, his grandfather would be delighted, saying 'Well done, Bobby lad, you'll be running against a whippet yet.' During his career, Bobby's electric pace was one of his greatest assets – George Best, a lightning-quick player himself, says that Bobby was the only man who could beat him in sprints during training at Manchester United.

Towards the end of his life, Tanner's eyesight was failing, so on

Saturday evenings he would send Bobby to buy the local football paper and then get him to read out all the scores. 'Even though he was dying, the most important thing was the football results,' remembers Bobby. It was an attitude that the grandson inherited. 'Football is my life. I eat, sleep and drink the game. When I wake up every day, I think of who we're playing in the next match. I think of nothing else, apart from my family. I wish I could play until I was 70,' said Bobby in an ITV documentary made when he was 30. The death of his grandfather hit him hard, for Bobby was a sensitive man who could be deeply affected by loss – as he was to show over Munich. 'When he died, I felt as though I'd lost my best friend and there was a gap in my life which was not filled for a long time, even though I was young,' wrote Bobby later.

Bobby was also a keen spectator. When he and Jack were babies, Cissie took them along in the pram to Ashington FC, and they would leap up at the roar of the crowd after a goal was scored. Later, they were sometimes allowed to work as ball boys at the club. Historian Mike Kirkup recalls: 'Their uncle Stan was playing for Ashington and he let them visit him in the dressing room or bring out the water magic sponge for the trainer. During the play, they sat behind the goals, which they thought was absolutely marvellous.' In the Charltons' youth, though Ashington FC had dropped down from the Third Division North into the North-Eastern League, there were still some big matches at the club. Stan Mortensen, the Blackpool and England striker, played at Ashington during the war, while in an FA Cup tie in 1950 against Rochdale, 12,000 people crammed into the ground, with some of them having to sit on the roof.

It has been claimed that Bobby, as a child, was a Sunderland supporter. In her autobiography Cissie said that Bobby's ambition was to play for the club, writing, 'He was a great admirer of Len Shackleton's team and would have jumped at the chance to join it.' But this view is disputed by those who grew up with Bobby. Ron Routledge, the schoolmate who went on to play for Sunderland, told me, 'I don't know where all this business about Bobby and

Sunderland comes from. It's just not true. Never once was he involved with Sunderland. We all followed Newcastle and I went with Bobby to most of the home games at St James' Park. I suppose some people might have thought that Bobby modelled himself on Len Shackleton, the Sunderland striker – for they had the same body swerve – but he didn't. Bobby was always just Bobby.'

Jack also remembers going to Newcastle with Bobby. 'Me and our kid would go to Newcastle to see Jackie Milburn. My father put us on the bus, and we'd get off at the Haymarket and go for something to eat at the British Home restaurant. Then we'd go and queue at St James' Park. We'd always leave it to the last minute so that we could get passed over everybody's heads in the crowd, ending up right at the front.' As usual, the difference surfaced between the brothers, for Jack was far more partisan in his support of Newcastle. He once told Mike Kirkup, 'I've always followed Newcastle United. To this day I'm a Newcastle fan and I was brought up black and white eyed. I don't think you ever change. Even when I was a player, the first results I looked for were those of Newcastle. When you're a Newcastle fan as a boy, you're a fan for life.' Indeed, one writer told me that he was recently in Jack's home during a Newcastle game which was being shown live on Sky TV. Just before the kick-off, Jack went down on his knees in front of the television screen in a mock act of worship to his beloved Magpies. Yet Bobby never felt the same attraction to Newcastle. 'I don't remember him ever being a great Newcastle supporter,' says Bobby's schoolfriend Evan Martin, who went with him a few times to St James'. Bobby himself says that after Manchester United won the FA Cup Final in 1948, they became his favourite team, though he always liked to watch good football wherever it was played.

And no-one played it better than Bobby Charlton. His natural talent was so enormous that anyone who saw him, even as a child, knew that he was destined to become a professional footballer. Ashington locals still speak with awe about the sight of the young Bobby, sailing past opponents twice his age and then producing a deadly shot from outside the box. Walter Lavery remembers: 'He stood out like a beacon. He was different, far above the rest of the young players, believe me. He was as near a genius as you could get. He was a great dribbler, with a real sense of style, even when he was young. He could run fast with the ball. He had techniques that the rest of us lads did not even realize existed until we went to professional clubs six years later. That gave him this special aura. Now don't get me wrong, he was a good mixer with the other lads. But, for all that he was in your company, you always had a sense that his mind was elsewhere, thinking about football. He knew that, with his talent, he was going to get away. And he was so passionate, competitive. I remember going to watch a school game one Saturday morning, and I caught sight of Bobby arguing with the referee.

"What's the matter over there?" I asked a spectator.

"It's young Chuckie. His team is winning seven-nowt and yet he's been arguing with the ref for the last five minutes that they should have been granted another goal."

That was so like Bobby. He wanted to win all the time.'

Rob Storey agrees. 'Bobby was always small for his age and went by the name of "Little Bobby". Maybe it was because of the low centre of gravity that he could control the ball so well. When we were playing in Hirst Park, everyone always wanted him in their team, because he was so much better than the rest of us, even though he was younger than most.' Evan Martin, who later went to grammar school with Bobby, recalls seeing him in a junior match: 'Bobby was only seven years old then, but already he was running rings round lads who were 11. He had terrific speed, one-touch skills and lovely balance. My father, who was a football fanatic and was also watching, turned to me and said, "Watch that kid Charlton. He'll make a name for himself."'

Bobby's talent was in direct contrast to Jack, who failed to shine amongst his contemporaries, as Rob Storey remembers: 'In all honesty, he was little better than me. Physically, he stood out a mile because of his height and long neck, but, when it came to football skills, though he was a solid full-back, he was so inferior to Bobby that it was an embarrassment.' Jackie Luthian says their destinies could not have looked more different. 'We all knew that Bobby would be a footballer, but we never thought Jack would be one. He was no better than anyone else. You see, he had no motivation. The thought of a career in the game had never entered his mind.'

Jack had the same character on the field as he was to show at Leeds, aggressive, uncompromising. But rather than playing centre-half, he was generally a full-back in his early games. And Bobby Whitehead says that this was his biggest problem. 'Being tall, he was good in the air but, at left-back, I think he was out of position. I kept him out of our school team for a few games when I was 14 and he was 15. But when we had a Cup match, our usual centre-half was off sick, so Jack moved in there. My father, who was watching, said afterwards, "That's the lad's position. He had a brilliant game."'

Perhaps the greatest myth about the Charlton upbringing in football is that Cissie taught Bobby how to play football. Folklore has it that, to quote Bobby, 'Being a Milburn with football coursing deep in her veins, she took me out on the slag heaps of Ashington and showed me everything from selling a dummy to scoring from 50 yards.' But this tale is untrue. For Bobby was a totally instinctive footballer, with a natural sense of how to play. Moreover, though Cissie provided exactly the right environment for her football-crazy son, she only once gave him direct, personal coaching. This happened when he was already 15, was at Manchester United and had played for the England Schoolboys. After one of these schoolboy internationals, Cissie had been talking to the chairman of the selectors, who said that Bobby's slowness on the turn was a serious weakness. When she returned to Ashington with Bobby, she decided to give him some specialized training. Adopting the methods that her own father, Tanner, had used when coaching sprinters, she took Bobby to Hirst Park early in the morning and had him running backwards and forwards until his speed on the turn gradually increased. 'I suppose that to a stranger it may have looked odd to see a 15 year old training like that with his mother, but this was Ashington and everyone knew I was football mad,' she said.

Cissie's own brothers were a bigger influence on Bobby,

particularly his Uncle George, who was at Chesterfield. In his summer holidays, Bobby went down to the club and joined in the training with the professionals. The hardened footballers were kind to him, allowing him to run all over the field and even to take penalties against goalkeeper Ray Middleton. After training, they took him to lunch or to the dog track or the golf club. If they went to the pub, Bobby sat outside with a tonic water. What really struck Bobby was the amount of swearing amongst the players. One incident particularly stood out in his memory, when a player who had been dropped had a ferocious, expletive-filled row with the manager. It brought home to Bobby, sitting quietly in the corner of the dressing room, the realities of life as a professional footballer.

In an interview with the *Sunday Telegraph* in 1973, Bobby spoke about the influence of Cissie's family and his youthful approach as footballer. 'My uncles made a big impression on me. They used to tell me I had a terrific backheel. That probably does not sound much now, but then, there was no-one doing it much, not even in the League. The game just came naturally to me. It surprised me when other boys couldn't kick or fell over. Why hadn't they the same balance? I thought they were unusual, rather than me. From watching as a kid and kicking around in the street, my philosophy of the game was always as an out-and-out forward. I never put my foot in – getting the ball was other players' work.'

It was an outlook that in later years would delight millions of fans – and enrage some of his closest colleagues.

CHAPTER TWO

The Migrants

Jack and Bobby had been on divergent paths since their earliest years, and the gap between them became much wider in adolescence, when they went to different secondary schools.

Both of them had attended the Hirst North Primary School, a traditional red-brick building in the heart of Ashington. Like so many others, the sports master of the school, Norman McGuinness, immediately recognized Bobby's outstanding gifts: 'There wasn't much he could be coached in. My first memory is seeing this small lad of nine, playing football with the 14-year-olds and just waltzing through them. It didn't take the wisdom of Solomon to see that he had great natural ability. Even at nine he had a body swerve and natural check that would take the other man the wrong way.' Inevitably, with Bobby as the captain, his school team was triumphant, winning the East Northumberland Junior Schools League Championship in 1949. In one match, Bobby's dominance had ensured that his side was leading 12–0 at half-time, and Norman McGuinness was forced to tell him, 'I want no more goals. You're humiliating the other side and that's bad sport.' It is a reflection of the austerity of post-war Britain that Bobby's team played in shorts fashioned from old blackout curtains by one of the teachers.

Bobby was not just much more successful than Jack on the soccer field. He also outshone him academically, as Jack later admitted: 'I'm afraid I was a bit of a non-starter. I just wasn't interested in subjects like English and maths. Robert was different. Not for him the wayward glances to what was happening outside the classroom. He was attentive and bright. And his handwriting was the envy of the whole class.'

In view of this testimony from Jack, he can hardly have been shocked when he failed his 11-plus and had to go to Hirst Park Secondary Modern School, while his younger brother won a scholarship to grammar school. But some of their contemporaries do not remember Bobby being as clever as Jack has claimed. In fact, Bobby, like Jack, initially failed his 11-plus, and only won a grammar school place after taking a second test, known as the 'review'. Alan Lavelle says: 'There were a lot in our class who were brighter than Bobby. To be honest, I was a bit surprised when Bobby got into grammar – I did not think he was that good a scholar.' Bobby himself has said that he was not the academic type. 'I neglected my lessons and found it difficult to do my homework because my mind was always on football. I was so totally convinced that I would be a footballer than I could not concentrate on anything else. But I regret not working harder. I wish I had studied my English and maths, so today I would be able to explain myself better.'

Nevertheless, for all such weaknesses, Bobby was proud to have gained his scholarship to Morpeth Grammar School. But then a complication arose. His family discovered Morpeth did not play soccer, preferring the socially superior game of rugby. Understandably, Bobby was distraught. The headmaster of Hirst Primary, James Hamilton, also thought it would be a 'tragic waste' to send Bobby to 'one of those snooty places that did not like football' – to use his phrase. So Hamilton, backed up by the formidable figure of Cissie Charlton, approached Northumberland County Council and explained the exceptional circumstances of Bobby's case. With a foresight not always shown by municipal bureaucrats, the education committee agreed that Bobby could be transferred to Bedlington Grammar, south of Ashington, a school which played football.

Bobby began at Bedlington in the autumn of 1949. Evan Martin, another Bedlington pupil, recalls that Bobby was eagerly awaited at the school. 'When he arrived we were already expecting him because of his local reputation. Everyone wanted him in their house so he could play for their house team. And then this kid comes in, with small, thin legs, looking anything but a footballer. But he soon showed that he could play. Even when he was 12, he was picked for teams of 18 year olds. He was that good, with wonderful silky skills. Bobby would get the ball with a man on him – he was always very heavily marked – and with his first touch he had beaten him. I never saw him head the ball much. If he got a high ball, he would chest it down. If he hit the ball anywhere around the penalty area, the keeper had no chance. He was even good in goal. Once, in a house match, the regular keeper was injured so Bobby went in and was fabulous. You could see he was gifted at all sports, whether it be snooker or cricket. As a batsman he would get into line and had all the shots. I once said to him, "Bobby, you could have been a good cricketer." He replied, "Ah, that stuff wasn't for me."'

Evan Martin, who was close to Bobby, has other memories of him as a grammar school pupil: 'He was very unassuming, a smashing lad really. He never, ever boasted, even when he was picked for England Schoolboys. He was reasonably bright, though, like me, he was not brilliant at mathematics or science. He was quiet, deep, never really let on what he was really thinking, though he was a good mixer and had a lovely sense of humour. There was a group of about five of us, led by a lad called Tucker Robinson, who was a character with greased back hair, like Henry Winkler as the Fonz. Bobby was a colliery lad first and foremost, and if there were any tricks going, he would be there. We used to go to the pictures a lot in Ashington, and I remember one night, after we had been to see *The Jolson Story*, he sang songs from the film all the way from the cinema to the bus stop. Bobby loved the music of people like Frank Sinatra and Nat King Cole.'

Evan Martin says that Bobby was neither especially good looking or popular with girls when he was at Bedlington. 'He was short and he had this problem with his hair, a double crown at the back which would stick up and he was always trying to plaster it down. But when he was14, he did go out with a lovely girl called Norma Outhwaite. She and Bobby were beautifully suited because they had the same temperaments: nice, straightforward, easy to get on with.'

Among the boys of Bedlington, according to Martin, 'There was a mystique about Bobby, because of his football. Everyone knew he was going to be a top professional, playing for England.' But this admiration was not shared by elements within the school establishment, which prided itself on academic attainment and frowned on the idea of a young lad thinking only of football as a professional career. Cissie Charlton wrote that this conflict between Bobby's interests and the school's 'meant that those days at Bedlington Grammar were not very happy ones'. The school's attitude was illustrated by two incidents which happened to Bobby. The first occurred during a lesson in the physics laboratory, which looked out on to the playing fields. Sitting on a bench by the window, Bobby was distracted by the sight of some boys having a football practice. Suddenly the teacher, Tommy Simmons, rounded on him: 'Charlton, you'd be wise to pay more attention to the blackboard than to the games outside. This is where your future lies, in your schoolwork. You'll never make a living as a footballer.'

The second arose when Bobby had been picked to play for England Schoolboys. Amazingly, the headmaster, Mr James, refused him permission to travel down to Wembley for the game. 'You're a scholar, first and foremost,' he said. The sports master, George Benson, was more understanding. Without the head's knowledge, he sneaked Bobby out of the school and drove him to Newcastle station for the rail trip to London.

George Benson was not the only Bedlington teacher to admire Bobby. Another was Tom Hedderley, the French master who was also involved with sport. Now in his eighties and living in Newcastle, he gave me his recollection of teaching Bobby: 'I will never forget my first sight of him. It was during a games lesson and, because it had been raining heavily, the football pitch was wet. We used heavy leather balls in those days, which were not waterproof. One of the balls came rolling out to this little kid, who was not the size of two penny-worth of copper. And he just smacked it. I can still see it, rising all the way from the edge of 18-yard area, thudding against the bar and then bouncing back halfway up the pitch.' Tom Hedderley remembers one match, the final of the local Blake Cup, when Bobby's tremendous local reputation worked against him. 'We were playing Blyth and it was a needle match. Blyth had worked out that their only hope of winning was to stifle Bobby – and they succeeded, winning 1–0. In desperation, our lads kept giving the ball to Bobby to see what he could do. But every time he got it, there were about six Blyth boys straight on to him. It was just impossible for him to get through.'

Hedderley continues: 'Bobby was naturally tremendously popular in school, but he never played on it, never became swell-headed. As in his later career, he was very gentlemanly on the football field. Everyone respected him, not only because he was a damn good footballer but also because of his nice nature. He was not an outstanding pupil, but he was in the upper stream for most of his time with us. In my subject French, for instance, he got by without showing any signs of being a linguist.' Hedderley disputes the view that Bobby was especially withdrawn. 'Yes, he did not like being thrust forward, but he was not reticent. I would have actually called him happy-go-lucky. He worked steadily, though it always seemed that his mind was on football. We talked about him a lot in the staffroom because we knew he was going to be someone special.' Like others, Tom Hedderley saw the graphic contrast in Bobby's parents. 'His dad was a really nice fella. Sometimes, he used to come and watch on Saturday mornings. He was a very quiet man, the opposite of Cissie.'

Bill Hodgkiss, Bobby's form master, told me that 'Bobby was an average academic pupil, a well-behaved, popular lad who was never in any trouble. In fact, he was the sort of boy who would try and quieten down trouble rather than cause it. He was relatively quiet, not outwardly vivacious, but I would not have called him withdrawn.'

Hodgkiss, like everyone else, knew that Bobby's only ambition was to play professional football. And, not long after his arrival at Bedlington, it became clear that he would soon achieve this goal. By the age of 14, Bobby was already the star, not just of his school, but also of East Northumberland District Boys and Northumberland County Juniors. News of his brilliance was now reaching top clubs across the country, and the first to act was the one Bobby eventually joined, Manchester United.

Ironically, it was Jack's secondary modern school, not Bedlington, that helped to secure the interest of United. For the Hirst Park School's headmaster, Stuart Hemingway, was a friend of the legendary United scout, Joe Armstrong, the man who secured so many of the Babes for Matt Busby. Having been told by Cissie about the lack of encouragement Bobby was receiving at Bedlington, Hemingway wrote to Joe Armstrong, urging him to come to the north-east to see Bobby. On 9 February 1953, Armstrong arrived at Hebburn to watch Bobby playing for East Northumberland Schoolboys. It was a bitterly cold day. A covering of ice lay on the rock-hard pitch. 'Oh, I can see it all now,' recalled Armstrong nearly 20 years later. 'It was a thin February morning and I had to peer through the mist. Bobby didn't do so much that day, but it was enough for me. He was like a gazelle and he had a shot as hard as any grown man, yet he was a kid of only 14.'

Armstrong was so impressed that immediately after the game, he approached Bobby and asked him if he would like to join United when he had finished school. Convinced of Bobby's talent, he did not raise the question of a month's trial, the usual condition for young players. To Cissie Charlton, who was also, inevitably, at the game, he said: 'I don't mean to flatter you, Missus, but your son will play for England before he is 21.' Armstrong then informed Matt Busby, the United manager, of his new find. On his scout's recommendation, Busby went to see Bobby play for England Schoolboys in a trial. He was just as impressed, marvelling at Bobby's grace, power and physique. 'I decided then that I wanted him for my team. He was a must, with his timing of a pass, his jinking run, his shooting. We needed no more qualifications,' recalled Busby.

Within weeks of this trial, Bobby was in the full England School-boys team, prompting a flattering profile in the *Newcastle Journal*: 'Bobby Charlton, a 15-year-old Bedlington Grammar School student, is the first member of the famous Ashington family of foot-ballers to have received this honour. The young inside-forward, whose ambition is to become a sports journalist, is the second son of Mr and Mrs R Charlton of 114 Beatrice Street, Ashington and the grandson of the late "Tanner" Milburn. It is interesting to recall that "Tanner" Milburn prophesied some time before his death that, of all the footballers in the family, Bobby would be the finest. This prophecy looks like materializing as Bobby possesses a remarkable record in school football, equally at home in either inside-forward position.' Bobby was part of a powerful young England team which drew with the Scots, beat Wales by four goals in Cardiff, and crushed the Irish by eight at Portsmouth. The most memorable game for Bobby was at Wembley, again against the Welsh, when, in front of 90,000 screaming young fans, he scored twice in a 3–3 draw. 'When I walked out on to the pitch, the stadium engulfed me and I played the game in a sort of trance. It was over before I realized what was happening,' he told the *Daily Express*. His first goal resulted from the kind of long-range shot which was to become his trade-mark, as he recalled. 'I whacked it and then saw it moving away from the keeper all the time. I knew it must be a goal as soon as I hit it.' His second goal was a poke through a mass of bodies, while he also made England's third, crossing for Maurice Pratt to head home.

By now an array of clubs was after Charlton, including many of the biggest in the country, like Wolves, Arsenal and Sunderland. Kenneth Wolstenholme, the renowned commentator, told me: 'I saw Bobby play for England Schoolboys and you could hardly get into Wembley for all the scouts who wanted to sign him.' This pres-sure was kept up at all hours of the day and night in the Charltons' home in Ashington. At one stage, no less than 18 top clubs were trying to take him on. Cissie recalled, 'I'd be cleaning the fireplace in the morning and I'd look round and there would be another one standing behind me. There were times when we had one scout in the living room and another in the kitchen. The Arsenal scout, in particular, always seemed to be on the doorstep.' In fact, Cissie was quite keen for Bobby to join Arsenal, because of the club's reputation for looking after young players, while Bobby himself has said that he was attracted to the fame of a big London club. 'I was very tempted to go to Arsenal. Since I was a northerner born and bred you would have thought that Highbury would be the last place for me. Yet the temptation was a very real one. Arsenal still has tremendous glamour and there's almost a physical attraction in going to a club which boasts such names as Hapgood, Bastin, James, Male and the Comptons.'

But, despite all the advances from Arsenal and the other clubs, Bobby decided to stick with the earlier offer from Manchester United. There were a number of reasons. One was that Joe Armstrong, the scout, had been the first on the scene, showing an interest before Bobby had even been selected for a schoolboy international. 'Whoever was going to be first was going to be in with a real shout. I wanted to be a footballer as quickly as possible and Joe was the first,' he told Tony Gubba in a 1993 BBC interview. Since that initial meeting, Armstrong had maintained regular contact with the Charltons – to such an extent that when the local education authority objected to all the scouts following Bobby from match to match, Armstrong passed himself off as his 'uncle', while his wife became 'Aunt Sally'.

Just as importantly, given the influence of Cissie on the Charlton household, Armstrong made sure he cultivated her. It was the kind of role he relished as much as talent hunting, for the tiny, grey-haired, crinkle-faced Armstrong delighted in his ability to charm the working-class mothers of his young quarries. As Eamon Dunphy, journalist and ex-Manchester United youth player, puts it: 'Joe was a delightful man with a shrewd mind and an instinctive grasp of the human condition. Women liked him. He was kindly yet flirtatious in a comforting way. Mothers were apt to be apprehensive about big city life with all its temptations. Joe understood their fears only too well.'

If Arsenal had glamour, then so did Manchester United in abundance. By the early 1950s, United had become the most exciting force in British soccer, winning the League in 1951/52 and gaining admirers across the country for their flowing style and brilliant young players like Johnny Berry, Duncan Edwards and Roger Byrne. When Bobby Charlton visited Maine Road for a schools trial match in March 1953 between East Northumberland Boys and Manchester Boys, another future United youth star, Wilf McGuinness, was in the Manchester team. 'I was captain most of the time of everything I played in and I was a bit cocky. I saw this young lad. He came up to me after the game when we had beaten them, and said, "We may both be going to United. My name is Bobby Charlton," and I thought, "Who the hell is Bobby Charlton?" He was very weak-looking in those days and made little impression on me. All I thought was, well, he's not a bad little player.'

By coincidence, this was the day that Tommy Taylor, the centre-forward, signed for United from Barnsley for a British transfer record of £29,999 – Matt Busby had knocked a pound off the fee so Taylor would not be lumbered with the title of the first £30,000 player. After Bobby's game, the local Manchester boys rushed off to see United, while Bobby had to travel home to Northumberland. As the bus took him to the rail station, he passed Old Trafford and glimpsed thousands of fans queuing eagerly to get into the ground. The whole experience only stoked the fires of his enthusiasm for the club.

Throughout his life, Bobby may have been unassuming, but he never lacked confidence in his ability. Certain that he could compete at the highest level, he therefore wanted a club which would provide him with the best training. Manchester United, he thought, fitted the bill because of its reputation for a strong youth policy. It was a policy born largely of necessity. Immediately after the war, when Matt Busby was appointed manager, the club had been desperately short of cash, largely because Old Trafford had been badly bombed by the Luftwaffe. Though the financial situation had improved by the turn of the decade, Busby was still reluctant to spend heavily in the transfer market. He preferred the acquisition of youthful excellence as the route to success, becoming particularly adept at exploiting the pool of talent available in schools football, a source largely ignored by other clubs. It is a remarkable fact that between 1951 and 1957, the golden years of the Busby Babes, United bought just one player, Tommy Taylor. So many of the other great names of that era, such as Albert Scanlon, David Pegg, Mark Jones, Wilf McGuinness and Eddie Colman, came directly from school, just as Bobby Charlton did. Ron Routledge, Bobby's Ashington contemporary, says that Bobby's desire to join United reflected his self-belief. 'He said to me, just before he signed, "Ronnie, I'm going to be the best." That is where you've really got to admire him. He could have gone to any other club and been quite comfortable. But he didn't because he wanted to be with the top young players – and United had the name then because of the Busby Babes. There was no way he was ever going anywhere else.'

When he signed for United, many in the north-east expressed surprise that he had not joined Newcastle, effectively his local side. In fact, his parents even received angry mail from several Newcastle fans, complaining about the decision to allow Bobby to leave the area. But, as Bobby later explained, it was Cissie's own cousin, 'Wor Jackie' Milburn, who was instrumental in ensuring that Bobby did not sign for Newcastle: 'He came armed with an offer to give me a job on a north-eastern newspaper but he was completely honest with me. He told me it was not such a good club at that time and that, what organization there was, was inefficient. He didn't believe in the way they treated their young players and the training was almost non-existent. They just went to the ground on Tuesday and Thursday evenings, kicked a ball around and there was no coaching.'

The other great club in the north-east, Sunderland, was never really in the running after an incident in which Bobby felt he was rebuffed by them. This happened on that frost-bitten morning in February 1953 when Joe Armstrong from United turned up to see Bobby playing for East Northumberland Boys. A scout from Sunderland was also at the match but at the final whistle, instead of going to see Bobby, he approached Ron Routledge, the East Northumberland goalkeeper, and made him an offer. According to Cissie, 'Bobby was really hurt to have been overlooked by Sunderland that day. Later, when Sunderland joined a long queue of major clubs trying to recruit Bobby, he had his own back. This time it was Bobby who did the turning down.' But Sunderland did not give up easily. Even when Bobby was travelling down to Manchester to sign formally for United, the Sunderland scout Charlie Ferguson followed him and got on the same train in the hope of persuading Bobby to change his mind.

Ray Wood, the former Manchester United and England goalkeeper who played throughout the 1950s with Bobby, says that Sunderland would have been absolutely the wrong club for him because of its mean spirit and lack of support for youngsters. 'Like Bobby, I'm from the north-east and Sunderland had wanted to sign me after I had played in the County Cup Final at Roker. They were known as the Bank of England team, they were so rich. After a meeting with the manager, Bill Murray, I was offered the forms to become a professional. Before I had looked at them, he asked, "How much were your expenses?" I said about one shilling, and ten-and-a-half pence. He gave me two shillings and asked for change. I could not believe it. I didn't sign after that. I don't think Bobby would have done as well if he had joined Sunderland or Newcastle. Neither wanted good young players to escape but, unlike United, they never give them a proper chance to develop.'

For all the high-minded talk of youth policies, there could also have been a simpler reason why United were able to win the battle for Bobby's signature: money. There were persistent claims that, as at some other top clubs, United offered financial rewards to the parents of talented youngsters – and this may have happened in Bobby's case. As Ron Routledge said to me, 'Bobby was off to

United , yes, because of the youth policy, but also because of the little incentives on offer.' Cissie denied, in her autobiography, that she or husband were ever tempted: 'The high-pressure tactics employed by the more unscrupulous scouts included some pretty lucrative bribes. Yet the plain fact of the matter was that taking bribes was illegal and we just couldn't bring ourselves to do it, even if they were an accepted fact of professional football life in those days. We were honest, working-class people with a very clear idea of right and wrong and no amount of money was going to change that.'

But the distinguished football writer Brian Glanville gave me a different account. 'I was once told by Jackie Milburn, with whom I was very friendly, that Bobby was all set to join Newcastle United. The deal had been done and dusted and Bobby was going to get a newspaper job. But Manchester United ensured it did not happen. According to Jackie's story, Cissie said to him, "I'm terribly sorry, but United offered us £750. What could I do?"' Brian Glanville continues: 'I have put that story to Jack Charlton and he has denied it but it would hardly be a surprise if it were true. At the time there were two clubs which were absolutely notorious for suborning young players and they were Manchester United and Chelsea. Matt Busby, for all his genial, incorruptible image, was actually a very ruthless man.' Glanville points to the example of Duncan Edwards, who was born in Dudley in the heart of the West Midlands. It would have been obvious for him to join Wolves or West Brom, both out-standing clubs in the 1950s, but instead he was enticed to Old Trafford. And, as John Kennedy wrote in his biography of Tommy Taylor, there were "rumours going around at the time of his transfer that Matt had offered all sorts of inducements to persuade Tommy".'

Rumours about such payments were given more credence in 1979, long after Matt Busby had retired, when a Granada *World in Action* programme revealed the web of unscrupulousness at Old Trafford. Most of the programme focused on the actions of United's late chairman, 'Champagne Louis' Edwards – father of the current chairman Martin – who made a fortune in the meat business, partly through the manipulation of local authority catering contracts, and used his wealth to gain control at Old Trafford in the1960s. Shortly after the programme was screened, he died of a heart attack while having a bath. Granada researchers uncovered a wealth of evidence suggesting that United were in the habit of paying more than just transfer fees. Particularly damning was the testimony of John Aston, one of United's great players of the post-war era and junior team coach since 1954, who, in a sworn affidavit, said, 'Some of these boys were induced to sign because United offered them or their parents backhand payments. In some cases I was personally involved in obtaining cash and handing it to the families of boys.' As Aston explained, money would be secretly raised through fictitious expense accounts, and then used to pay off families. Such was the strength of Aston's evidence that Matt made little real effort to dispute it, while two other books repeated the claims. One, Michael Crick and David Smith's *Betrayal of a Legend*, states: '£500 or £1,000 might be handed over in banknotes. Alternatively, the father of a promising young player might be employed as a part-time scout, though, of course, he was not expected to do anything for this.' And Eamon Dunphy, in his brilliantly vivid and subtle biography of Sir Matt, *A Strange Kind of Glory*, writes: 'Year by year, Matt Busby had found himself sucked into a moral quagmire. A few quid in an envelope to the father of a talented youngster for scouting, no bribe intended.' This does not, of course, necessarily mean that all young players, like Bobby, were acquired through such methods, or that they would have been aware of such approaches by United. But it does put into perspective some of the sugary guff that is written about United and Busby, as if he was too virtuous ever to be involved in the more mercenary aspects of professional football.

On 16 June 1953 Busby finally got what he wanted, when Bobby officially signed for United, thus beginning an association with the club that lasts to this day. So highly regarded was Bobby that the *Daily Mail* recorded the event. 'This may sound a minor signing but it is of major importance in a soccer world which is acutely aware of the value of developing youngsters. Charlton, the star of the

England v Wales match last season, has superb positional sense and ball control.' Before leaving for Manchester he played out his last season for Bedlington. Evan Martin recalls, 'We had a hell of a team in 1952/53, thanks mainly to Bobby's skills. We used to go to really hard secondary schools, like North Shields, and win easily. In the very last match of the season, we were on the coach and Bobby asked Tucker Robinson, "What's the highest individual score this season?"

"I got three against Alnwick," replied Tucker.

"Well, I'll get four today."

And he did. Two of them were 30-yard piledrivers. The goalkeeper did not even see them.'

Elder brother Jack had played no role in the saga of Bobby's move to United. There was no army of scouts after him, no club representative offering Cissie a fistful of cash for his services. Yet it is one of the strange twists of this story that Jack was actually taken on by a League club before Bobby. For most of his early years, Jack had rarely impressed anyone with his football. He was merely another competent youngster, a decent stopper of the kind that could be found throughout the north-east. He played for his school, district and YMCA side, but did not come near to his county team, never mind the England Schoolboys. In fact, he was dropped for several games from his district because of his habit of standing still, as if wondering what had happened, when he was beaten by a winger. 'You'll have to sharpen your wits up,' he was told. Evan Martin says: 'I remember watching Jack playing for the East Northumberland Juniors. He was at left-back and he was big, gangly and awkward. He did not impress me one bit.'

Indeed, it is a remarkable fact that the man who later gained a World Cup winner's medal could not even get in the Ashington FC junior team. Ken Prior, who grew up with Jack, explains: 'Jimmy Denmark, the former Newcastle centre-half, came to manage Ashington and the club decided to have a junior side. So the call went out for all the budding youngsters to come to Portland Park. We had a trial and Jack did not even get picked for the final squad. I didn't think he played too badly but he did not stand out, certainly not for his size. Jack went home, a bit upset, and after he'd gone, Jimmy Denmark said, "You know, that lad will never make a player."'

Yet, as he approached his 15th birthday, there was something about Jack – his size, his strength, above all his 'Milburn' heritage – which meant that he could attract the interest of a League club. After playing well for the Ashington YMCA Under-18 side in a match against Barkworth, he was approached by a Leeds scout, who offered him a trial at Elland Road. In his later career, Jack would sometimes maintain that he, like Bobby, was always destined to be a professional footballer. 'Neither of us had ever considered anything but playing the game for a living,' he told the *News of the World* in April 1973.

But this was hardly true. For Jack had never shown any inclination towards professional football, and, in a rare moment of self-doubt, he feared that if he took up the offer from Leeds, he might not make the grade because of his lack of talent. He saw himself as a big, gangly lad who was not really good enough. Going to Leeds risked the pain of rejection. As he once explained to Mike Kirkup, 'The only way you could get away from Ashington was to play football. But there was always the worry that you might not make it, and would get sent home again. Then you would come back as a failure.' Moreover, Jack loved the teenage life he had created for himself in the Northumberland countryside. If he left home for a big city like Leeds, he would no longer be able to fish and poach and shoot. Nor were his parents enthusiastic. In another illustration of how Jack felt he was excluded by his mother in favour of Bobby, he says that 'She didn't think I was good enough for professional football.' Indeed, Cissie held Jack's skills in such contempt that, when she first heard of the interest from Leeds, she felt that there had been some mistake. The club must have confused him with Bobby. 'I was amazed because although Jack enjoyed his football, he just wasn't the same calibre as Bobby,' she wrote.

Due to his mother's dismissive attitude and his own reluctance, Jack told Leeds that he was not interested. Now, with the end of his time at school approaching, he had to find a job. And the obvious one was coalmining. 'At that time in Ashington there were only the pits; there was very little else, really,' he recalls. So he followed his father into work at the Linton colliery. Initially, because he was serving his apprenticeship, Jack did not have to go underground. Instead, his first job was to stand by a conveyor belt for eight hours, sorting out the coal from debris as it came up from the mine. Never a patient man – except on the river – Jack found the work unbearably dull and kept asking for a move.

His badgering paid off. He was transferred to the weigh-cabin, where his task was to weigh the wagons before and after they were filled with coal, calculate the difference, then write the weight on the trucks before they were shunted into the sidings. Jack enjoyed his work there. 'Sometimes there was a quiet period when no coal was coming down and that was great. You could draw little things with a piece of stone. It was an artist's paradise. There were footballers, goals, nudes, everything. Some men worked there forever.' The other great advantage for Jack was that the sidings ran out on to land full of rabbits. This provided ample scope for his homemade snares, and Jack would regularly catch three or four a day, selling them on to the other miners. 'I usually left the pit at least two shillings richer than when I arrived.'

But it could not last. Jack was told that he had been selected to go on a 16-week training course in preparation for becoming a fully-fledged miner. As part of this induction, he was shown what work was like in the pit. Jack was appalled by the experience of his first trip underground: the cramped conditions, crawling on his hands and knees along a seam only three feet high; the noise from the explosives; the dust which went everywhere, including eyes and lungs; the gale force blasts of air from the ventilation system.

Returning to the surface, Jack handed in his resignation straight away, to the anger of the colliery manager.

'We've just spent a fortune training you. If you walk away now, I'll see that you never get another job in the pit   anywhere.'

'I don't want another job in the pit.'

Jack already had another option lined up. Two weeks earlier, with a sense of foreboding about the job in the colliery, he had applied to become a police cadet. Now Jack could not be regarded as one of nature's law enforcers, and his motivation was suitably vague. 'I was getting close to six feet in height. That, to my young mind, seemed as good a reason as any why I should try for the police.' Impressed with Jack's application, the Northumberland Constabulary summoned him to an interview.

But then fate, in the form of Leeds United, intervened. Despite the earlier rebuff, the club had not given up hope of attracting Jack and now another invitation arrived for a trial. This time Jack, having seen the misery of life underground, was much more receptive to the idea of becoming a professional footballer. He knew the truth, though, that Leeds' interest was partly motivated by his close family connection with the club, with three of his uncles having been players there and one of them, Jimmy, still in the squad. 'When I got the offer of a trial, I knew it was right nepotism,' Jack once said.

The immediate problem for Jack was a logistical one. His police interview was in Morpeth on Friday afternoon, while his trial at Leeds was early the following Saturday morning. In the days before motorways, there was no physical way he could get to both places within this timescale. So Jack decided to abandon the police interview, instead travelling down on Friday to Leeds with his parents. The trial was to be the most important match of his young life. If he succeeded, a new future in soccer beckoned. If he failed, there was little chance that any other club would show an interest.

Snow was falling that Saturday morning at Elland Road as Jack ran out to play for Leeds Juniors against the Newcastle youth team. He was in his customary left-back position, and, in the difficult conditions, he was not sure he had done enough to impress. But the club thought otherwise, admiring his height and solid style. After the game he was summoned into the office of the club secretary, Arthur Crowther.

'We'd like you to join the ground staff, Charlton.'

'Do you really think I'm good enough?'

'Of course. Why do you think we'd want you if we didn't.'

Jack went home with his parents on Sunday to pick up his belongings, before returning to Leeds to report for duty on the Monday. Any ideas about becoming a policeman had been ditched as quickly as the career in mining. Despite barely giving the matter a thought, he had somehow become a professional footballer. His only anxiety now was whether he would succeed. What he dreaded, above all else, was being forced to return to Ashington, labelled a failure.

CHAPTER THREE

The Rebel

Jack and Bobby might have gone to two of the biggest cities in
Britain, but they had joined very different clubs. Manchester United
were one of the soccer powers in the land, capturing the imagination of the public with their dynamic style and young stars. On the
other hand, Leeds United were languishing in the Second Division,
an ordinary side full of ordinary players. What particularly surprised
Jack when he arrived at Elland Road was the shabbiness of the
ground, the disrepair symbolic of the state of the ailing club. 'I
always regarded Leeds as a big club but I must confess that I had the
wind knocked out of my sails when I saw the place for the first time.
The terraces were made from ashes, not concrete, and there was
more than a liberal sprinkling of weeds sprouting around the
ground. In general the ground had a look of untidiness and at first I
was disappointed. Frankly, I don't know just what I expected but it
did not quite come up to the standard I had envisaged as a youngster,' wrote Jack in one of his testimonial programmes when he
retired in 1973.

The only thing the clubs had in common was the reputation of
their managers. When Bobby joined Manchester in 1953, Matt
Busby had already been in charge for eight years, building teams
which combined a dazzling creative flair with a powerful competitive

edge. Born in a poor Lanarkshire mining village, Busby had been a highly effective wing-half for Manchester City, Liverpool and Scotland in the inter-war years, his ability to read the game making up for his lack of pace. A family man and a Catholic, he exuded a natural charisma and authority as manager, rarely having to raise his voice. His judgement of a footballer, both in terms of talent and character, was almost impeccable. All players held him in respect, the younger ones in awe. 'In his control of the club, there is a lot of the character of a stern devoted grandfather, making all the big decisions, ordering and disciplining in some huge, unpredictably gifted household,' wrote Arthur Hopcraft in *The Football Man*. John Docherty, one of the United players of the 1950s, says of Busby: 'There was always this impression of him being such a gentleman, but, in fact, he was as hard as fucking nails. Remember, he was from the Scottish coalfields. You don't build great sides by being a nice guy. In private, he was a hard bastard.'

Jack's first manager at Leeds, Major Frank Buckley, was an equally powerful figure in the football world. Unlike Busby, who could terrify a professional with just a raised eyebrow, Buckley was much more volcanic, using loud, foul-mouthed tirades to impose his will. Born in 1883, he fought in both the Boer War and the First World War, where he acquired the title of Major. He was a good enough footballer to have played for England, while his finest spell of management was at Wolves just before the Second World War. An autocrat with a flair for publicity, he captured the headlines in 1938 by announcing that he had given his players 'monkey gland' injections to increase their energy levels. Stan Cullis, the Wolves captain of the 1930s and later Busby's biggest managerial rival of the 1950s, once said of Buckley's authoritarian style: 'He was never one of those equivocal people. He was a one-man band, who knew exactly what he wanted and where he was going' – an approach that some might argue Jack Charlton was to adopt in his managerial career. When Jack arrived at Leeds in 1950, Buckley was past his best. But signs of the old dictatorial spirit still lingered. Bobby Forrest, who joined Leeds at the same time as Jack, recalls: 'When we were training, Major Buckley used to sit in the old stand with a megaphone. If you did anything wrong, you'd get a real blast. The language was unbelievable. If I played a ball and it was cut out, he would scream, "You're fucking useless, Forrest." The residents nearby would regularly complain and eventually Leeds had to take the megaphone off him.' Buckley could be witty as well. In one dressing-room talk he admonished his centre-forward: 'Jesus Christ was a clever man, but if he'd played football he would never have found you.'

As a member of the ground staff, Jack also experienced the sharp end of the major's tongue. On one occasion he was on the Elland Road pitch with another boy, carrying out the monotonous task of removing weeds and replacing them with grass seed. For once, the cold heart of the major softened, for when he saw the two lads, he promised them each five shillings for every bucket they filled with weeds. When the boys had finished, they had filled six pails, so, with characteristic impertinence, Jack walked straight up to the major's office.

'What the hell do you want?'

'My 30 bob for the buckets of weeds.'

'Get out of here! You're already getting paid to do that work. Don't ever let me see you up here again with your buckets.'

In fact this kind of menial task was typical of the life of the ground staff. 'It was a hard apprenticeship,' said Jack in a 1968 television interview. 'You were basically a lackey, cleaning out the toilets, sweeping the terraces, painting and oiling the turnstiles, cleaning piles and piles of boots, putting studs in them, pumping up balls and brushing the car park.'

Traditionalists would say that such a routine taught the teenagers discipline, but Jack's friend and fellow manager, Ian Greaves, thinks it was a nonsense. 'I found it really odd the way these clubs exploited the future stars. It stuck with me for years. There is no way you could get away with that nowadays – and quite right too. You are either a cleaner or a footballer. When I became a manager, I never insulted young boys that way.' But Jack, in a rare submission to officialdom, knuckled down, still haunted by the fear that if he did not stick at it, he would be forced to return to Ashington. As he wrote in his autobiography, 'There was shame for the lads who were rejected. That was the fear that drove me during my first two years at Leeds. I did not regard myself as anything special when it came to playing football, otherwise I would have jumped at the first offer from Leeds and never gone near the mines. But now I had been given a second chance, I was determined that, come hell or high water, I'd take it.'

He worked just as hard on the pitch, training rigorously five days a week and playing for both the youth and third teams. Sometimes, he would even turn out twice on the same day. Such was his enthusiasm that he was willing to act as linesman if the appointed official failed to show. The thirds provided a particularly tough learning environment, because they played in the Yorkshire League, which was basically a miners' competition. 'I was just 16, playing against hard, fully mature men, big strong buggers who clattered into you with no quarter asked or given.' It was the hardest league he was ever to experience in his life, and Jack says it was the making of him.

In his later years, Jack became well known for his relaxed approach to life, enjoying a pint and a cigarette most evenings. But in this mood of youthful determination, he shunned such indulgences. Living in a boarding house near Elland Road, run by Mary Crowther and her spinster daughter Laura, he ignored the nightlife of Leeds except for occasional visits to the local cinema. Astonishingly, in his first two years at the club, he went into the city centre just twice. He was good about money, too, sending home £1 out of his limited weekly earnings of just £4 10s a week. Jack was pleased to be living in digs, for it was the first time in his life that he had been able to sleep in a bed on his own. Yet he also found it odd that his mother had not asked either of her two brothers to put him up. After all, one of the supposed advantages of going to Leeds was the family connection, with Cissie having claimed that Jack 'would be well looked after' in Leeds.

Jack's increasingly impressive performances and hard work paid off. After years of mediocrity, he was developing fast as a player. In his second year at Leeds, he was given occasional appearances in the reserve team, while in a practice match he played at centre-half and was given the job of marking the giant John Charles, the awesome Welsh international who could play up front or at the back. Jack felt he dealt with Charles quite well that day. Meanwhile, the dictatorial and profane Major Buckley, aged 69, had retired from Leeds United, his place taken by Raich Carter, the former Sunderland, Derby and England striker, whose success as a manager never matched his prowess in front of goal. Carter now had Jack's future in his hands, for League regulations stipulated that, at the age of 17, a member of the ground staff had either to be given a contract or released. Having heard nothing, Jack walked into the secretary's office on 8 May 1952.

'It's my 17th birthday today. Are you going to sign me or not?'

'I'm afraid the first team's in Holland, and Mr Carter has left no instructions,' replied Arthur Crowther. Jack was now worried, feeling that the dreaded journey back to Ashington now beckoned. But the next day, he was summoned to see Raich Carter. To his immense relief, Jack was offered terms as a professional, a £10 signing-on fee, plus £14 a week, the maximum wage, more than three times the amount he was earning as an apprentice, and the highest wage of any young professional at the club.

After receiving this good news, Jack went across the road to a newsagent's shop run by Jim Johnson.

'Well, have you signed yet?' asked Johnson.

'Just now,' replied Jack, surprised at the question.

'Thank God for that. I've had scouts from other clubs, about a dozen of the buggers, in and out of here all week, wanting to know if you'd signed.'

'What, to know if I'd signed?' said Jack, astonished at this level of interest.

'You, yes. They've been sweating on the highest line, over the road.'

Jack walked out of the shop, sensing that after all the doubts, he might at last have a real future in the game.

That feeling was only enhanced when, after a year of further progress with the reserves, he was elevated to the first team on 24 April 1953, the last day of the season. He was not yet 18 and it was only four years since he had been a struggling left-back in the East Northumberland Juniors, yet here he was, making his League debut against Doncaster Rovers, a full month before his more talented younger brother had officially signed for United. Despite his in-experience, Jack received little support from either management or players. He was merely informed that he would be at centre-half while John Charles would play centre-forward. As he recalled, 'Incredibly, Raich Carter never came near me that day, never told me why he had put me in the team. And when I climbed aboard the first-team bus taking us to Doncaster the next day, I was left completely alone, without as much as a word from my new team-mates. I mean, nobody told me what I was expected to do, no tactical talk, nothing.' But Jack acquitted himself well against Eddie McMorran, the Doncaster and Northern Ireland centre-forward, who himself was a player at Leeds in the late 1940s. 'Charlton did not let his side down,' was the verdict of the *Yorkshire Post*.

Soon after his League debut, Jack was called up to do his National Service. Because of his physique, he was selected for the Horse Guards and, during his two years of duty, he was based mainly at Windsor. It was through the army that Jack discovered two of the vices he had been carefully avoiding at Leeds: girls and cigarettes. Jack learnt that Windsor was a Mecca for young women, who came up from London to admire both the sights and the soldiers. For the first time in his life, he went to dances, and with his easy confidence and striking appearance, he was rarely short of female company. 'I had a girlfriend in Slough and a girlfriend in Maidenhead, but it was never very serious,' he later explained.

Smoking was a habit that Jack started during his years as a cavalryman. But he has always been an eccentric sort of a smoker, rarely getting through more than 10 cigarettes a day, unlike the real addict who cannot go long without lighting up. More interestingly, because he often does not have his own packet, he has become notorious in the football world for taking cigarettes off others, usually without their permission. Peter Lorimer, his colleague at Leeds, recalls: 'The funny thing is that he did not really smoke that much, yet was always cadging fags. He would not mind who he asked, even total strangers. I have seen him on the train just reach over to the fags on another table. If the Queen Mother was sitting next to him, he would ask her if he could borrow one.' In fact, when he was on guard duty at Windsor, Jack once went to have a cigarette break in the bushes. Finding that he was without any matches, he came out from the foliage to ask a passer-by for a light. To his embarrassment, he was face to face with Prince Philip. Jack ran faster than he usually did at Elland Road.

Jack later said that his two years of National Service were amongst the happiest of his life, especially because the budding manager in him emerged. In an interview in 1994, Jack said, 'My spell in the army did me the world of good. When I was with the Guards at Windsor I really began to enjoy myself. I was made captain of the army football team, the first private to be given such an honour in the history of the Guards. For about a year I organized the training and everything we needed. I made sure that I got myself and all the lads the cushy jobs. We had all the time off we needed, no guard duty and a late breakfast everyday. Because we had a couple of other professionals like me, we had a good team and we did bloody well. We flew to Germany and won the Cavalry Cup.'

Due to the amount of football he played in the army , Jack turned out only occasionally for Leeds reserves when he was on leave, while he made a solitary appearance for the first team – in August 1954 against Lincoln City. But the army had a profound effect on his character. Jack had gone into the Horse Guards as a diligent young apprentice, only too grateful just to be part of the Elland Road squad. He returned the captain of an army cup-winning side, certain of his own leadership abilities and used to ordering around other players. In short, he had become a rather brash, presumptuous young man.

And, now he was available again, that could only spell problems with the other Leeds professionals and officials. The next few years at Elland Road were to be filled with so many clashes that it frequently looked like Jack would be forced to leave the club.

Albert Nightingale, the Leeds striker in this period, told me: 'I know he was only starting his career but he was terribly confident about himself, even arrogant. He used to give real stick to the players around him if anything went wrong, even to me – and I was in the forward line. Big Jack did not care what he said to anyone, he was that cocky. He would not speak to you properly. If you were having a bad game, he would lose his head and start swearing at you. He would bad-mouth players on the pitch, and that would lead to a lot of rows. Nobody liked him really. His head was too big for his shoulders. Because he was always shouting at them, people found it difficult to play with him. And, though he was a strong character, he was only a 50-50 footballer, decent in the air but not much skill on the ground. He was mean as well, never spent two ha'pennies. It was a joke in the team, the way he never put his hand in his pocket. But Big Jack took it all in his stride.' John Charles, the star of that Leeds team, was frequently infuriated with Jack's attitude. On one occasion, Leeds were playing Fulham and John Charles was playing centre-forward. With just 10 minutes left and Leeds 1–0 up, Buckley decided to bring Charles back to strengthen the defence. 'Fuck off back up the field,' said Jack when the Welshman arrived. Charles was so annoyed that, in the bath afterwards, he grabbed Jack and pushed him right under the water. 'That will bloody show him,' he said. Another time, when Jack questioned an instruction, Charles pinned him against the wall and said, 'Listen, I'll give you a bloody hammering next time.'

Bobby Forrest, who also played with Jack and became a good friend, recalls: 'He was always outspoken. He never worried about having a go at anyone, never held anything back. He let you know if he thought you'd done wrong. With his quick temper, he encouraged mickey-taking. Because he had a long neck, some of us nicknamed him "Turkey". I remember we played up at Sunderland on

Boxing Day and we stayed in a hotel in Seaburn the night before. Jack was, typically, the last one down to the dining room that evening, and while we were waiting for him, I had gone into the kitchen, where there was a turkey with its head chopped off. So I grabbed the head and put it on Jack's plate. When he came in and saw this, he was absolutely furious. He really lost his temper. All the lads started laughing so he picked it up and threw it at me. But I ducked and it went crashing into a table behind, where a couple were quietly having their Christmas dinner.'

Bobby Forrest also remembers what Jack was like as a footballer in the 1950s: 'In his later career, he was so strong in the air, but in his first years, it was very different. It was striking the number of times in practice that he would try to head the ball and it would just shoot straight up instead of in the direction he wanted. There was no way, when I first saw him, that I would have ever thought he might one day become an England player.' But, unlike some, Bobby was fond of Jack. 'For all his confidence and hardness on the field, there was never an edge to him. He was just one of the lads, good for a laugh.' Jimmy Dunn, the Scottish-born defender, speaks of both Jack's resilience and his interest in money-making schemes, what Jack has always called his 'little earners'. 'Jack would stand no bloody nonsense. He could be bloody hard and was never intimidated by anyone at all. He was tough, confident, a strong devil. I got quite close to him. During the summer, when we reported for training and the team were building up a sweat in the hot weather, Jack and I would buy several litres of pop from over the road, then charge each player tuppence for a drink.'

Jack himself admits that, on his return from National Service, he could be a pain, though he put a lot of the blame on the organization of Leeds. He told the author Rick Broadbent: 'I thought I knew a thing or two because I'd been away and I'd suggest things; but they'd just say, "Stop moaning and get on with it – this is how we do it." The thing is, we didn't have any coaching in Leeds in those days. A day's training would consist of turning up, running the long side of the pitch and walking the short side. For variety, they'd say turn around and go the other way. Then we'd go to the tarmac car park and play seven-a-side. Nobody taught you anything and nobody learned anything. It was ridiculous and I got bloody fed up with it.' The point about training is reinforced by Albert Nightingale: 'Did we ever go through manoeuvres or tactics? Did we heck. We never practised anything in training.'

In such an atmosphere, it was predictable that Jack should clash with his managers. He regarded Raich Carter as a poor coach, and was not afraid to say so. 'We never had any team talks and we never had a run-down on the opposition. Leeds was not what I would call a professional club in those days,' he wrote later. To be fair to Jack, most other Leeds players shared this low opinion of Carter, who was unable to relate to his squad. Team captain Tommy Burden, for instance, left the club in 1954 following a bitter fallout with Carter. In a dressing-room row after a defeat by Bury, Burden was furious that Carter blamed the Leeds keeper for a goal conceded from a free-kick. 'I said to him, "You're the one who's bloody well to blame." I always felt that Raich suffered from thinking that there were no players any better than him.' John Charles said of Carter: 'He was very opinionated. He had the view, "I do it this way, so you do it this way." He loved himself. He would take the credit for what you'd done.'

Even in the face of such failings, Raich Carter had a strong enough side to win promotion from the Second Division in the 1955/56 season. But within a year, he had been forced to sell John Charles, the player around whom this success had been built. Transferred to Juventus for a world record fee of £65,000 in April 1957, Charles benefited hugely from the move, gaining an international reputation, a trio of Italian championship medals and the award of European Footballer of the Year. Jack Charlton also benefited for, with Charles gone, his place as centre-half now seemed secure. The transfer, however, was highly damaging to Leeds. Without the dominant figure of Charles in defence or attack, the club struggled in the First Division. Carter complained that he was not allowed to use the revenue from the deal to rebuild his side with new players, but by December 1958, the board had lost faith in him and he was sacked.

Bill Lambton, the man who replaced Carter, commanded even less authority amongst the players. A former goalkeeper with Nottingham Forest, Exeter City and Doncaster Rovers, he had been appointed by Raich Carter in 1957 as part of the Elland Road back-up staff. Almost as soon as he took over, his inadequacy as a manager was brutally exposed. His unorthodox training routines were regarded as absurd, his tactical advice negligible. Jack said later with typical honesty: 'Lambton wasn't a player, he wasn't a coach, he wasn't anything.' One of Lambton's bizarre ideas was to ask the players to wear running spikes during five-a-side matches. 'It was so silly. No-one would go near anyone else. I couldn't see the purpose,' recalls Bobby Forrest. During a practice session on a windy day, the players complained that the balls had been pumped up too hard, making them difficult to kick. Lambton came on to the pitch and announced: 'Nonsense. Good players should be able to kick balls like that in their bare feet and not hurt themselves.'

'Well, go on then, show us,' said Jack.

This the manager did, taking off his boots and hitting the balls in his bare feet. Though he refused to admit his pain, he winced with every kick and had to limp away at the end of the session. Jack despised Lambton at this moment for his stupidity and stubbornness. For Jimmy Dunn, this sort of foolish behaviour was typical of the manager: 'He was so bad it was comic. I could not believe he was made manager. I don't know how he got the job. He knew nothing about tactics, nothing about playing, nothing about football. I had no respect for him. No-one did.'

Jack clashed with Lambton off the field as well. At a team dinner in a Nottingham hotel, Jack created a scene when he was asked by the waiter which starter he had chosen from the set menu. Jack, feeling particularly hungry, said he would have both melon and soup. Lambton heard the request and exploded. 'You're not having both. Nobody has both.'

'What are you talking about?' asked Jack. 'It's on the menu –

two if you want it. I can have it if I want it, can't I?' asked Jack.

'No. You'll just have one or the other. Nobody eats those things together. It just isn't done,' continued Lambton.

'It is done in the best restaurants, better restaurants than this one. Now I would like both. Can I have them?'

'No.'

'All right. You can stick it,' said Jack, and he walked out of the dining room in a rage. Later he told the journalist Jimmy Mossop, who, like so many, became a close friend: 'Ignorance and dishonesty are two things I cannot tolerate. To try and con me into believing that you can't have soup and melon together is like trying to prove I was ignorant. I reacted because I knew I wasn't ignorant and I knew how things were done.'

There were other aspects of the club which angered Jack, such as the requirement that he sign an attendance book when he turned up for training, or the failure to clamp down on players who were drinking before matches. Perhaps what aggrieved him most were the double standards. A club rule had been imposed that only players and directors were allowed to travel on the team coach. After a game at the Valley, Charlton Athletic's ground in south-west London, when Jack tried to get a lift for two relatives who lived in north London, he was firmly told that the rule applied. No exceptions could be made. Yet two weeks later, when Leeds were playing again in London, he found that Lambton had allowed on to the bus four people who had nothing to do with the club – they actually turned out to be waiters from the team hotel. Jack stood up and angrily confronted Lambton.

'A fortnight ago my relatives had to miss their train and spent hours getting home. Now there's four complete strangers sitting on our coach.'

'It's got nothing to do with you,' said Lambton, 'I make the rules around here. You do as you're told.'

'I won't. You made a rule. You made me stick to it. Now you stick to it. If they're not getting off, I am,' said Jack, gesturing to the waiters.

'Please yourself,' replied Lambton.

With that, Jack made an angry exit from the bus. But then, as Jack stood on the kerbside, a Leeds director intervened. 'Get them off the coach – and get him on.'

Lambton's authority, always weak, had been utterly destroyed by Jack's action. A few days later, in March 1959, a crisis meeting was called at Elland Road, involving the chairman, directors, players and manager. Knowing he was under threat, Lambton made a pathetic plea: 'If you let me stay, we'll have a new start.' But it was too late. Such was the unanimous strength of feeling expressed against the manager that the club had no alternative but to sack him.

Still in his early twenties, Jack had proved that he could be a real influence in the club. Yet, he was still not an especially respected or popular figure amongst his contemporaries. For all his willingness to challenge the establishment, he was still regarded as too bombastic and ill-disciplined to be a good professional. 'My problems in those days were of concentration,' he told Jimmy Mossop. 'Training could not hold my interest. I could not concentrate on playing in practice matches. They never seemed to prove anything.' And he had become just as wayward off the field: 'I was boozing, staying out late and there were girls. I had a bit of a chip on my shoulder and I was causing a fair bit of aggravation at the club.'

Yet for all the problems that he experienced at this time, two crucial events happened in 1958 that were to change his life forever. First, he married. And, second, Don Revie, the most influential figure in Jack's football career, joined Leeds United as a player.

CHAPTER FOUR

The Conformist

'It was forbidding, in many ways, coming to such a big city but I didn't have any fear. It was an adventure for me. I just wanted to play professional football,' Bobby once explained. Like Jack, Bobby had rarely been away from home when he began his adventure in soccer aged just 15 in the summer of 1953. And, just as Jack had been disappointed by his first sight of Elland Road, so Bobby was surprised at the grime and ugliness of Manchester when he arrived in the city. 'When I got off that train at Exchange Station and looked around me, I saw all the buildings completely covered in a thick layer of black. There was so much smoke belching out of all the factories and mills that it clung to the buildings. Ashington, though it was a mining town, was never like that. It wasn't black,' said Charlton in a recent interview.

In the 1950s Manchester was notorious for its thick smog, so dense that it frequently shrouded the city in darkness and made even the shortest journey a nightmare. Joe Carolan, who joined United in 1956, told me, 'The pollution was unbelievable. I remember once getting off the train with some other players, and trying to walk through the centre of the city to my home. There was not a taxi, bus or car to be found anywhere because of the smog. It was so thick and black we could hardly see a thing in front of us. So we walked down the middle of the Stretford Road, and every few hundred yards, one of us would go off to the left or right to check if there was any landmark we might recognize.'

When he disembarked from the train, Bobby was met by Jimmy Murphy, Manchester United assistant manager, who was to have a bigger influence than Matt Busby over the development of Bobby Charlton as a footballer. Murphy, who never learnt to drive, took Bobby by taxi to digs run by a Mrs Watson near the Old Trafford cricket ground. Throughout the journey, as Bobby later recalled, Murphy spent the time extolling the virtues of Duncan Edwards, 'Great left foot, great right foot, strong in the tackle, great in the air, reads the game, can play in any position, is fast and has tremendous enthusiasm.' Bobby was in awe of Duncan before he had met him.

Unlike Jack, Bobby was not appointed a member of the club's ground staff when he joined United. And this again highlights the difference in the treatment of Bobby and Jack. For Cissie had been quite happy for Jack to join the Leeds ground staff at 15, even if it meant tedious and degrading work. But very different standards were applied to Bobby. 'My parents had been told that all you had to do on the ground staff was sweep up and clean toilets and all that, and my mum and dad didn't want me to do that,' said Bobby later. It was a classic case of favouritism, where the elder brother had to carry out duties which were seen as too demeaning for the younger.

Instead of acting as an orderly, it was arranged for Bobby to carry on with his education. Bedlington Grammar, which had strongly disapproved of Bobby's move into League football, had persuaded his parents to transfer him to Stretford Grammar in Manchester, so he might be able to gain some GCE (General Certificate of Education) qualifications. But the move turned out to be a disastrous one for Bobby, as both his studies and his football suffered. He rose at 7.30am, got to school at 9am, and then, as soon as his classes were finished, he went to Old Trafford for three hours of training. Returning to his digs at about 9pm, he then tried to do his homework. The task was beyond him. 'I was making a complete fool of myself in lessons; they were totally different from the work at

Bedlington because the GCE papers were different. I hardly knew what time of day it was and I found myself going to bed at midnight with unfinished homework which I just could not do. I was only 15 and I was in a terrible quandary because on one hand I could not go on living like that and on the other I did not want to let down my mother,' he wrote. As usual, he was much more concerned about his mother's judgement than his father's.

What made the problem worse was that Stretford Grammar had not been informed about Bobby's decision to sign for United. Understandably, given Bobby's talent, the school expected him to turn out for their side, while Bobby had his commitments with the Old Trafford youth teams. Conflict was inevitable. Within three weeks of the start of term, Bobby had been picked for two different matches on the same day. The moment of truth had arrived, he knew. So he rang his mother to tell her that he wanted to leave the school. Cissie proved understanding, agreeing that there was no point in struggling on at Stretford, and advised him to see the head-master. Now Bobby was always a shy, nervous man – throughout his career at Old Trafford he hardly dared to approach the patriarchal figure of Sir Matt Busby. But he was rarely more apprehensive than the day he had to explain his situation to the headmaster. 'Shaking like a leaf, I said I had no ambition to be an intellectual, that I was going to be a footballer and that I wanted to leave Stretford. He answered in four memorable words, "You are perfectly right."'

Bobby never had any doubts in his early years that he would make it as a professional. It is yet another striking difference between them: Jack the loud bombastic teenager, inwardly plagued by insecurity, and Bobby the quiet, retiring youngster who was certain of his talent. 'I was good and I found it easy,' he once said. After leaving Stretford Grammar, he would have loved to have become a full-time professional at Old Trafford, but his was impossible because he had not yet reached the age of 17. With his mother still reluctant for him to join the ground staff, Bobby had to find a job for a year. He therefore enrolled as an apprentice electrical engineer at the firm of Switch Gear, whose owner was a football enthusiast.

If his schoolwork had been difficult, this position was just dull. Dreaming all the time of soccer, Bobby wasted his day filing pieces of metal, making tea and running errands. Like so many trapped in the dreary routine of the workplace, he indulged in clock watching, frequently going to the lavatory to gaze at the clockface on the top of Stretford Town Hall, willing the hands to speed up so he would be free to go for training.

What made up for the tedium of the job was the atmosphere in Mrs Watson's house. He shared with seven other Busby Babes, including Billy Whelan, David Pegg and Duncan Edwards and they brought him out of his shell. He remembers: 'At first I was a bit homesick and inclined to keep to myself but the others soon accepted me for what I was. It was good fun. Everybody ribbed everyone else and the gags rattled off like machine gun fire. Mark Jones' idea of looking after us was to take us to a horror film in town and then march us all of five miles home. I shared a room with him for a time and then I roomed with Billy Whelan – he was like a big brother to me.' In fact, Bobby felt a far greater affinity to Billy than he did to his real elder brother, for Billy, a devout, teetotal Catholic from Dublin, shared Bobby's qualities of self-effacement and reticence. It is a reflection of the kindness of his fellow lodgers that they would give him articles of clothing and other presents, knowing that he was only earning £2 a week, barely half of what the ground staff apprentices were paid. 'Once Duncan Edwards gave me a new shirt which he said was too small for him. I don't think it really was, but it was a very welcome addition to my sparse wardrobe,' recalled Bobby. Albert Scanlon, the left wing who became a United professional in 1952, thinks that Mrs Watson's was the ideal environment for Bobby. 'When he came to Old Trafford, he was very shy and quiet, though he was a different lad if his mother turned up – he was much more open with her, and she always had such a loud, laughing presence. But Mrs Watson's house did the world of good for him, because he was mixing with other players. They had a great social life together, going to the films in Manchester, or playing football and tennis in the park. Bobby was always comfortable with that group.'

When he reached the age of 17, Bobby was finally able to give up his hated engineering job and become a full professional with United. The morning after he had signed, he went down to the United ground full of enthusiasm. The first person he saw was the trainer, Tom Curry, who gave Bobby a response he did not expect.

'What are you doing here? Shouldn't you be at work?'

'I've just signed my forms,' replied Bobby, expecting a word of congratulation.

'Stupid lad. You should have stuck to your trade. Don't you know what a hard game football is?'

The realities of Curry's remark were soon brought home to Bobby. Until now, at school, in Ashington, and in the county and England junior sides, he had been the dazzling star of the show. But at United, a club already awash with talent, he was just another young pro trying to make his way. Moreover, because he had never received any proper training before, Bobby had fallen into some poor habits. At the highest level, his reliance only on instinct and natural ability would not be enough. Bobby Harrop, who also joined United in 1953, told me: 'Bobby was just another player to me when I joined United. Most of us thought we were equally good. He had his good shot and pace, but he did not seem anything exceptional. In practice matches, we were usually as good as him. He did not stand out.' It is a point reinforced by Albert Scanlon: 'The turnover of youngsters at Old Trafford was phenomenal. Hundreds of lads came through its gates every year, and for every one who signed as a professional they probably let 50 go. With so many good players around, it was hard for someone like Bobby Charlton to shine. When I first saw him, I knew he was good but it would be false to say I knew he'd be one of the greats. He lacked consistency and would run around, trying to do everything at 400 miles an hour.'

Fortunately, Bobby Charlton's training was in the hands of Jimmy Murphy, one of the toughest and shrewdest taskmasters in British football. Like Busby, a practising Catholic born in a coal-mining village, Murphy hailed from the Rhondda valley. He had been a ferocious wing-half for Wales and West Brom in the inter-war years before Matt brought him to Old Trafford as his assistant. Murphy could have been a great manager himself, as he proved in taking Wales to the quarter-finals of the World Cup in 1958 in Sweden, but he preferred to remain at United, turning down lucrative offers from Arsenal and continental sides. Ex-United player John Docherty says that he made the right decision: 'Jimmy was magnificent but he was a natural number two. I think he would have found it hard to be under the constant glare of the press. He liked working with players, being with kids, knocking the shit out of you on the training ground to make you into a better footballer. All the players of my time will tell you that Jimmy Murphy was our greatest single influence, because he could make or break us.' It is a sentiment echoed by Bobby Charlton himself, who once wrote: 'There have been few better teachers of the game and I am greatly in his debt. Alf Ramsey helped me a lot when he became manager of England and so, of course, in many ways, did Matt Busby. But Jimmy got to my guts.'

Murphy could hardly have been a greater contrast to his serene, dignified boss. He was a man of dark Celtic passion: fiery, tempera-mental, aggressive, chain-smoking, foul-mouthed, 'with a voice like a cement mixer in full throttle', in the vivid phrase of Busby's. 'He shuffled these little steps,' says John Aston, 'a bit like Jimmy Cagney. He looked like a gangster. But he was a very warm, emotional man.' His favourite expression, which summed up his philosophy, was 'get stuck in'. Nobby Lawton, another contemporary of Bobby's, gave me this memory: 'He toughened us up, taught us to stand up for ourselves. When we played five-a-side at the training ground, Jimmy would join in and kick you to the ground. "What's going on here?" "That's what it's like in professional football," Jimmy would reply. His team talks were inspiring. After listening to one of them, I could not wait to get out on the pitch. All the managers I met in my career after Jimmy were ordinary.'

Several of Bobby's contemporaries say that he was a favourite of Jimmy's. But this was only because Jimmy, who was as brilliant a judge of a player as Matt Busby, knew that Bobby had a unique gift. He therefore gave individual tuition to Bobby in the evenings and on Sunday mornings, putting him through a rigorous training schedule to mould him into a true professional. In the *Sun* in 1975 Murphy explained: 'Bobby was loaded with talent but it needed harnessing. He was one of the hardest pupils I ever had to work on. He had so much going for him, perhaps too much. We had to bully him.' For example, one of Bobby's biggest weaknesses was his love of hitting long, 50-yard balls, and then standing to admire the result. Jimmy kept drumming into him the need to be part of a cohesive team build-up, moving with other players, being prepared to make a quick pass and then getting ready for the return. 'Keep it simple, give it to a red shirt,' Jimmy would remind him. As Bobby explained in a *Sunday Telegraph* article in 1972: 'I thought that the first thing I had to do as an inside-forward was to show how I could pass. But the full-back would cut it off and three or four people would be put out of the game. I was just showing off. Jimmy showed me the importance of the short game, that I had to work for the glory of the team, not for myself.'

Murphy also worked on building up Bobby's stamina. On Sundays, when everyone else had a day off, Jimmy took Bobby into the middle of the training ground, then proceeded to kick balls to all four corners of the field and demand that Bobby chase them. Even when Bobby was an exhausted, breathless wreck, Murphy carried on smashing his long balls out of the centre-circle, yelling, 'No-one has died of a heart attack on the pitch with me.' One Sunday, Bobby had grown so sick of this routine that he dared to challenge Jimmy.

'Why are you always on my back? Why don't you get on to the others?'

'Listen, son,' said Jimmy, putting his arm around Bobby's shoulder, 'we've got a lot of good young players here. Some of them will make it; some of them won't. We feel certain you will. That's why we give you so much of our time. Listen and learn.' Bobby never argued with Jimmy after that.

As a schoolboy, Bobby had been renowned for the power of his shooting and though he was naturally right-footed, he had been almost as devastating with his left. But this was another aspect of his game where Jimmy Murphy felt that there was room for improvement. Emphasizing the need for equal strength in either foot, he made Bobby spend hours kicking a ball from long range at a wall behind the Stretford End at Old Trafford. By drawing a line on the wall at a height of three feet and telling Bobby to hit below it, Jimmy taught Bobby to keep the ball down as he shot. But he never tried to stifle Bobby's urge to shoot from long range. In an article in 1991, Bobby explained how he developed his scoring potential under Murphy's tutelage. 'Most of my goals came from outside the box – I was always encouraged by Jimmy Murphy to have a shot if the window of opportunity presented itself. I used to practice against a brick wall at Old Trafford. I spent my afternoons perfecting my timing and building up my confidence.' It is a tribute to Bobby's diligence that many of those closest to him could not even tell that he was born right-footed. His own brother Jack wrote in his autobiography, 'People often ask me, "Which was your Bobby's natural foot in his playing days?" And I tell them, "I simply don't know."'

One of the great falsehoods about Bobby's shooting, beloved of hysterical commentators, was that he was able to 'pick his spot' in the goal. The truth is that all he tried to do was hit the ball on target and hope that, occasionally, one of his shots might be wide of the keeper. Again, it was Jimmy Murphy who was responsible for this approach. 'I was given a lovely piece of advice by Jimmy. He said, "The goals don't move. You know the general direction they are in and so, if you get the space, just smack the ball towards them." The principle was sound. I just concentrated on making the proper contact and then hoped that the ball would scream into the net. Sometimes it did, sometimes it didn't.'

As well as working on his technique, Jimmy Murphy also tried to educate Bobby out of some of his more immature behaviour on the field. John Docherty recalls, 'Bobby had this habit of indulging in gestures, or shouting at himself, if he had hit a bad ball or was disappointed with his play. Jimmy would say to him: "What's all this arm waving? We know you hit a crap ball. Now just get on with the game." And Jimmy told me, "That's the schoolboy coming out. He throws a tantrum because he doesn't want people to think that he can't do better. As soon as we can get rid of that, we've got a chance with him."'

For all Jimmy Murphy's tutelage, it should not be thought that Manchester United had attained perfection in its coaching. In truth, the system was disorganized and the facilities poor, particularly at the United training ground, The Cliff. Wilf McGuinness recalls: 'Looking back, it was bloody awful. The floodlights were dreadful, you could hardly see. The training kit was the worst imaginable. It was never washed, no-one knows what disease could have spread all over the place. When you arrived you just grabbed what you could from the table. Those big woollen sweaters, and the shoes, big heavy things. Afterwards you'd get in the bath – 40 of you – it was black within two minutes. When you got out you'd have to have a cold shower to get the muck off.' Equally disturbing were the informal practice matches organized by the players themselves on an old plot of land at Old Trafford, wedged between the back of the stadium and the railway line. These sessions were epics of almost gladiatorial savagery. Anyone who could not take a pummelling would not last long. 'Oh, those games were rough,' remembers Joe Carolan. 'We would be kicking the hell out of each other. Jeff Whitefoot once got cut very badly on his head and all the trainer, Tom Curry, did was give him a towel. That's the way it was. Bobby was as brave as anyone. He gave as good as he got.'

Increasingly tough and skilful, Bobby soon began to work his way up the hierarchy of United. He had started in the fifth team, which played in the Altrincham League and, thanks largely to Bobby's shooting, regularly scored 15 or 20 goals a game. He then graduated into the 'A' team, which was effectively the thirds. As Bobby recalled: 'They played in the Manchester Amateur League. You were 16 and this was open-age football with big dockers and guys from factory teams kicking lumps out of you. But it was another fantastic education.' In May 1954, Bobby was elevated to

Manchester's youth team. With names like Duncan Edwards, Eddie Colman and David Pegg – and now Bobby Charlton and Wilf McGuinness – it was by far the best junior team in the country, winning the FA Youth Cup five years in succession from 1953 to 1957. The fluent approach, based on Busby's philosophy of skill and simplicity of movement, captivated the public. Huge crowds would gather to see the young players – now christened the 'Busby Babes' – wherever they went. 30,000, for instance, turned out at Molineux for the second leg of the 1954 Youth Cup Final against Wolves.

The reputation of 'the Babes' now spread beyond Britain's shores. That summer, the team travelled to Switzerland for a youth tournament. They won it easily, remaining unbeaten in their seven games, scoring 21 goals and conceding just two. They won it again the following year in equally emphatic style. By this time, Bobby was a key member of the side, as Nobby Lawton, who went with him on that 1955 Swiss trip, recalls: 'We absolutely dominated the competition. We always seemed to be about 3–0 up after 10 minutes, with Bobby getting most of the goals. I could hardly believe how good he was. He was sensational. The way he struck the ball was so much better than anyone else. His timing was beautiful. He was a superb athlete, so quick on his feet. Don't forget that there were a hell of a lot of players who were trying to kick him. It was a very physical game when he started. People really went out to clatter him but they could not catch him. He would just skip away.' Reg Hunter was another who went on a youth trip to Switzerland. Like so many others, he was immediately struck by Bobby's talent: 'My first sight of Bobby was when he was playing for the reserves against the first team, and he scored two tremendous goals. I did not know then who he was and when I asked, I was told "Bobby Charlton". And I thought to myself, "Superb. He is really going places." Both the goals were classic Bobby, from a distance. He seemed to glide over the ground, and all of a sudden he would be away in one flowing movement. Bobby was inspirational on those youth trips abroad. You could tell that he was a special player, destined for great things, not just by his performances on the field but also by the way

Jimmy Murphy and Matt Busby looked after him. They spent a lot of time with him. He was a good leader in the youth team, though he was very quiet. But when he had to make a point on the pitch, he made it.'

Bobby's famous body swerve, which bewitched so many opponents throughout his career, was in evidence in the youth team. Ian Greaves, who also joined United in 1953, gave me this description of Bobby in action: 'Close your eyes, and picture Bobby Charlton with the ball, attacking a defender, dropping his shoulder, and going the other way. Now that is very simple. It is done every Saturday afternoon but never in the way Bob did. We would play against him in training every Tuesday and Thursday morning. Bob would use that trick four or five times. We knew the bloody trick was coming but we could not stop him doing it. He had this wonderful way of approaching you with the ball. You were quite confident. You were on two feet. The next thing you knew, he had sent you the wrong way. To do that at League level and at international level was remarkable. The other great feature of his play was that he was never frightened of going for goal. Some of the goals he scored led us to gasp, because he had no right to be shooting from there. He had such a powerful shot on him, especially with that left peg. If he was given half an inch of space 25 yards from goal, he was in with a chance because he had this uncanny gift of knowing where to shoot.'

Despite such prodigious talent, Bobby was not immediately selected for the first team on becoming a professional. There had been talk that after an astonishing run in the reserve and junior sides, when he hit 56 goals in 47 games, Bobby might be included in the line-up of the side that had won the First Division Championship in 1955/56. The *Manchester Evening News* reported on 10 April 1956: 'Manchester United just want one more thing from Matt Busby before the end of a great championship season. They want to see shooting star Bobby Charlton in a First Division setting for the first time. Some of Charlton's goals in the reserves have been acrobatic feats that no other English footballer would attempt.

Manager Busby is not one to keep youth – or the customers – waiting longer than necessary. He is sure to give Charlton his chance, either against Sunderland on Saturday or in the wind-up game against Portsmouth.'

But the call-up never came, and his mother, with her keen sense of her favourite's worth, was infuriated by what she interpreted as a wilful snub to Bobby. She decided that, since both Matt Busby and Jimmy Murphy were Catholics, then religious prejudice must have been the cause of her son's exclusion. As she wrote later, 'I'm not the type to dwell on my thoughts, so I grabbed the bull by the horns. I went to Matt and asked him straight: "Is Bobby being left out because he isn't a Catholic?" I could not have been more blunt. Neither could Matt. I knew from the expression on his face that I had really offended him. "How could you even think something like that? You are an intelligent woman, Cis. Don't ever ask me anything like that again."' In fact, Cissie had, in her blundering way, been correct in believing that there was a strong Catholic influence at Manchester United. The city's large Irish population identified with the club; over the years many of the best young players, such as Nobby Stiles, were drawn from local Catholic schools, while Matt Busby, in the words of his biographer Eamon Dunphy, 'was the most prominent Catholic in Manchester public life, a symbol of the faith to which he belonged, a Catholic admired and respected, around whom his co-religionists could rally'. Where she went horribly wrong was in believing that religion played any part in team selection. If it had, why would United have gone after George Best, who was brought up in a Free Presbyterian family in Belfast? It was always talent that mattered with Matt, not background.

Soon after the beginning of the next season, in October 1956, Matt proved Cissie's error by finally giving Bobby a place in the first team in the match against Charlton Athletic. Interestingly, Bobby was just a few days from his 19th birthday when he made his League debut, whereas Jack, always regarded as the inferior footballer, had been more than a year younger when he had his first game for Leeds. But that, of course, had been in the Second Division in a much less effective side. The news of Bobby's selection was proclaimed by Tom Jackson in the *Evening News*: 'It's happened at last. Bobby Charlton, 18-year-old "wonder boy" of Manchester United's reserve and FA Youth Cup-winning teams and pride of the Old Trafford nursery, steps out on the big soccer parade for the first time tomorrow. Who is this boy Charlton whom Don Revie describes as "one of the most complete footballers one could ever wish to see"? Well, he's another of the Matt Busby finds from schoolboy international football who has made great strides through United's junior and Youth Cup teams. He's not big physically, standing 5 feet 8 inches and weighing around 11 stone 8 pounds, but he combines a fierce shot with an uncanny positional sense.' After a nervous start, Bobby lived up to this star billing in his debut, scoring twice with typically powerful shots in United 4–2 victory. Sir Matt Busby wrote this account of the game: 'Bobby began his debut as if he was in his bare feet kicking a hot potato. He "got rid" too quickly, very hard but too quickly. That must have been the only spell in which Bobby Charlton was ever nervous on a football pitch. The nerves did not last many minutes. Suddenly, he began to play his own game, and his own game was slipping gracefully past two opponents as if they were stakes in the ground, putting in a good pass or whacking a terrific shot.' A great League career had begun. It was to last another 17 years.

There were two important physical legacies for Bobby from this debut. The first was the immediate realization of how exhausting League football could be. 'When the final whistle blew at the end of the match, my legs felt like rubber and I wondered where my next breath was coming from. I could not for the life of me understand how Stanley Matthews and Tom Finney had gone on playing for so long,' he wrote in his 1967 book *Forward for England*. Now he saw why Jimmy Murphy had pushed him so hard on the training ground. The second was that he gained complete confidence in his left foot. The fact was that Bobby was not fully fit for the game against Charlton, having badly injured his right ankle playing against Manchester City reserves three weeks earlier. Though the swelling had gone down, the ankle was still giving him real discomfort on the eve of his debut. But so determined was Bobby to play that when Matt asked, 'How's the ankle?' he lied and said, 'It's great.' That was enough for Busby. So Bobby went into the match virtually carrying his right foot – and did so for the next fortnight. He maintains, however, it was an invaluable experience, as he told George Best's biographer, Joe Lovejoy: 'It was enforced practice really. I probably would not have done it without the injury, but it did improve my left peg a lot. My "other" foot was never that bad, but it's amazing how, when you've only got one to use, your whole technique – your timing, your positional sense and your thinking – has to change.'

Bobby had actually taken the field that October afternoon as Lance Corporal Charlton, for by 1956 he was in the middle of his National Service. When he had been summoned to join the army, he had been told by Busby to apply for the Royal Army Ordnance Corps. This was because their base was in Shrewsbury, not too far from Manchester, so Bobby could still play at weekends. But when he had finished his basic RAOC training at Portsmouth, he received his orders to go out to Malaya, where the British Army had been fighting a long campaign against the communist insurrection led by Ching Peng. The threat to young servicemen was very real, for almost 500 of them lost their lives during this 12-year conflict. In a sense of panic, Bobby phoned Old Trafford to explain his predicament. He was told not to worry: 'We are certain your orders are to travel to Shropshire, not Malaya. It will be sorted out,' the club informed him. Manchester United obviously had friends at the top of the War Office. The next day, Bobby was instructed to take the train to Shrewsbury.

After his initial bout of anxiety, Bobby spent two uneventful but physically demanding years at the RAOC barracks there, humping around shells, equipment and crates of bullets. 'I didn't like the army simply because it seemed to be interfering with my progress as a footballer,' he said later. But this was hardly true. Bobby was allowed almost as much leave as he wanted to play for United.

Furthermore, he was part of a brilliant army team which would have beaten most sides in the First Division. Its players included internationals like Dave Mackay, Cliff Jones, Graham Shaw, Alex Parker and the England keeper Alan Hodgkinson. Above all there was Duncan Edwards, who happened to be serving in the same Shrewsbury depot as Bobby. Just as he had done at Mrs Watson's digs in Manchester, the giant, kindly Duncan looked after Bobby. 'Duncan was a year older than I was and he took charge of me the moment I arrived in the army camp. He had my billet arranged and everything. When he showed me to the billet, he noticed there was a spring sticking out of the bed. "We can't have that," he said. It was a great big iron bed, but he hoisted it over his shoulder, mattress, frame and all, and went off in search of a better one for me,' recalled Bobby.

Still in the army during United's championship-winning season of 1956/57, Bobby played in 14 League matches, as well as the Cup Final against Aston Villa, in which Peter McParland's vicious, jaw-breaking challenge on keeper Ray Wood probably cost United the Double. When Wood had to go off for treatment, Bobby was an obvious candidate to take his place between the posts. He had always loved keeping in practice sessions, and, according to Bobby Harrop, 'He could have been a professional goalkeeper. We used to stay out after training, I would go in goal while he shot and then we would change over. I said to him, "You could be a keeper." He had it all, speed, good reflexes, could cover the ground and deal with crosses and chips.' But on this occasion at Wembley, United captain Roger Byrne signalled the Ulsterman Jackie Blanchflower to take over.

By the middle of the 1958 season, Bobby was establishing himself in that great United team. There was even speculation about an England place. John Giles, who joined United in 1955, is full of admiration for him at this time. 'He was only 19 but he was brilliant, absolutely brilliant. Even amidst all that talent at United, he stood out for me because he could do it on his own, instinctively. He was a very instinctive player. He had such natural ability, with pace and beautiful balance. I have to admit that he was not always so enjoyable to play with as to watch. It was hard to relate to him on the pitch, in terms of working together on the ball, because he would be doing his own thing. When I first went to Old Trafford, I was taught by Matt and Jimmy: "As soon as you get in a nice position, find another player, let the ball go simple and quick." But playing with Bobby, I found that, sometimes, when I got in a good position, I did not get the ball from him. And I would be thinking, "Oh come on Bobby." Then I saw that he had suddenly gone past three or four players and was threatening the goal. He could break all the rules because of his individualism.'

Giles also remembers Bobby, in this period, as a 'shy individual but always friendly. We got to know each other because we were both young, living in separate digs and, in the evening, there was often very little to do. So we would wander up to the park and play bowls. In the right company, with people he trusted, he was one of the lads, enjoyed a drink, a game of cards, a song – he loved Frank Sinatra and had a good voice. He could be funny as well, with a dry sense of humour. Yet if a stranger came into the group, he would switch off immediately. He just would not be the same. And he could also be moody. If someone said what he considered to be the wrong thing, then he would take it to heart. Again, he was not a big drinker, but he liked a beer.'

Wilf McGuinness, one of his closest friends at this time, agrees about his shyness. 'Bobby used to come in to Mrs Watson's, just pick up a paper and start reading it. He did not converse that well, partly because he had a very strong Geordie accent.' But, for all his shy nature, Bobby should not be thought of as a loner. For he revelled in the company of the Babes. It is no exaggeration to say that this period was probably Bobby's happiest in football, when he was surrounded by friends of his own age and was enjoying the first freedom of adulthood. In later years, he would use the word 'paradise' to describe the pre-Munich years he spent with Duncan Edwards, Eddie Colman and the other United greats of that era. He was particularly fond of the streetwise Eddie Colman, as he told

Eamon Dunphy: 'I had come from the north-east which was, I suppose, a bit parochial and Eddie was the flash little townie. He was the first person I ever saw in drainpipe trousers. But he was brilliant. I was very close to Eddie. We were all close at that time. At Christmas I would stay with him. We'd play in the morning, then go back to his place for the turkey. His family were nice, lived in a tiny little street, where there was a real community spirit.'

The Babes also enjoyed the Manchester nightlife, going to the Bodega jazz club or the Plaza, run by Jimmy Savile, or the Continental, run by Eric Morley. Bobby's Manchester in the 1950s was a much more exciting place than Jack's Leeds. Wilf McGuinness recalls: 'We were just ordinary lads. We'd go to the Plaza, have a bit of a snogging session if we were lucky. Maybe we would see them again, maybe not.' A more sedate activity was going to the pictures. As one of the perks of being on the staff, United players had free passes to all the cinemas in the city, as well as to the dog tracks at Belle Vue and the White City. 'You'd be in the cinema on Saturday night, and suddenly you'd hear an "aaah" and a big "uggh". It was the sound of footballers with cramp in their thighs and their hamstrings. We didn't have rubdowns as they do today,' remembers McGuinness. Bobby adored the cinema, according to Albert Scanlon: 'A perfect day for Bobby would go: training, lunch in town, and then, in the afternoon, a visit to the News Theatre on Oxford Street to watch cartoons. He loved cartoons and would watch any that were showing. He regularly went into town two or three times a week, even by himself.'

Bobby could be high-spirited as well. Ronnie Cope, who was at United between 1950 and 1961, told me, 'Bobby was a cheeky little kid. He, Wilf and Shay Brennan were so close, they always liked a joke, taking the mickey out of someone. We used to call them "The Three Musketeers".' Twice as a young player Bobby was hauled up before Matt Busby for rather puerile offences. The first occurred when he and some other young players, travelling through Manchester by bus, started firing off water pistols at pedestrians in the street. In fact, according to Ronnie Cope, the toy guns contained urine rather than water, which made the incident all the more serious when it was reported to Old Trafford. The second difficulty arose when, still under the legal age limit, he was reported for having a beer in a pub. As Busby wrote in his memoirs, *Soccer at the Top*: 'When he was a mere lad, I had to put him right. He was very young and I heard he had been seen to have a drink of beer. So I sent for him and I told him, "If I ever hear you have been drinking beer again before you are old enough, you will be for it." It was a long time before he had his next glass of beer.'

On a more sophisticated level, Bobby further incurred the disapproval of Matt when the manager found out that he, Shay and Wilf McGuinness were planning to open a nightclub in Manchester. McGuinness explains, 'Wherever we went, there were always a lot of girls around, especially because Shay was a good looking lad. We thought we could make some money out of our popularity.' So in the summer of 1959 negotiations were started with local businessman Nipper Leonard to take over his nightclub in Queen Street, with an agreement concluded late one night. Yet when McGuinness turned up at training the very next morning he was confronted by an angry Busby: 'What's this I've heard about you buying a nightclub?' McGuinness continues, 'I could not believe how he knew because it was after midnight when we had reached the deal. By 9.45 the next morning it had got back to Matt. But he had a lot of informers all over the place. He warned me: "I think you three go into enough nightclubs without owning one. Just take a look at your contracts." We had to have permission if we wanted to go into another business. That was the end of it. It was never discussed ever again.'

Nor, in his less serious youth, did Bobby always show the commitment that was later to mark him out as a model professional – especially if he was not being supervised by Jimmy Murphy. 'I used to clown around with Dave Pegg and Eddie Colman. Even when we were training we used to lark about. Our trainer, Tom Curry, was getting old and he couldn't get around with us kids. He used to have a terrible time with us ducking out of training periods,' said Bobby in an interview in 1961. John Docherty says that Bobby, for all his quietness, was just like any other young lad. 'He would sometimes get pissed out of his head. I remember after a European Cup game, in 1957, we were in a nightclub, chatting up a few birds. Then an argument started and all of a sudden we've wrecked the place. Bobby was involved in that. He was no different.'

Interestingly, Jack and Bobby were probably closer in this period than they were at any other time in their lives. After years of moving in different directions, their lives were now dominated by the same adventure into professional football. At last they had something truly in common, and they began to enjoy each other's company. Jack would travel over to Manchester or Bobby to Leeds. Sometimes, they would go to David Pegg's house in Doncaster. Together, they played golf, went to the pictures or the pub, listened to Bobby's collection of records, took girls on dates or even went fishing, more happily than they had ever done in childhood. On occasional Sundays, Bobby would drive with Jack to Ashington to see their parents – this was when Bobby, before the rift with his mother, was still very happy to visit his home town. In a reflection of this better relationship, when Jack got married to his girlfriend, Leeds shop-worker Pat Kemp, in January 1958, Bobby was his best man at the wedding. As Jack told the journalist Norman Harris, 'It was not through convention but because he was my best friend.' Yet even in the new mood of harmony, some still detected a sense of distance between them. Laura Crowther, the daughter of Jack's landlady in Leeds, saw Bobby on his regular visits and knew the Charlton family well. She told me, 'Bobby came over a lot and stayed here the night of the wedding. But I'll tell you something, he and Jack never appeared close. He was very quiet, still seemed a bit of a mother's boy and that would get on Jack's nerves.'

With Leeds having won promotion in 1956, Jack and Bobby played regularly against each other in the last four years of the 1950s. In one game at Elland Road in 1958, Bobby humiliated Jack by nutmegging him. 'Come back, you little bugger,' cried Jack as his younger brother raced towards the goal. But Jack has always maintained that he felt no jealousy towards Bobby, only delight in his achievements at United. What he did feel envy towards was the glamour of Bobby's club compared to his own. 'It didn't worry me at all when our kid began to get write-ups as the greatest thing since the Archangel Gabriel. All I was jealous about was the club he had joined – Manchester United. I was jealous about their success, their traditions, the way people thought about them as a team. That's the way I wanted people to think about Leeds,' he said in 1970. John Giles recalls, 'I met Jack at Old Trafford a few times because he would come over and see Bobby. I used to feel a bit for him then, because he was out of it, while Bobby was starting to do so well. I don't think Jack liked the way that he was always referred to as Bobby's elder brother. I don't think it was jealousy – he was proud of Bobby and wished him all the best – but he found it awkward.'

Though he was sympathetic to Jack, Bobby could not have been happier in his own position. He loved the whole unique atmosphere of the Babes, their special companionship on and off the field. Tragically, that idyllic life was about to be shattered.

CHAPTER FIVE

The Victim

The United players were in high spirits as they gathered at Manchester's Ringway airport on Monday 3 February 1958, ready for the long flight to Yugoslavia for a vital European Cup tie.

The Busby Babes were in the form of their lives, having just achieved a sensational victory over Arsenal at Highbury two days earlier. It had been the most exhilarating game of the season, with United 3–0 up at half-time before winning 5–4. And victory had been won in the daring style that epitomized the Babes. Never once, even after Arsenal had equalized, did United seek to consolidate in defence. Instead, they stepped up their attacks, with Duncan Edwards and Eddie Colman continually driving through the midfield, while Kenny Morgans and Albert Scanlon mesmerized the Arsenal full-backs as they tore down the flanks. 'They just kept coming at us, and the score could have easily been 10–7. It was the finest match I ever played in,' said Arsenal keeper Jack Kelsey. Bobby Charlton, fast becoming a regular member of the side, played his part in this dramatic win, scoring United's second after a brilliant run by Scanlon. Charlton later gave this description of the goal, recalling how exhausted he was by the hectic pace of the game: 'After reaching the corner flag, Albert crossed a perfect pass for me. My breath was coming in great gasps and my stockings were sagging around my ankles, but somehow I managed to muster some reserve strength to hit the ball into the back of the net.'

United might have been enthralling crowds at home and across the continent, but, with typical narrow-mindedness, the English football establishment had not approved of the foray into European competition. When the European Cup was established in the 1955/56 season, the Football League refused permission for the reigning champions, Chelsea, to take part. It was the same insular attitude that had prevented England participating in the World Cup before 1950 and its spirit was encapsulated by the words of Alan Hardaker, League Secretary, about continental football: 'too many wogs and dagoes'. But Matt Busby, a far more cosmopolitan, expansive figure than most League mandarins, had no time for such an isolationist mentality. So when United were crowned champions in 1956, Busby defied the League and took up the challenge of Europe. The first season proved memorable. Through a string of brilliant performances, most notably a 10–0 demolition of Belgian champions Anderlecht at home, United reached the semi-finals, where they were narrowly beaten by the mighty Real Madrid.

Now there was a chance of reaching the semi-finals of the European Cup again. Making the second visit of that season behind the Iron Curtain, having earlier beaten Dukla Prague, United took a 2–1 lead into their away fixture with Red Star Belgrade. Though Bobby had played the previous year against Real Madrid at home, this was to be his first trip to Europe. His naivety about travel led to some ribbing from his team-mates, as Jackie Blanchflower recalled: 'He had been kidded about the shortage of food in Eastern Europe and packed his suitcase with biscuits and sweets.'

But, in taking such precautions, Bobby had not been as foolish as his colleagues imagined. For when the team arrived from Manchester after an uneventful flight, they found Belgrade to be a city of depressing bleakness and poverty. The icy grip of totalitarian communist rule could be felt everywhere, as Albert Scanlon recalls: 'We arrived in Belgrade at Monday teatime and went to this hotel. For some reason there were armed guards on every floor. By the time we got our meals they were stone cold. After we unpacked, a few of us went out for a walk and we saw people wearing shoes from old car tyres. It was incredible, and in all the shops people had to queue for everything. On the whole, Belgrade was a dismal place with not much to do and nowhere to go.'

The arrival of the United team was the most exciting event to happen in the city for years. As the team coach made its way to the stadium for the match against Red Star, thousands lined the streets to try and catch a glimpse of the players, all the while shouting out, 'Busby Babes' and 'Red Devils'. Immediately after the kick-off United showed why they had built such a reputation. As against Arsenal, they were 3–0 up before half-time, and, again, Bobby Charlton played a vital role, scoring two goals. Frank Taylor, the journalist with the *News Chronicle*, wrote of his second effort, 'Out of his goal came the acrobatic Mr Beara in his black jersey, to be shattered by a pile-driving shot which hurtled from Charlton's boot well outside the penalty by some 25 yards – to thud into the back of the net. Belgrade couldn't believe it. No-one ever shot from so far out and beat Beara. But Charlton did.' Albert Scanlon says of Bobby in that game: 'It was probably the best I had ever seen him play. He was just outstanding. His shooting was so ferocious, his balance so perfect.' Though Belgrade stormed back in the second half, supported by some rather dubious refereeing, United managed to draw 3–3, maintaining their aggregate lead.

There were a few sore heads the next morning when the United party made its way to Zemun Airport. The night before, the celebrations, which had started with an official banquet at the British Embassy, had gone on into the early hours of the morning. It was 3am when captain Roger Byrne and centre-half Mark Jones finally arrived back at the team hotel, two hours later than Matt Busby's imposed curfew. More sedately, Bobby, David Pegg and Dennis Viollet had been drinking at the hotel bar, while goalkeeper Harry Gregg – the big Ulsterman recently bought by Matt Busby from Doncaster Rovers – organized a serious card school in his room.

As they prepared to embark on the journey home, there was a

delay over Johnny Berry's papers, as Harry Gregg remembers: 'Digger Berry had lost his passport and you didn't get out of there without it. So everybody's pockets were turned out – no luck. It was a huge, overbearing lady who handled the immigration and eventually it was decided to unload the hold, where they found Johnny's passport in his suitcase. So we set off late.' Already tired and hungover, the team had seen quite enough of Belgrade by the time they were finally allowed to get on board the plane, a BEA twin engine Elizabethan specially chartered by United for the Yugoslavian trip. Those in the know were pleased to be flying in an Elizabethan, for not only was this the aircraft used by the Queen, but it also had an excellent safety record. Not one of this type had ever crashed.

After the exertions of the last few days, the passengers were only too anxious to get home, especially because United had an important League game against Wolves, their biggest rivals, on Saturday. But the journey back to Manchester was not a direct one, for the plane had to stop for refuelling at Munich. It was a bright, crisp morning when the airliner left Yugoslavia. As the Elizabethan made its way across the German border, however, the sky began to darken, turning from blue to dull grey, while the temperature fell dramatically. By the time the pilots began their descent, a thick layer of snow and slush was forming on the tarmac of Munich airport. Once the plane had landed, the passengers were told to disembark, for the refuelling was due to take at least 40 minutes. The *Chronicle* journalist Frank Taylor described the experience of leaving the cabin: 'As soon as the door was opened the wind gusted in, bitingly cold, as though it had blown in from the frozen wastes of Siberia. Duncan Edwards led the rush down the airliner's steps, with sleet lashing into the face like a razor. "Get your snow shoes on, lads. Short studs are no use in this stuff," he called over his shoulder as he picked his way carefully over the squelchy treacherous surface of slush into the warmth of the airport lounge.'

Inside the airport, Bobby, like some of the others, wandered around the shops looking at souvenirs, and then had a coffee. At 2.15pm, an announcement was made that the refuelled aircraft was now ready for boarding. As the players trooped back through the biting gale, Roger Byrne noticed that the wheel tracks of the plane, made only 40 minutes earlier on landing, were now almost invisible because of the snow. Yet, despite the poor weather, there was little sense of unease amongst the passengers. They were looking forward to lunch, a game of cards, and a kip. 'We'll be landing in Manchester around 7pm,' a steward told Bill Foulkes, the big full-back.

At 2.19pm, the pilots, Captain James Thain, the commander of the flight, and his co-pilot, Captain Ken Rayment, were given permission to taxi for take-off. The passengers heard the familiar purr of the engines revving up, and then the Elizabethan began to move down the runway. 'I remember looking out of the window as I always did to see the wheels leave the ground and mark the moment we became airborne. But just as the twin engines burst into a full-throated roar and we started to gather speed, the brakes were jammed hard and the Elizabethan came to a grinding halt. Dennis Viollet and I grinned at each other as we were jolted forward and everybody laughed and joked about the incident. We had stopped halfway down the runway – nobody knew why,' wrote Bobby later.

The reason the plane had stopped was because the pilots had noticed an uneven tone in the engines and a sudden fluctuation in the port pressure gauge. This was caused by a problem known as 'boost surging', as Captain James Thain later explained: 'Boost surging was not uncommon with Elizabethans at the time, particularly at airports like Munich because of their height above sea level. Over-rich mixture caused the power surge, but though the engines sounded uneven there was not much danger that the take-off power of the aircraft would be affected. The Elizabethans were very powerful in their day and you could have taken off on one engine.' Confident in the effectiveness of his aircraft, Thain decided to make a second attempt at taking off. But this time, he and Rayment agreed to open the throttles more slowly, because a quick opening was known to be one of the causes of boost surging.

At 2.34pm, the plane raced down the runway but once more the take-off had to be abandoned halfway down the runway when Captain Thain noticed that the port pressure was still fluctuating wildly. There was now a mounting sense of anxiety in the cabin. 'What the hell is going on here,' yelled Frank Swift, the huge former England goalkeeper who was now working for the *News of the World*. Some of the passengers lapsed into empty theorizing – one journalist suggested the sludge had short-circuited the plane's electrical system, a patently absurd idea given that the lights were still working in the cabin. Then a stewardess emerged to tell everyone that there was a slight technical fault. 'We hope to have it corrected soon but, in the meantime, please disembark and wait in the airport for a further announcement,' she said. Once again the players and press marched through the snow. 'Don't worry, no matter what the fault is, we're not in any danger. There is a point of no return on the runway where, if the pilot is not happy about the plane, he can still pull up quite safely,' Frank Taylor, who had served in the RAF, told Bobby as they walked together to the terminal.

It was at this moment that a fateful decision was made by the crew of the Elizabethan. William Black, the station engineer, had been summoned to the cockpit to discuss with Captains Thain and Rayment the problem of boost surging. The pilots explained that they had taken all the recommended steps – such as the more gentle release of the throttle – to eliminate it. Black said that the only alternative was to re-tune the engines, but that would involve an overnight stop. 'I don't think that is necessary. After all, the starboard engine has performed normally,' replied Captain Thain, who decided he would have another go at take-off. He was only reflecting the desire of everyone, manager, players and reporters, to be in Manchester by nightfall.

The passengers, who had just reached the terminal, were now told to return. 'We had ordered coffees, but we never got them because we had to go back on to the plane,' recalls Ray Wood, the United reserve keeper. Bill Foulkes felt that the order to return came too suddenly. 'There was something wrong. I wasn't happy.' Some of the journalists were equally surprised that a mechanical fault could have been mended so quickly, for it was barely ten minutes since they had last left their seats. Frank Taylor, with his wartime flying experience, was also worried about the possibility of ice on the wings. In appallingly cold, snowy conditions, he did not see how the wings could have been properly cleared of ice in such a short space of time. He was right to be concerned, for Captain Thain later admitted: 'Ken and I had not been out of the cockpit but we talked about the snow and looked at the wings from the flight deck. We had lost the film of snow we had noticed before our first departure and decided not to have the wings swept.'

There was now a palpable sense of nervousness as the passengers took their seats. 'I went into the aircraft and saw the steward, Tom Cable, white as a sheet, strapping himself into the very rear seat. I thought to myself, "There's something seriously wrong here,"' recalls Harry Gregg. It was often asked later why none of the travellers simply refused to board the plane. 'We were footballers. We just did what we were told,' says Albert Scanlon, though he does remember Frank Taylor telling him, 'Sod this. If you don't take off first time in the RAF, you scrap it.' Most of the passengers went back to the same places they had taken throughout the journey, but, crucially, Bobby and Dennis Viollet decided to move further up to the front of the plane, swapping with Tommy Taylor and Dave Pegg, who – in a tragic miscalculation – believed they would be safer at the back.

There was a brief delay when it was discovered, after a headcount, that one of the passengers was missing. True to his journalistic instincts, Alf Clarke of the *Manchester Evening Chronicle* had got on the phone the moment he arrived in the terminal to give his paper the story of the aircraft's problems. He arrived just as the plane was about to taxi. 'I had to tell the office. After all, we might have had to stay in Munich all night,' he explained. 'Oh, blimey, don't say that, Alf,' came a chorus from the other newsmen.

At 2.56pm Captain Thain requested permission to move out to the runway. It was immediately given and, after further routine checks, the aircraft started rolling. At precisely 3.02pm came a vital message from the control tower: 'Your clearance void if not airborne by zero four.' In effect, Thain had been given just two minutes to decide whether to make another attempt at take-off. If he was not in the air within the next 120 seconds, then there was little chance that the Elizabethan would be heading for Manchester that day.

Captain Thain decided to press ahead. A hush descended on the passengers. The usual footballers' banter had disappeared completely. 'I tightened my safety belt and glanced at my watch,' recalled Bobby Charlton later. 'It was just after three. There was a nervous kind of quietness in the cabin. I turned to Dennis Viollet and said, "I'm not taking my coat off this time." Once again we set off down the runway, the fields slipping past the window in a kaleidoscope as we gathered speed. I looked out of the window to see the wheels lift and I am sure they didn't rise more than two inches. Then, as I moved my head, I saw the fence at the end of the runway and I knew we couldn't clear it.' Up in the cockpit, the two pilots knew only too well that something was disastrously amiss. Captain Thain had watched in horror as the needle on the speed indicator reached 117 knots per hour, then suddenly dropped to 105. The plane had already passed the point of no return. He looked up from the instrument panel to see the fence looming ahead. And at that terrifying moment, he heard his co-pilot Ken Rayment scream, 'Christ, we're not going to make it.'

Ray Wood remembers the sense of foreboding as the plane hurtled down the runway for the third time, with one engine again sounding as if it was struggling to maintain power. He turned to Roger Byrne, who was showing real fear as he gripped the armrests of his seat, and said: 'Roger, what's happening?'

'We're all going to be killed,' replied the United captain.

'Well, I'm ready,' said Billy Whelan, the devout Catholic. They were the last words that Billy Whelan ever spoke.

Seconds later, the Elizabethan drove through the perimeter fence and ploughed on across a road. Its port wing crashed into a house, setting the building on fire. Miraculously, those inside, Mrs Anna

Winkler and her three young children, managed to escape without being hurt. But the impact tore off the wing and part of the tail, sending the plane spinning further through the snow. Amidst a deafening sound of grinding metal, the disintegrating fuselage then hit a tree and a wooden hut, where there was a truck filled with fuel and tyres. As the twisted wreck came to a juddering halt, flames lit up the wintry Bavarian sky.

Harry Gregg, who emerged as the real hero of the Munich disaster, gave me this account of what happened to him: 'As we crashed, I thought I was about to die. I thought I would never see my wife and little girl again. I was thumped on the head and didn't know what was happening. Everything was breaking up around me and there was this terrible noise, the noise of ripping and tearing. I could sense smoke and flames. Then suddenly the noise stopped. It was pitch black. I thought I must be in hell because of the blackness. I lay there for a while and felt blood running down my face. Eventually I realized I could not be dead. Above me to the right, I saw a hole. So I crawled over to it and looked out. Below me I could see Bert Whalley, one of the trainers, lying on the ground. I kicked at the hole to make it bigger and then dropped down beside Bert. In the distance, I could see people rushing away from the plane. Then Captain Jim Thain appeared with a fire extinguisher and shouted at me, "Run, you stupid bastard, it's about to explode."'

But Gregg ignored the captain's advice when he heard the sound of a baby crying. (This was the 22-month-old daughter of Vera Lukic, whose husband was the Yugoslavian air attache in London. United had agreed to give mother and child a lift back to England.) He went into the wreckage, pulled the child to safety, and then crawled back to rescue the mother. Moments later, he came across his fellow keeper Ray Wood, who recalls: 'I was trapped in the plane, under a wheel, and Harry and some others got me out. They actually broke my leg with a crowbar as they lifted the wheel off me. I was laid out in the snow. I remember two stewardesses standing in front of me, alongside Peter Howell, the *Daily Mail*'s photographer.

"How are you son?"

"Peter, give us a fag." I was shivering in the snow and I badly needed a cigarette. I was about to light it when I was quickly stopped. It would, of course, have been madness.'

Bill Foulkes was another who survived: 'I got out and ran as fast as I could. I must have been thinking that the plane would blow up any second but I can't remember having a clear thought in my head. I must have run about 300 yards through thick snow. When I was out of breath I stopped and looked round for the first time. I could not believe my eyes. The plane was cut in half – a mass of jagged metal. Bodies were strewn from it in a neat line in slush and water, where the snow had been melted. The tail end of the plane was ablaze in a petrol dump.'

In this scene of utter desolation lay the figure of 20-year-old Bobby Charlton. As the plane had broken up, he had fallen out of the cabin, still strapped into his seat, and landed near the tailplane. When Harry Gregg found him, lying in a pool of water made by the melted snow, he thought he was dead. Alongside Bobby was the equally cold and motionless body of Dennis Viollet. But, still fearing that the plane was about to explode, he grabbed both Bobby and Dennis by the waistbands of their trousers and dragged their bodies, like ragdolls, away from the wreckage. 'I didn't stop to think. They seemed to be dead. Dennis had a terrible cut on his head but Bobby was not badly marked. I pulled them through the snow and left them by a pile of debris,' he told me. Yet again, Gregg returned to the burning mess, this time finding Matt Busby, lying in agony in the snow, and Jackie Blanchflower, with blood pouring from his arm. He continues his account, 'Blanchy's arm was half-hanging off. I ripped off my tie and used it as a tourniquet. I had just finished tightening it, when I turned round and got the biggest shock. There were Bobby and Dennis standing up, staring into the fire. Well, that nearly killed me. I was sure they had been dead. I sank to my knees and wept, thanking God some of us had been saved.' Moments earlier Bill Foulkes had returned to the scene, where he had seen Bobby Charlton strapped into his seat. He then went over to Busby, and sat holding his hand. 'At that moment, I thought Harry Gregg and I must be the only ones on our feet. And then suddenly Bobby Charlton woke up, as if he had been enjoying a nap, and without a word, walked over to us. I asked him if was all right and he just kept looking.'

It is often claimed that Bobby Charlton has never talked about his experience of the crash. Now, while it is true that he is extremely reticent on the subject, he has, in fact, given several accounts, including an interview in the *Daily Mail* just a day after the crash. 'There was a terrible grinding crash as the plane went through some railings. A split second later it had smashed into a house or a building. I can remember being hurled through the side of the plane. I must have been knocked out. When I came round I was in the middle of a field about 40 yards from the wreck. I was aching all over as I tried to get up.' In an interview in 1964, he gave this graphic description of what he felt on the moment of waking: 'I could hear nothing but the howling of the wind, and I could see nothing but a couple of bodies. Neither was moving.' Bobby did not know that he had been dragged away from the plane by Harry Gregg and was puzzled by the distance he had travelled. 'Four of us were lying in the slush,' he wrote in his 1967 book *Forward for England*. 'I can only guess that the aircraft had spun round as it hit the house and tipped us out. There seems to have been no other reason four of us should have got out and I cannot believe we were physically thrown all that way. I saw Dennis Viollet next to me, also still strapped into his seat, with a nasty gash on his head. The boss was lying a few yards to our right and seemed to be having trouble with his legs. I released my safety belt and stumbled over to him. I felt as if I was in the middle of a painting, standing there with the action frozen in an atmosphere of stricken unreality.' Before he died in 1999, Dennis Viollet gave an equally vivid recollection of that devastating landscape. 'My head was split wide open and I was covered in blood but Bob seemed to have received only a slight knock to the back of his head. It's strange what people do in certain circumstances. I was not really conscious. I remember walking back to the plane and Bob was there with Bill Foulkes and Harry Gregg. Bob put his arm round me and I asked him a stupid question. 'Have we crashed, Bob?' It was then that I understood what had happened for I could see the carnage all around me. It was an absolute nightmare, a scene of utter destruction, with mangled wreckage and bodies lying in the snow. I felt terribly angry. I just wanted to dash into the plane, find the pilot and attack him.'

A Volkswagen van appeared. Matt was placed on a stretcher and put at the back along with Jackie Blanchflower and Johnny Berry, while Bobby, Dennis Viollet, Harry Gregg and Bill Foulkes were told to sit in the front. The van sped away, but before it had travelled far, it was stopped to load a stretcher carrying the badly burned Mrs Miklos, wife of the Manchester travel agent Bela Miklos. The Volkswagen moved off again, bouncing over the snow. Bill Foulkes takes up the story: 'The driver was speeding for all he was worth and we were lurching all over the road. I must have been in a state of shock. I could not stand it. I told the driver to slow down and asked him, "What the hell are you doing? Trying to get us all killed?" I got no response, so I punched him on the back of the head. I must have thumped him half-a-dozen times, but he just ignored me. I shouted for Bobby and Dennis to do something. They just stared ahead, with a vacant expression on their faces.'

When they arrived at the Rechts der Isar hospital, Bobby, Harry and Bill initially walked round the corridors in a kind of trance, unable to grasp the enormity of what had happened. They were then seen by a doctor, who explained that they would each be given an injection. All three protested that they were not badly injured, but, without listening, a nurse got hold of Bobby's arm and started to give him the jab. The moment the needle pierced his skin, he fainted and was caught by the doctor as he fell. Bill Foulkes and Harry Gregg were having none of this. They ran down the corridor and out of the hospital. Eventually, it was agreed by the doctors and BEA that they could stay in a hotel. Neither of them were big drinkers, but they worked their way through a bottle of whisky that night.

Meanwhile, Bobby was put in a small ward. Amazingly, given the carnage all around him, he was only suffering from shock and minor head injuries, which required just two stitches and a bandage. But, having collapsed once, the doctors wanted to keep him in for observation. The first Bobby knew of the extent of the disaster was the next day, from a German sitting in the bed next to him. As he later recalled in *Weekend* magazine, 'The German began to read out loud from a newspaper. When he went on to say that Dave Pegg, Eddie Colman and Tommy Taylor were dead, I didn't want to hear any more. I couldn't believe it and I didn't want to. I shut my ears to him but he just went on and on. I thought he would never stop. It was the worst moment of my life.'

Bobby was kept in for a week. During that time he and the other survivors were visited by Jimmy Murphy, who would normally have been on the flight to Belgrade but instead, in his capacity as part-time manager of the Welsh national team, had been in Cardiff for a vital World Cup qualifying tie. In the absence of Matt Busby, Murphy had the daunting task of trying to rebuild the team. In an attempt to boost the morale of those who were injured, Murphy had asked Bill Foulkes and Harry Gregg to go round the wards. They saw Matt Busby in his oxygen tent, hovering on the verge of death before making an astonishing recovery, thanks partly to the medical care of Professor Georg Maurer, the Chief Surgeon of the Rechts der Isar Hospital. Gregg remembers, too, the moment when he and Murphy came to the bed of Duncan Edwards, whose injuries were so extensive that he had been given only a 50-50 chance of survival. 'He was lying still as we approached, then he suddenly opened his eyes. "What time's kick-off?" Jimmy, trying to hold back the tears, just whispered, "Three o'clock son, three o'clock." Duncan replied, "Get stuck in."' Less than a fortnight later, Edwards was dead.

Ray Wood, who initially shared the same ward as Bobby, gave me this insight into what it was like for him in those weeks after the crash. 'When I first woke up I saw Bobby in the bed opposite. I was absolutely freezing cold. There was a doctor beside my bed holding my hand. Now I had seen films where people have lost their leg and they think their foot is freezing. That is exactly how I felt.' Wood's condition worsened and he was transferred to another ward. 'I had concussion and double vision. I could hear music playing all the time. My leg was in agony and, such was the pain, that I was drifting in and out of consciousness. I didn't even know what day it was. When my wife turned up, I asked her, "Where did you come from?" Harry Gregg tells me that when he visited the hospital, he found me in the operating theatre, where the doctors were working on my eye. They actually had it right out of its socket, sitting on the cheekbone. Typical Harry, dear man, he says that the thought passed through his mind, "Well, Ray won't be troubling me for the keeper's position any more."'

But for all their agonies, Ray Wood, Matt Busby – and Bobby – were the lucky ones. Of the 43 people on board the BEA Elizabethan, 23 died in the crash or soon afterwards. The tragic roll call included the co-pilot Kenneth Rayment, three Manchester United officials: Walter Crickmer (secretary), Tom Curry (trainer) and Bert Whalley (coach), and eight players: Roger Byrne, Geoff Bent, Eddie Colman, Mark Jones, David Pegg, Tommy Taylor, Billy Whelan and Duncan Edwards – 'all my mates' said Bobby later.

Two subsequent inquiries by German investigators concluded that ice on the wings was the chief cause of the accident. This was a verdict fiercely disputed by Captain Thain, who spent 11 years fighting to clear his name. In the eyes of his supporters, he was vindicated in 1969 by an official British inquiry which stated that sludge on the runway was to blame. But there was little hope of his returning to work as a pilot. He had been dismissed by BEA in 1960 for his failure to check for ice, as well as for breaching airline regulations – his other technical offence had been to swap places with Kenneth Rayment on the journey back from Munich. BEA rules stipulated that, even if the co-pilot was flying the plane, the commander of the flight had to remain on the left-hand side of the cockpit. The enforcement of this requirement might seem the height of pettiness, and Thain put forward a strong defence for his behaviour. First, he pointed out that Rayment was an experienced pilot, indeed more experienced than he was in flying Elizabethans. Second, he argued that he had a better view of the instrument panels from the right-hand side. But this did not wash with BEA, and for good reason. For the change of seats may have left, as Frank Taylor wrote in his book *The Day a Team Died*, 'a suggestion of divided responsibility in the cockpit', which resulted in a tragic disharmony of action. There is the possibility that in the last seconds on the runway, just as Thain was pushing the throttle for more power and trying to retract the under-carriage to achieve take-off, Rayment may have been working in exactly the opposite cause, slamming on the brakes to bring the plane to a halt.

Whatever the cause, Munich left a gaping wound on Manchester United, which has still not healed to this day. And, emotionally, Bobby Charlton was to suffer more than most. On 14 February 1958, he was the first of the survivors to leave the hospital. But his real pain was only just beginning.

CHAPTER SIX

The Survivor

'Deep down the sorrow is there all the time. You never rid yourself of it. It becomes part of you. You might be alone and it comes back to you, like a kind of roundabout, and you weep,' Sir Matt Busby once said, explaining how he was haunted for the rest of his life by the Munich crash.

Since the afternoon of 6 February 1958, Bobby Charlton has always been gripped by the same feelings. In a BBC interview in 2001 with Hunter Davies, he said, 'I still think about Munich every day. I was really fond of the players who died. David Pegg and Tommy Taylor were really close to me, I think because they came from a mining background like me.' Eamon Dunphy gave me this illustration of how the trauma of Munich remained with Bobby, even more than 30 years after the crash. 'In 1990 I interviewed him for my book on Matt Busby. We were talking alone in a room together and when he was recalling the events of Munich, he became very upset and began to cry. The crash had such a big impact on him. He is an intelligent, sensitive man and he felt it very deeply.'

As well as the sense of loss, there was also an element of survivor's guilt in Bobby's reaction. 'There was very little wrong with me physically but I could not stop thinking about the accident. I couldn't accept it for a long time and I felt drained of all emotion.

I kept asking myself, "Why me? Why should I be left?"' he wrote in 1967.

Bobby kept focusing on such dark thoughts as he lay in the Rechts der Isar hospital, his introspection made all the deeper because, unlike most of the other victims, he received no visits from his family. Cissie had, of course, been desperate to fly out to see her beloved son, and she had actually been offered a seat on a plane specially chartered by Manchester United for the relatives of the survivors. But only three months earlier she had undergone major surgery for breast cancer. Her doctor had warned her not to travel unless Bobby was desperately ill. And because of their respective commitments with the Coal Board and Leeds United, there had never been any question of either her husband Bob or her elder son Jack going to Munich.

Before the disaster, Cissie Charlton claimed to have known, though a sense of psychic intuition, that something was about to go wrong. 'On the morning of that tragic flight, I was more worried that I had ever been in my life,' she wrote later. 'I just couldn't settle, but neither could I explain why. A black worry had settled on me and I just couldn't shake it off.' Snow was falling in Ashington as well as Munich when Cissie decided to call on a neighbour to explain how anxious she was. Not long after she had waded back home through the snow, Ted Cockburn, the local newsagent, came to her yard. Cissie knew what he was about to say before he had opened his mouth.

'It's Bobby, isn't it?' she said.

'Yes, but I wanted you to know before it went on the placards. The paper has produced our bills about Bobby being in a plane crash and I wanted to make sure you knew first before I put them up,' said the newsagent. But, even though she had heard nothing officially, she felt she already knew what had happened to the plane.

The worst aspect for her was that the first radio and press reports to reach Ashington said that there were no survivors. Cissie desperately tried to ring Old Trafford from a call box to find out if this was true, but because of the poor weather the telephone lines had come down. Fearing that Bobby now lay dead in the Munich snow, she suddenly became hysterical in the phone booth, crying and screaming out his name, before being helped home by Cockburn.

Further south in Leeds, Jack had also received news of the tragedy. Having just finished his bath after a training session, he was standing naked in the dressing room, drying himself off, when Arthur Crowther, the club secretary, entered. Bobby Forrest, Jack's colleague at Leeds, recalls, 'We were joking and having a laugh when Arthur Crowther walked in, looking very serious. He said: "Quiet, I've got something very important to tell you. The plane carrying the Manchester team from Munich has crashed. They don't know if there are any survivors." An immediate, terrible silence descended on the dressing room. Inevitably, everyone looked at Jack, who turned white, truly white. You could see that he was shattered, but no-one said a word. I have never known a silence like it in my life. Nothing like it. The room was completely still. He got dressed quickly and went out.'

Jack went up to the club office to see if anyone had any more information, but Crowther was having the same difficulty as Cissie in contacting Old Trafford. Jack then decided to go back to Ashington, though, because his parents had no phone, he could not let them know he was on his way. He telephoned his new wife Pat – they had been married less than a month – to arrange to meet at the station for the grim journey north, still thinking that his younger brother was probably dead. As soon as he started talking to Pat on the phone, he burst into tears, the first time in his life he had broken down like that. On the way to the station, he called at Bobby Forrest's house to see if there had been any further reports about the disaster on the wireless. But Bobby's wife could give tell him no new details.

Jack and Pat found the rail trip to Ashington unbearable. Not recognizing Jack, some of the other passengers in their carriage talked blithely about the crash, even asking each other how much compensation the families of the dead victims might receive from BEA. No wonder Jack later wrote, 'The bloody rail journey lasted ages.' On arrival at Newcastle, Jack and Pat went to the Haymarket to catch the bus to Ashington. On their way, they saw a newspaper vendor selling late editions of the *Evening Chronicle*. Though he dreaded what he might find inside, Jack decided he had to buy a copy. Then, as he approached the stall, he could see a folded paper on the vendor's arm bearing the stop press news: 'Charlton among the survivors'. Just as Cissie had wailed in anguish in that phone box, so Jack now shouted out in joy, 'Bloody hell, he's OK,' before grabbing Pat and dancing a very public jig with her.

Thinking he was the bearer of good news, Jack walked into the Ashington family home with a large grin on his face. But, by now, Cissie had heard that Bobby was alive. Just before he had fainted in Rechts der Isar hospital, Bobby had managed to contact the British Consul in Munich, requesting a message be sent to his parents informing them of his survival. It was a Northumberland copper who delivered the Foreign Office telegram with the joyous words 'Alive and well, see you later, Bobby.'

Understandably, Cissie still wanted more news, so she decided to go to Manchester. The Charltons did not own a car, while all buses had been cancelled because of the heavy snow, so she hitched a lift to Newcastle from an early morning delivery van, and then caught the train to Manchester. Once she arrived at Old Trafford she received confirmation that Bobby was suffering from nothing more than a cut head, but she was appalled by the death toll of Bobby's friends. Unable to travel to Munich, she tried to take her mind off the disaster by helping in the club office, dealing with the avalanche of work brought on by the tragedy. For all Cissie's good motives, this may have been the moment when Bobby started to distance himself from her. According to Harry Gregg: 'I don't think Bobby was too happy about her being in the offices there. He felt she should not be there. He was slightly embarrassed by her.'

Old Trafford was in a state of shock in the wake of the disaster. Alma George, Matt Busby's secretary, had been one of the first to hear the news that Thursday afternoon. She later recalled: 'I was living in a nightmare. Like everyone else I was too numb to take in the awful grief. Agony piled on agony as the hours ticked by. Thousands hurried to the ground to see if they could help; the police threw a protective cordon around the relatives and friends who had lost their loved ones. Those of us left at the ground did our best to calm and console the grief stricken. But what word of sympathy could I find to comfort the bereaved?' Perhaps the most poignant symbol of despair was the transformation of the Old Trafford gymnasium into a temporary mortuary, filled with the coffins of the players who only days earlier had been gracing the pitch outside with their youthful brilliance.

But even in the pit of darkness, the club had to find the will to continue. Fixtures had to be completed, players bought, squads trained, tickets issued. When Jimmy Murphy had visited Matt Busby in his Munich oxygen tent, the broken manager had croaked in his deputy's ear, 'Keep the flag flying, Jimmy.' It was a duty that Murphy fulfilled with heroic zeal over the next few months, pulling the battered remnants of his team into a fighting unit. To the bewildered players left at Old Trafford, Murphy never showed anything but a brave face. Ian Greaves says: 'When we got the full truth of the disaster, we just didn't know what we were doing. There was a numbness about the place, especially when we started to go to all the funerals. But Jimmy forced us to carry on, working on us as if nothing had happened. But he had to do that. I mean, if he was going around in tears, what would the rest of us be like.' In private, away from his responsibilities, the passion in Jimmy's soul would engulf him in sorrow, as Harry Gregg remembered: 'In Munich, I was walking up the stairs to my hotel room when I heard this terrible crying. At first, I couldn't figure it out but as I got nearer I could just make out Jimmy sitting in the dark on the empty staircase, crying his eyes out. I just walked quietly away.' During this period, Jimmy started to drink heavily, a habit which Cissie quickly recognized and understood. 'Jimmy often said to me, "Make us a cup of tea, Cis," and I knew what he meant. I put a little drop of tea in the cup and filled the rest with whisky. It helped him to keep going during that terrible time. But it was a pitiful sight to see him wandering around the empty football ground at night, all alone with his thoughts in the darkness,' she wrote.

Shattered by the events of 6 February, Bobby could not be part of Murphy's immediate plans for rebuilding United. As he left the Munich hospital, he was told by Murphy to go home to Ashington and only return to Old Trafford when he felt ready. But there would be a time, in the coming weeks, when he would seriously contemplate giving up football altogether. In his black mood, it seemed that the game which had been his lifeblood, his driving force, had brought him only misery and bereavement.

Unsurprisingly, Bobby could not face a plane journey back to England from Germany, so he took the train and boat to London. At Liverpool Street station, he was met by Jack and his mother, who was shocked at his dejected appearance. As Cissie later recalled, 'When he got off the train he was a pathetic sight. He just stood beside his case looking lost. The platform was cordoned off but the station was swarming with pressmen and spectators. Jack said, "Let's just get him away from here."' Jack ushered Bobby and his mother into a car and then drove them north. It was during this journey that Bobby told them his disjointed, painful memories of the crash. Then he said, when he had concluded the story, 'That's it. I don't want you to ask me about it again. I want to forget all about it.' He could never, of course, forget about it, but Bobby hardly ever spoke about Munich again to his family or, indeed, to the other Manchester United players. 'In my eight years at Old Trafford I never heard him mention the issue of Munich once,' says the former United captain Noel Cantwell, echoing the views of all those who played with Bobby. It was a subject that no-one dared to raise with him. Only through a medium of his choosing – in a book or interview – would he talk about it.

Bobby says that it was even more difficult to cope once he arrived home. 'The sense of the tragedy seemed nearer. The papers were full of the crash – they couldn't leave the sensation alone in spite of the people they were hurting,' he said later. He found it particularly difficult to deal with the horde of reporters and photographers who gathered outside the family house, 113 Beatrice Street. Initially, he refused to see any of them. But his mother explained that they were only doing their job, adding that he had once harboured ambitions to be a journalist himself. So he posed for some rather stagey pictures, in one struggling to maintain a grin as he had a cup of tea and in another kicking a football in the street with two small boys who were dressed in Sunderland and Newcastle strips.

Cissie, as always, was not one to shy away from the limelight and she could be seen in some of the papers with a maternal arm around Bobby. But it is telling that her husband Bob had so little involvement with the public saga of the Munich air crash. All the dramatic moments of the family's response to the crisis had Cissie, not Bob, at their centre: the frantic phonecalls, the early morning trip to Old Trafford, the receipt of the Foreign Office telegram, the collection of Bobby from Liverpool Street, the handling of the media circus in Ashington.

Upbeat news stories, which accompanied the photographs, claimed that Bobby's first words, on walking through his front door, were 'Mum, is there a football in the house?' But in her autobiography, Cissie wrote that this was pure fiction. In reality, 'After the cameramen and reporters had left, Bobby announced that he was giving up football for good. He said that he had lost all his mates and never wanted to play again.' In his first weeks at home, there was little doubt that he was gripped by depression. He lay on the floor in his room, listening to his Frank Sinatra's records. The late 1950s was the time when Sinatra was working at Capitol under the direction of Nelson Riddle, producing some of the most heart-breaking albums ever recorded. Songs like *In the Wee Small Hours* and *I'll Never Smile Again* perfectly captured the desperate loneliness that had gripped Bobby.

The worst moment for him came the morning he realized that Duncan Edwards had lost his fight for life. In a contribution for Iain McCartney's 1988 biography of Edwards, Bobby stated unequivocally that Edwards was the finest footballer he had ever seen. 'Over the years, I have played with and against many world-class players, but in my mind Duncan Edwards is the greatest of them all. Pele and Di Stefano were marvellous, but they needed help to play. Duncan could do it all himself.' Bobby also recalled his torment at the death of Edwards. 'I last saw Duncan alive on the day I left hospital in Munich. He was still battling away, calling on his immense reserves of strength to defeat the inevitable. Tears stained my face as I left that room, praying he would make it. Back home in Ashington, my mother would greet me each morning with the latest newspaper reports from the hospital. Sometimes the bulletins were optimistic and my hopes grew.'

Then one morning, explained Bobby, there was no news.

'Where's the paper?' he asked his mother

'It hasn't come yet. Now eat up your breakfast.' She had cooked him his favourite meal of ham, egg and mushrooms.

'I don't want any breakfast. Duncan's dead, isn't he?' He knew the truth before she had time to say yes.

His despondency became only greater. Ron Routledge, the former Sunderland keeper who had grown up with him, told me how Bobby felt then. 'He was particularly upset about Duncan Edwards. He just locked himself away. He wanted nothing to do with anyone. It was terrible. After about a fortnight of this, his mother came up to me and asked: "Has he mentioned anything to you about football?" I told her, "Not really. He seems more concerned about what's going on in the hospital at Munich." Then Cissie replied, "He's said to me that he doesn't want to play again, that he won't go back to Old Trafford." I wanted to do something. So I went to a local school, got a football, and said to Bobby, "Right, let's go up the park." He didn't want to go but I pushed him. So we went to the park and we were there for a good three hours. I wasn't going to leave it there. I decided I was going to keep pushing him. We did that a few more times and gradually he opened up. At first he had been really down, hated the idea of kicking a football around, but eventually he got into it, and after a few sessions, he told his mother, "Look, I want to get back. I feel like getting back to United." But he never mentioned the crash once during our kickarounds, not once.'

Bobby was also encouraged in his return to soccer by his mother's GP, Dr MacPherson. Apprehensive about the future and needing some tangible, physical excuse to avoid confronting it, Bobby had been reluctant to have his two stitches taken out, though his injury had healed. But eventually he was persuaded to see the doctor, who, as well as removing the stitches, took the opportunity to give Bobby some advice about the need to start his life in football again. As Bobby later explained, 'He told me he had been in the RAF during the war and had seen his friends shot down repeatedly and that I had to learn to carry on as he had done.' After urging Bobby to begin kicking a ball again, the doctor finished with these prophetic words: 'I expect to see you at Wembley.'

Though Bobby now returned to Old Trafford, the scars of Munich were to stay with him forever. The crash turned out to be the pivotal moment of his life, defining his character, sharpening his relationships with both club and family, and building the footballer who was to become a world beater.

Bobby Charlton had always been a quiet young man, right back to his childhood. But the trauma of the crash greatly exacerbated his traits of shyness and reservation. The boyish exuberance which had often been displayed in his years at school and Old Trafford now disappeared, to be replaced by a streak of moody introspection. Where he had been a high-spirited, sometimes irresponsible, youth before 6 February, he now quickly matured into a serious adult. The dour, unsmiling, exterior, which was to become so much part of his public image, was formed in the aftermath of the crash. Having lost so many of his friends in one savage blow, he found it much harder to trust people.

The change in his personality was clearly seen by those around him. One of his Ashington neighbours, Ronnie Cameron, says: 'I knew Bobby before he was famous and he was pretty straight-forward, easy, polite. He used to get on very well with my mother, who said he was a gentleman. But Munich changed Bobby a lot, I thought. He was happy go lucky before that. He loved Frank Sinatra, had quite a few of his records and he used to walk around the place singing them. I never heard him singing out loud again after Munich. He became very quiet and sullen.' At Old Trafford, others saw a new quietness about him. Albert Scanlon says, 'Bobby did not seem to have an immediate physical reaction to the crash but he certainly grew up as a man. He became more withdrawn and said less.' Harry Gregg adds, 'To be nice about it, Bobby was deep and introverted, almost to the point of being surly.' And Bobby himself, in that 1961 interview in *Weekend*, admitted that the crash affected him in this way: 'I knew the road ahead would be different from the moment I woke up in the Munich hospital. I'm quieter now because I haven't got my old mates to go out with.'

A graphic example of this darker trait was given to me by Ronnie Cope who shared a room with Bobby during a week-long United trip to Blackpool soon after the crash. 'Bobby altered unbelievably after Munich. He never got back to being a joker, the Bobby Charlton I had known as a lad. He became more withdrawn. There were great mood swings. Some days, when we were in the hotel in Blackpool, he would wake up and he would jump on my bed, trying to wrestle with me. Yet the next day he would not even say hello, as if I was not there. It was almost as if he were having a blackout, he seemed to go so deep. You would say things to him and I am sure he would not hear you, because he would not answer. The days he didn't speak, I just left him alone. But then he would come out of it and he could enjoy a drink and a laugh.'

Jack sensed the change keenly, particularly because in the immediate aftermath of the crash he had felt more warmth to Bobby than at any previous time in his life. The fraternal affection was at its strongest on the car trip home from Liverpool Street, as Bobby wrote later: 'Jack didn't say much and there were long silences during the journey. But I felt very close to him then.' Yet this bond soon began to loosen. As Bobby brooded on the tragedy, Jack felt the shutters coming down and he came to see himself as an intruder on his younger brother's private grief. 'In a way,' wrote Jack, 'Robert was never the same lad to me after Munich. I saw a big change in our kid from that day on. He stopped smiling, a trait which continues to this day. Friends come up to me and say, "Your Bob goes around as if he has the weight of the world on his shoulders" – and I have to agree.' In an interview in 1980, Jack said: 'Something happened after Munich. We were very close until then, but after the plane crash, he didn't come home as often, and there was a barrier between us that I have never been able to fathom.'

But Bobby's change was more complex than merely a descent into taciturnity. With most of the great United side wiped out, Bobby was now the most talented player in the club. No longer just another member of the orchestra, he was now its lead violinist. Given this status, he believed he had to take on the mantle of responsibility for the performance of the team, even though he was only 20 years old. It was a burden that drove him to a new sense of involvement with the club, a new intensity in his play. For a while, he took the field like a man possessed by some inner force. 'When he came back from Munich,' says Reg Hunter, 'I noticed he improved tremendously. All of a sudden he moved into brilliance. It was because he had to grow up so quickly. He was a different player altogether after the crash. He had always been quiet, never said a lot, but he was certainly much more mature after Munich, especially in the big matches. He was more involved, wanted the ball all the time, held on to it, took responsibility for everything. People came to rely on him. Before Munich he was in and out of the first team but it was very different when he returned. He took over the side, in effect.'

Bobby's new dominance saw him quickly transformed by the press into the most exciting star in British football. His story had all the right ingredients to fascinate the media: the drama of his survival in the snow; the virtuosity of his skill on the ball; the tragic loss of team-mates; the coalmining background; the family foot-balling heritage; and there was also the added piquancy that, at the time of the crash, he was still a lance corporal doing his National Service in the British army with three months to go before his official demobilization, though the War Office bowed to public pressure and released him early. Some sportsmen with big egos might have revelled in all this attention, but for Bobby, with his retiring nature, it was an added burden. And the bigger a star he became, the more his caution and reticence grew. John Giles, that shrewdest of judges, who was at United from 1956 to 1963, thinks this is one of the keys to his personality. 'Bobby changed after Munich, because he was suddenly thrust into the position of being a superstar, in the full glare of publicity all the time. I don't think he enjoyed it. I would say it was a big culture shock for him, just as big a shock as it was later to be for George Best and David Beckham. Because he was such a conscientious lad, such a decent human being, he was not comfortable with being a star. With his talent, he would probably have achieved that status anyway during his career, but the glare of fame would not have arrived so quickly had it not been for Munich. And because he became so aware of the need to behave the right way in public, he was more withdrawn, more shy after Munich.'

The death of so many colleagues also had a profound effect on Bobby's attitude towards both soccer and Manchester United. Though he became such a major figure at the club after Munich, he has often said that he was never again to derive the same enjoyment from playing. After February 1958 the game was more of a job than a pleasure. The carefree days had gone forever. And he felt the same way about his new team-mates at Old Trafford. He never developed the same rapport with those who arrived after the crash. Having grown up with the Babes, he always seemed to view their replacements as outsiders, not part of the true Busby tradition. It was almost like he had drawn an invisible dividing line in the dressing room between who had played with him before Munich and those who joined the club after the disaster. For Bobby, paradise had existed with Duncan and Tommy and Eddie. It had been lost on that German runway and could never be replaced. Eamon Dunphy believes this is crucial to any understanding of Bobby. 'The key to Bobby is that he was one of the Munich lads. He went to the club as a 15 year old and became United right through. After the crash, Busby, realizing he could not build another set of Babes, started to flash the cheque book, buying in people from other clubs. Bobby was never easy with the change in culture. He had a feeling of alienation from the new club. There was a big split between the pre- and post-Munich lads. Bobby harboured – perhaps to an unreasonable degree – a resentment against the people who had been brought in.'

For all his diplomacy, Bobby was never afraid to express his feeling that the post-1958 United sides he played in never measured up to the standards of his heroes, certainly not in terms of commitment. 'That pre-Munich team was special in many ways,' he said in 1973. 'They were playing because they were dedicated to the club. I can't honestly say that the present team is the same way. Maybe it's me, perhaps I don't want to believe that they are as good. But with the old team, if they were losing by three of four goals, which was not often, they'd go flat out, still try to save something, their pride in the club. We were committed to the club, the game, the gaffer. Now it's a career. People have their minds outside the game.' In an interview with John Roberts for his superb book about the Busby Babes, *The Team That Wouldn't Die*, Bobby said: 'For me, the football in the late 1950s was the best it's ever been and, from a selfish football point of view, that United team could not have been lost at a worse time. The difference after Munich was the commitment of the side. The team that played before the crash had nothing to prove. Those players knew they were great. Afterwards, we had everything to prove.'

Noel Cantwell, who joined United after 1960, bears out this point about Bobby's disillusion. 'It seemed, when I arrived at Old Trafford, that Bobby resented the new people that had come in. I got the feeling that he saw us as intruders. So when you were introduced to Bobby, he shook your hand, was very polite, but he stuck to his own pre-Munich crowd. He was in a group with the likes of Wilf McGuinness and Shay Brennan, the lads he'd grown up with. They were his mates, and, if we were on the bus, they would spend all their time playing cards together. But I could understand the way he wanted to be with the lads he'd known since he was young.'

For all Bobby's mental anguish after Munich, he was not long out of the Manchester United side. The club was in the middle of perhaps the most romantic cup run in British history, having beaten Sheffield Wednesday 3–0 in a highly-charged, emotionally wrought fifth-round tie at Old Trafford on 19 February. So makeshift was the team against Wednesday that the match programme contained eleven blank spaces where the names of the Manchester players should have been.

Bobby was brought into the team for the next round, against West Bromwich Albion. Having drawn at the Hawthorns 2–2, United then had a replay at home. Such was the excitement that United were now generating, such was the willingness of the city to identify with a club still in mourning, that not only was the ground again packed to capacity, but no less than 20,000 people were locked outside. It was in this game that Bobby demonstrated how quickly he was developing. Playing on the left wing instead of his usual position as inside-left, he produced a piece of magic that was to linger in the memory of all who saw it. The match was heading towards another stalemate – this one goalless – when, in the 89th minute, Bobby received the ball from the tiny forward Ernie Taylor, who had been signed by Jimmy Murphy from Blackpool just six days after the crash. In the *Daily Herald*, Bobby gave this description of what happened next: 'Before I knew it I had the ball and was flying down the wing. I seemed to be tackled a dozen times, but somehow I got past all of them, full speed ahead. Now I was coming along the byline, now I was cutting back a low centre across goal, somehow beating the entire defence. And there was Colin Webster, thundering up the middle, side-footing the ball in full stride into the empty net. They say I just kept on running and running until I reached Webster, then grabbed him and hoisted him in the air.' Bobby later called it the greatest Cup tie he had ever played in. Frank Haydock, a United player, says of that goal. 'It was such a wonderful move, I could not get over what he'd done, the way he beat people with both pace and the body swerve. That was a real eye-opener for me, showing what sort of player he would become.'

Though United fell behind in the League and were knocked out 5–2 on aggregate by Real Madrid in the European Cup semi-final,

Bobby's superb form ensured that the team went all the way to Wembley in the FA Cup. Bolton, however, showed none of the sentiment that had swayed the nation after Munich, winning an undistinguished match 2–0. Their cynical professionalism was summed up by their second goal, when Nat Lofthouse barged Harry Gregg into the United net. Yet United's inadequacy had also been exposed, as Bill Foulkes recalled: 'Our forwards had never been in the game. Bobby, who had played so brilliantly between the disaster and Wembley was jaded on the big day. He had been required to play in too many matches – because there could be no thought of dropping him. He was too good a player to rest, and who could replace him, anyway?' In public, Bobby said he did not really mind losing to Bolton. He was more relieved that the team had not disgraced itself, that it had achieved something for the battered manager. He wrote later, 'What mattered was that we maintained our position in the game, the glamour and identity in being a top-class club. Matt, who had only recently come out of hospital, came to give us a pep talk at Old Trafford before the final. He couldn't. He just cried. Those fellows who died were his family.' In private, however, Bobby was dispirited after the Final, as Ronnie Cope recalls. 'There was some mix-up at the ceremony and Bobby, by mistake, got a winner's medal. Afterwards, he just threw it on the floor in the dressing room. It didn't mean a thing to him. He had a tremendous love for United and the club was everything to him.'

Up until the Cup Final, Bobby's form for United had led to a national clamour for him to be selected for the England team. This mood, as Bobby understood, was tinged with a degree of sympathy for what he had been through. Nevertheless, there was a genuine recognition that here was an outstanding young talent who could be one of the saviours of English football. The early and mid-1950s had been a dire period for the national side, with the successive 6–3 and 7–1 defeats by Hungary in 1953 emblematic of England's lack of vision and organization. Bobby Charlton represented hope for the future.

When Kevin Keegan was dropped by England in 1982, he

complained bitterly that he had only learned about the decision through the press. 'Bobby Robson should have had the guts to tell me to my face,' he wailed. But Keegan's case is hardly unique. This is the way so many players have been informed about international selection or exclusion, particularly in the pre-Ramsey days when an FA committee chose the England side. And so it was with Bobby Charlton. On one of his visits to Ashington he had been to the pictures with Jack in the late afternoon. As they came out of the cinema, Jack picked up an evening paper. There was the news, in the stop press column, that his younger brother had been selected for England. True to their natures, Jack was much more demonstrative, letting out, in his words, 'a whoop of joy', while Bobby just smiled. Jack says that his elation was completely genuine. 'There was no jealousy. There couldn't be. He was the great player of the two of us, and I never in my wildest dreams thought I was good enough to play for England. I was just proud and thrilled for him.'

Six years later when Jack contradicted his own prediction by winning his first cap for England – coincidentally against Scotland as well – Bobby's response was very different. In April 1965 Leeds and Manchester United were playing in an FA Cup semi-final at Hillsborough as the news came through to Leeds boss Don Revie that Jack had been picked for the England squad. He told Jack after the game, a typically stormy Cup tie which Leeds won narrowly. Unable to contain his glee at the news, Jack ran along to the United dressing room to see his brother, who recalls: 'I was sitting slumped when our kid came beaming through the door. "Go away," I thought, "we don't need you at this moment." But Jack just stood there, the smile getting wider and wider. "Hey," he said, "I'm in the England team with you."' The announcement was greeted with a resounding silence, only broken for a moment by Bobby's brief two words of congratulations, 'That's terrific.' Then another United player said, 'Now fuck off out of here.' Jack then knew he could not have chosen a worse time to tell his brother, walking into the dressing room of the team he had just helped to knock out of the FA Cup. 'But that's the kind of tact I'm famous for,' he once joked.

Interviewed in 1959 about his selection for England, Bobby made the predictable noises about achieving his childhood ambition. 'This is what I have been dreaming about since I was nine. I've never wanted to be anything else but an England footballer,' he told the *Daily Mail*. As always, Cissie loomed large in his thoughts: 'I know who will be happiest of all – my mother.' Interestingly, however, he said later that he was so emotionally focused on United's Cup run that he felt indifference towards the game. 'I went up to Scotland completely unworried, with no pre-match nerves at all.' Now this was very different to the way Bobby Charlton was to feel throughout the rest of his career. Though a master on the field, he would usually be gripped by pre-match nerves off it. Nobby Lawton game me this description of Bobby in the dressing room before a big game: 'At ten to three, Bobby was like a great performer, waiting in the wings, building himself up as he prepared to go out on stage. "This is me, this is what I'm good at," you could see him saying to himself. Bobby would be shaking. That was how much he cared about his performance. That's why he was great – every game mattered. He would often have a cigarette before the game, his hands shaking. Jimmy Murphy would sometimes put a bottle of whisky on the table in the dressing room, and Bobby and a few others would take a swig. It wasn't like a drink, really just a gulp, Dutch courage before the conflict. He was always the same before every game at Old Trafford, very, very nervous.'

The selectors thought he would be anxious so they made him share a room with Billy Wright, the Wolves and England captain. Intriguingly, Bobby, who always had such respect for authority throughout his career, was not especially impressed with the leadership of Billy Wright, the ultimate 'establishment' man. 'He was a nice fellow but I didn't feel he had much influence as captain other than by his example as a player. There was such a turnover in those days in the team that he was reluctant to criticize players in case they thought it was his fault,' says Bobby.

Bobby had an excellent first game for England, making the first goal and scoring the last in a 4–0 win at Hampden. His strike came in the 85th minute, when he hit a thunderous volley from a cross by Tom Finney. So impressed was Scottish goalkeeper Tommy Younger at this shot that he actually ran out of his area to congratulate Bobby, something that would be unimaginable today. 'Well done, son, that was a fantastic goal,' he said. Players on both sides were amazed at Bobby's spectacular effort. Tommy Docherty, later to be Charlton's last manager at United, recalls: 'It was one of the greatest goals ever seen at Hampden. I was on the receiving end. Bobby left me flat-footed as he met a cross from my Preston team-mate Tom Finney. The ball came in at hip height and Bobby caught it on the volley. Our goalkeeper was still diving when the ball hit the net.' Bryan Douglas, the Blackburn winger, says, 'I can remember Bobby's debut as if it were yesterday. That goal of his showed me what he was all about – two wonderful feet and a great temperament. He did not need to be near a goal to score. He could fire them in from anywhere. I once watched him in training, cracking ball after ball into an empty net. I could see that it just gave him a thrill to see the ball rocketing into the goal.' In praising such shooting, Douglas also exposes the absurdity of the idea that Bobby ever 'picked his spot'. He continues. 'Bobby was always modest about his skill, honest as well. I remember once playing against him in a League game. There was a throw-in, he dummied, let the ball run past him, and then he hit it from about 30 yards with his left foot. When I complimented him on this fabulous goal, he said, "Well, I just hit it. I knew the goal was somewhere over there."' Bobby was just as successful in his second game for England at Wembley against Portugal. Every time he received the ball a roar went around the ground and he scored twice in England's 2–1 triumph, both his goals from long-range shots. But already critics in the England set-up were privately expressing reservations about his workrate.

From these dizzy heights, Bobby's performances went into swift decline. It was as if he had been running on adrenalin after Munich, and now, as the end of the season approached, he was suffering from delayed shock. 'Jaded' was the word that Bill Foulkes used about Bobby's appearances in the Cup Final and the international against Yugoslavia. Albert Scanlon said to me: 'The press had build up this romantic image of Bobby, the player who had emerged from the debris of Munich to appear in the Cup Final and become an international. It was in a reaction to all this publicity that he lost his confidence.' Bobby admits that, ever since the calamity, he had been feeling under unrelenting pressure. 'I was just an ordinary footballer, yet every move I made was watched. I can't remember whether I wondered if my best days were already behind. I just went out and played, never in touch with the pace of the game, playing in little spurts, hating every minute.' It was this idea that he could only play 'in little spurts' that was to cause Bobby particular aggravation in the coming months.

But the biggest problem facing Bobby now was that England were due to play in Belgrade, the scene of his last United game before the Munich disaster. Bobby was never a tough player in the conventional, hard man, David Batty, sense – 'he couldn't tackle a fish supper,' in the words of John Docherty – but he was never lacking in true moral courage. It is a tribute to his bravery that, only three months after Munich, he was willing to undertake the same journey to Belgrade that had resulted in the deaths of so many of his colleagues. Arsenal must be wishing that Dennis Bergkamp, who has never been through any experience to match Bobby's ordeal, could show the same fortitude. 'I don't feel like flying again but I realize to achieve my ambitions I shall have to face it again in the future,' Bobby said just after the disaster.

What made Bobby's first flight after Munich all the more of a strain was not only the media attention on him in London, but also the difficulties the plane experienced on the way out to Yugoslavia. On a scheduled stop in Zurich, there was a hold-up of around three hours before the BEA Vickers Viscount could take off again. Bobby must have felt a shudder of disbelief when he heard the loudspeaker announcement, 'the flight from London to Belgrade will be delayed owing to a technical fault' – almost exactly the same phrase that had been used just 15 minutes before the doomed third take-off attempt on 6 February. Yet no matter what agonies he was feeling, he never once flinched. Instead, as the England team waited at the Swiss airport, he carried on drinking lemonade and writing postcards. It was a different story once he was on board again, as Bernard Joy recorded in the *Evening Standard*: 'It was distressing sitting immediately behind him. He fidgeted, sweated profusely and constantly looked back, seeking assurance and diversion.' Johnny Haynes, the Fulham midfield general who was also on that trip, has nothing but admiration for Bobby's gumption. 'It must have been difficult for him. But, to his great credit, he knew that the more quickly he got back in the air, the better. Yes, he was nervous when we were flying again but once he got out of the plane, he was a different person. You could almost see the physical relief all over him. He had done it. And I don't think flying ever bothered him that much again.'

Apart from the problems of travel and the memories of Munich, Bobby also hated Belgrade itself, because of the oppressive trappings of communist dictatorship – 'too many policemen and soldiers for my liking'. The result was as bad anything else about the trip. England were thrashed 5–0 by Yugoslavia, one of the worst defeats of the post-war era, and Bobby himself admits that his own performance was 'a nightmare'. The stifling heat was one reason why the England players performed so badly, as Ronnie Clayton told me: 'Bobby's reputation took a dent after that game in Yugoslavia but that was true of a few of us because we played in 95 degrees heat in the shade. After a quarter of an hour, we were flagging. It was a terribly difficult game. Everyone was off form, not just Bobby.'

It was on the evidence of his form in Belgrade that the selectors took the strange decision to drop him from the England team during the World Cup finals in Sweden in 1958. England subsequently did not win a single game and came home after failing to progress from their qualifying group, while both Wales and Northern Ireland reached the quarter-finals. The decision to leave out Charlton for all the games provoked a national outcry. It was the biggest controversy about England's participation in the 1958 competition. Yes, Bobby was inexperienced, youthful and inconsistent, but he could also turn a game in a single move. In contrast, the man that the selectors clung to up front, the West Brom striker Derek Kevan, lacked all such daring and creativity. He was just another heavyweight of a League centre-forward, whose nickname 'The Tank' was all too indicative of his inelegant approach.

England supporters of every age simply could not understand how a struggling side could take the field without Charlton. When the England manager Walter Winterbottom arrived back at Heathrow after the World Cup, he was met by his wife, daughter and son. He put his arm round his wife and kissed her, and did the same to his daughter. With his son, he thought a more masculine greeting would be appropriate, so he stretched out his hand. But his son refused to take it. Instead, he just scowled and put the question the whole nation was asking: 'Why didn't you choose Bobby Charlton?' In the *Daily Express*, Desmond Hackett spoke for many when he expressed outrage at the action of the selectors. 'I want to know what every football fan in England wants to know. Why was Charlton missing from an England team that demanded a player who could shoot?' I accuse the England selectors and team manager Walter Winterbottom of deliberately killing the individual talents of the players they took with them.' Hackett went on to explain that the line from the selectors was that 'Bobby Charlton was not a 90-minute player, that he was, in fact, a slacker'.

In view of Charlton's subsequent career, it seems an extraordinary criticism. In the 1960s and early 1970s, he was always seen as the model professional, who would never stop running for his side. In fact, the biggest complaint against him was that, far from being a 'slacker', he wanted to be involved too much. Nevertheless, this was the view of the England decision-makers in 1958. He was a lightweight, unable to contribute more than the occasional spectacular shot. There is a fascinating passage in the 1960 book *Soccer Partnership*, written with the co-operation of Winterbottom and Billy Wright, in which the case against Bobby Charlton is spelt out clearly. The English vice of emphasizing hard work rather than flair is all too apparent in these words: 'Even against Portugal, when he scored both of England's goals, little was seen of Charlton as a footballer helping his team and being part of the team effort. He did not feature in progressive, linked movements and his defensive play was non-existent. People who watched him closely concluded that he was immature and by no means of international standards.' Turning to the World Cup in Sweden, the book states: 'England could just not afford specialist players. Consistency was England's need in this competition, and the assurance that every player would give his maximum effort and efficiency.' It is the old battle cry of English footballing mediocrity, which led to the blighted international careers of a host of intuitive players, from Stanley Matthews to Glenn Hoddle.

Tom Finney, who himself missed most of the games in the World Cup through injury, could not understand the fuss over Charlton. He saw Bobby only as a potentially good player, not yet the finished article, and thought the whole row 'hopelessly exaggerated'. On his return to England in 1958 Finney, the most respected member of the side, set out his view: 'There is no "real" Bobby Charlton story, no hidden mystery about his rejection by the England selectors, no backroom squabbles or misbehaviour calling for disciplinary action. On the contrary, Bobby Charlton has always appeared to me one of the quietest lads with whom one could travel on soccer business. I am certain that the only reason for his missing the World Cup lay in the decision that he was considered too inexperienced for the series. Now my own assessment of Charlton as a player is that he shows great potentialities. Given normal progress, I have no doubts about his talent proving big enough for a regular berth in the international team. At the same time, I cannot understand how the non-selection of a promising youngster could cause such a hysterical outburst among the followers of football.'

Hysterical or not, most people thought the selectors had done Charlton a terrible disservice. The decision showed them to be idiots, devoid of any real understanding of the game. And this perception was not wrong. Bryan Douglas, a star England player throughout this period, told me a story which highlights how out of touch the selectors were. 'We had a woeful set-up before Ramsey. I was on the World Cup tour of 1962 in Chile and we had gone to the British Embassy for a reception. Just before I went in, one of the selectors pulled me to the side and said, "Will you stand with me, Bryan, and tell me the names of the players as they come in." I thought to myself, "Well, that's great. Here's a selector and he does not even know the names of the people he is supposed to be choosing."'

Yet such officials now had Bobby's international destiny in their hands.

CHAPTER SEVEN

The Bighead

Nostalgia can be a dangerous emotion. In retirement, the great player watches as his career become one long series of triumphs. His medals and cups are endlessly celebrated, his virtues continually lauded. In such romantic storytelling, even the few setbacks are treated as challenges that were heroically overcome on the march towards inevitable glory.

But at the time, the picture can be very different. Without the benefit of hindsight, the player's progress seems more stumbling, more complicated. Nothing is fixed about the route to success. When failure is encountered, there is no certainty that he will overcome it. From the contemporaneous angle, a run of poor performances – glossed over decades later – can seem like the death-knell for a career.

Thus in 1990 Alex Ferguson was seen as a failure as United manager. After four years in charge and without a trophy to his name, his future at Old Trafford looked doomed. No-one would have been surprised if he had been sacked then. Yet now he is widely regarded as the greatest manager in the history of British football. Similarly, when Tottenham sold Pat Jennings in 1977 for just £45,000, thinking he was finished, little could the club have imagined that nine years later he would be one of the stars of the 1986 World

Cup. And Peter Reid looked an injury-plagued footballer of unfulfilled promise before Howard Kendall turned him into the lynchpin of his all-conquering Everton side. Ironically, it was Everton that had released Reid five years earlier, thinking he would not make the grade.

The same could be said of the Charlton brothers. Today, they are amongst the most revered figures in football, holders of more than 140 England caps between them, World Cup winners and acclaimed international ambassadors. But, in the early 1960s, anyone making a prediction of such a future for Bobby and Jack would have been met with incredulity, even though the pair had been involved in top-flight football for a decade. Bobby was seen as a troubled soul, an enigma, who had failed to live up to his potential. There were complaints about his workrate, his lack of vision, his mercurial nature. 'The problem of Bobby Charlton' was raised frequently in the press. Looking back, it is amazing to read an article like that written by Peter Lorenzo in the *Sun* in October 1964, less than two years before the World Cup victory, when the decision to drop Bobby from the England team led him to ask: 'Is this the end of the road for Charlton?' In this piece Lorenzo argued that Alf Ramsey may be 'finally convinced that the undisciplined skills of Charlton are luxuries England can no longer afford. In the past three seasons his scoring rate has declined. I wonder if we shall ever see the Bobby Charlton of old? Unless we do, I think his international days are over. Against all his qualities stands an unforgivable soccer sin, the inability to perform or contribute as a member of an England team. As an individualist, Charlton can be supreme. As a team man he is the Prince of Unpredictables.'

Lower down the scale, Jack was having just as many problems as his brother. His early years at Leeds had been characterized by rows with players on the field and with managers off it. In the late 1950s and early 1960s his belligerence became even worse. Pig-headed, boorish and aggrieved, he made life awkward for all around him. Full of his own opinions, he was intolerant of the views of others, almost becoming something of a bully. 'You've always got plenty to say for yourself, Big Man', the little Scottish forward Jim Storrie, would tell him. So infuriated did Jack become with Storrie that, on one occasion in the baths, he grabbed Storrie and almost thumped him. He hated being part of a mediocre team, yet he did little himself to raise the standards. Despising his managers and coaches, he refused to take training seriously. Instead of listening to their advice, he did his own thing, charging around the field or remaining static as the mood took him. He was no more diligent about fitness sessions. One time the Leeds players were out on a cross-country run, panting as they struggled up a hill. Then a lorry came past, and there was Jack, sitting in the back, cigarette in hand, just waving at them. It was not the sort of gesture likely to enhance his popularity. 'He was a one-man awkward squad,' wrote the late Billy Bremner, Jack's captain during Leeds' years at the top. 'There was a time when he was ready to feud and almost to fight with anyone who crossed his path. He was at odds with club, manager, coaching and training staff.'

Nor was Jack anything like the commanding centre-half he was to become in the mid-1960s. Jimmy Dunn, who left Leeds in 1959, says, 'When I was with him, I would never have thought he would become an international, not at all.' In fact, Jack was a pretty moderate player, who only stood out because of his height and the amount of noise he made on the pitch. Ian St John, the renowned Liverpool striker and later ITV commentator, told me this story: 'When I was at Motherwell, I played in a friendly against Leeds. Jack was at centre-half and it was the first time I had seen him. We had a good team and we put seven past Leeds. I got a hat-trick and Jack was useless, absolutely useless. I asked myself afterwards, "Is he really Bobby Charlton's brother?" It was always good to play against Jack then, because you were usually guaranteed a few goals.' In a match in 1960, when Leeds were beaten 3–0 by Wolves, Eric Todd of the *Guardian* wrote: 'Charlton booted the ball to such ridiculous heights that only a giraffe could have hoped to beat Slater and his men in the air.' Alan Peacock, the Middlesbrough striker who was to join Leeds in 1962, explains one of Jack's weaknesses in this period:

'When I was at Boro, I used to come up against Jack. We used to have some right ding-dongs. But I never minded playing against him then, because he was often trying things he couldn't really do. Like he would bring the ball down and try to play a bit, and then he would give you a chance of nicking the ball off him. He wasn't skilful enough to carry it off so he always gave you a chance.' Jack has admitted to this fault, telling the *Evening Standard* in 1967: 'I thought that I was another John Charles. I fancied myself as bursting forward from the 18-yard line, dribbling through opponents and cracking in goals from the 18-yard box. But I wasn't as good on the ball as I thought I was and that landed the team – and myself – in trouble.'

As we have seen, Jack clashed bitterly with Raich Carter and Bill Lambton, the Leeds managers between 1953 and 1959. The first he saw as an uncommunicative martinet, the second as an amateurish incompetent. He got on better with his next boss, the easy-going Jack Taylor, who had done a solid job for seven years at QPR. Taylor brought along his own brother Frank as coach, and Jack had more respect for him than the previous holders of that position. 'Frank Taylor was the first guy who ever took me out on a pitch and taught me how to kick a ball properly – following it through, keeping it low, chipping balls. One thing he did was to lay down two bricks and place the ball between them, then ask you to run up and hit it full on,' he wrote in his autobiography. Yet though Jack says he established a rapport with the Taylors because of their interest in the technical side of the game, Jack also exploited the soft approach of his manager, refusing to obey his instructions and continuing on his own sweet way in training. Bob English, the Leeds physiotherapist at the time, says: 'Jack Taylor didn't crack the whip enough. Training was slack. He never came to watch people and I remember him only once getting out his tracksuit.' Freddie Goodwin, who came from United to Leeds in 1960, told me: 'There was a huge difference in atmosphere between the clubs. At United, we had played for the team, whereas at Leeds, so many of the side just seemed to play for themselves. And Jack was part of that. He was an indisciplined player when I joined.' Thanks partly to Taylor's unwillingness to impose discipline on his team Leeds were relegated into Division Two. Pretty soon, they were faced with the drop into Division Three.

One of the reasons Jack was so insufferable was that he thought he knew more about football than anyone else at the club. And this, in turn, was because he had become a fully qualified FA coach. It was the former Leeds player, George Ainsley, who fired Jack's interest in coaching in 1958, when he took him along for a lesson at a school in Batley. Watching Ainsley work with the pupils, Jack became fascinated with the process of coaching and soon afterwards enrolled at the FA academy at Lilleshall. Here he was taught by the England manager, Walter Winterbottom, alongside the likes of Bobby Robson and Billy Bingham, who, like Jack, were later to become big managerial stars. Tony Waiters, the Blackpool goalkeeper, who emigrated to the USA and went on to international management with Canada, was another on those courses at Lilleshall. He says: 'I spent a lot of time with him then. It was pretty obvious then that he had what it takes to be a successful manager. He knew the game, knew the players and what made them tick, and he was not afraid to mix it with them if necessary. Yet he always retained his sense of humour. I know people have often referred to Jack as a dominant, almost aggressive figure but I never saw him that way. He was a leader, definitely, but I never found his manner to be offensive. As a coach, he was strong, outspoken, simple in what he said, certainly not wishy-washy. But I never found him dogmatic or bombastic. Interestingly, I always thought he would have made a brilliant referee, because he had such understanding of how to handle players. He taught me one very useful thing about crossing the ball into the box. Now the traditional thinking was always that the player should get down to the byline before crossing. But in a discussion with Jack, he pointed out that it could often be more effective to cross from the angle of the penalty area over to the far post. Jack said, "Listen, the worst that can happen is that the ball goes out for a goal kick and then it can't be counter-attacked." I was very taken with this and started to use the approach in my demonstrations. It caused a lot of controversy then but you see it used all the time today.'

Jack, showing more dedication than he did at Elland Road, soon received his FA badge and began working in schools and boys' clubs around Yorkshire. He quickly became so enthusiastic that he would not only take coaching sessions in the afternoon, but sometimes he would try to cram one in before training at Leeds at 10am. Willie Bell, who joined Leeds in 1959, remembers how he was infected by Jack's passion for this work. 'Jack was the one who introduced me to coaching. He collared me one day and said, "Listen, Willie, I have to do these sessions in school halls in the middle of nowhere. Would you like to share some of them with me." So Jack and I went to work together. Now the pay didn't amount to much, probably only about 19 shillings, but it provided me with valuable experience. And it was wonderful to see him working with kids. He was so constructive, so able to put across his ideas. After that, I always felt he would make a great manager.'

Two intriguing points are raised about Jack's early involvement in coaching. The first is that it highlights yet another serious difference with Bobby, who had no interest in analysing the game. Whereas Jack was fascinated by tactics and loved to think about different patterns of play, Bobby always relied on his instincts and indeed was suspicious of coaching. Jack once said that he actually preferred coaching to playing. In contrast, Bobby, on becoming manager of Preston, took the opposite view: 'I don't like coaching. The great teams just come together and click.' Noel Cantwell, who before his transfer to United had been a key member of the famous 'West Ham Academy', gave me this illustration of Bobby's attitude towards analysis. 'I remember sitting on the United bus and I was discussing our last match with Harry Gregg and Maurice Setters. Bobby came past and said, "You're not bloody talking about football again, are you?" He just didn't like to think about the game in that way. In all the team talks during my years at Old Trafford, I can't recall Bobby ever once making a contribution.' Today, looking back on his time at Preston, Bobby is not so dismissive of coaching. 'Top players can have it too easy. We jump the queue when we're asked to run a club, without getting any coaching qualifications. If I were doing it again, I would get them.'

Secondly, Lilleshall showed that Jack, in the right environment, could be a much more intelligent footballer than the difficult professional who turned out every Saturday for Leeds. When there was a feeling of mutual respect – as existed among the trainee coaches – then Jack lost his sullen resentment. But in the short term, the experience of Lilleshall only deepened his contempt for the Leeds set-up, making him even more awkward. He had been mixing with the stars at Lilleshall, discussing the future of English football with people like Bill Shankly, and then he had to return to a Second Division outfit where, in his view, 'The players just came into the club to do their bit of training, played their matches and then buggered off. They weren't interested in developing their skills or any theory or anything like that.' So Jack felt no motivation to improve his game. To use an old-fashioned term, Jack became thoroughly 'Bolshie', as he himself admitted in his 1973 Ashington testimonial programme. 'Looking back on those times now makes me realize that I must have been an awkward customer to deal with. I was feeling sorry for myself.'

One player at Leeds was particularly contemptuous of Jack's attitude. He was Don Revie, who had been bought by the club from Sunderland in November 1958 for £14,000. Now reaching the end of his career, Revie was still one of the most perceptive footballers of his generation. At Manchester City he had transformed the fortunes of the club through his role as a deep-lying centre-forward, continually breaching defences with his long, accurate passes and delicate chips to the two City strikers up front. This pattern of attack, loosely modelled on the Hungarian approach which had ripped England apart in 1953, became known as the 'Revie plan' and helped City win the FA Cup in 1956. The term itself was a tribute to the influence that Revie had within the game. Incidentally, when he was at City, Revie had been desperate for the club to sign Bobby, having seen him play in that schoolboys trial at Maine Road. As he later recorded, 'The simple way Bobby hit his passes, went past defenders and the fierce way he shot marked him out as a cert world beater. I told Les McDowell, the City manager, that the kid was a must for us.' But by then Bobby was already on his way to Old Trafford.

On arriving at Elland Road, Revie found that Jack brought precious little of his brother's application to his football. 'When I joined Leeds United as a player, I was amazed to find how undisciplined Jack was. He was one of the most awkward customers it had ever been my misfortune to meet. Whether it was because the club had never had much success or not I have no idea. But in all matches, Jack wanted to run about all over the place. He seemed to think that if he didn't do it, no-one else would,' wrote Revie on Jack's retirement. What also enraged Revie, as a player, was Jack's behaviour in practice matches, which Jack seemed to treat as a joke. Even Jack admits that his habit of racing about all over the park was 'totally unprofessional'. After one such selfish move, Revie turned on Jack, 'The best thing that could happen to you would be for the club to leave you out. You're ruining it for the rest of us with that chip on your shoulder.' Then Revie added a final, cutting sentence: 'If I were manager, you'd never do for me.' Les Cocker, the trainer, who had played as a professional at Stockport County and Accrington Stanley, recalls how difficult Jack was at this time: 'I remember we played Raith Rovers in a friendly. Jack was having one of those days when he was casual, lethargic, could not care less. Jack Taylor, the manager, had a word with him at half-time and Jack's reaction was to pull his jersey off, throw it to the ground and say, "Get yourself a fresh player." That was his attitude.'

Jack admits that, when it came to Les Cocker, he was just 'facetious and nasty'. Soon after his arrival at the club, Cocker found himself being sneered at by Jack: 'What are we doing then, Cocker?' or 'You know best, Cocker' Jack would say. Eventually Les Cocker had heard enough of Jack's sarcasm. He stopped Jack in the car park and said, 'Listen, if you don't stop calling me Cocker . . .'

'Well,' said Jack, 'tell me what you'd bloody well like to be called, if it's not by your name.'

'I've got a bloody handle, you know, and it's Les.'

By mid-1960, Jack was so fed up with Leeds that he wanted out. Other clubs learnt of his disillusion and showed an interest in buying him. One of them was Liverpool, where Bill Shankly had just taken over as manager. Now Liverpool were hardly a major force in British soccer at the time. They had been languishing in the Second Division for even longer than Leeds, having been relegated in 1954, and were short of class and cash. Nor was Shankly regarded then as a titan of management. Since 1949, he had wandered through a series of dismal outposts in the old Third Division North, including Workington and Grimsby, while he had achieved little in his five years at Second Division Huddersfield Town. But Shankly was consumed with a passionate ambition for his new club. Having seen Jack in action many times, he thought he could mould him into the centre-half he needed at the heart of his defence. But Leeds, for all Jack's faults, were reluctant to sell him, especially because they were in a battle to avoid relegation. So the fee quoted to Shankly was £20,000 plus, which the Liverpool board thought was too high. According to his biographer, Stephen Kelly, 'Shankly reckoned Charlton was worth every penny' of this fee, but his views did not wash with the directors, who would allow no more than £18,000 to be spent on Jack. The strict limit meant that the negotiations went nowhere and the potential deal collapsed, much to the annoyance of Shankly and Jack.

A year later, another, much bigger club declared its interest in the still dissatisfied Jack, who was now refusing to sign his contract for the new season. This, he was surprised to discover, was his brother's own Manchester United. In fact, Harry Gregg says that it was Bobby who told the club that Jack was unsettled at Leeds. Leeds still held Jack's registration, which meant he could not go to another club without their approval. But by the summer of 1961, while Leeds continued to pressurize him into signing new terms, Jack had become increasingly excited at the idea of moving across the Pennines to play under the direction of Matt Busby, who was still trying to rebuild his team following the carnage of Munich. However, the fee demanded by the Leeds board this time was even higher at £26,000, reflecting the club's increasing reluctance to let go of one of its few assets. Matt baulked at the figure, and finally decided that, rather than buying a new centre-half for the start of the new season, he would give an extended run to 21-year-old Frank Haydock, who had just come through from the United youth team. Jack was furious at the way he felt Manchester United had misled him, and went to Old Trafford to confront Busby, 'No messing about, up the stairs and into the Old Man's office. Then Matt started to flannel, saying the boy Haydock had not done too badly, could we leave it for a while and so on,' says Harry Gregg. According to his own account, Jack responded: 'I can't believe what I'm hearing. I have caused ructions at Elland Road. I have refused to sign a contract. Nobody there is speaking to me. I have caused bloody havoc in the club. I have been offered a deal and turned it down, and now you are telling me that I have got to wait until the beginning of the new season, until you have had a look at someone else?' Bobby would never have dared to speak to Busby like that.

Bitter and embarrassed, Jack now agreed to accept his new contract. The deal meant a loss of face and money for him, but, in his self-pitying mood, he did not want to negotiate over the details. Instead he put forward that rarest of Jack Charlton statements: an apology.

It is interesting that throughout the saga of Jack's abortive attempts to get out of Elland Road, some of the biggest names in British football management showed an appreciation of his talent. Jack, as we have seen, was not highly regarded by his fellow professionals. Like his own mother and his Ashington schoolfriends, they saw him as little more than a decent stopper. Yet there were no shrewder judges of a player than Bill Shankly and Matt Busby, who recognized that, beneath Jack's blustering indiscipline, he had real courage and authority. They sensed that, given the right direction, Jack could become a top-class footballer. It is a remarkable fact that, on his retirement, Matt Busby said the greatest regret of his entire career at Old Trafford was his failure to sign Jack Charlton. As he explained, 'Munich had crippled United financially and I decided I could not afford it. I converted Bill Foulkes into a centre-half, but I often wondered how much stronger we would have been with Big Jack at number five.'

Equally appreciative of Jack's potential was the new Leeds manager, Don Revie, who had taken over in March 1961 after the sacking of Jack Taylor. Revie was to be the most instrumental figure in Jack's career, for without his guidance, it is doubtful if Jack would have come near to England standard. In truth, Revie was probably a much bigger influence over Jack's development than Busby was over Bobby's. Matt was always a distant figure, a patriarch who left much of the day-to-day work to his deputy Jimmy Murphy. He was never very interested in coaching, relying on the right creative blend rather than organization to achieve results. Bobby once gave this insight into his style. 'My first real glimpse of Matt was at a Youth Cup tie. There was a bit of a hush in the dressing room, wondering what he would say. "Get the ball first" was about the lot but we all sat there and thought, "Fantastic, what a great man!" He had this aura, a strange kind of ability to inspire you to play above yourself without actually saying much. I think he was frightened of blinding people with science. He wanted to let ability express itself. Compared with the coaching stuff the FA churn out today, he was a laugh.'

Revie was the opposite. His experience with the 'Revie plan' at Manchester City encouraged him in his belief that the system was more important than the players. While Matt told his team, 'Go out and enjoy yourselves', Revie produced dossiers for each match, analysing every opponent and every possible manoeuvre. His attention to detail was legendary. If Leeds were to play a Cup tie against a lower division side on a sloping pitch, then Revie would trawl all around the city looking for a local pitch with a similar slope so his side could practice on it. After Munich, Busby rarely appeared on the training ground, whereas Revie was always there in his tracksuit.

Revie also liked to get close to his players, even literally so – after practice games, he sometimes liked to give each member of his team a powerful, soapy massage with his own hands. For all his tough Geordie masculinity, Jack says he loved the experience. Revie's passionate concern for his players' welfare was further reflected in the way, for example, he improved their travel arrangements and hotel accommodation. Terry Cooper says, 'He was a great man and a great manager who looked after us by wrapping us in cotton wool.' In such ways, he succeeded in building a team spirit at Leeds which has probably never been bettered at any club. '95 per cent of the players would have run through a brick wall for him,' was the view of Billy Bremner.

But there was also a darker aspect to Revie, much darker than any side to Matt Busby's character. He was an obsessive, neurotic individual, his life governed by the need to achieve results. So compulsive was this streak that he became highly superstitious, once going a whole season wearing the same blue suit because he thought it would bring him luck. Peter Lorimer says, 'Sometimes you would think he was barmy. He would have to walk to the same lamppost every day and his lucky suit was so worn that the arse was hanging out of it.' Revie also had a paranoia about anyone taking a photograph of his players on the day of a game. He once went berserk before a Cup final when a young journalist tried to take a picture of two Leeds stars, grabbing the camera and smashing it against the wall – behaviour that would be utterly unthinkable for Busby. More disturbing were the widespread suggestions of his corruptibility. Like all too many managers, he offered illegal payments to attract players to his club. Alan Ball recounts how Don handed over three separate cash bundles of £100 to entice him to Leeds from Blackpool in 1966. '"I need you badly in my team," he said. "Don't worry about the money. I'll pay you as long as it takes to get you."'

Such petty bribery was standard practice for club managers. What was not was Revie's apparent willingness to pay money to fix matches. There were strong allegations that he tried to influence the result of the League game in 1972 against Wolves, when Leeds needed just a point to win the Double. Just as worryingly, Bob Stokoe said that when he was player-manager of Bury in 1962, Revie had tried to bribe him as Leeds fought to avoid relegation to the Third Division. Stokoe claimed, 'He offered me £500 to take it easy. I said no and then he asked if he could approach my players. I said under no circumstances. After that match, I lost all respect for Revie.' Revie lost the respect of the entire nation more than a decade later through his woeful performance as an England manager, when his siege mentality and fixation with planning were all too evident. 'He seemed to think you could work it all out on a computer and that's what would happen when you got on the field. His dossiers must rank as the most boring bedtime reading of all time and what's more, they were complete nonsense. They put fear into players and it must be obvious you can't play football that way,' says Alan Ball.

But perhaps the biggest indictment of Revie is the way that his Leeds teams played. During his time in charge, they became a byword for cynical professionalism. In their cold, ruthless way, they robbed the game of all its glamour and romance. 'Keep on fighting' was the notice that captain Billy Bremner pinned up in the dressing room, and most of his players carried that instruction out to the letter: committing a stream of vicious fouls, abusing referees, over-reacting to every incident, bending every rule. In an era of physical contact in soccer, they were undoubtedly the dirtiest team in the League. George Best says that the only time he ever needed to wear shinpads was when he was playing Leeds. Under Revie, the club won many trophies but no friends. Anyone who dared to criticize their tactics was met with a barrage of hysterical abuse. In a typically memorable phrase, Brian Clough once said that 'Don Revie's so-called family had more in keeping with the Mafia than Mothercare.' It is telling that, unlike Busby at Manchester United, Don Revie started no great tradition at the club. The1960s left a host of golden memories at Old Trafford but only a legacy of sourness at Elland Road.

The tone for Leeds' descent into opportunistic aggression was set by Revie's purchase in 1962 of Bobby Collins from Everton.

Scottish-born Collins was one of the nastiest players in British football, specializing in the 'over-the-top' tackle which had more chance of causing an injury than winning the ball. Yet it was also Collins' ferocity which helped to instil in Leeds the hard-nosed, ultra competitive outlook of the Revie era. 'Leeds were real hard, but that's better than getting beat. You've got to win. The game's all about winning,' Collins said recently. To be fair to Jack Charlton, he never approved of this approach, unlike his manager, and frequently had arguments in the dressing room over such tactics. In his own autobiography, he wrote that he was 'uncomfortable' with the attitude that Collins and Revie bred. 'We were getting a reputation for intimidating teams rather than outplaying them.' Jack's relationship with Collins was at times a tempestuous one. During one pre-season tour, after a game against AC Roma, they clashed so bitterly in the dressing room that Collins followed Jack angrily into the showers, punches were thrown and Don Revie had to go into the cubicle, in his suit, to separate them. Another time, in March 1965, at a hotel in Harrogate, Jack threw a jug of water over Collins, only to be chased down the corridor by the angry Scot. In his desperation to catch Jack, Collins put his arm through a glass door and required 16 stitches on the wound. Typically, he played in the match the next day, with his arm in a heavy bandage.

Apart from his opposition to this kind of football, Jack came to be a huge admirer of Revie. True to his straightforward nature, Jack remained a loyal friend when Revie was ostracized by the English footballing world in 1977 for abandoning the national side in favour of a lucrative new position with the United Arab Emirates. And as Revie decayed slowly and tragically from motor neurone disease, Jack visited him regularly before his death in 1986.

Twenty-five years earlier, their relationship did not have the happiest of starts. As the 1961/62 season began, Jack was still simmering from his failure to leave the club. 'He spent quite a long time trying to get away from Elland Road and he made a bit of a nuisance of himself in the process,' said Billy Bremner. Feeling out of place, Jack took out his anger on his coach, Syd Owen, the former

Luton centre-forward. On one occasion, when Owen tried to ask Jack why he was fed up at Leeds, he was told to 'shove off'. Jack also became infuriated with the way Owen shouted at him during practice matches, feeling that he was being singled out for attention. He marched into Don Revie's office and, shaking his right fist, declared, 'If Owen doesn't get off my bloody back, then I'll not be responsible for my actions.'

Jack also took out his temper on the new manager. In a game against Rotherham, Leeds had conceded a goal in the first half from a header on the edge of the 18-yard box. Revie was angry about this error and said so in his half-time talk, blaming Jack for failing to pick up the centre-forward. Jack, who thought the keeper should have saved the header easily, was so resentful at this accusation that he threw his teacup at Don Revie. It narrowly missed the manager, smashing into the wall behind him. A stunned silence fell on the Leeds dressing room, as Revie left the room without saying a word.

Jack's unsettled attitude was reflected in his changing position within the side. When Revie first took over, he had the rather quaint idea that Jack might make a useful centre-forward, because of his power in the air. In fact, Jack did not do badly, scoring in his first match against Portsmouth and averaging a goal a game in a five-match run. In the 1961/62 season, when Revie again had him playing occasionally at centre-forward, he hit 10 goals in 19 League and Cup games. But for such a creditable record, Jack hated being a striker. 'You are the wrong way round up there. The ball comes to you when you have your back to the goal and I prefer to be facing it,' he explained.

At other times, Revie was so frustrated by Jack's attitude that he pushed him down into the reserves. But then, towards the end of that 1961/62 season, with Leeds desperately fighting to avoid the drop to the Third Division, Revie felt he had to bring Jack back at centre-half. For the first time in months, Jack was playing where he wanted. There was a new fire and purpose in his play as he led the battle against relegation. Team spirit suddenly rose. Leeds went through the final games of the season without defeat. Then something happened which would have seemed laughable only a few weeks earlier. He was summoned to the office of the manager, where he was astonished by what Don Revie had to say to him.

'Listen Jack, I'm sorry about what I said last year.'

'Eh?'

'When I told you that you were not my type of player. The fact is that you've really impressed me the way you've played in the last few games and dedicated yourself. You've made yourself one of the best centre-halves in England. If you keep going like that, you'll play for England.'

Jack, who had never considered himself England material, thought Revie was talking nonsense and told him so. But the manager persisted.

'I mean it. As long as you screw the nut. All the time. Not just some of the time.'

A seed had been planted in Jack's mind which was to reach full bloom within less than three years. Surprisingly, though, it was not the first occasion that Jack had been told he could reach a higher standard. A year earlier he had been playing in a benefit match against Tommy Lawton, widely regarded as the finest header of a ball ever to appear in English football. As Jack recalled later in the *Daily Mail*: 'At this time at Leeds, there was no method abut the way we played. You just ran your guts out. Coming off the field, Lawton said to me, "You know, you'd make a good player sometime if you'd only let somebody else do some of the work."' Despite the source, Jack was not in the mood to listen to such praise. But now, in the new environment of Leeds under Revie, Jack was much more receptive.

Part of this new regime was a much greater emphasis on fitness, something that had long been ignored in professional football where training usually meant nothing more than a few laps of the ground. Willie Bell gives this insight into the rigorous approach that Revie introduced: 'I remember when Don took over. We went for pre-season training and I thought we were just going to kick a ball around. But no. Instead, we were divided into teams of six and points were awarded for running, for relay races, even for carrying huge telegraph poles the length of the field. You do that twice and you can't move the next day. I think at Leeds we trained harder than any other side. Don Revie pushed us right to the limit. Our first game of the new season was against Sunderland at Elland Road. It was a warm day, everyone was in their shirt sleeves. We came out and we were like supermen. We were so fit and we were running so well that Sunderland just couldn't keep up. After 15 minutes some of them were so exhausted trying to keep up, that they were sick.'

Thanks to Revie's new sense of direction and encouragement, the change in Jack was dramatic. He suddenly became a leader, organizing the back four. With his new-found responsibility, he persuaded Revie to switch from the former defensive system of man-to-man marking to a new, more fluid method of zonal marking, where each defender had to pick up the opponent when he was in his area. After being a rebel for years on the field, Jack was now the one giving orders at the back. Peter Lorimer, who joined Leeds in 1962, pays this tribute to the change in Jack. 'When I came to Elland Road, there was no doubting Jack's ability. It was just that he was so casual, anti-training, lacking in concentration. The older players did not rate him at all. That was where Don Revie did a great job with him. Don was one of the great disciplinarians and he won the battle with Jack. Jack had been very domineering at the club but Don soon had him in his pocket, no question. Once Don got hold of Jack, he turned him into a great player, a total professional.' Jack only partially agrees with Lorimer's verdict. In an interview with the *Daily Express* in 1973 he explained, 'Some have said that I was a poor professional when Revie started to shake the dust out of Elland Road. They have said I was shuffling away from any real future in the game. I do not accept this. What I do say is that at the time I had no-one to look to, no example to follow. Revie filled a great vacuum in my career. He gave it purpose. He told me and the rest of the club that the only limits we had were those we placed on ourselves.'

In 1963/64 Revie's hard work paid off when Leeds won promotion to the First Division. Both the club and Jack were going places.

CHAPTER EIGHT

The Winger

While Jack was struggling at Leeds in the late 1950s, Bobby's career with both United and England appeared to be progressing like an express train. After the disappointment of the World Cup in Sweden in 1958, Bobby regained his place in the England team that autumn. Immediately his brilliant form left the public and press wondering why he had been excluded from the national side in the summer.

His first game back for England was against Northern Ireland in Belfast in October. This was probably the greatest Northern Irish side in history, led by Spurs captain Danny Blanchflower and also containing the likes of Billy Bingham, Jimmy McIlroy and, in goal, Bobby Charlton's own United colleague Harry Gregg, who had recently been voted the best goalkeeper in the World Cup tournament. A classic encounter in front of a huge crowd of 58,000 at Windsor Park ended in a 3–3 draw, in which Bobby Charlton, playing as centre-forward, scored two of England's goals, both of them rockets from outside the penalty area.

It has often been said that Bobby Charlton was not a great goalscorer but a scorer of great goals. While this might be true of later in his career, when he was operating more as a midfielder, it certainly does not hold good for the 1958/59 season, when Bobby hit eight goals in nine appearances for England, and, just as impressively, 29 in 38 League games for United. Doug Holden, the Bolton winger who played with him for England at this time, says 'I cannot think of anyone in England now as good as him. There is no-one around with his attributes. He was technically head and shoulders above all the other players of his generation. He had such natural ability, a wonderful shot, and, like Stanley Matthews, he had phenomenal acceleration from a standing start. Another of his great skills was that he would be running fast with the ball and then would stop dead suddenly, taking his opponent straight past him. And he had that great body swerve and change of direction. The moment I played with him, I knew he was something special.'

Joe Baker made his debut in that Irish game in Belfast. A centre-forward with Hibernian, he enjoys the distinction of being the first Scottish League player to have been picked for England. He gave me this view of Bobby: 'I had first got to know him in the England Under-23s and he was an excellent player, with two tremendous feet. He could really crack them in from 25 yards. Now, in the modern game, we see that all the time, but then it was unusual to hit the ball from far because it was so much heavier and the pitches were worse. Bobby really stood out as a powerful striker of the ball. There were, of course, games when he disappeared but that is bound to happen. It is impossible to be brilliant every week. But even when he was not scoring, he was still firing balls out to the wings or through the centre. I got a lot of good service from him during my time with England. On the field he was pretty quiet, though he would get annoyed if he shot over the bar. Off the field he was even quieter, very reserved. He never said anything in the dressing room, not a thing. He was a very deep thinker – at least it seemed so. Cautious, never opened up. When you were on England duty, you sat at meals and had a chat. But Bobby always sat back and just listened. Sometimes you would not even know he was there. He was friendly enough if you engaged him in conversation, but he would only go so far. Getting anything out of him was like getting blood out of a stone. He was the total opposite of Jack. In the England dressing room, Jack was all noise, Bobby just silence.'

All Bobby's youthful talent could not disguise the fact that he was part of a mediocre England set-up that had been performing dismally for more than a decade. The manager since 1946 had been Walter Winterbottom, who had played briefly as centre-half for United in the mid-1930s before an injury finished his career. He then became a schoolmaster and a coach, quickly winning a reputation for his innovative training methods. Though some of his admirers hailed him as a revolutionary who laid the foundations for Ramsey's triumph in 1966, the fact is that during his 16 years in charge, England's record was a dismal one, flopping in every major tournament and rarely challenging teams abroad. In his defence, it could be argued that, in the World Cup of 1958, England suffered grievously from the loss of Munich victims Roger Byrne, Tommy Taylor and, above all, Duncan Edwards. Moreover, he was hampered by his inability to pick his own teams, for, as noted previously, that was the task of the selection committee. And the values he was trying to promote, of technical excellence and organizational systems, ran totally counter to the clattering, muddy world of English League football. Yet, even when all this is acknowledged, no-one could dispute that Winterbottom failed in the fundamental task of winning the respect of his players. He was too scholarly, refined and theoretical to relate to the tough professionals in his charge, many of whom despised the very concept of coaching. Jimmy Greaves once said: 'Walter was a joy, although I never understood a word he said. He came out with some marvellous phrases. I used to think, "What on earth is he talking about?"' Tommy Lawton, who called Winterbottom 'that PT instructor and Man United reserve', was less tolerant: 'You're going to tell Stan Matthews how to play outside-right? And me how to score goals? You've another think coming.'

Bobby could never have been so dismissive to Winterbottom's face, but he had little time for him as a manager, as he explained in 1973: 'He'd never been properly in the professional game. He didn't know how to handle players, how to talk to them. He spoke too well, too precisely, like a schoolmaster. Walter had this impeccable accent, whereas football's a poor man's game, players expect to be sworn at, a bit of industrial language. He didn't criticize you enough individually. If you played badly, you wouldn't know till the next team was picked and you weren't in it. There was no feeling of belonging in the team. It was all theory with Walter. It had to be serious all the time. Even a five-a-side game you weren't allowed to enjoy. I didn't mind coaching at the club, but Walter used to go through things that I felt were obvious to people who were supposed to be good players.' Bobby recalled with a shudder one incident when he showed insufficient respect to the England manager, during the 1958 tour of Sweden. The team were at the swimming pool one morning and a naked Winterbottom decided he would use the slide. 'He hit the water with a huge splash. Trying to appear an old hand, I shouted, "Good old Walter!" There was silence. All the other players just looked at me. I realized that, even in the nude, Walter had to be taken seriously and that a junior must not make himself too at home.'

A year after the failure of Sweden, England went on a tour of the Americas which turned out to be even more disastrous. England played four games, and lost the first three to Brazil, Peru and Mexico, only slightly redeeming themselves with an 8–1 win over the USA in Los Angeles, a match in which Bobby scored a hat-trick. 'England had no mental attitude for playing abroad at that time,' said Bobby. For all the poor results, though, Bobby loved the tour. He had never been anywhere more distant before than Belgrade, and, after the coal-darkened bleakness of Ashington and Manchester, he revelled in the exciting sights on the other side of the Atlantic, sunbathing on Copacabana Beach, gazing at the skyscrapers of Rio, meeting film stars in Hollywood, and watching his first game of baseball. His fellow Manchester United player, Warren Bradley, gave me his memories of being with Bobby on that tour. 'Bobby, like me, was quite new to the England team. He was quiet, not a big mixer, but I found him a pleasant, low-key personality, perfectly approachable. There was an air of single minded determination about him. The only time he would get upset was if he was annoyed with himself, if he had not lived up to his own standards. He was still in the process of developing as a player, but I could tell he was going to be really effective. We were poor on that tour, losing all but one of the games. It was desperately hot in Mexico, where we were playing at 7,000 feet. We came off at half-time, gasping for air and had to use the oxygen masks in the dressing room. It was worse than pre-season training. The press crucified us, even after we beat the USA. I remember that game in Los Angeles well, because there were several strange features. It was played on a baseball pitch and there was a pitcher's mound right in the middle. And we came out on to the field one by one, while this booming loudspeaker introduced each of us. We all felt like real Charlies. But we were hosted very well throughout, getting to places like Disneyworld. We were also taken to a nightclub, where there were these poles that stretched from the floor to the ceiling. I wondered what they were for. Suddenly a firebell went and all these scantily-clad women came sliding down.' Like Bobby, Bradley was not impressed with Winterbottom: 'He was a gentleman but he was not close to the professionals. When we went to Brazil, he had myself, Ronnie Clayton and Johnny Haynes – the winger, inside-forward and the half-back – running up and down to practice our passing in the 'triangle'. Remember these were international players and it was about 90 degrees, following the end of a tough League season. That was Walter's approach, a bit simplistic.'

Johnny Haynes remembers that this trip deepened Bobby's devotion to American vocalists. 'With people he trusted, Bobby was great. I used to go out with him and have a drink, a laugh, a bit of a song. When we were in the hotel in Los Angeles, me, Jimmy Armfield and Bobby went out for a stroll one evening. We walked into this place which we thought was just a bar but it turned out to be a cabaret venue, with one of those long walkways where the entertainer can go right into the audience. Then who should come on but Sammy Davis. Bobby was a huge fan of his. He loved that evening.'

Despite the setbacks of that tour, Bobby continued to hammer in the goals for England and United with his cannonball shots. Tony Waiters, the Blackpool and England goalkeeper, gave me this insight into Bobby's shooting. 'I was in goal at Bloomfield Road when he hit this big, booming shot. It crashed into the crossbar so hard that it must have gone about 50 feet up in the air. I had never seen anything like it. It was remarkable, especially considering the old leather ball we used then. The ball came through pretty straight from Bobby. There was not a lot of swerve on it. But it was the pace and power that made him so difficult to deal with. And it all seemed so effortless, it didn't look as if it was being hit with power. In that way he was quite deceptive. I also remember his lovely, flowing movement. He would play crossfield, which was quite unusual. Nowadays, with the treated ball, you get a lot more of those long, crossfield passes. But Bobby was pretty much on his own then in being able to spray the ball from one side of the field to the other. Johnny Haynes was a great passer but he did not have the same length as Bobby.'

The press were becoming equally generous in their praise. In a beautiful profile of Bobby in November 1961 for *World Sports*, entitled 'The Silent Hero', Doug Gardner wrote: 'The blond left winger gets the ball halfway inside the opposing half and near the touchline. Setting it in motion with a characteristic little tap with the outside of his left foot, he covers 40 yards with the speed and elusive wriggling of a snake – and is just as deadly when he decides to strike. Having drawn the whole defence, he suddenly turns in his tracks and with one, swift thudding blow sends the ball high into the left-hand corner of the net. That is Bobby Charlton.' In another passage, Gardner highlighted Bobby's quietness, that sense of isolation from the rest of his colleagues which meant that he could sit 'silent and morose' at a party or in the dressing room, while he was also 'invariably the most silent member of the group at team conferences'. But Gardner thought that this was the key to his playing style. 'When Charlton explodes into action with either an exhilarating run or a cannonball shot, he is not so different from the seemingly gloomy partygoer who suddenly leaps to the nightclub stage microphone.'

Bobby's shyness was often remarked upon by those who met him at this time. Arthur Hopcraft, in his book *The Football Man*, describes interviewing him in his lodgings around 1959: 'I had some fairly harmless questions to ask him for the newspaper I was working on, and the whole interview was conducted on the doorstep, with Charlton holding on to the doorknob, not being in the least obstructive but blushing and leaving words trailing indistinctly and ambiguously in the air. He said that he had always found it hard to answer questions about himself.' As Gardner points out, Bobby can be seen as a classic example of the shy, self-conscious individual who suddenly comes to life when performing in public. Such people can feel diffident in groups, where they are anxious about being made to look foolish. But in a public setting which allows them to display their talents, they are much more confident. They are engaged in the one activity they instinctively understand, one that involves no awkwardness or embarrassment. Like an actor going on stage, they know that, for all their nerves beforehand, this is what they do best. The performance is where they can truly be themselves; the rest is superfluous. It is interesting that Sir Stanley Matthews, another brilliant but misunderstood forward, had exactly the same sense of awkwardness. 'He is not a good talker, and smiles come sparingly from him. The overriding impression he gave in his home was of acute, conscious wariness,' wrote Hopcraft.

By 1962, Bobby's achievements had made him one of the stars of the national side. But he still could not drag England out of their long run of second-rate performances against the best international sides. That summer, England went to Chile for the World Cup but, yet again, failed to impress. The tournament was one of the most poorly organized of modern times, with many of the games held in venues barely fit for a Fourth Division contest. England's own base for the qualifying rounds was at the American Braden Copper Company high up in the mountains at Coya. To travel to the town of Rancagua, where England played their matches, the team had to take a train down a miniature railway into the valley, but such was the dire poverty of the local peasants and the inadequacy of the decrepit stadium that tiny crowds turned up to watch. According to Ray Wilson, then an emerging full-back with Huddersfield, 'It was like playing in a village, a little stand on one side and a hut on the other, and that was it. I can't imagine a country like Chile getting the World Cup now.' England's camp up in the hills was better appointed, with a swimming pool, training ground, tennis court, golf course and well-kept gardens. The biggest problem with the place, says Bryan Douglas, was the 'sheer boredom'. There could be no complaints about the food. England brought in their own specialist cook to make roast beef and chicken, though this arrangement was not to cause anything like the controversy that Alf Ramsey provoked in the World Cup of 1970, when he insisted on the import of British food for his team, thereby insulting his Mexican hosts.

One of the England party, Stan Anderson, recalls: 'Our mountain retreat was adequate but it was a bit primitive, to say the least. We stayed in miners' accommodation. I don't think the players would put up with it today. The only place of any interest was the golf course and we had to borrow some clubs to use it. But it was an amazing experience in that high altitude because the ball flew miles. I played with Bobby then. He was a pretty keen golfer, a nice steady player, on about eight or nine. There was also a ten-pin bowling alley. The Americans who were there made us very welcome and we played bridge with some of them. But it was very isolated, hardly the ideal preparation for a World Cup. Bobby was a quiet lad on that tour, though people looked up to him as a player. He was totally different to his brother, who was more aggressive. Now there was nothing aggressive about Bobby at all, neither in his football nor his manners. But he was a real, class player. The beauty of him was that he was so two-footed. Any ball that came to him he could hit it with either foot with equal power. That is almost unique in football. He was a very determined character, everything had to be right. He would sometimes moan if people misplaced passes or did not give the right ball.'

England's first game in Rancagua was against their arch-enemy Hungary, who had won the previous three fixtures and scored 15 goals in the process. Despite this being a World Cup fixture between two of the most famous names in international football, the crowd numbered only around 7,000 spectators. 'Accrington Stanley went out of the League playing in front of more people,' jokes Bryan Douglas. Once again, England were defeated, losing 2–1, though the game was more closely fought than previous encounters with Hungary. But England came good against Argentina, winning 3–1, with the second a typical Charlton drive from 20 yards after a surge down the left flank. Thanks to this victory, England only needed a draw in the next game against Bulgaria to progress through to the quarter-finals. The decision was taken by Winterbottom that, rather than go for victory, England would concentrate on keeping possession. The England team was racked by nerves before the kick-off, says Johnny Haynes: 'I cannot remember a bunch of England players more nervous about a match than we were over this one.' With Bulgaria also anxious to keep it tight, the consequence was an epic stalemate, as Ray Wilson recalled. 'I remember Bobby Charlton shouting, "What the hell's going on? Get the bloody ball up here!" It was a frightening game, one of the worst I have every played in. We were in our half and they were in theirs. It must have been the most boring game of all time.'

Jack would, of course, have been very satisfied with such a result – it was just the sort of draw that Ireland regularly achieved under his leadership when the score mattered more than the style. But to Bobby, always a passionate believer in attacking football, England's performance was a disgrace. 'I was getting more and more frustrated every minute,' he wrote later. 'Towards the end I was trying to beat four players at a time and losing the ball. Ron Flowers and Maurice Norman were yelling to me, "Don't go at them. We'll settle for a draw." I couldn't understand them at all because here we were representing England in the World Cup and if you are to have a chance of winning it, you have to play football. Yet we were passing from full-back to half-back to inside-forward and back again. I really was furious.'

For once Bobby abandoned his usual reticence and expressed

his feelings in the dressing room. While the rest of the team were delighted to have qualified, Bobby fumed at the way they had played, even having a go at his captain, Johnny Haynes:

'Well, we've qualified.'

'Hell yes, but we've not bloody frightened anyone. We've not made anyone think what we might do. Some of our play was ridiculous. It was a waste of time going out on that field. I never want to play in a match like that again,' said Bobby.

England's weaknesses were exposed in the quarter-final against Brazil, when they lost 3–1, though Bobby again played well, especially in the first half. What disappointed him most was the attitude of the team, which he felt lacked dedication and cohesion. 'Some of the lads were wanting to get home and there was even talk that one of them had cheered for Brazil. We were a very good side that became dilapidated,' he told the journalist David Miller. Jimmy Armfield agreed about the demoralization of the team. 'We could have won against Brazil, I am convinced, in the right frame of mind.'

Though the World Cup had been a failure for England, it had been something of a triumph for Bobby, who was voted one of the outstanding players of the tournament. What made his achievement all the more impressive was that he felt he was playing out of position. Since the autumn of 1960, Bobby had been picked mainly on the left wing for England and Manchester United. Busby, unlike Ramsey, always believed in the value of wingers as part of his formation, and, when Albert Scanlon left for Newcastle after the 1959/60 season, he decided that Bobby could fill the role. Similarly, at England level, the selectors had been searching for an outside-left since the retirement of Tom Finney, the death of David Pegg at Munich and the failure of either Doug Holden or Alan A'Court of Liverpool to impress in the job. It was a job Bobby intensely disliked, for he thought that he was not involved enough with the play, depending on others to give him the ball rather than winning it himself. He told Eamon Dunphy: 'I hated playing on the wing, waiting, depending on other people. I wanted to get into the game, to get something out of it. I remember once at Notts Forest I didn't touch the ball for 20 minutes. So I started going inside to look for it and Jimmy Murphy was there saying stay wide. But I said, "Jimmy, I'm not getting a kick here." I hated it but I never really questioned it. If that was what the boss wanted, I did it.' John Giles, who played on the right wing for United, says: 'I know how Bobby felt. I was never happy out on the wing because I didn't get into the action so much. Bobby was a natural, could play anywhere, but winger was not his best position.' Most players and observers felt that Bobby was at his most dangerous in his roving, advanced midfield role, the position he held in his golden period in the mid-1960s, though one of the few to disagree is his Manchester United colleague Denis Law. He believes that Bobby should have stuck to the wing: 'I could never understand why we didn't use Bobby more on the wing. To me he was one of the finest wingers in the world. Playing in midfield, he would invariably hit long raking passes out to the flanks, which was fine from the spectator point of view because it looked spectacular. But it was also terrific for the opposition because it gave defenders time to reorganize. Whenever Scotland met England we were happy to see Bobby in midfield – he wouldn't cause us problems from there, but put him on the wing and it was a different story. He had phenomenal speed which could take him past any full-back. He could get to the byline and either chip balls back or across with that magical left foot, and cause all sorts of problems. I've always believed that United would have scored far more goals if Bobby had been used more in that way.'

For all Bobby's reservations about the position, it was as a winger that he had stamped his authority on the international stage. The world's press rhapsodized about his grace and power, his athletic running and glorious shooting. As one Brazilian journalist said after Chile, 'He has the foot magic, the simple natural rhythm and feeling for football which makes him so like Brazilian players.' The foreign appreciation of Bobby also came in something far more tangible than fulsome press notices. By the time of the World Cup in Chile, there had been attempts by a host of Europe's top clubs – including

Barcelona, Real Madrid and Roma – to sign him. This was the era when several of the biggest British stars, such as Jimmy Greaves, Denis Law, and John Charles, had been lured to the continent, largely because of the financial rewards on offer. When Jimmy Greaves signed for AC Milan in 1961 in an £80,000 transfer deal, his signing-on fee was no less than £10,000 – a considerable sum when, under the doomed maximum wage rules, even the best-paid British footballers were only earning £20 per week. 'Without doubt, the strong appeal of Italy was the money,' admitted Denis Law when talking about his £110,000 move to Torino.

Yet these figures pale beside the money that Barcelona were apparently willing to pay for Bobby. During the 1962 World Cup, the club's coach Ladislav Kubula watched Bobby in his three qualifying matches for England. He was so impressed by his displays that he sent a telegram to his club president, raving about Bobby's dashing style and urging that the club acquire him 'at all costs'. Specifically, it was reported that Barcelona were willing to go up to £300,000, a sum so astronomical that the British press described it as 'absurd'. But Kubula thought Bobby was worth almost any price: 'I like Charlton's rhythm, flair, ball skill and natural instinct for football. He also has a wonderful shot. He has everything we want.' However, no firm offer materialized. Besides, Bobby was not interested in moving. He was settled at Manchester, having made the city his adopted home since his move in 1953. Nor were the examples of Law and Greaves inspiring; both had hated their spells abroad and had returned to England within a year. The pay for top English footballers was rapidly improving – with the abolition of the maximum wage in 1961 Johnny Haynes was now on £100 a week at Fulham. More importantly, less than a year earlier Bobby had married Norma Ball, who worked at a model agency, and they were about to start a family – she was heavily pregnant with their first child Suzanne at the time of the 1962 World Cup. And there was a fervently patriotic streak in Charlton which meant that he would never consider living anywhere except England. As he told the papers at the time, 'I don't want to leave England. I am quite satisfied with what I am getting at Manchester United. In any case, the England players who have gone abroad seem to have found nothing but trouble.' There was also the formidable obstacle of Matt Busby, who had turned down an £80,000 bid from Roma in 1961. 'Roma asked us if there was any chance of buying Charlton. I told them there was none. The lad wants to stay with us and I said we want to reach the top as well and we don't intend selling our best players.'

The most intriguing aspect of the foreign interest in Bobby was that he appeared to be appreciated more abroad than at home. His reliance on intuition rather than workrate, on skill rather than aggression, on movement rather than obstruction was often at odds with the robust English First Division. During these years, despite all the plaudits he received during the World Cup, there were persistent complaints within Britain that Bobby was an 'enigma', a 'self-indulgent' player who did not understand the needs of his side. It was said that he would drift out of games and would contribute little beyond a few extravagant shots or passes. That lyrical journalist Brian Glanville had written, after Bobby had scored twice in an England game in 1959: 'Charlton's great merit is that one never knows when the brooding, rumbling volcano will explode, when the burst of speed and mighty shot will transform a match.'

But it was precisely this inconsistency which so infuriated others. His England captain at the time, Johnny Haynes, told me: 'He was not the sort of guy you could rely on to produce at every game. He could suddenly do something extraordinary but then he would disappear and you would not see him for a while. When he got the ball he could be brilliant, but if didn't have it, he would sort of vanish out of the game.' It is amusing, in the light of those words, to read what Matt Busby once wrote in a tribute to Sir Stanley Matthews: 'He might not be in it for three-quarters of the game, and then in the other quarter he would destroy you.' But Haynes' view was widely shared. It was the complaint which had been made against him ever since his England debut in 1958: that he failed to pull his weight. Typical was the comment from Joe Mercer, when he was manager of Aston Villa, in 1961: 'The lad has so much talent and we are all willing for him to do well every time he pulls on an England shirt. But something always seems to be holding him back. If only he would go forward and tear them apart like we know he can.'

The gap between the continental and British attitudes towards Charlton in the early 1960s is striking. Compare Mercer's statement with that of Gigi Peronace, the Italian agent who brought John Charles and a string of other British players to Serie A: 'We would have dearly loved to have taken Bobby Charlton to Italy. He could not have failed. His flowing, graceful skills and his explosive shooting would have made him a great favourite.' This difference reflected a fundamental clash between the Latin footballing culture and that of Britain, where the practical was celebrated before the aesthetic, the artisan before the artist. Alan Hoby pointed out in an article in the *Sunday Express* in June 1962, just after the World Cup, 'When Charlton plays abroad he is hailed as a world beater – a wonder winger whose name is coupled with startling six-figure bids from clubs like Barcelona. But, when he plays at home he is too often labelled moody, unpredictable and the biggest false alarm in English football. The answer to this baffling and ironic mystery lies, I believe, in the dynamic make-up and dramatic, free-as-a-bird temperament of Latin crowds and officials. Abroad, particularly in South America and Spain, Charlton is admired for what he is – a 'natural', one of the outstanding instinctive footballers of our time. Yet, in the stereotyped, mechanical rut of so much League football today we do our damnest to stamp out natural talent and steamroller the individual.' Hoby concluded his article with a warning against Charlton's critics: 'It is up to us to learn the lesson – before it is too late and England's growing regiment of soccer robots trample the last vestiges of magic from our game.'

Unfortunately for Bobby, some of his critics were within his own dressing room, for Manchester United was a club beset by cliques and personality clashes. The five years after Munich were probably the darkest of Matt Busby's reign, when playing standards fell so low that, at one stage, the club was faced with the genuine prospect of relegation, while there were continual rumblings of discontent from certain players over everything from money to tactics. The facilities were as poor as the coaching. For all the caring, powerful image that Busby projected to the outside world, Old Trafford was not the happiest place in the early 1960s.

One of the central problems was that Busby, who had been manager since February 1945, was still recovering from the emotional and physical scars of Munich. He was therefore not able to exert the same authority as he had done previously. 'He was never the same man after the crash,' says Eamon Dunphy. 'He was a wreck when I first went to Old Trafford in 1960.' Furthermore, as we have seen, his need to buy in players from outside caused resentment to those, like Bobby, who had grown up in the era of the Busby Babes. Nor were all his decisions wise. In September 1958, he paid £45,000 – a British transfer record at the time – to Sheffield Wednesday for the striker Albert Quixall, who was far too highly strung to cope with the pressures of leading the front line. A nervous, slightly hysterical individual, he was best known among his colleagues not for his goalscoring achievement but his repulsive practice of defecating into someone else's boots as a practical joke. Moreover, Jimmy Murphy was no longer the force he was in the 1950s. Broken by the strain of Munich and now drinking heavily, he did not command the same respect amongst the imported players that he once enjoyed from the Babes.

One of the other players that Busby bought was the Irish international and left-back Noel Cantwell, whose transfer from West Ham in 1960 cost £30,000. Cantwell, one of the most sophisticated and thoughtful players of his generation, was appalled by the shambolic nature of Old Trafford. 'There was no proper coaching whatsoever. Nobody, but nobody at Old Trafford knew anything about coaching. Training was so boring it would drive you mad. We would just have a few laps, a five-a-side, and sometimes a game at the back of the stands, where people kicked the fuck out of each other. With people like Bill Foulkes and Harry Gregg around anything could happen there. I remember Harry once bit Shay Brennan, sank his teeth right into him because Shay didn't pass him the ball. Out on

Above: Bobby Charlton's 'paradise' – the brilliant United youth team of 1954/55.
Eddie Colman is holding the FA Youth Cup, with Wilf McGuinness and Bobby to his left.

Below: April 1956: Jack Charlton toasts promotion to Division One with Leeds United.
Manager Raich Carter pours the champagne for the great John Charles.

Award-winning brothers – Bobby as
European Footballer of the Year 1966
(above) and Jack as the Football Writers'
Footballer of the Year 1967 (right).

One of the most famous Wembley goals.
In front of a crowd of 92,000, Bobby
Charlton's pile-driver past Calderon sets
up England's 2–0 victory over Mexico in
the 1966 World Cup.

the field, there did not seem to be any system or pattern. We were just a team of individuals and I wanted to see us playing for each other. People would not come and help, as they had done at West Ham.' Cantwell says that when he tried to impose a sense of organization, it led to more rows. 'I had many fallouts with the trainer, Jack Crompton. He didn't like me. He would deliberately give me all the worst kit. So many were not interested in discussing tactics. I remember once, at a team talk, Denis Law said to me, "For Christ's sake, don't say anything today, because I've got to get away."'

Thinking he was going to one of the biggest clubs in Europe, Cantwell was shocked at the poor facilities of the club: 'At West Ham we'd had modern training gear. But at Old Trafford, it was all great big old sweaters and socks full of holes. We were given boots in training that were like cut-off wellingtons. It would remind you of being in prison.' It is a point reinforced by Denis Law: 'When it came to training, Manchester United were still in the dark ages. We were lucky if we had five balls for the whole team. When we came in for training, they slung a pile of old jerseys on the table and you had to sort through it like at a jumble sale. On a good day you might get one which only had a big hole in the sleeve, and a decaying tracksuit to go with it. If you wanted a pair of boots, they looked at you as if you were asking for the moon. If you wanted a second pair of boots, forget it. The facilities were more fit for horses than for men.'

Noel Cantwell's disillusion extended to Bobby's effectiveness as a player. 'His rate of scoring was not that high for the ability he had. He was brave, quick, had a cannon in both feet, he had everything. He was a truly great player. Yet the end product was not always as good as what I imagined it would be. He should have scored 20 goals a season with what he had. But he did not want to get into the box. You look at Martin Peters. If the ball arrived in the box, he'd be on the end of it. Now Bobby didn't do that, though he had the ability. And he sprayed the ball everywhere, was a beautiful passer left and right. But for me, as a fellow professional, I felt he could have contributed more.' Cantwell echoes the criticism of Denis Law over Bobby's long-range passes. 'He could batter the ball across the field, get applause from the crowd as if he had scored a goal, but, at the end of the day, it didn't beat anybody. The defence was still in place. Over lunch or a beer, some of us would talk about the last game. Of course, the subject of Bobby would come up. And we would ask each other, "Now what was his contribution? What did he do so well?" Often we would be disappointed. When you played with him, when you knew the ability he had, you'd think, "We should have had more. He should finish better. Put more shots on goal."' On Bobby's reluctance to analyse the game, Cantwell is struck by the difference with Bobby Moore. 'Bobby Moore was always searching for ways to improve his game. He would ask me questions every day. Now Bobby Charlton never searched. He just had a wonderful gift and he went out and did it. So he wasn't that influential on the playing side. He wasn't a leader, a dominant personality. I don't think the boss ever took him into his confidence during my time at Old Trafford.'

Noel Cantwell is equally interesting on Bobby Charlton's temperament. 'He was tremendously brave, in the sense that you couldn't frighten him at all. He was unbelievable that way. People would whack him and kick him and all sorts, but he stayed on his feet, just got on and played. And I never saw him lose his temper. We had a few punch-ups over the years at Old Trafford, but I never saw Bobby get involved in anything like that. Not that he didn't complain, though. He was a right moaner on the field, always moaning about something. But nobody took any notice of him. He was a sulker, he would sulk if things went wrong. There's no doubt that Munich must have changed him. He never seemed very happy. He wasn't bubbly or a joker. He had his own little group, him and Shay Brennan and some others, and they would play cards all the time. He was not a confident guy, very nervous. God love him, he used to smoke, and if you gave him a cigarette, you would see his hand shaking.'

Harry Gregg, who came to be an admirer of Bobby, echoes, in even more forthright terms, some of the early criticisms of Bobby's football. 'In his later years at Old Trafford he deserved all the tributes he received. But I have always maintained that during the first part of his career he did not earn one sentence, one letter of all the praise he was getting. As a player he had everything Joe Public loved. And most of the team hated playing with him because he hadn't a brain in his head, no footballing brain at all. He didn't know when to keep it and when to give it.' Harry Gregg recalls a match in 1961 against the Double-winning Spurs side when he was badly injured. These were the days before substitutes, so Gregg, though he could not stay in goal, went upfield. 'Bobby Charlton picked up the ball in his own half. I was crippled but I went out to outside-left, hoping to pull Spurs centre-half, Maurice Norman, with me. By now, Bobby was going through the middle. But Maurice didn't go with me so I'm out there, in space on my own. I was screaming at Bobby, "Play it, Charlie, play it!" But instead, he tried to take everyone on and lost the ball. I pigeon-toed over to him as he lay down in the mud.

"You fucking brainless bastard," I said.

"What's wrong with you?"

And I replied, "Thank Christ I don't have to play up here with you every week. Because you're brain dead."

I remember I was giving a lift to Pat Crerand, soon after he arrived at Old Trafford and he turned to me in the car and said, "Does he play like that every week?"

"Who are you on about?"

"That bastard Charlton."

But I have always said – and this annoys some of the ex-players – that, later on, Bobby deserved all the great things that were said about him, because his brain and his feet came together.'

Whatever his perceived weaknesses, no-one disputed that Bobby Charlton was a model for others in his commitment to his job and his club. 'A good pro' is the term constantly used about him. Unlike his elder brother at the time, he was never self-indulgent or self-pitying. He never caused his club managers any trouble by messing around in training. He might be introverted, but he was also reliable. Unlike some other top players, he would shrug off the knocks and niggles that are part of a sporting life. 'He was, in many ways, the perfect professional,' says Nobby Lawton. 'He was there on time every day. He trained every day. He never complained. One of the most striking features of his career was how he was so rarely laid off with an injury.' On the field, he could be exasperating, but he never wanted to opt out of his responsibilities. 'He always tried his hardest, no matter what the circumstances. He would never try to hide on the field, even if he was not playing well. I never saw him give anything but his best,' says Johnny Giles.

It is striking how, unlike some of the cynical pros of the senior dressing room, so many of the younger players at Old Trafford were full of admiration for Bobby. Their number included the Belfast-born striker Sammy McMillan, who joined immediately after Munich. 'I was in awe of Bobby Charlton when I went to Old Trafford,' McMillan says, 'but he was totally modest. He was down to earth, without any airs. He never acted the star. He was always decent to youth and reserve players. He was very helpful to me, giving me tips in training. I was naturally right-footed and he told me that I should keep practising on my left. He also worked with me on my shooting, encouraging me to keep my head down when I hit it. I have nothing but praise for him.' The same is true of Barry Fry, presently the manager of Peterborough, but in the early 1960s a youth team player at Old Trafford. He told me: 'Though Bobby was pretty young himself, he was like a god to us. He had a great aura around him so we all looked up to him. He was very serious about his football, never a Jack the lad. If you did not show a serious head on the pitch, you soon got a fucking bollocking from him. He was very helpful, though, always gave you solid advice about eating right and sleeping right. He was insistent on being a good pro, telling us to listen not only to Matt but also to Jimmy Murphy. Bobby thought the world of Jimmy. He was totally unlike the usual big star footballer who thought he was God's gift. He was modest, feet firmly on the ground. I was substitute for the first team twice, and, in the dressing room, Bobby was very determined, serious – just the way he played.' Barry Fry, of course, got to know Jack through management and, like so many others, says he is 'the complete opposite' to Bobby. 'Jack's a laugh a minute, outgoing. He would tell you to fuck off to your face in front of 100 people, whereas Bobby would call you out to a private room to do it.'

Sadly, for these youngsters, they were joining a troubled club. A festering mood of recalcitrance gripped the team. There was none of the feeling of 'all for one and one for all' which characterized Ramsey's England or Revie's Leeds. As Noel Cantwell says, 'It was a strange dressing room, when you think about it. You'd be standing, stripping, and talking to people every day, maybe five days a week, and half of them did not get on very well together.' Harry Gregg and Bill Foulkes, for instance, could not stand each other. Denis Law, who came to United in a £115,000 move from Torino, 'never saw eye to eye' with Bobby, to use his own phrase. Pat Crerand, who joined from Celtic in 1962, regarded Bobby as overrated, complaining that Bobby was an 'impostor', while Bobby thought Pat was a loudmouth. He was not surprised one evening when Crerand, a dogmatic Irish republican for all his Scottish nationality, threw a pint of beer over Sammy McMillan for starting to sing an Orange anthem. John Giles and David Herd did not like each other. The despised Albert Quixall, regarded as a second rater, was subjected to regular verbal assaults from the senior pros. 'Everyone would shout at him all the time, he got some real bollockings,' remembers Noel Cantwell.

Maurice Setters, the defender signed from West Brom for £30,000, was another loud, bellicose personality, described by one ex-player as a 'crude, nasty, bullying guy of the sergeant major type'. Interestingly, for all that he was a post-Munich outsider with a completely different temperament, he and Bobby had a good rapport, partly because they had known each other in the army. There was almost an air of protectiveness from Setters towards Bobby – once, when they were drinking together in a bar during Manchester United's 1961 tour of the USA, Maurice threatened to hit another customer for making an offensive remark to Bobby. Each also had a mutual respect for the other's football. 'I was pleased to have

Maurice around. He didn't like losing. He gave the side some spirit,' said Bobby once. Today, Maurice describes Bobby, 'as a natural, the complete product. He seemed to glide along the ground, and could play anywhere. The only problem he ever caused me was that he wanted the ball all the time. Sometimes he would even try to take it off another United player. I'd have to say to him, "Listen, get back up the bloody field. It's our job back here."' Setters acknowledges the big difference in their characters. 'Bobby was not like me. I would speak to anyone, but he was much quieter, very much a loner. But we got on great. We'd play golf and he'd come down to my family home in Devon. I became close to him; he was decent, polite, unassuming.' Indeed they became such good friends that Maurice was the best man at Bobby's wedding.

But this sort of relationship was untypical of the divided Old Trafford. And discontent in the club was further deepened in 1961 by the grievance over salaries. United were one of the biggest clubs in Britain but also, with regard to pay, one of the meanest. When the maximum wage was abolished, the Old Trafford professionals thought, understandably, that they would receive a large rise. Yet all that was put forward was a basic £25, plus some appearance and bonus money, an offer Eamon Dunphy rightly describes as 'outrageous'. Ironically, just as Jack was refusing to sign again for Leeds in the hope that he could reach a deal with United, so his younger brother was caught up in talk of a mass protest at Old Trafford against the new contracts. The whiff of rebellion evaporated, however, when the players were made to confront Busby in person, one by one, over their demands. All of them signed with barely a murmur of argument. That they did so is an indicator of the strength of Busby's charisma, his almost mystical powers of persuasion, which enabled him to convince a player that he had done him a favour by dropping him.

Busby might have won this battle, but the mood of disgruntlement still lingered. It came to a head during the 1962/63 season, when the group around Noel Cantwell and Maurice Setters were making ever louder complaints about the lack of direction at Old

Trafford, particularly the inadequacy of Jack Crompton's training regime. A crisis meeting called by Busby with all the players failed in its purpose of 'clearing the air'. John Giles thought the meeting was a 'waste of time', while the big personalities continued to argue. Typically, Bobby Charlton said nothing at the meeting. He just wanted to get on with playing football.

John Giles, fed up with Busby and Old Trafford, left in 1963 to join Leeds, where he was to be a crucial figure in the rise of the club – and Jack Charlton's future. 'It was certainly not the happiest of times at Old Trafford. I had felt things were not right for a long time. It was obvious Matt did not want to keep me – and I wanted to go. Matt was a believer in players, get them in, give them freedom to play. If we didn't do well one week, there was no big inquest. Now I don't believe that is entirely correct, because there needs to be some analysis. When I arrived at Leeds, it was totally different. There was great attention to detail. Don would be out there on the training field, putting things right week by week. And the atmosphere at Elland Road was different from Old Trafford, where there were a lot of players who just did not get on.'

Perhaps the most glaring indicator of that difficult climate is the suggestion that United may have been tainted by the match-fixing scandal which cast its shadow over football in the early 1960s. In 1965, after an in-depth investigation by the *Sunday People* – later dramatized in the TV programme *The Fix* – three Sheffield Wednesday players, Tony Kay, Peter Swan and David Layne, were sent to prison after being found guilty of taking bribes to under-perform. But the web of corruption may have been spread much more widely. In line with Stokoe's claims of Don Revie's attempted bribery in 1962, there have been allegations that some professionals at Manchester United may also have been involved in a conspiracy to fix certain matches between 1960 and 1962. Nothing was ever proven but the charges were serious enough for *Daily Mail* journalists to confront a group of players in a hotel in Blackpool, while Busby was so concerned that he delivered a dressing-room lecture on the need to avoid any involvement in a betting coup. Harry

Gregg has actually gone on record to say that he was offered money to throw games, and one player told me that in a game at Highbury, he was surprised at the muted celebrations which greeted a United goal. In his acclaimed biography of Busby, *A Strange Kind of Glory*, Eamon Dunphy wrote: 'There is no doubt in my mind that Manchester United players did conspire to fix the result of at least three games during the 1960 to 1963 period. It is widely accepted within the game that those who were convicted in the ensuing scandal were not the only prominent players involved in match rigging.'

Certainly, as Dunphy puts it, 'There did appear to be something odd about United's performances' during the early 1960s. In 1959/60 they finished seventh in the League, their defeats including a 7–2 drubbing by Newcastle and a 4–0 loss to Preston North End. They did not climb higher than fifth in the next two seasons, and plummeted to 19th in 1962/63, their worst League position since the Busby era began. The only redeeming feature was a triumph in the FA Cup, when they beat Leicester City 3–1. It is a reflection of how low United had sunk from the glory days of the Babes that Leicester were the strong favourites.

For Bobby it was his first trophy since before the Munich disaster. Bill Foulkes wrote later: 'There was a particularly poignant moment after the match. As the other lads went tearing round the field, Bobby and I just stood there and looked at each other. We had been there twice before and lost. We had been to Munich, and came back, and at this moment it was impossible to think of anyone but the lads we had left behind there, never to return. We went off to join in the gallivanting, because it was expected of us, but we both slipped away before the rest of the team.'

There were three other events that happened in football in 1963: a certain young Ulsterman called George Best made his debut for United; a Dagenham-born ex-Ipswich manager called Alf Ramsey had his first game in charge for England; and, at the end of the year, Bobby Charlton was switched away from the wing by Busby to a central role. 'Will this new position now bring out the full measure of greatness in him?' asked the *Daily Herald*.

CHAPTER NINE

The Husbands

Marital breakdown, serial infidelity and inexhaustible promiscuity have long seemed essential parts of the glamorous footballer's lifestyle. From George Best to Ally McCoist, no group has embraced the modern sexual revolution with more enthusiasm than soccer stars. Arsenal's Peter Storey spoke for many when he said: 'From the first time I kicked a ball as a professional, I began to learn what the game was all about. It's about drunken parties that go on for days. The orgies, the birds and all the fabulous money. Football is just a distraction, but you're so fit you can carry on with all the high living in secret and still play the game.'

Even those footballers who were far too honourable or restrained to subscribe to Storey's extreme philosophy could still experience difficulties in their personal lives. Of Bob and Jack's contemporaries, such dignified names as Gordon Banks, Bobby Moore and Stanley Matthews all went through crisis or divorce. Jimmy Greaves, another Charlton contemporary, saw his marriage fall apart, though in his case the mistress was alcohol rather than a woman.

Yet Jack and Bobby have escaped such a fate. Both of them have been with their wives for more than 40 years, and, in both cases, their marriages appear solid. For all the opportunities that must have presented themselves in years of travelling around England and the globe, both have remained strong family men. Through my research for this book, I have not heard one whiff of scandal attached to either of them. Indeed, their fidelity is one of the few characteristics they have in common. 'Temptation would never cross my mind. Never in a million years would I leave home for someone else. Geordies don't get divorced,' said Jack in 1996. Tony Cascarino, the most capped Irish player of the Jack Charlton era, told me 'Jack's marriage was certainly very strong. During all the time I knew him there was never the slightest hint of his messing around. And, anyway, he wouldn't want to waste the money on a girlfriend.' The same could hardly be said of Cascarino. During the 1994 World Cup in the USA, he met a girl in a bar and took her back to his hotel room. Such behaviour was strictly against Jack's instructions, and the Irish team floor had been cordoned off on grounds of security. Unfortunately for Cascarino, CCTV cameras had picked up the visitor, though her identity and that of the player were unclear from the pictures.

'Who was the fucker with the bird in his room?' No-one owned up, so Jack went round the team, asking each player if he was guilty. After being greeted with a barrage of 'not me, boss' answers, Jack gave up before he reached Cascarino. But later in the day, while the Irish team were training, Cascarino became sufficiently troubled by his conscience to confess.

'It was me, Jack.'

'What do you mean?'

'It was me. I brought the girl back to my room.'

Cascarino says that Jack completely lost his head, frothing at the mouth with rage: 'What? We're training for the fucking World Cup and you take a bird back to the room.'

'I'm really sorry Jack.'

'I should fucking send you home.' Cascarino now had visions of boarding the next plane back across the Atlantic, before the World Cup had even started. Then, after grumbling more, Jack looked Cascarino in the eye.

'Well, I hope she was fucking worth it.' With that, Jack laughed and the subject was never raised again.

Bobby has been equally loyal. Alec McGivan, the football entrepreneur, who worked with him on England's bid for the 2006 World Cup, says: 'One of the many impressive things about Bobby is that he is incredibly devoted to Norma. For a couple who have been married 40 years, they are obviously very, very fond of each other. When we were travelling around the world, he was always ringing her up and making sure he sent her flowers. They seem a very happy couple. When I first asked him to work on the bid, he said: "I am very willing to do this but there will be occasions when I want my wife to come with me because it is a long haul and I don't want her left on her own all the time." He was always happiest when she was there because I think they are good company for each other.'

As Jack's row with Tony Cascarino demonstrates, he hardly had a puritan or other-worldly outlook on life. Nor had his brother Bobby, who has been known to express an amused envy at some of the wilder antics of George Best. When he was just 17 and staying in Mrs Watson's lodgings in Manchester with the Babes, Bobby quickly learnt the truth about adultery. At Christmas 1954, there was a tremendous row in the house after Mrs Watson caught her husband Albert in bed with one of the maids. Christian morality does not seem to have been the basis of the Charltons' restraint, for they are not men of religious convictions. Like many respectable working class children of their generation, they attended an Anglican church in Ashington, but have not shown a strong spirit of devotion since. 'I suppose I'm like 70 per cent of the population as far as religion goes, in that I just don't know,' Jack told the *Sheffield Morning Telegraph* in 1980.

No, the answer to their domestic happiness is that they have both been fortunate enough to marry people with whom they feel totally compatible, who have helped them build close and loving families. 'We've been terribly lucky,' said Norma Charlton in 1973. 'I just can't think of any bad moments in our marriage. Just lots of good ones.' Pat is just as devoted to Jack. But given Jack's traits of insensitivity and self-centredness, she has probably had a harder time than

Norma over the years. She joked once when asked how she felt about being married to Jack for 36 years, 'Not even the great train robbers got that.'

There had been a few girlfriends in Jack's life before Pat. Laura Crowther, the daughter of Jack's landlady says that, before his marriage, 'He always did his own thing and was certainly never shy. There were quite a few girlfriends before Pat, though she was the only one he ever went out with properly.' There had also been a few encounters with gays, though of a purely mercenary, non-sexual kind. Jack admits that when he was doing his National Service at Windsor, he discovered that the local homosexuals could be ruthlessly exploited. 'We used to call them queers. We used to go to a certain pub where they would buy you drinks all night. They would become very friendly at closing time, but we'd just say, "Well, thanks very much, see you now," and walk off,' he wrote in his autobiography.

It was in 1957 that he first met Pat Kemp. They were both 22 years old. He was a young professional at Leeds; she worked in a local furniture store. One evening, Jack had gone with two Elland Road colleagues to the cinema below the Majestic Ballroom in Leeds. There was a dance on and, once the film was over, he went upstairs to find out what was happening. Immediately he saw Pat, he was taken with her, though, typically, Jack does not express this attraction in the most romantic terms. 'She was a bonny girl with lovely teeth,' he once recalled. Jack walked over to introduce himself but Pat, who had been brought reluctantly to the dance by her sister, was not particularly impressed by the 6′ 3″ soccer player. She knew nothing of football and had never been to a match.

'I'm Jack Charlton,' he said.

'And I'm Doris Day,' she replied.

Just as he was launching into a conversation with her, a man came on the stage and announced, 'Ladies and gentlemen, we've got a bit of a celebrity here, Jack Charlton.' Jack was summoned on to the stage to give out a spot prize, though Pat still refused to be starstruck: 'That sort of thing doesn't impress me. I'm funny like that,' she said later. It was precisely this down-to-earth approach that would help to make such a successful marriage.

Though unimpressed by Jack's status as a micro sporting celebrity, she liked Jack sufficiently to agree to go on several dates with him. 'I was comfortable and easy with her and soon started taking her to various football functions. After we'd been going for a time, people asked when we were going to get married. I said "Next year" and when next year came, that's what we did,' he said in an interview in 1996. Jack and Pat held their wedding at St Peter's Church, Bramley, Leeds, in January 1958. As well as Bobby as best man, other guests included David Pegg, Tommy Taylor and Billy Whelan, all three of them to be dead within a month in the snows of Munich. At the time Jack was earning just £16 a week and could not afford to run a car. He therefore had to borrow one from a friend for the wedding. Unfortunately the car developed a flat tyre on the way to the church. 'So we had to change it then and there, and eventually arrived in a lather of sweat and confusion.' The honeymoon was not the most luxurious affair either, lasting just two days in a hotel in Scarborough before Jack had to return to duty at Leeds. But Pat, in her practical way, was more interested in Jack's reliability as a husband than his glamour as a footballer. 'He was always a good worker. From carrying firewood at the age of 10, he's always done something,' she said in 1994.

Over the next eight years, they went on to have three children, John, Debbie and Peter. None of them have either achieved or sought the fame of their father, though Peter, as an infant, achieved a vicarious kind of national celebrity through the fact that he was born just two days after the 1966 World Cup Final. The name of World Cup Willie – the soubriquet of the FA's rather tiresome mascot – was inevitably bestowed on him by the press. John has worked as a football coach, most recently at the north-eastern club of Blyth Spartans, while Debbie, having married a surgeon, lives in Leeds and Peter is in the packaging business. Both Peter and John also worked with their father behind the scenes when he was manager of Ireland.

Peter once inadvertently caused physical agony and a permanent injury to his father's right hand, through precisely the kind of dangerous high spirits that characterized Jack as a child. Ian St John, who was Jack's assistant manager at Sheffield Wednesday, recalls the incident: 'We were sitting in the house in the afternoon, watching a bit of racing on the telly. Young Peter was about 12 years old, and he came in with a big cane from the garden. He was whipping it around, and despite Jack telling him not to, he kept on waving it. Then he flicked an ornament, and over it went, crashing to the ground. Peter then rushed out of the room, with Jack chasing after him. As he went out, he slammed the door behind him, squeezing Jack's finger as it closed. I was up, into the hall, and shoved Peter upstairs, while Jack is screaming like a banshee, saying, "I'll kill him, I'll kill him." Pat runs in from the kitchen to put some cloth on it, trying to stop the bleeding. We all get into the car, I'm driving with Jack and Pat in the back. Jack is in absolute agony. We get to Emergency, take Jack up to the desk. The nurse behind the desk took one look at him and said. "Jackie Charlton? Oh, can you give me your autograph?" But it was serious. Jack lost the top of one of his fingers. I saved Peter's life that day. If Jack had got his one good hand around Peter's neck, he'd have probably strangled him.'

Pat has been much more than just a homemaker to Jack. She has also helped to organize his finances, do his paperwork and sort out his VAT and tax. At Leeds, she ran the set of souvenir stalls for which Jack had the franchise and did the books for his clothing business. At Middlesbrough she assisted at the supporters' club, while at Wednesday she was a housekeeper for several of the younger players. Mack Squires, one of Jack and Pat's neighbours in Northumberland, has said, 'Jack is a good manager, but Pat is a pretty good manager of Jack too. She is very much her own woman. They make a great team.' In her forthright way, Pat is similar to Cissie, a point made to me by Mike Pickering, who grew close to Jack during his years as captain of Sheffield Wednesday. 'I went up to stay with Jack's parents many times and I was struck at how like Jack's mother Pat was – both were very decent, warm, down to earth, welcoming, no airs. I got on really well with both of them.' Brian Hornsby, another Wednesday player who stayed in Jack's house while he and his wife were house hunting in Sheffield, says, 'We had wonderful times there, like when Cissie came down and we would have barbecues at the back. It was a really happy, great family. Pat was wonderful. She would do anything for Jack and Cissie.' Jack was proud of the good relationship between his wife and his mother, which could hardly have been in starker contrast to Cissie's view of Norma. 'Pat and Mum got on magnificently and became very good friends,' he said.

For all his gratitude to his wife, Jack has an old-fashioned chauvinistic streak in him. Indeed, he even uses such chauvinism to explain why his marriage has worked. 'I supply the resources, like a nice home and holidays, and she looks after our kids. That's how it has worked and that's how we've survived,' Jack told the *Daily Mirror* in June 1994. Brian Hornsby recalls of the time he and his wife spent with the Charltons: 'Pat and Jack had a very strong marriage. They got on so well. Mind you, Jack was hardly a new man. I remember once sitting with my wife in the living room and the fire was dying down. Jack was on the opposite sofa. He looked over and said to my wife, "Anne, the fire's going out. You'd better do something about it." That's the way he was. If he wanted something doing, he'd get someone else to do it.'

'Pat is a lovely person, though you sometimes wonder how she has put up with Jack,' says Andy McCulloch, another professional who served under Jack. 'Poor Pat would be cleaning and then Jack would stride in, sit on the couch and put his feet up. I once got up to help Pat with the dishes and he said, "No way, that's a woman's job," and made me sit down again. Jack's a man's man. I don't think women would always take to him.' One surprising side of Jack's character, which runs against this stereotype, is his fondness for cooking. 'He was very proud of his cooking. When he'd caught some trout and we were having a barbecue, Jack would bake the fish for a long time in silver foil. He would boast, "This is a special way that I learnt in Argentina."'

A hilarious snapshot of life in the Charlton home is provided by

Ian Mellor, who now works for the PFA and, as a player in the 1980s, served under Jack at Wednesday: 'Managers usually put you up in a hotel but not Jackie – he put us up in his home. I always remember when I was joining Wednesday, I brought my wife and my young son with me and we were met by Jack at his house. He was wearing green wellingtons. He started to show us round the house, still with the boots on. He takes us upstairs and shows us his daughter's room, Debbie's. There is a pink carpet there but he just walks straight in. Me and my wife looked at each other. We had been thinking that we should take our shoes off, and here he is, walking right across a spotless carpet in his boots, saying "This our Debbie's room. Lovely, isn't it?" Andy McCulloch and I lived with him for about three months. I remember one day, pre-season, we got back around 3pm. We had a game of Scrabble, while he sat on the sofa watching TV. Then we had a couple of brews from Pat. About 5pm we had our tea, so Jack wheeled himself off the settee, ate his and then went back. His son Peter was also around, and he liked to tease the little Jack Russell terrier, making it jump around and bark. So Pat has two strangers in the house, a dog barking its head off, and Peter by now has put on an ELO album full blast. More tea is brought in, Andy and I have another game of scrabble. About 10pm Jack is brought in a butty. By this time, the noise was almost deafening, with the music, TV and the dog. At 11pm she screamed at Jack, "Jack, for God's sake, will you sort this noise out?"

"Can't I have two minutes peace, woman?" He'd been on the settee non-stop from 3pm until 11pm, and here he was complaining about being asked to do something.'

It is interesting to hear Pat's views on her husband. 'Jack would never gloss over anything to spare your feelings. He never thinks, "Now will this hurt?"' she said in an interview in 1972. 'I get upset a lot. We're not speaking at the moment, to tell you the truth. He has this hard, mean streak, this obsession to win, to be the best. He hates losing, he wants to be good at anything he does. He packed up golf for that very reason. He kept going and going to the club. But he wasn't improving so one day he threw his clubs down in disgust and has never played since.' Jack had just been dropped by Leeds before this interview and Pat was finding it difficult to cope: 'I so want to show sympathy for Jack, but he just puts his head up in the air and says, "I don't care; it doesn't worry me." You know it does but he can't stand you feeling sorry for him. I can't show him how much I feel and, yes, that does hurt me. He has two ways of showing he's upset. Sometimes he's quiet and nobody else really would know he was bothered. Other times he rants and raves and goes berserk. He does that a lot. It's part of him, really.' Even in Jack's moments of despair, Pat could only remember one occasion in their marriage when her husband was in tears, 'when he thought Bobby had been killed in the plane crash at Munich. He cried then.' In another interview with the *Sunday Express* in 1994, she said: 'Jack is a man of strong convictions. He has his beliefs. And he is never ever wrong – even when he is.' That is a phrase that anyone who has played with Jack will recognize. Pat also explained how untidy Jack can be around the house. 'He has his office, his den. He answers his mail in there, watches television, and ties his fishing flies. It's a bit of a tip, to be honest.'

Through the years spent with Jack, Pat developed a love of football. Her technical understanding became so deep that Jack would even discuss tactics with her when he was in charge of Ireland, though she never directly advised him – 'now that would be going too far,' she says. Noel Cantwell, who was close to Jack during those years in Ireland, recalls: 'Jack consulted her about the team and everything. He would often say to her, "What do you think?" She's become something of a connoisseur of football. I've been on team buses with her and we've had very constructive chats about the game. She has strong, intelligent opinions about it.' Again, there is the similarity with Jack's mother Cissie.

The family home that Jack built with Pat can be seen as an extension of his personality: noisy, open, hospitable, sometimes relaxed, sometimes tempestuous. In the same way, Bobby's much more private home reflects his shy, reserved character. Where Jack welcomes the world in, Bobby sees the home as a refuge from the world outside. 'An Englishman's home is his castle,' he says, 'I like to keep that side of my life very private.' The atmosphere of cheerful chaos to which the Sheffield Wednesday players referred is very different from the elegant serenity of Bobby and Norma's luxurious home in Cheshire.

At 23, Bobby was just a year older than Jack when he married Norma Ball. As with Jack, Bobby had enjoyed a few relationships in his life before Norma. For all his quietness, there was no sense of his being an innocent, as Albert Scanlon recalls: 'He was never a Jack the lad, but he was something of a dark horse.' With his blond hair, good manners and prowess on the field, Bobby was seen as one of football's most eligible bachelors. On his 21st birthday, for instance, in 1959, he received more than 200 fan letters, many of them from girls – what was called then, in a predictable little pun, his 'bobbysox' following.

The most high profile of these partners was a stunning young fashion model called Marlene Shapiro, described by the *Manchester Evening News* as 'tall, slim and auburn-haired'. They first met in 1958 at a dance organized by the Manchester Jewry, where Marlene was awarded the title of 'Personality Girl of the Year'. The next year, Bobby – in a reflection of his growing fame in the city – was the judge for this contest, and thus met Marlene again when she had to place the sash around her successor. This time, Bobby plucked up the courage to ask her out, and they started a serious, if brief, romance, seeing each other almost every day. So close were they that friends even expected Bobby to propose. Marlene said that it was Bobby's shyness that first attracted her. 'I grew to be very fond of him. We were content if we just sat in my home talking as all young people do.' For his part, Bobby was smitten, saying, 'I like her very much. She is a very nice and lovely girl – the only one I have liked so much.'

Yet, after only five weeks of intense companionship, Bobby and Marlene split up. The cause was not anything to do with a cooling of ardour – in fact, when they split, they were more devoted than ever. 'I was very much in love with Bobby,' said Marlene. Strange as it may seem in our age of multicultural tolerance, the reason was a clash of religious faiths, for Marlene was Jewish while Bobby had been brought up a Protestant. The objection did not come from the Charltons, for Cissie was not a religious person, but from the Shapiros, who told their daughter there was no future in the relationship. In the 1950s, parental authority still meant something and Marlene accepted this advice. In April 1959, Marlene announced that the romance was at an end. 'My parents are not bigoted about religion, but they advised me for my sake and for Bobby's that it would be futile to go on and each of us would be upset. So we have mutually agreed to end it. I know it's best for us both. I know Bobby's hurt terribly, too, though he tries hard not to show it.' As Marlene recognized, Bobby wanted to put on a brave face over the end of the affair. 'Ours was a wonderful friendship that grew and grew, though from the beginning I also realized that nothing could ever come of it because of religion. I knew that a long time ago but Marlene is great company and it's not easy for a young man to stop going out with a girl he has grown to more than like – whatever the religious difference.'

Bobby was not only attracted to dark-haired beauties. Around this time, he also asked out Jean Clarke, a blonde model who was the hostess of the hit ITV quiz show *Double Your Money*. 'He was very shy,' said Jean, echoing the words of so many others. Bobby had actually met her while he was taking part in the programme, not as some celebrity guest, but as a real contestant. Hosted by Hughie Green, *Double Your Money* ran on ITV between 1955 and 1968 and was one of the biggest quiz shows of its generation. The format of the show, filmed at the Redifusion studios just 300 yards from Wembley Stadium, was simple. Over a period of weeks, a participant had to answer a series of questions from a chosen, fixed subject. Every correct answer meant that the winnings were doubled until a £1,000 jackpot was reached. The one twist of the show was that contestants were required to answer the questions from a soundproof booth, so they could not get any help from the audience.

Bobby Charlton took part in January 1959, choosing pop music as his specialist category. To the surprise of colleagues at United, who were not aware of his large record collection, he performed brilliantly, answering every question successfully until he reached the £500 mark. But the great problem for him was the stipulation that he enter the soundproof box. With each week that passed, he became increasingly nervous until he simply refused to go into it. There can be no doubt that this claustrophobia was awakened by his terrible memories of being in the cabin of the BEA Elizabethan at Munich. 'I don't like being shut in there not being able to see anyone. I start to shake as soon as I get inside that box. I can hardly put on the headphones. It wasn't so bad when I answered the first question, but it has got progressively worse each time,' he explained to ITV. Hughie Green was perplexed to see how much Bobby was suffering, saying: 'This guy takes a bigger beating in the box than anyone else I have ever had on the programme. He really gets me worried because he is so nervous in there.'

Having won £500, Bobby said he would not move on to the next round unless he could answer questions from the stage rather than the box. His demand was so unprecedented that Hughie Green told him, 'We're going to have to get guidance from management on what we're going to do. Come back and see us next week and we'll let you know the result.' ITV's management agreed to let Bobby stay on the stage and the next week he duly won his £1,000. The prize money, he promised, would be used to buy his father a car. 'He's a miner so he can't afford it himself,' said Bobby.

Later in 1959, Marlene Shapiro began to express regrets over the hasty break-up with Bobby. 'Often I wonder whether I did the right thing in ending our friendship. But then, what's the use of wondering now? Even if I changed my mind, Bobby would never take me back. I remember how hurt and embarrassed he was when we decided not to see each other again,' she said in September 1959. But pride was not the only reason Bobby would not take her back. For by then he had met another striking dark-haired woman, Norma Ball, who worked as a receptionist at a Manchester fashion agency. In a BBC interview, Bobby described how they met: 'I fell in love with her immediately. I was introduced to her coming out of the ice rink in Derby Street in Manchester. As soon as I saw her, I thought, "That's the girl for me."' But Bobby and Norma did not start dating immediately: 'She probably thought I was a bit pushy because now and again I would phone her up and say that I would like to take her out. She would then knock my legs from under me. "No, I'm not going," she would say. She thought I was a little bit presumptuous. It shocked me but I knew she was the one. She was beautiful.' As with some other women, it was Bobby's shyness that she liked. 'He was a lot quieter than the other boys. That was the first thing I noticed about him,' she says. Lynda Lee-Potter, the distinguished *Daily Mail* journalist who interviewed Norma in the 1960s, agrees with Bobby's assessment of her looks. 'She really was stunningly beautiful. That is what struck me more than anything. She obviously adored Bobby and they seemed to have a very happy marriage,' she told me.

Their wedding was held at St Gabriel's Church in Middleton, Manchester on 22 June 1961. Both wanted a low-key occasion. Wilf McGuinness was the obvious candidate to be Bobby's best man, but, as he explains, 'I was a Roman Catholic and the Church said it would not be right for me to play a role in weddings and baptisms.' So the job went to Maurice Setters, who has this recollection of the event: 'It was a lovely day, went really well. But it was held in midweek so it was not a big flash event. It was the first time I had ever been best man so I got a bit of stick off the other United lads, but I think my speech was OK. I liked Norma a lot. She was good for Bobby. She was helpful as well. She and Bobby used to babysit for me so I could take my wife out.' The only incident in the wedding day that annoyed Bobby was when a group of Manchester United supporters turned up to cheer and wave rattles. He found their behaviour invasive and lacking in dignity. Unlike Jack and Pat, Bobby and Norma went abroad for their honeymoon, enjoying a week's holiday in Majorca.

Almost everyone who knows Jack says that he has never changed since his early years. And marriage did not alter him in any recognizable way – he was just as pig-headed at Leeds in the immediate aftermath of his wedding as he was before it. But the same was not true of Bobby. Apart from the experience of Munich, his decision to marry Norma was the most important event of his young life. Before he met her, he had led a slightly aimless existence, living in digs and having no real interests except football, swing music and the occasional night out with the lads. After setting up home with her, he became much more mature and better organized. 'Like most footballers,' says John Giles, 'getting married was a good thing for him. Norma settled him down, made him responsible. He was never a great one for the high life, and when you're not a playboy, you're always happier when you're married. And don't forget, Bobby, like most of us, was living in digs, so to move into a home was so much more comfortable.' Noel Cantwell remembers the change in Bobby's lifestyle: 'When Bobby was single, he would join us on our Wednesday nights out. We would often go to the Continental, one of the clubs in town. Basically, it was unmarried guys – though Dennis Viollet would often come along because he was not having a good time with his wife. Bobby was a normal guy, good company, liked a beer. Some evenings, if there were a few birds around, our luck might be in. There was a reporter in Manchester then called Tony Stratton Smith who worked for the *Daily Sketch*. He would throw these great parties and provide the birds. Bobby would be up there and he'd be as wild as anyone else. Oh yeah, he wasn't Mr Perfect in his youth. In fact, Norma was a good influence on him because, before she arrived, he could be a bit wayward, led astray by Shay Brennan.' Brennan, who sadly died in June 2000, was renowned for his fondness for a drink and a bet. Within a few years, he was also to be accused of leading George Best astray, though that can hardly have been a difficult task to accomplish. Cantwell continues, 'When Norma arrived on the scene, Bobby immediately disappeared from our weekly get-togethers. When we saw him we'd tease him and say, "What are you doing? Getting settled down? Oh Bob." But it was obvious he was in love.'

One of the particular ways that Bobby had been led astray by Shay

Brennan was through money. In fact, Bobby admits that occasionally he would lose half a week's salary through a misplaced bet. As Ronnie Cope recalls, there was a culture of gambling at the club amongst young players. 'Bobby and Shay were involved in that and I could not believe the sums they were playing for. One day, when a card game was going on in the players' lounge at Old Trafford, the boss came in. The place went deathly quiet. He went over to the table, picked up all the notes, said, "That's going to the Blind School" and walked out. That stopped gambling at the club but it went on elsewhere.' Ronnie Cope thinks that marrying Norma made Bobby more responsible in his behaviour. 'I have always said that marrying her was the best thing that ever happened to Bobby. He no longer acted like a kid. She was a smashing girl, very attractive and seemed to have an influence on him straight away. He knew from then on he would be focused on his career.'

Bobby did not, however, become some saintly figure after marrying. On away football trips, he could still enjoy the occasional heavy session, as Harry Gregg remembers: 'That great, wonderful image he has – Bobby Charlton could drink Jordan dry if the mood took him. In 1965, we were playing Vorwaerts, behind the Iron Curtain. The morning after, when we flew back, Bobby was so hungover we virtually had to carry him out and hide him at the back of the bus. Another time, when we were playing a friendly match in Belfast, involving an old England team, Bobby and the rest of were bevying all night in their hotel. Bobby was sitting there, blocked out of his mind, and he turned to me and said, "Harry, I'll allow you to buy the great Bobby Charlton a Bacardi and Coke."'

The physical manifestation of Bobby's change was that he became much smarter. Today, across the football world, he is known for being well groomed, but this concern for his appearance can be dated to Norma's arrival in his life. When he was a carefree bachelor at Old Trafford, he was notorious for being unkempt. Sammy McMillan recalls: 'Before he got married, he was a bit of a scruff. I remember once, when he got on the coach, the boss had to say to him, "Bob, will you brush your shoes." Norma put him on the right track.' Harry Gregg says, 'He was so scruffy it wasn't true. He wouldn't get his hair cut and would arrive at the ground with it all over the place. He wore a pair of shoes till they were done. He once went into a shop, bought a new pair and just left the old ones lying there. He used to get a lot of stick from Bill Foulkes, whose wife Theresa had done a bit of modelling so Bill thought he was a male model.'

There were also hopes that Norma might help Bobby's football, for this was the period when he was widely regarded as an unpredictable enigma, 'For too long,' wrote one newspaper in 1961 shortly before his wedding, 'Bobby Charlton has been a youngster not too sure of where he was going. That is why pretty Norma Ball is important to English football. She will provide the link that has been so long missing in the life of Bobby Charlton, the basically shy, outwardly mixed up kid who has that rare, indefinable talent which makes him an artist.' Managers always like their key players to be married because they believe it provides them with more stability. Matt Busby certainly took that view with Bobby: 'Many things happened to Bobby after Munich. Suddenly he became something of an idol and he was not happy about the fan worship heaped on him. With a settled home life, I am sure he will be a better player.' Busby's outlook was shared in Europe. Team manager of Real Madrid, Emil Osterreicher, against whom United had fought so many fine battles, praised the potential effect of marital life on Bobby. 'He is the one player in Britain who really interests us. He has both the grace and the instinct of a great player. He is, however, inconsistent. But this will probably be ironed out when he is married. Many players I have known have revealed their true ability for the first time when they have accepted the responsibilities of marriage.'

The responsibilities of marriage became quickly apparent, when Norma gave birth to Suzanne and Andrea. Suzanne is the only one of Jack and Bobby's offspring to have gone into public life, having become a household name across Britain as a TV weather presenter. Indeed, like her father, she became pre-eminent in her field – a 1998 BBC survey revealed that she was the most accurate forecaster in the country, beating the likes of Bill Giles and Michael Fish. And she also married a professional sportsman. Her husband Nick Brown, who was introduced to Suzanne by Bobby in 1991 at a sports charity function, was once ranked Britain's number two tennis player.

As Bobby is much quieter than Jack, he is sometimes portrayed as being under the thumb of Norma. It is an unfortunate commentary on the continuing misogynistic values of the football world, that no man can be seen as preferring his home to the bar without incurring accusations of being emasculated. Willie Morgan, who had something of a bad boy image during his spell at United, told me: 'I don't suppose Bobby liked our lifestyles. Clubbing was never his scene. He was more of a family man – though that was by order. Norma ruled the roost. Bobby did what he was told.' It was not the only time I heard that sort of disparaging comment. 'Norma has a big say in anything that goes on. I know her. She's very nice to me, but she is the power in the home,' says Harry Gregg. Just as with Bobby, some have said that she was too aloof. One of Bobby's contemporaries, watching her at a reception, said to me, 'I have to say that she had a snooty look about her. I could not get it out of my mind. When I saw that, I thought that Cissie, who never liked Norma, may have been right about her. She was perfectly pleasant, but not what you would call warm.'

Norma herself accepts that she was viewed by some in the football world in this way, even at Manchester United. 'I don't think I'm very popular with some of the wives,' she said in an interview in 1968. 'Some of them get a bit of reflected glory and it goes to their heads. I know I am a bit older than some of them but I've never been what you'd call a dizzy girl.' The very fact that Norma had the poise to handle Bobby's international fame, never showing any anxiety about being Lady Charlton, was a cause of resentment. 'It sounds very snobbish but Norma was a cut above most players' wives,' says the journalist Brian James, who knows Bobby well. 'Footballers tended to marry the local shop girl, who was not always capable of rising with his career. But Norma was very different. She was a smart young lady, very respectable and a very suitable partner for Bobby. She was the type of woman most parents would be only too delighted to see their son bring home – except if their mother happened to be Cissie Charlton.'

Former Manchester United Secretary and Director Les Olive, who grew to know the Charltons well during his four decades with the club, is equally dismissive of Norma's critics. 'She is naturally charming and has given wonderful support to Bobby. She comes with him to Old Trafford for most games and we have a meal beforehand. She is very good company. She's also pretty shrewd about football, having been involved with the game so long.'

As with Pat, it is intriguing to hear Norma's views about her husband. She said in 1973: 'He's really changed very little from the quiet shy man I met more than 15 years ago. He's a hard worker above all things and terribly conscientious. His dad's always been proud of doing a good day's work for a good day's pay and that's the way Bobby thinks too. With him, football is always very, very serious.' In her 1968 interview with Lynda Lee-Potter, she revealed: 'People think Bobby's stand-offish but he's not really. He's not a born leader but he's easy with the people he likes. Soccer isn't a job to him, it's his whole life. I have to accept that. When we got married, I just slotted in behind. Because it's important to him, it's important to me as well. I wouldn't flatter myself so much as to think that I mattered more to him than football.' But Norma gave some credence to the view that she was in charge off the field. 'Bobby's very thrilled with his home, but I usually have the last say when we buy anything. I get my own way most of the time, but he's like most very quiet people, when he gets mad he goes berserk. He bawls and shouts and gets really violent.'

That insight into Bobby's rare bouts of foul temper was fascinating enough, but perhaps most telling was Norma's comment about her husband's relationship with Jack and Cissie: 'People think that he and Jackie are very close but they're not. Jackie takes after his mother – he always wants to be in the front line of everything.'

The rift was to widen dramatically in the years to come.

CHAPTER TEN

The Internationals

Like Bobby and Jack, Alf Ramsey had a tough but respectable up-bringing which taught him the value of hard work. Bobby once said that he and Jack were so diligent because they followed the example of their father: 'He never shirked, never took a day off work. He was frightened to death that someone might accuse him of being lazy. He had great pride.' Alf Ramsey's father had a similar mentality. He was a small farmer in Dagenham, which in the 1920s was a rural suburb of London, but he had to supplement his income by driving a municipal dustcart. It was largely through sheer application that young Alf, once he became a professional football, reached inter-national standard as a full-back. He was not blessed with great natural talent or pace but, as Dave Bowler wrote in his excellent biography of Ramsey, 'He was a slave to practice, returning to work on certain skills in the afternoon, working on facets of his game back home in Dagenham in the close season. He set himself a task, to become a thoroughly competent and utterly reliable player.' It was a goal he achieved, winning 32 England caps during his career with Southampton and Tottenham. But what elevated Ramsey above the merely competent was his superb sense of vision, for few players could read the game better. Though he lacked pace, he was rarely caught out of position because he could anticipate his opponents' moves so well.

After his retirement as a player in 1955, Ramsey became manager of Ipswich, then just a minor backwater club in the East Anglian countryside which had never won anything – today's closest equivalents are probably Peterborough or Cambridge United. Yet Ramsey took this Third Division side all the way to the League Championship in 1961/62. It was a feat made all the more remarkable by the fact that Ramsey used essentially the same side on his march through the divisions towards the title, only purchasing one player before the 1961/62 season – and even he, Dougie Moran from Falkirk, cost only £12,300. One can take all the trophies of Sir Alex Ferguson, Bob Paisley and Brian Clough, but none of them ever achieved anything on this scale. Ramsey built his success on two key platforms: a strong team spirit and a workable, simple system, the 4-3-3 wingless formation that was to be the basis of his England triumph. Interestingly, these two elements were exactly the same as the ones that, nearly 30 years later, enabled Jack to turn Ireland into one of the world's best sides. Jimmy Leadbetter of Ipswich, talking about Ramsey's approach in the early 1960s, sounds just like one of the Irish players of the late 1980s: 'It was about trusting each other. We were there to win. Alf always wanted you to play your natural game and, before you realized what you were doing, you were fitting into the team pattern. He was a great one for putting players into their best positions. Our minds were not full of tactics. There were certain rules, things we didn't do in defence. We wouldn't play square balls because there was a chance of nipping in on goal.' The square ball at the back was also a particular hatred of Jack's.

The parallels between Ramsey and the Charlton brothers do not end there. Each of them also had a strong competitive edge, hating to be defeated at anything they did. All three of them were passionately devoted to England rather than Britain, while Jack and Alf shared a heartfelt dislike of the Scots. If Jack had to fill in his nationality on an official form, he always put 'English' rather than British, while Ramsey, on a trip north was once greeted by a representative of the Scottish press with the words: 'Welcome to Scotland, Mr Ramsey,' to which he replied, 'You must be joking.'

It is also interesting that Jack Charlton's playing relationship with Bobby Moore in the England team was very like Alf's own with his captain Billy Wright in the early 1950s. Jack both admired and was disturbed by Moore's skills as a ball player, just as Ramsey wrote that he found Billy Wright's 'attacking tendencies rather worrisome, for he was prone to carry the ball forward and, if things went wrong, was caught out of position, which made things rather difficult for me'. Ramsey once told Jack that one of the reasons he brought him into the England team was because 'I know you don't trust Bobby Moore.'

'What do you mean? Bobby's a tremendous player,' replied Jack.

'Yes Jack, but you and he are different. If Gordon Banks gives you the ball on the edge of the box, you'll give it back to him and say, "Keep the bloody thing", but if Gordon gives the ball to Bobby, he will play through the midfield, all the way to a forward position if he has to. I've watched you play and I know that as soon as Bobby goes, you'll always fill in behind him. That way, if Bobby makes a mistake, you're there to cover it.'

If Alf's defensive play was like Jack's, his character was like Bobby's: cautious, dignified, polite, stubborn and so wary of strangers and the media that he was often regarded as 'aloof'. His team-mate at Southampton, goalkeeper Ian Black, gave this description of working with Alf: 'He wasn't disagreeable in any way, he was easy enough to get along with, but he didn't mix a lot with the rest of the players – apart from training and matchdays, we didn't see him a lot. He was very reserved, wouldn't go out of his way to talk to anybody but if you wanted his advice, he would give it.' Those words could easily have been spoken by a Manchester United colleague about Bobby Charlton.

Ramsey, however, did not have Bobby's shyness and nervousness. On the contrary, he had a streak of confidence bordering on arrogance. That is why he, unlike Bobby, made such a good manager – he knew exactly what he wanted and was not willing to debate his opinion. Geoff Hurst recounts two occasions, both of them involving Bobby, which show how Ramsey was his own man. The respect in which he was held by the rest of the 1966 team meant that Bobby Charlton was sometimes asked to act as spokesman for the players. But his status was never enough to sway Ramsey, as Hurst recalls. 'When we were issued with our grey flannel suits in 1966, Bobby was chosen to ask Alf if, on less formal occasions, we could dress casually. "No," said Alf firmly.' Another time, the England squad were becoming fed up with the distance they had to travel between their hotel at Hendon in north London and their training ground at Roehampton, south of the river. Sometimes the round trip could take more than three hours. 'We asked Bobby to suggest to Alf that we should train at a ground closer to the hotel. Bobby waited for his moment and one day, when the team bus was stuck in traffic on the way to Roehampton, Bobby went to the front of the coach and put the suggestion to Alf. "Bobby, I'll give it some consideration," said Alf. Before Bobby had returned to his seat, Alf turned and called down the bus, "I've considered it and we'll stay as we are."'

On another occasion, in 1969, when England were flying to South America, Ramsey heard laughter from the back of the plane. He walked down the aisle and saw newcomer Allan Clarke.

'You enjoying yourself Allan?'

'Yes, Alf, great, thanks.'

'Well you don't fucking enjoy yourself with me. Remember that.'

He could be painfully awkward as well. One exchange on a radio interview went:

'Are your parents still alive, Mr Ramsey?'

'Oh yes.'

'And where do they live?'

'Dagenham, I believe.'

Incidentally, for all his refinement, Ramsey was the manager who coined the soccer cliché 'over the moon' – after Ipswich won the title in 1962, he told the press that he 'felt like jumping over the moon'.

Bobby and some of the other England players experienced the

angrier side of Ramsey when they disobeyed his instructions on a matter of team discipline. As well as showing Ramsey's toughness, this episode demonstrates that Bobby's stainless image could occasionally be at odds with reality. In May 1964, just a year after Ramsey had taken charge, the England team gathered at the Lancaster Gate Hotel on the eve of flying to Lisbon for an international against Portugal. Despite Ramsey's imposition of a curfew, in the late evening seven players, Bobby Moore, Jimmy Greaves, George Eastham, Gordon Banks, Johnny Byrne, Ray Wilson and Bobby Charlton, decided to take a stroll into the West End. It was Jimmy Greaves, himself on the descent into alcoholism, who said of Bobby Moore, 'I would have to put him pretty high in the table of international drinkers. There were not many footballers who could match him in a drinking contest.' So with Moore and Greaves leading the way, 'It was odds-on the stroll becoming something of a stagger before the night was through.' The party found its way to a bar called The Beachcomber, where, according to Greaves, 'We got stuck into a drink called a "Zombie", rum-based with a real kick.' It was after 1am, says Gordon Banks, by the time the team returned to the hotel. At first the players thought they had not been spotted when they crept back, but as soon as they reached their rooms they knew they were in trouble, for Ramsey had ostentatiously left their passports lying on their beds.

Nothing was said the next morning, though Alf was very quiet. Then, after the final training session in Lisbon, Alf dismissed the rest of the team and said, in his stilted voice, 'I think there are seven gentlemen who would like to stay behind and see me.' Gordon Banks recalls, 'We felt like little boys as we shuffled with embarrassment in front of an obviously angry Alf. "If I had enough players here with me, none of you would be playing in this match," he said. "Just learn a lesson that I will not tolerate the sort of thing that happened in London before we left. You are here to do a job for England and so am I. Thank you, gentlemen, and don't let it happen again."' Ramsey had handled the situation well, letting the players know of his displeasure, while not creating a scene in London.

Bobby Moore, however, refused to bow to his authority, and caused more trouble by going out drinking with Greaves during a trip to the USA a fortnight later. For a time, Ramsey seriously considered dropping Moore. Their relationship did not recover properly until the eve of the World Cup. Bobby Charlton himself learnt a lot about Ramsey from the affair: 'He was the boss and let you know that, no doubt about it. You were under him and you had to listen and there were plenty who were prepared to take your place if you didn't. And he could be intimidating too, if he wanted.'

When Ramsey first took over the management of England in 1963, one of his first acts was to get rid of the selection committee which had been such a bane on Winterbottom. But even with Ramsey in sole charge, it was not clear that either of the Charlton brothers would necessarily feature much in his plans. Jack was still playing in the Second Division, and only Don Revie had talked privately of him as an England prospect. Despite the hopes invested in his marriage, Bobby continued to be seen as inconsistent, unable to recapture the form of his youth. His Manchester team-mate Bill Foulkes summed up the views of many in the football world when he said before the World Cup: 'Bobby Charlton is the complete enigma. He is one of the most natural footballers I have seen, so graceful with the ball – beautiful to watch. But he is completely different in temperament from Denis Law, and sometimes gets lost in a kind of dream. When he has one of those days, he looks one of the worst players in the world. He hits the heights and plumbs the depths. There are no in-betweens with Bobby.'

One of Bobby's problems was that he was still on the wing with both England and United. But at the end of 1963, Bobby was gradually switched to an inside position by Busby, playing as a deep-lying striker. Since this gave him a much more central role, feeding the ball through the midfield to Denis Law and the flanks, Bobby was much more comfortable. He told the *Daily Herald* in January 1964: 'As a winger, I can only get into a game in spasmodic flashes. As a centre-forward I'm in the game all the time. I could not be happier about my change of fortune.'

Bobby was perhaps even luckier when it came to the England manager. Ramsey, an uncannily perceptive judge of both character and talent, saw that Bobby was being wasted on the left wing. So he decided to shift him to the centre, putting him at the front of England's midfield, as Alf moved towards the 4-3-3 formation. Alf was coming to the view that Bobby, if utilized better, could be one of the keys to winning the World Cup. With a more central role, thought Ramsey, he could become the co-ordinator of England's attacks. George Cohen, his World Cup team-mate, feels the move was absolutely right for Bobby: 'Bob used to get chewed off by the crowd at Wembley when he was on the wing, and I don't think he was as suited to playing out there. But moving him into the middle, like George Best, gave him greater freedom. He had that great acceleration, beautiful balance that gives the great players half a chance at goal when there isn't one.'

Apart from the shift in position, there were three other developments under Ramsey that were to benefit Bobby's England career hugely. The first was Ramsey's phenomenal attention to detail – at Ipswich he had even personally ordered the grass seed to make sure it was right for the pitch. In an interview with Martin Tyler, now Sky TV's chief commentator, Bobby recalled: 'His professionalism showed through straight away. When we were on his first real tour, in 1963, the first game was in Bratislava, and he told everybody that when they were doing their warm-up they had to do it in the particular areas of the pitch that they were most likely to play in. I was a left winger then, and I had to do all my warm-up down the left-side touchlines. I had to practice taking corners in case there was a difficult run-up to the ball, across a running track or something. Alf used to say that you might only get one corner in the match, so you should be fully prepared to make the most of it.'

The second was that he made Bobby work harder on his fitness. A natural athlete with a powerful physique and great pace, Bobby had never had a slack attitude towards training. But now, just as Jimmy Murphy had done a decade earlier, Alf Ramsey pushed him to new heights, driving him to the point of exhaustion. 'With the World

Cup in view, Ramsey sentenced Charlton to 100 hours of training torture. He made Bobby run harder than ever before. He made Bobby more mobile than he has ever been in his whole career. It was sweat and murder, but Bobby did it,' wrote Alan Hoby in a *Sunday Express* April 1966 profile of Bobby. The third change was for Ramsey to bring Bobby out of his shell, by encouraging him to take part in team discussions. It was another crucial step in the making of the mature footballer. 'Previously we had been used to being talked at by the manager, but now he forced everybody to talk among themselves,' wrote Bobby. 'This was a bit embarrassing for some people who normally don't say much at their clubs. I was one of them at first but slowly I began to say a lot more than I usually do. It helped me enormously, because before this I had kept my thoughts about other players to myself.'

The transition of Bobby into the lynchpin of the England team in the run-up to 1966 was not without its problems. For a start, Bobby's position was never fixed as Ramsey struggled to find the right combination in attack. In the 1964/65 season alone, Ramsey tried 15 different forwards, while in the three years up to the World Cup, no less that 25 forwards were picked. In this unsettled atmosphere, Bobby's form continued to fluctuate, so much so that he was dropped by Ramsey in October 1964 following a poor performance in midfield against Northern Ireland, when England almost squandered a four-goal lead before winning 4–3. His place was taken by Terry Venables. 'Because Bobby did not measure up to the job of linkman in Belfast and is now out of the side, it would be very wrong to say that his England career is over,' warned Ramsey. But that is exactly what the English press were saying. Gourmet, politician and writer Clement Freud was sent to Manchester by his editor to see Charlton 'and find out how a man feels when his international career is over, when the writing is on the wall'. Over a lunch with 'good champagne', Bobby assured Freud: 'Oh I'll play for England again. I'm not worried about getting my place back.'

He was right. Before the end of the 1964/65 season, Bobby had returned to the side. Yet his performances could still be uneven as he came to terms with his new central role. In October 1965, for instance, when England drew 0–0 with Wales in Cardiff and then were beaten 2–3 at home by Austria, Eric Todd of the *Guardian* wrote: 'What R Charlton's part in the plan of campaign – if any – was supposed to be, I have no idea. Linkman? More like a member of the chain gang.' But, some of his moves could also be brilliant, as Fred Pickering, the Everton striker who made a trio of England appearances at this time, says. 'It was just great to play alongside him. I remember one wonderful moment when he feinted to play the one-two with Jimmy Greaves. But instead of actually playing it, he let the ball go through his legs, completely deceiving the centre-half, who had moved to cut off the return. With the defender now taken out, he turned, and slid the ball into the path of Jimmy, who put it in the back of the net. Any normal player, like me, would have just played the ordinary one-two but Bobby had that extra dimension to his play. He was so natural, so committed.' It was precisely these qualities of flair and commitment which ensured that, as the World Cup approached, he became one of the fixtures in the England team. As Jimmy Armfield put it, 'We had a trump card – every great team has one and we had Bobby Charlton. Alf found a role for Bobby which suited him, and that was good managing.'

Looking back on Bobby's growing ascendancy, Alf Ramsey said in 1970: 'He has always been gifted and an exceptional international, but in his early days he was never a very good reader of the game. He was instinctively attracted to the ball. There was perhaps a lack of concentration and an inability to play with those around him. He often had no other thought but to get as near as possible to it all the time. But when he matured, he became not just a brilliant individual but a collective team player.' Ramsey highlighted one moment, in a friendly against Yugoslavia just before the World Cup, when he realized that Bobby had become the complete player. 'Bobby was in midfield when an England attack had broken down on the left wing. Normally Bobby would have instinctively chased the ball out to that wing towards the play when suddenly he stopped, as if remembering something. He looked about him and when the Yugoslav defence switched the ball to the other side of the field and started to come away in attack, Bobby was there, looking to see if there was danger from the blind side. In that match, he became a great player for me.'

By April 1965, Bobby had been joined in the England side by his elder brother Jack, who was just a month short of his 30th birthday when he made his debut against Scotland at Wembley. Jack's rise into the England team was widely greeted as an indicator that Ramsey was becoming increasingly desperate in his search for the right blend of players for the World Cup. In the popular imagination, Jack was just an ordinary, ageing defender, who used aggression to make up for his lack of creativity. That view was only reinforced by his behaviour on the day his call-up to international honours was announced. Playing in an FA Cup semi-final against Manchester United at Hillsborough, he became involved in a lurid flare-up with Denis Law. 'I was going for the ball,' said Denis, 'but my shirt was not going with me. Jack Charlton had grabbed a handful of it and was trying to hold me back. It was literally being ripped off my back. I lashed out at Jack and we began swapping punches. I was unaware that our team-mates had joined the fray and there were fists flying all over the place. It took a few minutes for the referee to calm the situation down.'

'You had to hang on to Denis,' said Jack by way of explanation, 'because he was so sharp and so good in the air. I used to hate playing against him.' Law despised the violence of Leeds during the Revie years, though he felt that the gamesmanship and professional fouls practised by the likes of Billy Bremner and Norman Hunter were far worse that anything Jack perpetrated.

Contrary to Busby's virtuous reputation, however, Manchester United could be as dirty as any side in the League and had an appalling record for cautions and sendings-off, thanks to the likes of Pat Crerand and Nobby Stiles. In fact, Busby once sent out Law in a match against Spurs with instructions to kick Danny Blanchflower black and blue. As the columnist Max Marquis wrote in 1970: 'It is an inescapable fact that the vast majority of commentators just do not want to say anything deprecatory about Busby; he is a personification of the Emperor in the story of the Emperor's Robe. Eyes are carefully turned away from the nakedness of Manchester United's disciplinary record.'

Jack's public reputation as little more than a bruiser was misplaced. Thanks to Don Revie's influence, Jack's whole game had improved to such an extent that when Leeds returned to the First Division for the 1964/65 season, he was one of the finest centre-halves in the country. Jack has been fond of downplaying his accomplishments as a defender, with lines such as 'I couldn't play, but I could stop others from playing.' He also says that when he asked Ramsey why he put him in the England side, he received this reply: 'Well, Jack, I have a pattern of play in mind – and I pick the best players to fit that pattern. I don't necessarily pick the best players, Jack.' This may have been an example of Ramsey's dry humour, for the fact was that, by 1965, Jack was probably the best English player in his position, particularly because Maurice Norman, winner of 23 caps at centre-half between 1962 and 1965, had lost form and reverted to being a full-back at Spurs. Ramsey later said, 'I had always admired Jack. He was a strong tackler and good in the air. He was a far better footballer than he was given credit for and in 1965, when I was building my World Cup squad, I saw him as my centre-half for the foreseeable future.' According to George Cohen, Jack was exactly Ramsey's type of footballer: 'Alf liked players who'd take a bad knock but still get up and play, the player who was absolutely knackered but would draw himself up for the next run. He could see through a person's character, which gave him a big edge on lots of other managers.'

Ramsey's view of Jack was shared by many in the football world who knew him better than the fans or the press. John Giles says: 'When I went to Leeds, they were in the Second Division but Jack was playing really, really well. When we went up, I think Jack was the best centre-half in England, by a long way. He was definitely the best. He was strong and he could cover the ground, though not like Bobby, who was a thoroughbred. He was always there, getting the vital headers in, clearing the ball. He was great when we were really up against it, when we had to defend. Away from home, in a tough match, he would always do his stuff.' Joe Baker, who played for Arsenal against Jack and with him for England, describes Jack's virtues thus: 'I was not surprised when he was picked for England because he was doing such a good job for Leeds. He was cumbersome, but he did his job well, great in the air and not trying anything fancy. I was very nippy as a striker and my forte was turning defenders with one touch. When I was playing for Arsenal against Leeds, many times I thought I was away from Jack when suddenly this big, long leg would stretch out and whip the ball away from me. For England, Jack's job was to win the ball and give it to Bobby Moore, that's how they worked. He was also there to give Bobby a kick up the arse.' For all Jack's success, Baker says that he had one tactic which was guaranteed to rile Jack. 'If the ball was coming over and I knew I was not going to win it, I would just take a step back before I jumped. Jack would then come over the top of me and I would get a foul. It was a simple thing to do but it usually worked. Jack absolutely hated it. He would go off his head with me.'

Inevitably, there was a great deal of media interest in Jack's appearance against Scotland on 10 April 1965, given that he and Bobby were the first brothers to represent England together since 1899, when Frank and Freddie Forman played against Ireland at Roker Park. The Forman brothers, unlike the Charltons, played for the same club, Nottingham Forest, and they were both on the scoresheet in that game at Sunderland – a feat that Bobby and Jack were to achieve once in their England career together, in the 5–1 demolition of Wales at Wembley in November 1966. The *Sunday Express* compared the two brothers: 'Facially, the resemblance is uncanny. There is the same quizzical look about the eyes, the same high cheekbones, the same clipped Northumbrian accent, and the same pawky grin. But whereas the more withdrawn Bobby is inclined to be reticent with strangers, Jackie's thoughts are an open book. The words and images spill from his lips in a spontaneous stream. In action, too, the Charlton brothers are as different as calm and storm. Bobby can change pace or the course of a game with a sway, a swerve or a thundering sledgehammer of a shot. But Jackie does his work so economically and without stress that you don't always notice him.' In the *Evening Standard*, Jack said that the difference also lay in talent. 'I never considered myself half the player that Bobby is and I still don't, even though I am now an international. He's got a natural aptitude and does things so easily. There's no comparison. I can never hope to be as good as he is.'

Like Bobby, Jack had an excellent international debut, performing solidly at the back in a 2–2 draw. The Scotland striker Ian St John, who had been so dismissive of Jack a few years earlier, was impressed: 'He had re-invented himself. I was amazed at the transformation; he was now playing to his strengths, in the air and the tackle, in his ability to read the game. He deserves real credit for turning his career around, a career that had been going nowhere. But Don Revie was vital as well. I spoke to Don many times about Jack, and he said that, when he first became manager, Jack was a big, dogmatic bugger who would not listen to anyone's opinion bar his own. But eventually the penny dropped and he became a real player.' Jack says that he found his entry into international football comparatively easy because 'There was always someone around to give the ball to.' He slotted so smoothly into the defence alongside Bobby Moore that, almost immediately, he became a permanent presence in the team. In only his fourth game, in a 1–0 victory over West Germany at Nuremberg, he was described in the press as 'a massive presence, simply magnificent'. There was now little doubt that he would play in next year's World Cup.

Having grown used to the unobtrusive, dapper presence of Bobby, the arrival of Jack came as something of a shock for some of the other England players. 'In the dressing room, you always knew where Jack's peg was. It had the trousers and braces hanging on it,' says Geoff Hurst. Derek Temple, who played for England in 1965, recalls: 'Jack was always confident, a noise on the field. He would have a go at people if he thought they were not doing their jobs. He was quite quick-tempered as well. Bobby was the opposite, very reserved, a deep thinker, though he had a nice dry humour. They were both smokers, though Jack never had any cigarettes. If you lit up, Jack would just reach over, take it off you and carry on.' Peter Thompson, the Liverpool winger, provides this insight into the pair: 'I shared a room with Bobby when we played against Holland in 1965. At first, I thought he was a bit snobbish, but he was actually just quiet. All we talked about was football. He was lovely really, very polite, a gentleman. Jack was the exact opposite. We had a meeting after one England game and Alf Ramsey explained how he saw the goal we had conceded. We then discussed it, and everybody agreed about the way we lost the goal – except Jack Charlton. He put his hand up and said, "No, that's not right, that's not the way it happened." Jack was quite aggressive about it. Here's another example of Jack's attitude. Sir Alf said: "Right, tonight, we are going to the cinema. When we come back at 10pm, it's tea and toast and then bed." Then Jack piped up, "I don't want to go to the pictures." The next night, Sir Alf said, "Right, we're all staying in tonight." So Jack had to say, "I want to go to the pictures." He always seemed to want to be different. He was such a contrast to Bobby. Bobby agreed with everything. I never heard him swear much. I certainly heard Jack swear. In one Liverpool-Leeds match, about halfway through, he was at the side of the pitch and there was a bit of skirmish going on, involving Billy Bremner. I was only a few yards away as Jack said to the referee, "Excuse me, what would you do if I called you a bastard?"

"I'd send you off."

"OK, in that case I'll just think you're a bastard."

'But Jack and I got on fine. After one game at Elland Road, I saw Jack and he invited me to his house for a party. When I turned up he said, "Hello Peter, I thought you were picked to play today. I never saw you." It was such a slap in the face. That was his sort of humour but I could not argue with him, because he was 6' 3". They were both great, though, in their own ways.'

By the end of 1965, Jack was part of a settled four-man defence, alongside Bobby Moore, Ray Wilson of Everton and George Cohen of Fulham, with Gordon Banks behind them in goal. It was a line-up that exuded authority and assurance, probably the most effective English defence of all time. Gordon Banks says: 'Jack Charlton was strong and commanding in the middle. We used to get on at each other during matches, but this was purely to keep each other on the alert. The somctimes rude and brutal things we yelled in the heat of the battle were always quickly forgotten once the final whistle had blown.' Jack's noise on the field is also remembered by Ray Wilson, 'Me and big Jack were mouthy players and it's very important that people talk. We never used to break, we tried to keep the back four solid, we never tackled until they got round the penalty area and the other lads put them under pressure, so they couldn't squeeze the ball through.'

In front of the back four, the short-sighted but terrier-like Nobby Stiles, Bobby's colleague at United, had been brought in as a ball-winning midfielder, while Bobby was growing into his central role, enjoying the licence to travel all over the field. Jack always felt that Stiles was crucial for both Bobby and the England team: 'The main factor in our winning the World Cup,' Jack said in 1986 BBC interview, 'was the introduction of Nobby. He could win the ball and allow Bobby not to have the responsibility of having to pick up and mark and hold up the people in the back four. Nobby gave the ball to Bobby and let him play. Once Nobby came in alongside our kid, not only did it work for England, it also worked for Man United.' This was a view echoed by George Cohen: 'It's not recognized that Nobby was a very good distributor of the ball, but he fed Bobby Charlton time and again. Bobby could see Nobby go into a tackle, was confident he'd come out with the ball, moved into space and Nobby would find him. That was a very good partnership.'

But, at the start of the 1965/66 season, Ramsey was still experimenting with both his system and the rest of his forward personnel. Then, on a bitterly cold December night at the Bernabeu Stadium in Madrid, Ramsey finally achieved the breakthrough he had been seeking. Playing against the European champions, Spain, England adopted a 4-3-3 formation, with Ball, Stiles and Bobby Charlton in midfield and George Eastham, Joe Baker and Roger Hunt up front. With this unorthodox strategy, rarely seen before in Europe, England tore Spain apart and would have won by much more than the 2–0 scoreline if the strikers had taken their chances. Bobby Charlton later recalled how bewildered the Spaniards were by England's tactics: 'The full-backs Reija and Sanchis were particularly at sea – frustration was written all over their faces. For three-quarters of the game, they were waiting for attacks to come down the wings so they could tackle the wingers. It was comical to see them wasting their time because we often had five players going through the middle and never had five forwards strung out across the field.'

Ramsey had tried 4-3-3 several times before, but never to such devastating effect. His famous 'wingless wonders' were truly born that wintry night in the Bernabeu. As he said later, 'It was after the Spain game that I realized England could win the World Cup with this system.' Inevitably, Jack Charlton, with his cantankerous trait, wanted to argue with Ramsey about the new approach. 'He was the only player who actively disagreed and opposed it,' said Ramsey in an interview in 1994. 'That was Jack Charlton, the rebel. He argued against it, queried it and left me in no doubt that he was not in favour. He didn't take kindly to changes and I had to tell him, "Do it my way or else." "Or else what?" he would say. "You are out," I replied. It was necessary to let him know who was boss, that I felt the system was successful and that our World Cup hopes might well depend upon it. Jack used to enjoy moaning, if he could make things difficult for me he would. But once he saw that the tactics worked, he held up his hands and admitted defeat. Jack was basically an uncompromising man, shrewd and calculating. He knew the game, that's why he tried to cross swords with me.'

Ramsey always maintained that 4-3-3, decried by observers as stifling, was actually a flexible system, allowing his side to attack or defend as the state of each match required. Given that he had the pivotal role in the formation, it is not surprising that Bobby agreed. 'The beauty of this system,' he wrote in 1967, 'is that while the defence should be virtually watertight, an attack can be built up in a second and midfield players can make a spearhead of six forwards by joining the strikers. I think it is more entertaining than traditional, orthodox football.'

Over the next six months, Ramsey continued to fine tune the tactic while England completed a tough round of friendly matches, concluding with a fine 1–0 win in Poland. England had started to take on the air of serious contenders, and Ramsey's pledge made in 1963 that 'England will win the World Cup' was beginning to look less foolish.

CHAPTER ELEVEN

The Winners

Before the 1966 World Cup tournament itself, the England players were given three weeks' holiday by Ramsey. Bobby went with Norma and young Suzanne to Majorca, though the large number of football fans there ensured that he had little peace. By now Bobby was one of the biggest names in European football, through his exploits with England and Manchester United. 'I couldn't stop thinking about football, and had to spend most of the day on the beach talking about it,' he explained. The local Spaniards were especially anxious to meet him after the dramatic win in the Bernabeu. According to Bernard Joy in the *Evening Standard*, 'Spanish fans liken Charlton to the "White Arrow", the great Alfredo di Stefano, because of his fluency, effortless acceleration and boyish enthusiasm.'

In a reversal of their childhood, when Jack was always wandering while Bobby stayed at home, Jack as an adult has never liked to travel as much as Bobby. So instead of going abroad, he opted to stay with his former Leeds colleague, Bob Forrest, who ran a guest house in Weymouth. Bob Forrest says: 'He came down with his wife, two kids and his mother. The local lads would knock on the door, asking for his autograph, while he did a bit of training with the Weymouth team and went running along the beach. He also did some functions and openings, so the town got a very good impression of him. He was very easy, enjoyable company. People even today stop me now to say how much they remember his visit.'

After their contrasting breaks, it was down to the serious business of training in June at the elegant Elizabethan manor of Lilleshall, the FA's academy in Staffordshire – or as Jimmy Greaves put it 'the fitness fanatics' paradise'. It was an extremely demanding month, reflecting Ramsey's belief in the importance of mental and physical discipline. From 9am until 9pm the players were made to follow a strictly regimented routine consisting of exercise, training films, and practice matches. With his characteristic attention to detail, Ramsey even had the team doctor, Alan Bass, give the players a demonstration of how to cut their toenails properly. Alcohol was prohibited and no-one was allowed to venture beyond the confines of the grounds. Once a small group led, inevitably, by Jimmy Greaves, managed to reach a nearby golf club. They were downing a few pints when England trainer Harold Shepherdson walked in. 'You,' he said to Greaves, 'would manage to find a bar in the middle of the Sahara.' Ramsey was furious and gave this warning: 'Gentlemen, if anybody gets the idea of popping out for a pint and I find out, he is finished with this squad forever.' 'Nobody went back after that,' says Jack, who described his time at Lilleshall as 'like being in a Stalag. Alf wanted to push us to the utmost limit of human endurance. It was a test of character as much as a physical training programme.'

As usual, Bobby took a different view: 'It was a monastic existence but I loved it. Football was my life and I was with footballers, playing football.' He told the journalist Ken Jones, 'The work was so strenuous that when the press lads were allowed in for a day they were convinced that a punishing session had been put on especially to impress them. That most definitely was not the case. Most nights we were looking for our beds long before lights out.' The purpose of Lilleshall was not just to raise the standards of physical fitness to a new peak, but also to strengthen the spirit of the team. In this Ramsey succeeded better than probably any England manager until the arrival of Eriksson. His 1966 side found the holy grail of international football, a genuine club atmosphere. Never one to dish out praise gratuitously, Jack says: 'Alf Ramsey had a feel for players. In a real team you can't have shit-stirrers around. If there's someone you can't trust, get rid of them. They were totally absent in that squad. I never once heard any player questioning the merits of another, whether he should or shouldn't be in.'

Jack's explosive presence did not always contribute to a relaxed atmosphere, as Wilf McGuinness, one of the England coaches, recalls: 'Jack was so stubborn. He had terrible rows with everyone. The way he used to argue with people, I sometimes thought to myself, "We'll never win anything if this carries on."' Paradoxically, though, Jack's openness may have helped to build a strong team spirit. During one practice match, Jack and Nobby Stiles, another high octane personality, had been trading verbal insults on the pitch. 'We were really slanging one another. We were at it like five-year-old schoolboys. It was a good job we didn't come to blows because I would have dropped him – if I'd had a stepladder to reach him,' says Nobby. At half-time, their argument escalated, as Geoff Hurst recalls: 'They didn't mince words. I remember Jack being very cutting about Nobby's performance when Partizan Belgrade beat United in the European Cup. Stiles, in turn, probed open an old wound by vividly describing Jack's performance for Leeds against Zaragoza. It really was pretty brutal stuff. But I was delighted. I realized then that if we had players who felt that they knew each other well enough to tear strips off each other's carcass, then we certainly knew each other well enough to act together. It certainly worked out that way. From that moment, the old shyness fell away. Players got into the habit of telling each other exactly what they thought. If anyone doubts the value of that bust-up, just let them remember how the England defence played as a unit during the World Cup.'

After all the toil at Lilleshall, the opening game of the tournament, on 11 July against Uruguay, was a severe disappointment. Uruguay, bent on survival, used a packed defence and achieved a 0–0 draw. 'They had ten full-backs and a goalkeeper,' said Ray Wilson. At the end of the game, Jack was walking towards the

England dressing room when he and Bobby Moore were hauled off by FIFA doctors to undertake a random dope test. Though he was given the all-clear, it was not his last such experience in 1966. 'Two players were selected at random after every World Cup game and big Jack got nabbed every time. Before the tournament ended we presented him with a potty and named him "England's Jimmy Riddle champion",' says Gordon Banks.

Jack had a more pleasant experience the next day, when the England team were taken to Pinewood studios. After a pleasant lunch with wine, they were given a guided tour in which they met Norman Wisdom, watched some filming of the James Bond movie *You Only Live Twice*, and were told to clear off another set by George Segal because a fit of the giggles – provoked by Ray Wilson – was affecting his concentration. Jack also had a central role in a press photocall with one of the Bond starlets. 'There was this lovely little girl, well endowed. They wanted a picture so I had to pick her up and hold her. I got a lot of stick from the lads about that,' said Jack.

Initially, the visit to Pinewood did not seem to have lifted England's performance for the next game against Mexico, as they again struggled to break through the defence. A lot of sweat was expended without much sign of penetration. But that suddenly changed in the 38th minute, when Bobby picked up the ball in the deep. As he told David Miller in the book *Boys of 66*: 'I thought, well, I'll just carry it into their area and see what develops. I didn't really expect them to allow me to keep going. Had someone come at me and challenged me, I would have laid it off to Geoff Hurst, or Roger Hunt or to Martin Peters or Alan Ball but I just kept going.' Bobby Charlton took the ball over the halfway line and, to his surprise, still remained unchallenged. Continuing on his run across the smooth Wembley turf, he was now only 25 yards from goal. 'I just knocked it to the right and I thought, well, I've always been taught just hit it in the general direction of the goal and let the keeper worry about it. I just banged it and it came off so sweetly. When it was on its way up, I thought, well, that's a goal.'

Bobby Charlton's awesome shot was the spark that lit England's campaign. Up until that moment, Ramsey's side had looked stodgy, timid, lacking in ideas. A miserable, early exit appeared a real possibility. But suddenly, thanks to a stroke of genius, England were on course – and they were never to look back. It was probably the most memorable goal of Bobby's career, not only for the sheer breathtaking quality of his shot, but also for its context. Looking at replays of the goal today, what is so impressive is that Bobby hits the ball with very little backlift and while still on the run. There is no sense of his winding up to take a blast – which is exactly why he surprised the Mexicans so much. Ramsey said later that this was one of Bobby's unique gifts. 'He is possibly the only player who can run full out and shoot in his stride without checking or any loss of pace.' At the other end of the field, Gordon Banks had a full view of Charlton's goal. 'The ball seemed to climb like a jet plane taking off and finished in the top corner with the goalkeeper Calderon totally beaten. No goalkeeper could have stopped it.' Banks once explained why Bobby was so difficult to face: 'The trouble with Bobby, from a keeper's point of view, is that he can suddenly challenge with shots from the most harmless-looking positions. But they come at you with such velocity that you know you've got to treat them as if they were deadly missiles. You've got to brace yourself against their power.'

England dominated the rest of the game against Mexico, winning 2–0. It was by the same scoreline that they beat a mediocre French team, thereby ensuring qualification from their group. The quarter-final against Argentina was the nastiest match of the tournament, with the South Americans displaying a ruthless cynicism which would have embarrassed even Don Revie's Leeds at their worst. The Argentinians were brimful of talent, but they decided to try to foul, play-act and abuse their way into the next round. Particularly negative was their captain, Antonio Rattin, who was sent off after spending most of his 35 minutes haranguing the West German referee, Rudolf Kreitlein. As Hugh McIlvanney wrote, it was not so much a football match, more of 'an international incident'. The

Charltons suffered as much as any other English players. 'I quickly discovered that whenever I beat an Argentinian, I could expect to be tripped, body-checked, spat at or dragged to the ground,' said Bobby later.

Bobby was even more infuriated at the punishment meted out to Jack, so much so that he picked up the only booking of his international career. It is widely thought that Bobby's 12 years and 106 caps with England were free from any such blemish, but this is not the case. Jack had gone up for an England corner, was battered by a defender, collided with the keeper and then, as he tried to get up, was given a kick straight in the ribs, knocking the wind out of him. Bobby was the nearest player to him and grabbed the Argentinian by the shirt, pulling him away. It was the first time he had ever taken such action in his career, and he later admitted that he almost lost control when he saw Jack being attacked on the ground. Referee Kreitlein was certainly losing control of the game, his difficulties made all the worse because he spoke neither English nor Spanish. In scenes of utter confusion, with the Argentinian keeper still lying prostrate, both Jack and Bobby were given cautions. But such was the mayhem at Wembley on that boiling afternoon that neither Charlton realized they had been booked. It was only in 1998, when FIFA was conducting some research into its archives, that the award of the cautions was confirmed. 'It was a misunderstanding, really,' said Bobby when informed of his offence. 'There was a lot of pushing and shoving in the goalmouth involving my brother and I was only trying to calm people down. It was a very intense match and feelings were running high.' It was after this chaotic game that FIFA decided to introduce the system of yellow and red cards. It was the English FIFA official, Ken Aston, who came up with the idea when, driving away from Wembley at the end of the quarter-final, he was stopped at a set of traffic lights.

Even though Rattin had been sent off, England still struggled to make their numerical superiority count, until, in the 77th minute, Martin Peters sent over a near-post cross from the left, which Geoff Hurst met with a glancing header. It was an instinctive goal, based on the telepathy between two West Ham colleagues; Peters, knowing where Hurst would be, did not even need to look up when he hit the ball. With typical modesty, Bobby Charlton has said that this goal 'was the best I ever saw in my time with the England squad, an unstoppable cross and header'. It was enough to see England through to the last four.

The malevolent atmosphere at Wembley continued after the final whistle, with Alf Ramsey rushing on to the field in an attempt to stop his players exchanging shirts with the Argentina team, whom he notoriously described as 'animals'. Spoiling for a fight, some Argentinians then threw a chair through the door of the England dressing room. Jack Charlton was ready to take them on: 'Send them in!' he screamed, 'send them in! I'll fight them all!' Fortunately, for Jack, the police arrived to clear the Argentinians away. That evening, back at the England base in the Hendon Hall hotel, Ramsey let the players celebrate, as Nobby Stiles recalls: 'We all got well and truly drunk, and Alf was over there in the corner and never said a word.'

The semi-final against Portugal could hardly have been a more different affair. The football was open and fluent, the sportsmanship of the highest class. With the brilliant Benfica striker Eusebio in the forward line, Portugal were probably the most exciting side in the tournament. But for sheer pace and power, England had a match for Eusebio in Bobby Charlton, who exploited to the full the space that he was given by the attack-minded Portuguese. If his goal against Mexico was the greatest of his international career, then this match was probably his finest. He ran non-stop, was at the heart of almost every forward thrust, and scored both England's goals. His performance was the ultimate fulfilment of Ramsey's vision of Bobby as the attacking, roaming midfielder. His captain, Bobby Moore, said of him: 'A lot of pros had their arguments against Bobby, but he was world class all right in every way. Sometimes he would lose possession by attempting the impossible or doing naïve things instead of playing the simple ball. But he had all that lovely skill and talent and that lovely habit of suddenly getting a ball in a nothing position on the halfway line, dropping one shoulder, then another, drifting past two people and plonking it in the back of the net from 35 yards. You'd find yourself still screaming at him to give the simple pass. So you'd break off in mid-sentence and go pat him on the cheek.' Like Ramsey, Moore felt that Bobby was much better suited to his central role. 'I had seen his first game for United, at outside-left. At times he looked the best winger in the world. But his irresponsibility was worse out there. Playing midfield for Alf, he used to run the game.'

Both Bobby's goals were typical flashes from a distance. The first came after the Portuguese keeper Pereira dived to save from Roger Hunt. The ball rolled out to Bobby who, from 15 yards, hit it first time. 'I was really pleased with that goal,' he told John Motson in a BBC interview, 'because I could have whacked it, tried to hit it as hard as I could. If I had done that I would probably have missed. But Wembley is such a beautiful playing surface that I could confidently push the ball in a straight line along the floor, knowing that it would not deviate at all. I trusted that lovely pitch. I went right through the gap between the two full-backs.' His second goal was made by Geoff Hurst, who chased a long ball down the right wing from George Cohen, took it into the box, turned and hit an inch-perfect pass for Bobby to smash home. The goal was a tribute to Hurst's team spirit. 'He was in a good position to shoot but was completely unselfish. Personally, I would have taken a chance and had a shot at goal, rather than waiting for someone else to get into a better position. But he put the ball right in the spot and I had little to do except hit it as crisply as I could.'

At the other end of the field, Jack was having a tougher time, trying to cope with the mighty Torres, who was one of the few players who could match him in the air. But he and the defence held out until, with just eight minutes to go, Banks went to collect a cross only to be beaten to the ball by Torres, whose header would have gone into the net had Jack not handled it. Eusebio scored from the penalty spot, the first goal Banks had conceded in the tournament. But, despite a desperate barrage in the dying minutes, it remained the only goal Portugal scored. 'At the end I was in tears as I hugged our kid. We were through to the final,' said Jack

Eusebio also left Wembley in tears, tears of disappointment after being superbly marked out of the game by Nobby Stiles, whose performance prompted the normally taciturn Ramsey to lead a round of applause for him in the England dressing room. But, for the rest of Britain, Stiles' Manchester colleague Bobby Charlton was the real star. The press the next day was unstinting in its praise, suggesting that he be given a knighthood or a seat in the House of Lords. 'If Nelson's statue was not so firmly based on its foundation in Trafalgar Square, there would be a risk today that Bobby Charlton would be in his place,' was one typical over-the-top comment. Gordon Banks gives a less hysterical assessment: 'The match belongs to Bobby Charlton more than anybody. He gave the greatest performance of his life.'

In the four days before the Wembley final, the biggest controversy was over whether Jimmy Greaves would be picked. Having been injured after the France game, his place had been taken by Geoff Hurst. But he was now fit again, and for many observers it was unthinkable that he could be left out, having scored 43 goals in his 54 games for England – an international striking rate unparalleled in post-war British football. But critics could point out that he had been ineffective not only in the first three matches of the 1966 tournament but also throughout the 1962 World Cup. They could also note that the majority of his England tally had been scored against the weaker nations – 26 out of the 43 goals were against just five countries: Wales, Northern Ireland, Peru, Luxembourg and Norway. Interestingly, Bobby Charlton was not a fan of Greaves. Bobby wrote in 1973: 'Jimmy was a bit of a luxury. I always felt that he'd score five if you won 8–0 but in matches where a single goal would decide, it was better to have someone like Hurst. You never saw Jimmy much in a game, he was waiting there to score and I suppose that's why he never materialized for Alf.'

True to his instincts for loyalty, Ramsey stuck with the side that had beaten Argentina and Portugal. On the evening of 29 July 1966,

Alf gathered his players before sending them to bed and told them: 'It is going to be the biggest day of your lives and you are going to win. Goodnight gentlemen.'

By the following morning, the mood of the country was at fever pitch. The World Cup Final was to be the biggest event ever held in Britain apart from war or a coronation. Bobby caught a glimpse of this sense of excited anticipation when he and his room-mate, Ray Wilson, took a walk into Golders Green to try to take their mind off the match: 'It was then,' wrote Bobby later, 'that I realized how much the game meant to the nation. People kept wishing us good luck, quietly, almost shyly, as though not wanting to unsettle us. Then, on the way to Wembley in the team bus we passed Hendon fire station. The polished appliances were out front, proudly on parade and bells were ringing for me and my mates. I shivered; if winning the World Cup meant so much to so many people what if we lost?'

But this was only a passing feeling, for Bobby and the rest of the England team were confident of victory over Germany. They were at home, they had a good recent record against Germany, and had already beaten two of the strongest sides in the tournament. 'I don't mean to discredit them, but they'd never beaten us at that time,' said Ray Wilson, 'and especially after playing Portugal in that super match in the semi-final – we were quite relaxed about it.' In the end, though the result was just what England wanted, the final never matched the entertainment of the Portuguese game. This was because the two most dangerous midfield players on the field, Bobby Charlton and Franz Beckenbauer, had each been given instructions by their managers to mark the other. 'Beckenbauer was a new star in 1966,' explained Bobby, 'he was doing things never seen before, going at respected players and taking them to the cleaners by getting behind them with his pace and speed and accuracy. It was my job in the Final to run with him and stop him. As I found out, that's the job he'd been given. We both really cancelled each other out and didn't make any great contribution to the game. I seemed to be with him permanently. Wherever he went, I was there. I had good legs, could run for 90 minutes, so I think that's why I had been designated to look after him.' Exactly the same sort of thinking had occurred in the German camp, which saw Bobby as the biggest threat. It is a tribute to Bobby's reputation that West Germany were willing to sacrifice their finest player in order to stifle him. As Beckenbauer himself recalled, 'Before the match, Helmut Schoen, our manager and his assistant coaches, decided that I should mark Bobby Charlton. They knew that if I did, it would reduce my own strength for attacking, but they were insistent. "It is very important," Schoen said, "because you're fast enough to stay with him, to control him." Bobby at the time was the best player in the world and he also had lungs like a horse. I never remember being so exhausted as I was at the finish that afternoon. Playing the role I did on that day meant that neither of us could really enjoy the match, neutralizing each other.'

Despite their confidence, England went behind early on, when Ray Wilson made a dreadful unforced error by tamely heading a long, speculative centre, which was going out for a goal kick, straight into the path of Helmut Haller. Haller's subsequent half-volleyed shot lacked power, but, thanks to a misunderstanding between Jack and Gordon Banks, it slid into the net. 'I remember standing there,' wrote Jack, 'and I could have stopped it.' But he let it go, because 'it looked as if it was going straight to Banksy'. Unfortunately, Banks had misread Jack's mind, as he later recalled: 'I left it because I thought Jack had made up his mind to clear the ball. We finally looked on in horror as the ball went on its uninterrupted way into the net. Jack can be an argumentative bugger in a crisis, but on this occasion he shrugged his shoulders and accepted that it was just one of those things.' But almost immediately England equalized, through a Geoff Hurst header.

Then they took the lead late in the second half. Following a goal-mouth melee, Hurst hit a drive which struck the German defender, Horst Hottges, and spun up in the air. At this moment Jack Charlton felt destiny calling, as he told TV's Martin Tyler: 'It was coming straight to me. Then all of a sudden Martin Peters popped up in front of me and whacked it into the net. I didn't feel cheated.

I'm glad the bugger never came to me because I'd have kicked it over the bar or something could have gone wrong.'

Something did go very wrong for Jack in the last seconds of the game, when he was adjudged to have fouled Ziggi Held as he went up for a header. Jack was adamant that he had committed no offence and Banks agreed. 'It certainly looked to me as if Held had backed into Jack.' But a free-kick was given, about ten yards from the box, and England lined up their wall. Lothar Emmerich fired a shot into the goalmouth, the ball hit George Cohen and then was deflected on to Karl-Heinz Schnellinger, who, in Jack Charlton's opinion, handled the ball. But the Swiss referee Gottfried Dienst thought any handling was purely accidental – and subsequent replays suggest he was right. The ball then fell to Wolfgang Weber who coolly sidefooted it past Banks. England could hardly believe what had happened. 'Our kid was just standing on the goal line looking at the ball lying at the back of the net, with the tears running down his face. All he could say was fucking hell, fucking hell,' recalled Jack. Just seconds after the kick-off, Dienst blew up for full-time.

It was at this moment that Alf Ramsey proved what a great manager he was. England could easily have gone to pieces, shattered emotionally and physically by seeing their hopes of victory so cruelly dashed. Indeed, Bobby admits that 'our spirits were sinking as we changed over,' a point reinforced by Geoff Hurst. 'One or two of our team, especially the Charlton brothers, looked so sick you would have thought we had been beaten.' But, with wonderful psychology, Ramsey rallied the team. His captain, Bobby Moore revealed how he did it: 'Alf was unbelievably good. He could have come on screaming and shouting, hollering and hooting, saying, "I thought you'd know better. I thought you'd have learned after all those years as professionals." Instead he said, 'All right. You've won the World Cup once. Now go and win it again. Look at the Germans. They're flat out. Down on the grass. Having massages. They can't live with you. Not for another half-hour. Not through extra-time.'

This was the message that England needed. In the next 30

minutes, the hard grind of Lilleshall showed its worth, as Ramsey's team out-ran the Germans and Geoff scored two more goals to achieve his unique hat-trick. The first was one of the most controversial of all time – Hurst admits he cannot be certain that the ball crossed the line – but there was no doubt about the second. That last thunderous goal, which was made by a beautiful long pass from Booby Moore, dramatically highlighted the difference between Jack and his captain. While Moore took a return from Alan Ball, controlled it, calmly looked up, moved forward and then stroked it out to Hurst, Jack Charlton was screaming alongside him, 'Kill it, kick the fucking thing out of the ground!'

Moments after Hurst's exhausted, epochal strike, the final whistle sounded. England were world champions. Jack sank to his knees. 'I suddenly realized that I was knackered. I put my head in my hands. I don't think I actually said a conscious prayer. It was just relief at the end of two hours of football.' When Jack rose to his feet, Bobby was beside him. They embraced each other.

'What is there to win now?' asked Bobby

'We'll just have to win it again,' replied Jack.

As England received the trophy from the Queen, Bobby was overcome, this time with tears of joy. 'I've never cried before over a football match. But the sound of the public just got to me. It was a very emotional thing. Afterwards I thought I was a wee bit unprofessional crying but now, when I look back, I don't see any other way I could have handled myself. It was lovely, a fantastic moment.'

Ramsey showed a famously stoical face through all these celebrations. He even told the trainer Harold Shepherdson to sit down at the end. And he showed the same spirit in the dressing room, as Bobby discovered. Instead of congratulating Bobby, he criticized him for some supposedly irresponsible play. 'He really went for me, saying "What the bloody hell do you think you were doing out there? Shooting when you should have been looking round for other people. We should have had it sewn up." I'd messed up a couple of chances before Geoff Hurst clouted the goal that made us safe, and Alf was still steaming. I began to mumble something about the ball being wet, but Alf was in no mood for excuses. He never was.'

That evening, vast throngs gathered in London to cheer the England team from its hotel in Hendon to the Royal Garden Hotel in Kensington. 'The streets were packed. Every window and door seemed to have someone in it and people ran beside the coach for two miles or more, shouting and waving their flags,' wrote Bobby. There followed an official banquet, attended by the other three semi-finalists, the England players' wives and that ultra-opportunist Harold Wilson. Bobby was presented with numerous gifts, including a case of port from the Portuguese team. Much of the night was a glorious alcoholic blur, particularly for Jack Charlton, who was on his own because his wife Pat, about to give birth to Peter, was confined to their home in Leeds.

His parents had been at the banquet, 'but you don't go out with your mother and father after winning the World Cup,' as Jack put it. Instead he teamed up with his old friend, the journalist Jimmy Mossop. Hoping to evade the huge crowds, they slipped out a side window in the hotel and jumped into a taxi. To their surprise, there was already a customer in it – a professional violinist who had just finished a concert and knew nothing about football – but he made no objection to Jack and Jimmy's presence. They were dropped at a West End club called the Astor: 'The whole place was one big party,' ran Jack's account. 'I got so drunk I don't remember much about it after that, except that Jimmy and I woke up in some house in Leytonstone on the floor and the settee. The house belonged to a lad called Lenny and his wife. The next morning, I went down to the garden and a woman popped her head over the wall and said, "Hello Jackie." I could not believe it. It was one of our neighbours from Ashington, Mrs Mather. She was visiting relatives who lived next door. "How are you going, Jackie?" she asked, a little suspiciously. I think she was wondering what I was doing in a garden in Leytonstone.'

Jack's mother was more worried than suspicious when he returned to the hotel the next day at noon. She was standing in the foyer waiting for him.

'Where have you been? I have been up to your room and the bed has not been slept in.'

Jack told her there had been no need to worry. From his top pocket he produced a card which read: 'This body is to be returned to Room 508, the Royal Garden Hotel.'

Less than a month later, on 18 August, the Charlton brothers and Cissie met up again at another celebratory reception, this one held in their home town of Ashington. Once more, huge numbers gathered to see the World Cup winners, who were ferried by a Rolls Royce from the family home in Beatrice Street to Ashington Town Hall. As the *Ashington Advertiser* reported, 'Football crazy kids stormed the car carrying the Charltons to their reception, chanting all the while "England, England". About 2,000 youngsters almost swept the brothers off their feet and waved their autograph books in the air. When order was restored, the two heroes made repeated appearances from the town hall window to acknowledge the cheering thousands in the main street.'

Yet even on this happy occasion, the differences between the brothers were once more apparent. Jack had arrived with all his family – including the newborn son – at Beatrice Street in the afternoon, but there was no sign of Bobby. 'We were beginning to think we would be making the journey on our own when Bobby and Norma turned up,' recalled Cissie. Bobby's explanation – which reflects both his dislike of large groups and his sense of growing unease with his immediate family – was that he and Norma had turned up earlier, but seeing the throng in Beatrice Street, had sought refuge with one of their relatives.

Once in the Rolls Royce, according to Cissie, Jack 'made the most of that half-mile trip, perched there on the back of the rear seat. He waved and grinned all the way to the town hall.' Bobby, however, 'looked worried and distinctly uncomfortable'. This is also the memory of Clive Crickmer, the north-east journalist who was amongst the Ashington crowds that day. 'I was covering the story for the old *Sun* at the time. They went round in an open car. It was noticeable – everyone commented upon it – how Jackie was waving,

Jackie was the extrovert, eagerly pointing to mates in the crowd, and Bobby looked very tense, rather sombre, and was obviously putting on an act. And we all wondered why, saying to ourselves, "He's a cold fish, isn't he?" But it was only later we discovered he felt ill at ease in Ashington. It was noticeable how tense he was. It should have been a happy occasion but he was uncomfortable, whereas Jack was enjoying every moment.' In the town hall, Bobby made the sort of diplomatic remarks for which he later became renowned, for example: 'You have given us a wonderful reception and I only wish everyone on the streets could be here to see our presentation.' Jack, on the other hand, was all passion: 'It's good to be back in the rows of streets where boys should be brought up. I am proud to belong to the largest mining village in the world.'

Twenty years earlier, Jack had been playing in those Ashington streets alongside his brother. No-one could possibly have thought then that one day he would be a World Cup winner.

CHAPTER TWELVE

The Players

1966 was the making of Bobby Charlton. Some 400 million watched the World Cup finals, by far the largest-ever television audience at the time, and Bobby's performances ensured that he became a household name, not just in Britain but internationally. The journalist Michael Parkinson tells how, on a visit to Lapland, he was approached by a man wearing ear muffs and smelling of reindeer. 'He knew only four words of English. They were, 'Bobby Charlton, Number One.'

All the previous doubts about his vision and his effectiveness as a team player had vanished. No longer the enigmatic under-achiever, he was now one of the most revered footballers of his generation, his stature surpassed perhaps only by Pele. The great Brazilian himself once paid this tribute: 'Bobby Charlton was a master footballer. His name is respected throughout the world both for his skill and the sportsmanship he showed at all times. He was a great ambassador for England and for football.' In fact Franz Beckenbauer thought that Charlton was even greater than Pele: 'I have more admiration for Charlton than any other player, even Pele, whose shirt is pinned to the wall in my lounge at home,' he revealed in 1975. The coach of Benfica, Bela Guttman spoke for many when he said: 'Bobby Charlton is the best midfield player in Europe. If I had Charlton in my team, we would not only win the European Cup but we would also be World Champions.' His new status was confirmed by winning the titles of both British and European Footballer of the Year in 1966.

But there was, perhaps, no bigger admirer of Bobby than his own elder brother. In fact, Jack often went so far as to describe his younger brother as the greatest midfielder of all time, and would argue passionately in defence of this judgement. Many of the Irish players told me that when the subject of Bobby cropped up during long bus journeys, Jack always said that 'Our kid' was the best. It is one of Jack's many endearing qualities that, for all his distance from Bobby, he was always fiercely proud of his brother, and would tolerate no criticism of him as a player. Bob McNab, the Arsenal and England full-back who shared a room with Jack during a 1969 tour, says, 'Whether those two guys got on or not, you could not say a bad word about Bobby in front of him. Jack thought Bobby was the greatest player there has ever been. There was no way he would allow anyone to say otherwise.' In an article in the *News of the World* in 1973, Jack explained his reasoning: 'Denis Law may have had more devil in his make-up, George Best may have been cheekier with the ball, Pele was stronger and also had marvellous skills. But I've weighed all this up and I'm convinced that Bob was the finest all-rounder in the world. He could put the lot together, make goals for others and his work-rate was outstanding. On top of that, we all know of his dramatic and thrilling goals.'

True to his cautious nature, Bobby has been much less lavish in his praise of Jack. In a television interview in 1967 he said, 'I always thought our Jackie was a good player. I thought he carried Leeds for a good few years before they became the team they are now. But I didn't want to flatter him by saying that because cynics would just say, "Oh well, he's just saying that because he's his brother." But I always felt it.' Yet Bobby has occasionally been more generous. In 1984, for instance, he described Jack as 'outstanding' and 'a marvellous player for England.' Bobby also gave this insight into Jack's work at the heart of the England defence. 'Gordon Banks had a lot to thank him for. A great goalkeeper in every other respect, Gordon didn't always get cleanly to crosses. So Alf Ramsey made Jack responsible for attacking the ball when it came high into the penalty area at corners and free kicks. Few people noticed, but Jack didn't mark anyone in those circumstances. He simply went for the ball with his head.'

Mutual respect was not always in evidence when Bobby and Jack were playing against each other. 'Now don't go kicking our Robert today,' Cissie frequently used to tell Jack. Before 1964, Jack had little chance, with Leeds spending so many years in the Second Division. But even when Jack and Bobby confronted each other at the peak of their careers, Jack hardly ever found himself disobeying his mother's instructions. This was not through fraternal affection, but because Bobby was usually too fast and skilful to be clattered to the ground by Jack. As Jack put it in a 1967 interview with LWT: 'I don't particularly like playing against Bobby. I always feel that he's going to run past me, leaving me sat on my backside and looking like a right fool.' Jack was obviously still haunted by that moment in the late 1950s when Bobby nutmegged him at Elland Road.

Just before the FA Cup semi-final between Leeds and Manchester in 1970, Jack claimed to feel some brotherly feeling when he saw Bobby under attack: 'For all my apparent hardness, I hate it when somebody knocks him, as one or two are tending to do at the moment.' But Jack was not so sentimental on the field, and he certainly never showed any favours to Bobby. Bobby recalled the time when they met in another FA Cup semi-final, this one in 1965. Moving towards the Leeds goal, Bobby faced the intimidating figure of Norman Hunter. 'Then I heard a familiar Geordie voice. "Clatter the little bastard!" yelled Our Kid. I pulled out, deciding in an instant not to offer Norman the opportunity. That was typical of Jack. He isn't as hard as he tried to make out, but being his brother didn't get me any privileges.'

One line from Jack confirms this. It was once put to him that he was so professional that he would even kick his own mother to stop her scoring. 'Mother? – Never. Our Kid? – Yes.'

Apart from England duty, Bobby and Jack rarely played on the same side except in charity occasions. Ian St John remembers one such match when they did: 'I played with Bobby and Jack in Buenos Aires during the 1978 World Cup – Jack and I were working for ITV. During the tournament they had a match between the European press and the South American press. We had a very good team, including the great Raymond Kopa of France and Di Stefano, who had always been my hero. It was a packed stadium, 50,000 people. We got a free kick, and Jack came loping up the field, his legs stretching, and shouting, 'Hang on!' so he could get up at the far post for the kick, as he had done so often with Leeds and England. But Kopa had a shot and it went right over the bar. Jack shouts at me, 'Tell that bugger to wait and let me get in place next time!' So next free kick, again in a good position, Jack comes loping up, wanting the header to the back post. 'Tell him to hang on,' he said. So I said to Kopa, 'Wait till Big Jack's in position.' But Kopa immediately ran up and smacked it over the bar. Jack is going really beserk by now and I said, 'Look, I'm doing all I can. I can't do anymore.' Five minutes later, another free kick and I am physically holding Kopa back, while Jack runs up to get in his place. I am still holding Kopa away from the ball, when Bobby ran up and smashed it over the bar. I can't repeat Jack's language.'

It would be difficult to find two players who were more different than Bobby and Jack, the elegant attacker full of grace and power, and the ruthless defender, pummelling his opponents into submission. 'I'm a destroyer. I'm not called on to do fancy, classic things,' Jack once said. It is typical of the contrast in the brothers that Bobby's two greatest weaknesses, his heading and his tackling, should be Jack's two biggest strengths. Whereas Bobby could admit that he was 'useless' with his head, Jack was widely regarded as Britain's finest player in the air. Matt Busby once compared Jack's heading to that of Dixie Dean, the Everton striker who still holds the record for most league goals in a season. In a technical analysis in the *Sunday Times* in November 1968, Jimmy Adamson, the chief coach of Burnley and a former Footballer of the Year, wrote: 'In modern defensive play, Jackie's ability at heading can create panic in the opposing teams; with his feet on the ground he can send a ball up to 50 yards.' Adamson said the secrets of Jack's unique skill with his head included: 'an explosive ability to jump some 22' to 26' or more after only four steps'; his strong neck muscles; his sense of positioning which meant he was so often 'in the right place at the right time'; and 'his courage which makes him unafraid of situations involving a great deal of physical contact.' Nor was Bobby anything like as good as Jack at winning the ball. 'Bobby was not the best of tacklers. Once he got the ball he was brilliant, he could get away because of his change of pace, but in 50:50 situations where he was challenging for the ball, the other fella would usually beat him,' says former United keeper Ray Wood.

Jack's tough physical approach was seen by many as the embodiment of the worst of Leeds' aggressive footballing culture. Jack was once speaking at a dinner in Newcastle, alongside the film director Colin Welland. As Welland started his speech, he picked up a mysterious heavy object, wrapped in newspaper, and took it over to Jack. He handed this strange parcel to Jack with the words: 'There you are Jack. There's something you always wanted.'

Jack, looking puzzled, opened it up and there was a bone covered with blood and some remains of meat.

'Colin, what the hell's this?' asked Jack.

'Derek Dougan's shin bone,' joked Welland, to uproarious laughter. But that was the way much of the public thought of Jack, an image only reinforced by his notorious claim in a 1970 TV interview that he had a 'black book' in which he kept a list of his enemies.

To be fair to Jack, he was a robust player but never a dirty one. His offences, like his shirt-ripping against Denis Law, were all too obvious and usually reflected an intemperate spirit. But he was incapable of the sort of insidious, cynical challenge that characterised other members of the Revie side. Ian St John says he never had 'that nastiness, that villainous outlook', while Peter Lorimer told me that Jack 'hated the dirty players, the guys who went over the top. He would fight and compete for every ball but he never believed in tackles that could break someone's leg. He had his rules about how the game should be played.'

Yet it would be absurd to argue that he was anything like his younger brother Bobby, who was universally acknowledged to be an exemplar of good behaviour. Whereas Jack picked up a string of bookings during his career, Bobby only had two cautions – one for remonstrating with the Argentinians after they had viciously kicked his brother in the mayhem of the World Cup quarter final of 1966, the other for failing to withdraw the correct distance at a free kick in the 1967 Charity Shield Final. In December 1966, in a poll of Football League Referees, Bobby was overwhelmingly voted the game's model player. Amongst the tributes to Bobby were these: 'He always picks himself up after a tackle, dusts himself down and gets on with the game,' and 'Always the perfect gentleman. He often comes under provocation but never hits back.'

This sort of comment could never be written about Jack. For all his dislike of nasty play, he was not averse to ignoring the law. Ian Storey-Moore, once of Forest and Manchester United, says, 'He was an awkward bugger to play against, to be honest. If you got past him, then you would pretty quickly feel the tug of the shirt. I don't think he was too averse to bringing you down. I think he would have many more bookings if he had been playing today.' Jack was regularly at the centre of trouble because of his short fuse. 'I have always been terribly fond of Jack,' says Brian Glanville. 'But there is a violence within him'. Again, Storey-Moore argues that, though 'Jack was not the worst of the Leeds, team, he did have a violent temper. If someone upset him in a game, I think he would certainly make sure he left his mark on that player.' In a European Fairs Cup tie against Valencia at Elland Road in the 1965/66 season, he went so beserk that the intervention of the Yorkshire constabulary was required. Jack recalls that after one corner, he was kicked on the ankle by the Valencia left-back. 'I looked across at him. He started to run away round behind the goal. I went after him. Next thing I was surrounded by Valencia players. The full-back stood behind them, cowering for protection. I had more or less calmed down when, right from the back, their goalkeeper leaned through and punched me straight on the mouth. As I wiped the blood away, the players opened up and I could see the keeper a few yards away. I went running after him but a policeman threw himself on top of me, driving his knee into my thigh.' Not surprisingly Jack and the full-back were sent off, while the goalkeeper, terrified of the wrath of Jack, had jumped over the fence and hidden amongst the spectators. At a subsequent FA hearing the referee, Leo Horn from Holland, said that he has never seen such madness as was in Jack's eyes that night. As Peter Lorimer puts it, 'That Valencia game showed Jack's temper. The keeper had a choice, jumping into the crowd or facing Jack. He chose the crowd. I would have done the same.' Jack was subsequently fined £50 with £30 costs, a verdict referee Horn thought was far too lenient: 'I am shocked and angered. Mr Charlton is a very lucky man.'

Unlike the reticent Bobby, Jack could be almost as aggressive with his own side. 'On the pitch, he was very critical. In the dressing after a game, he would sometimes explode, throwing a cup at the wall.' 'With Jack,' says Lorimer, 'the keeper should have saved every shot. Jack would give him a bollocking after every goal, no matter how it was scored. Of course, he would never take any of the blame himself.' Jack's legendary fellow Leeds defender, Norman Hunter, told me: 'You knew when Jack was really mad. His bottom lip used to start to quiver. That's when you got out of the way. He would always have plenty to say at half-time, plenty. Nothing was ever the Big Man's fault, it was always someone else's.' Yet it was one of Jack's interesting traits that he often played better when he was riled. Sometimes, he would just want to stroll through a game, then he would take a knock from the opposition and would suddenly play with the fiery intensity that Leeds needed. 'I think that was a throwback to his younger days, when he'd tried to play football,' says Lorimer. 'There were times when he could be very casual, as if he was just trying to glide through the match. Then someone would upset him and he'd roll his sleeves up and get right into the battle. There was no-one better than him then.'

Again, in contrast to Bobby's lack of interest in strategy, Jack regularly argued with his Leeds colleagues over their approach. As he showed during his management career, Jack loathed players stroking the ball around in his own half and always felt it was much better take the shortest possible route into the opposition penalty box. But Giles preferred Jack to build attacks from the back and through midfield. 'I had row after row with Jack about this,' says Giles. 'We had different philosophies. He always saw the game through the eyes of a centre-half. He didn't believe I should come deep for the ball. He thought if we moved it out from the back, we would have a goal scored against us. He had strong views on the game and wouldn't listen to anyone else, which is fair enough.'

David Harvey the Leeds goalkeeper of the Revie era, remembers an incident which illustrated the clash between the styles of Charlton and Giles. 'We would get a free kick, well inside our half, and Gilesy would come back and take it. This would infuriate Jack. He would say, 'I could do that. Why don't you fuck off and go thirty or forty yards up the field?' On one occasion, we had one of these free kicks and John let Jack take it. Leeds lined up on the opposing 18-yard box. Jack took the free kick and whacked it straight over the crossbar and into the crowd. John was standing just ten yards away.

"That's why I bloody take them," he said.

Yet, for all their differences as players, there were also some striking parallels between Jack and Bobby. Perhaps the most obvious one was their total commitment to their side's cause, whether it be at international or club level. Of Bobby, Sir Alf Ramsey said that his 'dedication is never less than 100 per cent', while he used the term 'magnificent professional' about Jack. David Sadler, who played alongside Bobby for almost a decade at United, says he was 'outstanding on the field. He had all the attributes you look for in a player. He had great natural ability, was enormously strong, had a terrific appetite for the game and worked so hard for the team.' The Italian-born Carlo Sartori, who arrived at Old Trafford in 1963, has this recollection of Bobby: 'Before the kick-off, he would try and gee us up, "Come on lads, let's get out there." He was always trying.

Even if we came in at half-time, 2–0 down, he'd be saying, "Come on lads, we can still win this." He always believed we could turn it round. I found him inspirational that way.'

In the same vein, his Leeds colleague Norman Hunter says that Jack 'was great to play alongside. He was so passionate, so committed. He was like a policeman on patrol duty. He used to wave his arms around, saying to us, "You go here and you go there." As a defender in front of goal, there was no-one better.' David Harvey, the Leeds goalkeeper, describes Jack as a 'bit of a Godfather, a big man in every way.' Harvey tells a story which shows how encouraging – and forgiving – Jack could be with him at Leeds. At the time, Jack was increasingly frustrated by the howling errors which regular keeper Gary Sprake continually committed, the most famous of which occurred when Sprake threw the ball into his own net against Liverpool at Anfield in 1967. So Jack persuaded Revie to select Harvey. 'I remember a game, soon after I started. I was still only 19 and I was feeling nervous. I don't think the game was 10 minutes old before I came for a cross and went to punch the ball. And in doing so, I knocked Jack out. I thought to myself, "Oh for fuck's sake, what have I done? What's Jack going to say?" The trainer came on with the cold water and brought Jack round. I was a trembling teenager, terrified of Jack. Yet he just got up and said, "Oh forget it." Maybe he admired me for the commitment I showed.' As he grew used to playing with him, Harvey became a huge admirer of Jack: 'You could not put a price on what he did for Leeds. He was just fantastic for the club. It gave me tremendous confidence playing behind him. I would not want to play behind anyone else. I felt protected. When I first got in the team, he made a point of looking after me. There are things that a centre-half can do when the ball is being crossed into the box and he sees the goalkeeper coming for it. He can lean on an incoming forward, or get in the way of a striker, or, on the blind side, sort someone out. And Jack did those things. He went out of his way to help me.'

It is also interesting that in their own specialisms of shooting and heading, neither Bobby nor Jack were strictly orthodox players.

When striking the ball, for instance, Bobby would sometimes lean back, contrary to all the coaching advice about 'getting your head over the ball.' Nor was he a dribbler in the classical sense. Unlike his childhood hero, Stanley Matthews, he did not mesmerize the opposition by keeping the ball close to his feet when he embarked on a twisting run. Instead he kicked the ball in front – sometimes quite a long way in front – and then beat defenders with his sudden acceleration and deceptive swerve, a move which always brought a huge cheer from spectators.

Through his heading ability, Jack adopted a revolutionary new technique at set-pieces, which proved so successful that it soon became an integral part of the game. This was his practice of coming up into the opposition's penalty box at corner kicks and standing on the goal-line by the near-post, thereby obscuring the view of the keeper. As the ball came over, Jack would flick it on or try to score himself. Even if he did not reach it, he caused enough confusion in the box to make it impossible for the keeper and other defenders to handle such a set piece with any comfort. The strategem arose more by accident than careful design. He had been messing about with his brother Bobby and Jimmy Greaves on the England training ground in Roehampton, practising crosses. When Bobby went into goal, Jack decided to annoy him by standing immediately in front of him as Greaves hit the ball. 'What are you doing? Get out of the way,' said a perplexed Bobby. Almost every time the cross came in, Jack was able to block Bobby and head the ball past him. Immediately he knew he was on to something, so he tried the trick again in training at Leeds. Without telling keeper Gary Sprake what he was up to, he got Peter Lorimer and Eddie Gray to curl in balls at the near post. Jack recalls. 'I was backing into Sprakey as the ball came in. And he couldn't handle it. He finished up on top of me, starting a fight in the middle of a training session.'

Leeds then started to use the tactic in competitive matches, and it caused just as much trouble for other goalkeepers. 'It was Jack's height and ability to spring that made it possible,' says Norman Hunter. 'Other clubs just did not know what was coming because it had never happened before. The number of goals, especially in European games, was incredible. Continental sides just could not cope.' The move provoked a huge controversy in the football world. There were accusations of cheating, of unfair conduct. While media pundits questioned the legitimacy of Jack's action, managers desperately tried to think of a way to counter this dangerous new weapon. Some said Jack should be surrounded, others that he should be left completely alone. Joe Mercer, the manager of Manchester City who lost an FA Cup tie against Leeds in 1968 due to a Jack Charlton corner, spoke of his mixture of appreciation and frustration over the move: 'I'll admit to admiring it, although often with clenched teeth. What I do know is that it's fiendishly clever. But they said that about the Great Train Robbery.'

The Blackpool and England keeper Tony Waiters had the unfortunate experience of punching the ball into his own net as a result of a Charlton corner. He told me of the problems that Jack generated in the goalmouth: 'Big Jack had that long neck of his so he stood out like a beacon and to an extent, he acted like a target for the crosser. But he was also very good at dealing with the ball that came in, making exactly the right judgement as to whether to head for goal or whether to glance it on to the far post. At Blackpool, we were not sure how to counter it. We brought back our centre-forward Ray Charmley to mark him. The ball was played in. I tried to get it. And I was impeded, not just by Jack but also by Ray. The ball spliced off my fist into the back of the net. We talked a lot about this and we decided that really it did not do a lot of good to bring someone back to defend against Jack because he was so effective there. The best bet was to leave him for me, the goalkeeper. It wasn't the perfect solution because Leeds were so good on the inswinging corners.' Harry Gregg, Manchester United's keeper, told me he had always adopted this approach with Jack: 'Goalkeepers were inclined to be drawn to him like metal to a magnet, instead of moving away from him. And when they were drawn to him they pulled their own defenders around him, which didn't make any sense to me because it meant that they were fighting Jack and their own players. My attitude was to leave him be, while I remained two or three yards from the back post. Jackie and I had a few tangles over the years, I think he got a thump from me one time, which left a bit of a bend in his nose. That was all part of the game in those days. There was no screaming and shouting about it. Jack didn't personally cause me any concern. He wasn't a hard man. But if you allowed Jack to be a bully, he would be a bully.'

Thanks to his eagerness to go into the box at set-pieces, Jack built up an impressive goal tally over his career. In all competitive games, from 1952/53 to 1972/73, he scored 102 goals, a total of which any midfielder might be proud. Indeed, he found the net more often for England than Andy Cole. For Leeds, he hit no less than 71 goals in the league. It an interesting fact that this is much more than the combined total of league goals from all his England defensive colleagues of 1966: Moore, Stiles, Wilson and Cohen. But as Peter Lorimer remembers, he was never effusive in his thanks to Leeds colleagues who helped him score. 'You would bend it right under the bar and he would just nudge it in. Then he would turn round and run back as if it was all his own work. He would never acknowledge that someone else had helped make the goal. He thought it was all down to him. That was how he was. He did not give out praise.'

Despite their growing stature as international players in the late 1960s, similar complaints were still made about Jack and Bobby's lack of footballing intelligence. Bobby himself admitted: 'A tendency to select the wrong option – long passes when shorter ones were more profitable and certainly safer – remained a flaw throughout my career.' When Alex Stepney joined United as goalkeeper in 1966, he was surprised to be warned not to throw the ball to Bobby outside the penalty area because he could be a liability in defensive positions. 'That advice held good until Bobby retired,' says Stepney, 'He could never resist the urge to push it past an opponent and run after it. It was a dangerous way of playing and sometimes put us in trouble.' Even at international level, the same charge was made against him by Ramsey: 'Bobby was never a very good reader of the game and could be prone to lapses of concentration. He was instinctively attracted to the ball and often had no other thought but to get as near as possible to it all the time. That could make it difficult for others around him.' Almost exactly the same assessment is made of Jack by Peter Lorimer. 'Jack's biggest weakness was that his mental concentration in matches would occasionally let him down. He would piss off, take it into his head that he had to score, even with an hour still to go. Or he would go off on one of those long, bloody runs of his, thinking he could go past five men. Then he would lose the ball and everyone was chasing back. He could be totally undisciplined and thoughtless that way.'

One more positive virtue which Jack and Bobby shared was their courage on the field. Jack was a famously brave player, never shirking his responsibilities or worrying about injury. That spirit was graphically demonstrated in the England v Scotland game at Wembley in April 1967, when a first-half tackle by Willie Johnston broke two bones in his foot. Yet, he emerged again after the interval to play up front and actually scored for England, poking home an Alan Ball pass in the home side 3–2 defeat. But nor was Bobby was a cowardly player. He could not have survived almost 20 years in professional football if he had been. According to the testimony of Nobby Stiles, who knew a few things about tackling, 'Bobby is not a 'jumper when it came to tackles and never flinches one. Yet he seems to glide away from attempted kicks that I have never been able to avoid.' Alan Gowling, another United colleague, gave me this explanation of how Bobby avoided tackles: 'Being a youngster at that stage, I faced the big centre-halves who wanted to make a point. I got a number of badly damaged ankle ligaments because I kept my feet on the ground in my attempts to get past people. But by watching Bobby, I learnt that if you can read the tackle and get your feet off the deck then you are less likely to get a serious injury. Naturally, when you keep your feet on the ground when you get hit, there's some resistance in your feet and joints.'

Moreover, Bobby had a streak of real moral courage in the way he was always gave his best and never tried to hide. This is what Harry Gregg admired most about him. 'There are people who, if the opposition is up their arse, won't accept the ball because they don't want to make a mistake. Bobby Charlton was never like that. He would take the ball anywhere, no matter what pressure he was under. And that's extremely important at the top level.' Ian St John agrees. 'But he was a brave player, a really brave one, because he always wanted the ball. He wasn't one of those who went hiding when the going got tough. People were coming at him from all angles, but he could ride their tackles, like Maradona.'

In another tribute to Bobby's courage, John Aston, who was one of the heroes of the 1968 European campaign, gave me this memory of Bobby: 'He was brave in the sense that he had faith in his own ability. I remember a match on a heavy pitch against Spurs, when about three of his shots had ended up in the stands. Then he got the ball again, far outside the area. Now most players, being human, would have played the percentage game and passed it on. Not Bobby. He had a pop from 35 yards and scored. I will never forget it. You get dozens of players who could shoot from that distance on the training pitch. But the big difference comes when you have to do it in front of 60,000 people. All your senses are heightened and you have that extra adrenalin rush. It takes real courage then to have a shot.'

Thanks partly to the influence of Jack, Leeds enjoyed an excellent return to the First Division after winning promotion in 1963/64. In their first season back in the top flight, they reached the FA Cup Final, losing to Liverpool 2–1 after extra-time, and finished runners-up in the League after an enthralling battle with Bobby's Manchester United. In the very last game of the season, Leeds needed to win at Birmingham to secure the title but could only manage a draw. Jack Charlton later admitted that his team had 'choked under pressure'. They were runners-up again the following season and beaten finalists in the European Fairs Cup of 1966/67. But for all such consolidation, Leeds' greatest period under Revie occurred after 1968.

In contrast, Bobby's golden spell with Manchester United was in the mid-1960s. The years after Munich had been a time of faction and failure for the club, but the FA Cup win in 1963 showed that

Busby's long process of rebuilding was finally achieving results. The improvement continued the following year, when United reached the FA Cup semi-finals and finished second in the league. At the peak of his form, Denis Law hit an astonishing total of 46 goals in the season and won the title of European Footballer of the Year. Law says that the shooting of Bobby – along with that of fellow striker David Herd – was vital to his success: 'Bobby and David were two tremendous strikers of the ball and whenever I saw either of them shaping up to shoot I would try to get in close to the keeper – because I reckoned that even if he got a hand to the ball, he probably wouldn't be able to hold on to it. I scored a good many goals for United in that way, picking up the rebounds.'

The next four seasons from 1964 were to be the finest in the club's history until the arrival of Sir Alex Ferguson, as United won two league titles and the biggest prize of all the European Cup. Just as had happened in the era of the Babes, United's success was built, not on defensive systems or work-rate, but on the right blend of skilful players given the freedom to attack. As Eamon Dunphy wrote of these four years: 'Football for Matt Busby was about the spirit. At its most glorious, football transcended the ordinary, the material. There was no formula, just people expressing themselves through this tantalisingly simple medium.' It was a style that made Busby's side exhilarating to watch when they were in their most creative, adventurous moods. It also made the forward line of Best-Law-Charlton part of footballing legend. At their peak, they were the three musketeers of British soccer, destroying opponents through their daring inter-play and rapier strikes.

Nothing better exemplified the United approach than the scintillating performance in the 1965/66 European quarter final against Benfica, whose stars were Eusebio and Torres, later to become familiar to British crowds as members of the Portugese World Cup side. United won the pulsating home leg 3–2, inspiring Geoffrey Green of the *Times* to write: 'Here was a match played at sizzling speed, full of creation and movement. For Manchester, Charlton was world class, the equal of Eusebio.' The 1–0 advantage was not expected to be enough for the away leg, especially after United's last woeful European game in Lisbon. But, in a ravishing demolition of Benfica, United won 5–1 in the Stadium of Light. Bobby hit the fifth goal but it was George Best who was the star, scoring two electrifying goals in the first half. Best himself says he was touched by genius that evening, and it was after this game he was christened 'El Beatle.' Sadly United were unable to sustain this form and crashed out to the more workmanlike Partizan Belgrade in the semi-final.

A harmonious dressing-room is not always a pre-requisite of success, as the late nineties spat between Andy Cole and Teddy Sheringham at Old Trafford proves. And the same was true of United in the mid-sixties, for there was always a degree of friction between Bobby, Best and Law. Bobby's relationship with George Best deteriorated so badly after 1968 that they would not even pass the ball to each other, but, even in the mid-sixties, they were, in George's phrase, 'never the biggest of mates, on-or-off the field.' As Best recorded in the third and most recent version of his autobiography, 'I think he thought I was a little greedy so-and-so who wouldn't give him the ball, but then I thought he was a bit of a glory hunter as well, looking for the chance to unleash one of those long range shots rather than giving the ball to me. He was always a bit dour, as well, and a real moaner on the pitch.' George is right about the way Bobby felt about his play in this mid-1960s period. 'He would drive you mad on the pitch, never pass, but you'd put up with him while he was scoring, doing the work. George did it all naturally, by instinct, without ever thinking about it. but he didn't, like the great players, like Duncan Edwards, make others play, pulling the strings all over the pitch.'

The distance between George and Bobby initially resulted, not from active mutual dislike, but from the age gap and different lifestyles. 'Bobby was married and didn't mix socially,' George has said, 'After matches, I'd be out and about while he went straight home to his wife and if we were training at the Cliff he'd finish, hurry off to his car and that was it.' Bobby himself agreed with this analysis: 'We had little in common beyond the colours of

Manchester United. Seven year's George's senior, I had settled down to a married life when he began to assume the image of a pop star. It was all there: the Beatle haircut, the trendy gear, the white Jaguar saloon, the braceleted entourage of hangers-on who persuaded him that conformity was for kicking into touch.' But the pair were perfectly civil. Sometimes, if the United players had been training at Old Trafford rather than the Cliff, George would sit in the tea-room chatting happily for ages with Bobby, Shay Brennan, Denis Law, Alex Stepney and Nobby Stiles. And once, after a game in Cardiff, Bobby took George home and, with Norma away, even cooked him a meal.

Similarly, Denis Law and Bobby were not close. Denis, a much wittier man than Bobby, found him unapproachable and too much of an establishment figure, nicknaming 'Sir Robert' long before Bobby had received his knighthood. For his part, Bobby thought Denis was a show-off – 'I would not understand the fuss he made about scoring, the hugging and the kissing.' He also disliked what he termed Denis's trouble-making side. 'You got the feeling sometimes that he wanted to create havoc, that he liked to cause a commotion. He talks common sense, but when he gets onto the field, something comes over him and he can be violent,' said Bobby in 1973. Bobby's relationship with Pat Crerand was equally difficult. Crerand, like some other United players did not rate Bobby and has often sneered about Bobby's reticence, saying that Bobby used to go into the bathroom and smile at the mirror, just to get it over with for the rest of the day. Meanwhile, Bobby saw Pat as sarcastic and opinionated. The football writer Ken James, who knew United well, says: 'Pat had a hard Scottish wit. And he terrified most of his team. If anyone shirked a tackle, they would turn round and see Pat's angry face and clenched fist. Then there would be the fearful bollocking to follow in the dressing room.' But the sense of resentment from Law and Crerand may have worked on a much deeper level than merely that of a personality clash, since both of the Scots had a fervent loathing for England. Denis Law refused to watch the World Cup Final, preferring to play golf, and once described

England's victory as 'the blackest day of my life.' Paddy Crerand, according to George Best, was 'about as anti-English a Scot as you could wish to meet.' Because of his Irish roots, Crerand's brand of Anglophobia was further inflamed by his attachment to the cause of hardline republicanism. 'Basically he was a provo,' one ex-United player told me, and Noel Cantwell says that Crerand would rather have played for Ireland than Scotland. After 1966, Bobby's embodiment of England's supremacy made him an obvious target of their anti-English envy and prejudice.

But not all of Bobby's relationships in the team were so awkward. He was particular friends with Nobby Stiles and Shay Brennan and could relax in their company over a meal or a game of cards. Before he died in June 2001, Shay said of Bobby: 'He was serious about the game and always gave 101 per cent. He was such an honest player. I remember, after the maximum wage was abolished, that Bobby was paid five pounds more than me. Five pounds? He should have been on three times as much.' Bobby's sense of loyalty to Shay – which contradicts the idea of Bobby being selfishly introspective – was shown in 1986 when Shay had been through a triple heart by-pass and was concerned about his financial future. Without any fuss, Bobby, now a director of United, organised a benefit match for him in Dublin against Shamrock Rovers. As John Giles says, 'I know people say Bobby can be hard work but his benefit for Shay shows the fundamental decency in Bobby. Though they were great pals, Shay was scared stiff about approaching Bobby. But there was no problem at all. He treated Shay with great respect, made him very comfortable about it, organised everything.'

Like Bobby's England room-mate Ray Wilson and Bobby himself, Nobby Stiles was not a great socialiser and disliked invasions of privacy. Of Bobby he once said, 'He is as genuine a guy as you'll ever meet. Bobby and Shay Brennan were the two who went out of their way to welcome me when I first moved up to the first team. He has always been very shy, a trait that is often mistaken for aloofness. His modesty is quite ridiculous.' Such warmth seemed to have rubbed off on Nobby. Francis Burns told me that he, Shay and

Bobby were the three most welcoming senior professionals when he joined the club in 1964: 'I remember being on my first trip away with United. We were actually in Hawaii and I was walking along the promenade when those three summoned me over for a drink. That's what they were like, very normal guys from working-class backgrounds, even though they were superstars. Once I got in the team, Bobby was wonderful to play with. Yes, he was a moaner on the pitch. There was no one worse for shouting and bitching and all the rest of it, but it wasn't personal, it was just his way of expressing his frustrations and trying to gee up the team. He was always nervous before a big game, but would use the pressure in the right way. I remember on Friday mornings, you could often see him sitting on his own in the stand at a deserted Old Trafford, smoking a fag and gazing out on the pitch. He was visualising the match the next day, focusing on the moves he would be making. I thought that was fantastic.'

This kind of view is supported by many other United players of the era, like David Sadler, the versatile all-rounder who came to the club in 1962. 'When I joined, Bobby was one of the quieter ones. He didn't do anything to put me off but nor was he overly en-couraging. I'd been at Old Trafford a few years before I felt he had accepted me. But, as I progressed, that changed and we became closer. When we were on tour, he was happy to be part of our group. He had a terrific sense of humour. He would play cards on the bus. He would go in for all the mickey-taking, the laughs that were part of footballing life. That is not something that is immediately obvious to outsiders. You really need to get to know him to see that. He is a very warm, funny guy, great fun to be with, but that side has not always come out because he is such a private person. Bobby is respected but not loved. Yet if people knew him like I do, then they would really like him much more.'

John Aston also tells an intriguing story which he believes sums up Bobby's essential decency. 'We were playing a pre-season friendly in a remote part of Austria. I was rooming with Bobby and we got on very well. One morning he came in and said, "Look what I've got, an English newspaper. He sat down to read it. Suddenly he started muttering, 'It's disgraceful. Ridiculous. Shouldn't be happening."

"What's the matter, Bob?" I asked.

'He explained that Lev Yashin, the great Russian goalkeeper, was having his testimonial in Moscow and two players and an FA official had all backed out at the last minute. He thought this was wrong. He went out of the room, went to see the Busby, came back, packed. Then he hired a car, drove from our resort, in the back of beyond, to Vienna, caught a Russian plane to Moscow, played in his testimonial, and came back the next day. When I next saw him I said, "You must be knackered, Bobby."

"John, I've never been so embarrassed in my life."

"Why?"

"Because there were people from all over the world, giving him presents, and I was on the only one who didn't have anything." Bobby didn't realize that he had given him the best present of all by turning up. It just shows what a gentleman he was.'

The compassionate side of Bobby was also revealed by his work with the Professional Footballers Association in the sixties, as Nobby Lawton, who served on a PFA committee with him, recalls. 'We used to meet in the Midland Hotel in Manchester. Terry Venables and Maurice Setters were on the committee as well. We had meetings every month Bobby was very good at them. I know public speaking did not come naturally to him, but he was fine then because he was with guys who knew him. So he felt free from the usual pressures of a public performance. He gave good advice, he was interesting to listen to. We used to have a lot of letters from ex-professionals, sometimes big names, who had fallen on bad times and we tried to help them. Bobby was always concerned about their welfare. I found him very sympathetic at those meetings, though it was a sad way to learn the hard facts about professional football.'

Bobby's morose image is further contradicted by the way several of the younger United professionals reacted to him. Frank Kopel says, 'He was a huge star when I joined in 1966 but he was still a very modest man. It was never a problem to speak to him. There were no airs or graces or anything like that. He was a genuine, down-to-earth person. On the training ground, he was just like a little schoolboy really. He was happy to play in a five-a-side, whether it be the first team or the thirds, so long as he was running about, kicking a ball.' Wilf Tranter, who came to the club as an eighteen year old in 1963, told me: 'The player we detested was Bill Foulkes. He was really old school, hard with everybody. In a five-a-side, he'd whack you. He didn't give a shit. But Bobby was very approachable. He was fabulous really. He remembered what it was like to be a young player. He would give lifts to us, take us to matches. Even though he was a superstar, he was shy, which could make him seem slightly furtive. But once he was relaxed with you, he was fine. He had a dry sense of humour – in fact it bordered on being so dry that you might not think he had one. For me, Bobby is United's greatest ever player. He did astounding things on the pitch. He did what Ryan Giggs does so well today, taking the ball from box to box. Most of his goals are remembered as long distance shots, but I watched him score in 1965 against Aston Villa, when he took the ball from David Herd, went round four people and put it in the net. There was such astonishment at this goal that a silence went round the ground before the spectators broke out in applause.'

Bobby was never more inspirational or emotional than on the night of the 29 May 1968, when he led United to victory over Benfica at Wembley in the European Cup Final. It was the most romantic night in the club's history, when the dream of the ultimate football prize in Europe, the dream which had gripped the club through trial and tragedy, finally became a reality. Exactly ten years earlier, in the quest for that title, the cream of United's talent had been scythed down in Munich. Every subsequent campaign was touched by the shadows of that crash; the desire to win, to vindicate the dead, became more intense with every failure. The Wembley victory was therefore not just a triumphant memorial to the fallen; it was almost like a moment of exorcism for the club. Busby himself said: 'The moment when Bobby took the Cup, it cleansed me. It eased the pain of the guilt of going into Europe. It was my justification.'

Bobby's sense of personal fulfilment was almost as strong as Busby's. It was not just that he was one of the survivors of Munich, but also that he had a strong devotion to both his club and the city of Manchester. Since arriving there as a fifteen-year-old, he had developed a powerful feeling of identity with his adopted home. Just as the greatest patriots often those who are attached to a nation by choice rather than birth – Napoleon was, after all a Corsican, and De Valera an American – so Bobby Charlton was more proud of Manchester than many Manucunians. He had fallen for the city during the golden years of 'paradise' with the Babes at Mrs Watson's, and had remained loyal ever since. This sense of belonging was, of course, bound up with his love of United, a love so deep that he would never consider moving to another club. Busby once said, 'When Bobby was twenty, I could have sold him to any one of three of four Italian clubs. Considering the extraordinary money he could have made in Italy, the opportunity had to be offered. His reply was always, "I am a Manchester United player. I don't want to play for any other club." He was such a club man that I find it hard to believe there will ever be better.' Tony Dunne, the Irish full-back who played in that 1968 campaign, reinforces this point: 'I always thought Bobby felt Manchester United more than anybody. He felt it if the crowds weren't up because the club might be losing money. He would get frustrated because he always wanted to win. He wanted the club to rise, and I think that stemmed from the crash.'

There is a wonderful symmetry about the milestones of Bobby's career: the European Cup final taking place exactly a decade after Munich; the two crucial games against Portuguese opponents in 1966 and 1968; Nobby Stiles twice fighting his epic duel with Eusebio; Bobby scoring twice in each game against the Portuguese; both the World and European finals being held at Wembley; both matches going to extra time; and in both of them, Charlton's team winning after scoring four goals. Given these parallels, it is often claimed that there was an air of destiny about United's march on the European title in 1968. Indeed, some of the United players had that feeling. 'As we progressed through the rounds, getting through some really tough away games, I began to feel that fate was taking a hand,' says David Sadler.

But this looked far from the case during the semi-final against their old adversaries Real Madrid. With only a 1–0 home advantage from the first leg, United were 3–1 down at half-time in front of a crowd of 120,000 at the Bernabeau stadium. A feeling of despondency hung over the United players as they trudged into their dressing room. Legend has it that this is the moment when Busby showed his true greatness as a manager, inspiring his players to lift their game with his half-time talk. Busby went along with this version, saying that 'I reminded the players that the aggregate score was only 3–2 and we were in fact only a goal down. I told them they should simply go out and play.' But Bobby Charlton's account is very different: 'I'll always remember going in at half-time and the old man was speechless. I've never known him speechless before, even Jimmy said nothing. We were gutted. Hardly anybody said anything. I remember thinking there must be something, someone must talk but no-one did. We were waiting for the Boss or Jimmy but they were down. Then someone said, "We only need one goal to get a replay in Lisbon." Someone else said, "Let's have a go." That was all.'

Yet even without any rhetoric from Busby, the side he had built showed the guts, the will to stage a daring fightback One trick Busby did pull off was to ask David Sadler to shift out of his defensive role and push forward. The move worked and in the seventieth minute Sadler scored with a header from a Crerand free kick. Then five minutes later, Bill Foulkes, who rarely ventured beyond the half-way line, was seized by some primal urge, charged up the field and hit home a George Best pass from the right wing. Thanks to Foulkes's eccentric run, United were now the first English team to reach the European Cup Final. Nobby Stiles recalls Bobby's mood afterwards: 'We were singing in the showers with our kit still on. Bobby laughed and cried. I don't think he knew what day it was, or cared, he was so pent up.' Later the players went out to celebrate but Bobby could not join them. He felt too ill, too drained. In the dressing room, he had taken a couple of beers and then started to shake. Lying down in his hotel was all he could manage.

After this victory, Bobby thought there was no way United could lose to Benfica: 'I can remember thinking that we had come too far and been through too much for us to fail in that final match. We had everything going for us, of course, playing on our own patch at Wembley. We also had a good record against teams from Portugal, and after coming from 3–2 down in Madrid I thought it would be impossible for us to get beaten.'

In the absence of Denis Law, who was in hospital having a knee operation, Bobby was captain for the match. According to Tony Dunne, 'Bobby was nervous and if he could be nervous it was no problem for me to be nervous.' The weather was almost as draining as the mental pressure, for it was an unusually hot, humid night at Wembley. After the excitement of the previous tie, United were anxious and sluggish in the first half, missing a series of chances. Then, early in the second half, Bobby broke the deadlock. What made his goal so improbable was not just that he scored with a header, but also that he did not intend to find the net. 'I actually went for a decoy run. Then David Sadler just knocked it in and I was only trying to flick the ball on but it went right into the bottom corner. Lovely.' Dave Sadler says, 'I know that it didn't happen too often but Bobby could actually be quite a good header of a ball. That night was very emotional, we were feeling the pressure, but Bobby's great goal set us on our way.' Benfica equalised, however, and the score was still 1–1 in the final minute of normal time when Eusebio burst through with only Stepney to beat. But the young keeper made a brilliant save at close range, and, just as England had done against Germany, United dominated extra-time, scoring three more times, with Bobby getting the last.

At the final whistle, amidst wild jubilation on the terraces, Bobby ran over to his manager. They hugged each silently, tears flowing down their cheeks. 'I didn't say anything to the old man because I didn't need to. I knew exactly what he was thinking and feeling. It was a big thing for the club but a bigger thing for him personally.

It was all very, very emotional,' said Bobby in the *Daily Telegraph* recently. 'How did I feel to be handed the trophy after ten years? It felt bloody heavy. I was so dehydrated I handed it on to someone else as quickly as possible.'

In fact once he reached the dressing room, the combination of exhaustion, dehydration and relief made Bobby feel even more ill than he had done in the semi-final against Real. He was not the only one. Pat Crerand, who had also run his heart out, was 'sick as a dog' – to use Bobby's phrase. So, to get some fresh air, he staggered out with Bobby across the track at Wembley and sat in one of the main stands. 'The stadium was empty, silent,' wrote Crerand later. 'And even in my awful state I remember thinking how hard it was to believe that more than 100,000 people had been there little more than half an hour before. I vaguely remember being sick again.' He and Bobby had still not recovered by the time they reached the Russell Hotel in Central London. Retiring to their rooms, they were forced to miss the celebratory reception and banquet. Bobby recalls: 'I'd consumed gallons of water immediately after the game and every time I tried to make it to the bedroom door, I fainted. It was a great pity because all the Munich survivors, plus the parents of the lads who died in the crash were all there. I desperately wanted to join them, but whenever I dragged myself out of bed, I fainted.' But it was the memory of Munich that was contributing to his collapse. As his wife Norma, who had to go to the reception on her own, explained at the time: 'He couldn't take it, with complete strangers coming up and slapping him on the back and telling him what a wonderful night it is. He's remembering the lads who cannot be here tonight.'

Downstairs that night, Matt Busby sang *It's a Wonderful World*. But the light was fading fast. The European Cup was to be his last trophy.

CHAPTER THIRTEEN

The Rivals

It was no secret in the football world that the two brothers were not close, even before the spectacular rift that surfaced on the death of their mother. The diplomatic Bobby once admitted that 'apart from a facial resemblance, we haven't much in common'. Ian Storey-Moore, who went on a football trip to South Africa with the two in 1980, says, 'It was interesting to see on that trip that Bobby and Jack just didn't mix. If we went out for a drink, invariably Bobby and Jack were not together. Most brothers have at least some characteristics in common, but not them.' Jack's colleague at Leeds, Peter Lorimer, has a similar memory. 'I remember once we were in Dublin airport, waiting for a flight after a pre-season friendly. Jack was there reading his paper. By coincidence, Manchester United were there as well and I saw Bobby at the duty free. I went back to Jack and said, "Jack, your Bob's over there." He just said, "Oh is he?" and then carried on reading his paper, as if it was of no interest to him. You would think you would want to go and say hello to your own brother. It was as if Jack was saying to himself, "Well, what am I going to talk to him about?"' Lorimer also went on a world cruise with a Bobby Charlton XI and was amazed at the difference between Bobby and Jack. 'Jack loves controversy, having a real debate. He would say that black was white, just for the sake of an argument.

There is an aura about him. But on that trip with Bobby, sometimes you thought that he was ignoring you. I think it was just shyness. There was a pretty wild group, including myself and Alan Ball, but Bobby would very rarely sit down with us. He was pleasant enough but he would not join in.' Though Jack always maintains that he was not jealous of Bobby, sometimes he could not disguise his resentment at all the attention focused on his younger brother. On one occasion in 1967, after a Leeds game against Manchester United, he was having a pint in the players' lounge at Elland Road when he was approached by Sam Leitch, the well-known journalist with the *Sunday Mirror* and BBC TV.

'Hello, Jack.'

'Hello, Sam.'

'How's your Bobby?'

At this question, Jack slammed his pint down on the table. 'Do you know what really gets me about you, Sam? Every time you see me, you always ask how our kid is. That's fine. But not once do you ever ask me how I am. I'm always seeing you after matches and it's always, Bobby, Bobby, Bobby with you. I'm an individual in my own right, you know, not just Bobby Charlton's brother. Ask me how I am for a change.' Taken aback by this outburst, Leitch apologised. 'I'm sorry, Jack. I never realised you felt that way. Thinking about it, you're absolutely right. It never occurred to me I was being tactless when we met.'

'Oh, it's all right, forget it,' said Jack.

'No, I've been thoughtless. How are you Jack?' continued Leitch. 'I'm fine.'

There followed an awkward silence as neither could think of anything to say. Eventually, Leitch put down his drink and turned to Jack. 'So how's your Bobby keeping?'

Ron Atkinson, who went through a bitter fallout with Bobby when he was sacked as Manchester United manager in 1986, recalled this incident when he was working as a TV analyst during the 1992 European Championships. He was up in the gantry with several great names, including Franz Beckenbauer, and Michel

Platini, as well as Bobby and Jack. 'At no time, even though they were merely feet apart, did the Charlton brothers even acknowledge or look at each other. I found it all a bit bizarre, so later I quizzed my favourite Charlton about the family silence. "Don't worry," Jack informed me, "we just don't get on. Our kid was a much better player than me, but I am a much better bloke."'

Stan Cummins, the former Middlesbrough striker whom Jack famously labelled in 1976 as potentially Britain's first million pound player, drew this analogy with the TV comedy *The Odd Couple*: 'I played with Bobby when I was 17, in a testimonial for John Hickton. It was amazing, as an amateur, asking the great Bobby Charlton to pass the ball to me. Bobby was a very nice man, a gentleman. I was so in awe at first I said, "Pass the ball, Mr Charlton." But he just said, "It's Bobby." He was totally different to Jack. Bobby was gracious, polite. Jack was blunt. He didn't care what people thought of him. They reminded me of *The Odd Couple* in that US TV series, played by Jack Klugman and Tony Randall. That is exactly how I picture them now.'

Even at the peak of their careers, the contrast between Bobby and Jack can be seen in so many other aspects of their lives, on and off the field. It existed, for example, in something as basic as their routine before a match. Jack was highly superstitious, whereas Bobby was not. Bobby did follow a set, orderly procedure, in which he usually started by having a rubdown on his legs and finished by taking a sniff of ammonia or a gulp of whisky. But there was nothing obsessive about his approach, unlike that of Jack. Brought up in the paranoid world of Revie's Leeds, where superstition was woven into the club's fabric – Revie once even brought a medium to the ground – Jack believed that he had to be the last out of the tunnel and he even gave up the Leeds captaincy because it required his going out first. There were other features of his pre-match ritual. He would always go and sit on the toilet, with a programme. Then he would leave the programme on the floor next to the toilet. If he was playing at home, he put it on the left-hand side of the seat, if away on the right. Then he put his boots on, left one first. The last thing he would do before leaving the dressing room was to put some Vick up his nose to clear his channels. In all, Jack admits, it took him nearly an hour to get changed. Once out on the field, according to Billy Bremner, 'Jack always has to score a goal during our kicking-in sessions before the match begins. So when Big Jack takes a swipe at the ball and it looks like going remotely near, Gary Sprake makes no attempt to save.'

Interestingly, Jack has said that he needed to follow this routine in order to get himself into the right mood for a big game. 'I find it very hard to build myself into a state of nervous tension. I try to do this artificially with a whole rigmarole of superstitions.' Bobby never needed anything like that because he was already nervous. In contrast to his usual behaviour, Jack would be very quiet and still before a game. Bobby was the opposite. Before the kick-off, according to Alex Stepney, 'He was the most nervous man in the dressing room, a non-stop chatterer. "Come on now, we can win this one," he would say repeatedly.' Even when he was player-manager at Preston, Bobby was the same. 'What really surprised me about Bobby,' says the ex-Preston keeper Roy Tunks, 'was how nervous he always got before games. I couldn't believe it. Here was the great Bobby Charlton still on edge after all he had done.' His United manager, Sir Matt Busby, once highlighted the anxiety that lay at the heart of Bobby's character: 'Bobby is a man who worries about his game, worries more than he should. There's nothing you can do to stop that. It's just his nature.'

Again, another graphic difference lay in their ease with public performances, which had become part of the life of an international soccer star. Jack Charlton had never been afraid of speaking his mind, whether it be in the Leeds dressing room or Hirst Park Primary School. The Sheffield journalist Pat Roberts once gave this vivid description of Jack's mode of speech: 'He talks fast, furiously and at a pitch which suggests that somewhere within his formidable frame is a built-in audio system – with speakers in every room.' So when Jack succeeded his brother in 1967 by winning the title of British Footballer of the Year, instead of mumbling a few words of thanks at the awards dinner as most of his predecessors had done, Jack gave a barnstorming performance, full of anecdotes and delivered with an assurance which a professional toastmaster might envy. Sam Leitch wrote in the *Sunday Mirror* on 21 May 1967: 'Big Jackie wowed more that 500 people at the annual Footballer of the Year banquet under the Café Royal's chandeliers. He made the most impressively honest and natural speech I have ever heard from a sportsman. The hardest, possibly toughest audience in soccer rose on their feet to give the man, who used to be known as Bobby Charlton's elder brother, a fantastic ovation. The Minister of Sport, Denis Howell, said he would have Jackie in the Commons any day. Footballers normally make lousy speeches. But Jackie could not put a word wrong.'

Jack's first public speech was such a success that that he started a whole new career as one of the finest after-dinner speakers in the country. His method is based, not on a string of polished jokes or witty one-liners, but on his ability to speak about his life in football in such a compelling, humorous and passionate manner that he can hold an audience spellbound for more than an hour. Jack's famous idiosyncrasies – his mispronunciations, his forgetfulness with names, his coruscating lack of diplomacy – only add to his appeal. Barry Fry, himself one of the great characters of football, says: 'When he stands up after dinner, he is just one of the lads and that's why everyone loves him. They can all relate to him, no matter how much money he has got. He is just Jack the lad. He doesn't tell jokes, he tells stories. He tells them in such a way that he has the audience in stitches because half the time he has to wait 10 minutes while he tries to remember the name of the fucking geezer he is talking about.'

Far more famous than Jack in the early 1960s, Bobby was occasionally asked to attend functions, but because of his almost chronic shyness, he hated the experience. It was his Manchester United captain Noel Cantwell who first persuaded him to take to the public stage in 1962. Cantwell had been invited to give a talk at a club in Altrincham and asked Bobby to join him. At first Bobby refused, saying 'Oh no, I can't do that sort of thing.' But Cantwell explained it was only a question and answer forum, so he would not have to give a speech. Rather reluctantly, Bobby agreed, but on the drive to the club he said: 'Honestly, Noel, I'm petrified. I would give £100 to get out of doing this.' Cantwell continues his account, 'I told him he would be fine. So we got to Altrincham. We sat down in a hall full of people and they started to fling their questions at us. Bobby actually handled his very well. I'll always remember, though, someone asked him what was the most pleasurable game he had played in, since he became a professional footballer. Now Bobby by this time had won around 30 England caps, had played in two Cup Finals, and been part of a European campaign. And he said, in all honesty, that it was in a match against Blackburn Rovers reserves at Ewood Park. He said it was so significant because it was Wilf McGuinness' first game back after breaking his leg. I could not believe it. He was so modest, thinking about someone else, thinking of his mate who'd been through a hard time. That's the type of person he was.'

Noel Cantwell believes that this was the start of Bobby 'breaking the ice' over speaking in front of others. But, despite the comparative success of his Altrincham outing, Bobby remained painfully diffident for many years. Indeed, it is only in recent years – through his ambassadorial work with England and Manchester United – that he has become more confident. That perceptive judge Alan Gowling, who once turned down a place at Cambridge University so he could continue playing for United, says of Bobby: 'I do think that he has improved tremendously over the years as a public speaker. When he started, he was very nervous. But he obviously worked at it. When I hear him now, I find him very interesting; he's relaxed and therefore comes across much more entertainingly.'

Mike Newlin, whose company MBN Promotions organizes sporting celebrity functions, has this analysis of Bobby's technique and impact as a performer: 'He has developed such confidence over the last 20 years. He is now one of the best speakers we have got. He speaks without notes, throws in some gags, but the best thing about him is the way he speaks from the heart about the great managers and great players. He knows exactly how to squeeze an audience. He is very emotional and you believe everything he tells you.' Newlin also explains that, for all his fame, Bobby retains his modesty. 'He is extremely down-to-earth. For instance, he will often drive himself to an event. If he arrives somewhere, he does not expect anything. He is happy just to sit down, have a cup of tea and read the paper. He has never given me a second's problem, never turned up late or argued about money or let anyone down. He could not be less starry.'

Jack has always loved to talk about himself; as John Giles puts it: 'He has a capacity to see the world entirely through his own eyes.' But Bobby has been loath to do so – one reason why, rare amongst great British sportsmen, he has never published his autobiography. Compared to Jack's own rumbustious and candid tale, a huge best-seller in 1996, there were two books from Bobby in the mid-1960s, *My Soccer Story* in 1964 and *Forward for England* in 1967 and since then there has only been an enjoyable compendium of anecdotes, *Bobby Charlton's Most Memorable Matches*, expertly written by Ken Jones in 1984. The football journalist Ken Montgomery gives this illustration of Bobby's incredible modesty and lack of ease, from a time when he was working on some articles about Bobby's career. 'I went up to see Bobby in Manchester, and we arranged to meet at Sam's Chop House which was a very famous restaurant in Manchester then. Bobby, of course, turned up right on time, very polite, charming. We went into the restaurant, were shown to our table, and within two or three minutes, several other football celebrities, including Malcolm Allison and some Manchester City team members, came in. Bobby became quite embarrassed, even though he was a far bigger name than any of them. He turned to me and said: "Ken, we have not ordered our meal yet. Would you mind if we went somewhere less conspicuous because it embarrasses me talking in front of them?" He obviously feared that his leg was going to be pulled. So we went off to his golf club near Cheadle at Cheshire, where we had a lovely lunch and I got my work done.

Bobby insisted on paying for the meal and then driving me to the station, because he said that his embarrassment had taken me out of my way. That was typical Bobby. He was so shy. He did not fancy being the butt of their humour, but he was so pleasant about it to me.' Yet those who witnessed that scene would have probably concluded, without knowing the circumstances, that Bobby was so aloof he had walked out.

Bobby's restraint is also shown in the way he has never indulged in foul language in his public appearances. He was not like that on the soccer field – indeed, as we have seen, his utterances could be as rich as anyone else's in the heat of the contest. But, when he has been representing club or country he has hated the idea of swearing, especially in female company. Alec McGivan, in charge of the 2006 World Cup bid, told me: 'He is very gentlemanly, old fashioned in his values and views. He expects people to behave properly and dress properly. He frowns on swearing in front of a lady.' Jack, inevitably, is the opposite. Most of those who go to hear him love his earthy humour. But his speeches are so peppered with obscenities that he has sometimes been the subject of complaints, as happened at a dinner in Sheffield in 1978 organized by local building societies, when his use of the f-word was greeted by the embarrassed silence of 400 guests. The dinner organizer, Denis Blundell, said: 'I didn't want to invite him but I was outnumbered. My colleagues thought he would be a colourful character. I think we might have got someone better who would have acted with decorum.' Jack's friend Ian St John says: 'Jack's language can be unbelievable, even in front of women. He was doing a function in Aberdeen, and there was the Lady Mayoress there. His first words were, "You need to excuse my language. I can't fucking help it." And then he's off.'

Bobby's sense of diplomacy is also shown in his unwillingness to discuss politics. He has neither professed any allegiance to a party nor shown much interest in the subject. 'To understand the game of politics, you have to go in for it and, as I have no intention of doing that, I pay my taxes and forget it,' he once said. However, like most professional footballers of his time, he is essentially conservative in outlook. All the values he propounds, like respect for discipline, private wealth, authority and tradition, reflect this. His Manchester United team mate, John Aston, says, 'Bobby always seemed an older man in attitude than age. He was socially conservative, a monarchist, a *Daily Mail* type of guy.'

Jack, of course, has to be different. Cissie once said that she always thought Jack would become a politician because he was so strong in his opinions. Though never a paid up member of the Labour Party, Jack has long boasted of his commitment to socialism. In the 1970 General Election, he even published a booklet, entitled *Why I am Labour*, setting out his reasons for backing Harold Wilson. Jack's instinctive left-wing outlook has never wavered. Even in 1980, when the Labour Party was sliding towards Bennism, Jack was demanding that the party 'get back to socialist principles', while he was a supporter of Arthur Scargill – who was a neighbour and friend – during the miners' dispute in 1984/85, lending money, food parcels and a car to his local strike committee. And today, he is disillusioned by the centrist drift of Labour. 'I wish I could argue for them as I used to. But they no longer know what they want.' Eamon Dunphy, though, feels that there was little coherence in Jack's socialism. 'Jack was boring about politics. He would quote Arthur Scargill and Brian Clough as founts of wisdom. There was no thought behind it. It was just knee-jerk stuff.'

Jack's socialism does not sit easily with the greatest passion of his life: field sports. His love of fishing and shooting is perhaps even stronger than his attachment to soccer – he once said that he would rather die on the river than on the football pitch. And when he was asked, in 1994, what was the first thing he would save from a fire, the answer was not his football trophies but 'probably my fishing rod or I might pick my gun.'

Just as with his after-dinner speaking, Jack managed to turn his interest in rod and gun into a lucrative media sideline, producing a number of TV programmes and books on the subject. In 1992, for example, he and Tony Francis presented a six part series for Yorkshire Television, called *Salmon Run,* which took them from

Balmoral in Scotland to Alaska. Far more controversial was the series he made for Channel Four in 1985 called *Jack's Game* in which he went ferreting, beagling and hunting wild mink. The scene that provoked the most outrage was when he killed a stag with a shot in the back. Defending the programme, Jack was coldly rational about the need for hunting: 'In 95 per cent of situations in field sports there has to be control. You can either feed an animal in the abattoir and then shoot it, or you can leave it on the hill and shoot it.' But animal rights campaigners were appalled at what they perceived to be propaganda for cruelty. 'The idea that anyone could get pleasure out of killing an animal or prolonging its death is terrible,' said the League Against Cruel Sports. Some militants went further than just issuing statements. An armed guard was placed on Jack after he received a number of threats from the Animal Liberation Front, who said that 'Jack is number one on our hitlist' – not the first time this has been said. Meanwhile the pitch at Highfield Road – where his Newcastle team were due to play Coventry – was sprinkled with glass in protest and further warnings were given of damage to Upton Park where Newcastle also had an imminent fixture.

None of this put Jack off. Indeed, nothing, not even football, was allowed to interfere too much with his expeditions, as Ian St John, one of his assistant managers at Sheffield Wednesday, recalls: 'Jack would occasionally say, "Look, I'm going up to Scotland fishing, but if the chairman comes in, tell him I'm looking at a player." Jack was such a countryman, with his wellies, cap, gun. And his car, it was absolutely stinking of everything: bits of animals, fish, birds, dogs. Absolutely minging. You virtually had to wear a mask to get into it.' Mark Smith, who played under Jack at Wednesday, describes the sort of chaos which helped to make such a mess: 'There was a group of us in his car, and Jack had been shooting. He had his little Jack Russell terrier with him and the dog took a few nibbles out of one of the dead birds. He then started to throw up over the back seat. It was some scene. Jack was trying to drive with one hand and slap the dog with the other, telling him to stop being sick.'

The chaos could almost be the same in Jack's home. Alan Peacock, the former Middlesbrough and Leeds striker, says: 'I remember going to see Jack when he was at Boro and we'd be sitting there in his living room, plucking pheasants while watching the telly. We had paper on the floor but there would be these bloody feathers all over the place.' So wrapped was Jack in his field sports that, at both Middlesbrough and Sheffield Wednesday, he used to take some of the club's apprentices with him on grouse shoots and get them to act as beaters. Stan Cummins recalls: 'At first he asked for volunteers and we put our hands up, but once we had found out what was involved we were more wary. It was a long, tiring day. Next time he asked for volunteers there were no takers. But he said, "Well, you're coming anyway." So we had to go. And when we were out beating the bushes, getting the birds to go in the air, he accidentally shot Graeme Hedley up the backside. It was no big deal. He wasn't using bullets, but just a pellet gun.' Despite the incident, Hedley bore Jack no ill will and later joined him at Wednesday.

When he was at Leeds, Jack was just as keen on country pursuits, though he had less time to pursue them. While he was still a player, he arranged to buy some shooting rights at a grouse moor at Coverdale, along with a farmhouse which he planned to turn into a weekend retreat. In an interview with the *Yorkshire Evening Post*, Jack explained his long-held affection for the gun: 'I learned to handle a gun when I was 13 but I gave up poaching when I was in my early twenties, when people started recognizing me. I never shoot anything I don't eat. I bag pheasant, pigeon and grouse and I am going to try squirrel next. I'm told it's delicious.' As always, though, there was the difference in the brothers. 'Bobby has been out once or twice with me but he doesn't like killing birds or animals.' If Jack had to be indoors, he liked traditional games such as darts or dominoes. 'His ideal night was in a pub or a working men's club, having a pint and playing dominoes with Billy Bremner. He was old fashioned that way,' says Peter Lorimer. Interestingly, for all his love of country sports, Jack never enjoyed fox hunting, simply because he was, as he once explained to the *Sheffield Star*, 'scared stiff of horses. I like the hunt atmosphere and everything connected with outdoor pursuits. But I can't go near horses.'

Bobby's tastes were more suburban than country, He was a relatively good golfer and to this day plays at Mere in Cheshire, with a handicap now of around 10. Norma is also a useful golfer, regularly taking part in competitions. One of Bobby's occasional golfing partners is Sir Alex Ferguson: 'I see a lot of Alex socially, mostly on the golf course,' said Bobby last year. 'It's best if I don't say too much about his golf – quite frankly it's pretty bad.' When he was with United, one of the team's set pre-match rituals was to go to Davyhulme Golf Club, have lunch, and then play a few gentle shots on the course, a routine Bobby always enjoyed because it was 'quiet and peaceful'. Nobby Stiles once gave this interesting analysis of Bobby as a golfer, saying that the sum of his game was less than its parts – a criticism sometimes made of his football: 'He can play all the shots in the book, but he cannot string them together. He hits a good length, and it annoys him he that does not play better. Perhaps the only time you'll get Bobby really stirring things up is on the golf course. Occasionally, he loses his temper at himself when playing, because he really could be quite good, but somehow does not seem to be able to make the best of it.'

With his restless soul, Jack was never a great spectator at anything except football, but, as well as football, Bobby enjoyed watching cricket, boxing and, above all, rugby league. He first saw a game in 1965 and soon became hooked on it. What he particularly admired about the game was its raw physical toughness allied to sportsmanship. 'I don't feel I'm a real man when I watch rugby league,' he once said, 'I feel I'm getting money under false pretences and wild horses wouldn't keep me away from Salford.' He was deeply impressed that, after a serious punch up at St Helens, 'The opposing team came into the club after the match and it was all forgotten as the lads chatted together. In soccer, we would have talked about that kind of incident for weeks.' Bobby was also a much better player at cards than Jack, because, as Noel Cantwell says, 'He had the right kind of face for poker.' If Jack had a good hand, he could not help but reveal it in his expression. As Peter Lorimer recalls, 'If we were playing, say, on a train or coach, Jack could never disguise his feelings. We could always tell when Jack was on the verge of cashing in so we would all lay our cards down. Jack would then lose and go mad and throw all the cards out the window and go away and sulk.'

Jack's lack of self-consciousness was shown in the way he paid little attention to his appearance. Again, where Bobby, after his marriage, was always neat and well organized, Jack never cared at all. Leeds goalkeeper David Harvey says of his first experience of sharing a room with Jack: 'I really had my eyes opened. We were staying away for three days and Jack had one shirt. He was so untidy, so disorganized. He would be wearing things like odd socks, one red and one blue. He left clothes lying everywhere. I was so shocked at his attitude that the first time we roomed together, I stayed awake all night. I remember Jack once said to me, "I don't trust anybody with dirty shoes." Then I looked down at his and they were absolutely filthy. He was endearing that way.' Norman Hunter claims that 'If Jack and Billy Bremner shared a room, it looked like a bomb had hit it.' One of the strangest aspects of Jack's lack of sartorial elegance is that he was involved in the running of two men's outfitters in Leeds but as England colleague Peter Thompson puts it, 'He was hardly the greatest advertisement for his shops. He was the scruffiest dresser, whereas Bobby was always immaculate in his blazer or suit.'

Allan 'Sniffer' Clarke says: 'If you put a £1,000 suit on Jack Charlton, it would look as if it was worth £50. That's because of the shape of his body. Gary Sprake was always immaculately dressed, probably the best dresser in Leeds, even in casual gear. I remember during one flight, Billy Bremner and I were laughing and Jack says, "What are you two laughing at?"

Billy said, "It's not me Jack, it's Sniffer, he's on about how you're dressed." Jack went absolutely potty. He said, "I'm not having that."

The gaffer hears us shouting and comes over, "What's happening?"

Jack says, "It's them two. They're taking the piss out of the way

I'm dressed. I wouldn't mind but there are only two people in this club with any dress sense, and that's Sprakey and myself." Well, that made it even worse. We were all laughing then. How Jack Charlton ever ran a gentleman's outfitters I do not know because he was the world's worst dresser. On quite a few occasions, when we were playing away in Europe, we would travel on the Monday, have the game on Wednesday night and come back on Thursday. You're away for the best part of a week. So we would report to Bradford airport. I would have a little bit of hand luggage, with a few bits of clothing and my toilet bag. I see Jack, just standing there, with no luggage. I say to him,

"Where's your gear?"

"I'm travelling light this trip."

At the top of his jacket pocket, there would just be a toothbrush. Scruffy bugger.'

In his management career, he still could not get it right. The Sheffield Wednesday player Ian Mellor, who lived with Jack for a while, shared this incident with me. 'Jack was doing an after-dinner speech and he come down in his suit, having changed. His trousers were at half-mast, at least six inches above his ankles. You know when you were going into assembly as a schoolkid, you polished your shoes by rubbing them on the backs of your trousers. Jack stands there, with his trousers halfway up his legs, and then rubs both shoes behind his legs. They were still barely clean. "As long as you look respectable, that's all that matters," he said as he walked out. I could hardly believe what I had just seen.'

Bobby was not only smarter, he was also more self-conscious. And nothing exemplified this more than his concern over his baldness. Born with blond hair, Bobby started losing it when he was just 17. The fallout spread rapidly and by his mid-twenties, when he was at the peak of his career, he had little left on top apart from a few wisps at the front. For any man to suffer such drastic hair loss so young would be trying, but in Bobby's case it was made much worse by his natural diffidence. Bobby Harrop of United recalls, 'He got some stick from the lads, he certainly did. It was nothing serious, all jokes.' In response, Bobby adopted the unconvincing tactic of grow-ing his hair long on his left-hand side and then brushing the strands across his pate. If he had been working in an office, he might have been able to maintain the delicately constructed edifice in place. But it was an absurdity in professional football, when the tendrils went flying within seconds of the kick-off, flopping across his face or falling over his collar. Throughout every game, Bobby could be seen, constantly trying to comb the errant hairs up and over his head with his left hand. So intense was this action that it sometimes led to con-fusion among his colleagues. Roy Tunks of Preston remembers one such occasion. 'We would have set signals at setpieces. And in one game at Deepdale, Bobby was about to take a corner when a gust of wind suddenly blew his hair up. He was desperately trying to put it back as he kicked and there was total confusion as no-one could understand his signal. It was hilarious really.'

Far from detracting from his baldness, Bobby's comb-over only emphasized it. He was not the first to cover up in this way, but he was certainly the most famous person to do so. In fact, along with the likes of Jennifer Aniston and the Beatles, he became one of the very few people in modern British culture to have given his name to a distinctive hairstyle. The 'Bobby Charlton' was instantly recogniz-able, whether it be practised by Peter Swales or Rab C Nesbitt. On the TV programme *Room 101* Lorraine Kelly of GMTV named the 'Bobby Charlton' comb-over as one of her personal pet hates. How Bobby must wish he could have played in today's Premiership, where baldness is a positive virtue and even the most youthfully hirsute of footballers, like Beckham and Gerrard, insist on shaving their heads. Eventually, in the mid-1980s, Bobby recognized that his hairstyle was absurd. In a 2001 BBC interview he said, 'The way I swept it across was really stupid. When I think about it now, I ask myself, "Why did I do that?" I said to Norma one night, "This is ridiculous." And I just cut it off. I realized that I did not need to worry any more.'

Interestingly, Bobby's premature baldness brought out the protective instincts of both his mother and elder brother. During the England-Scotland game at Wembley in 1967, Cissie Charlton was watching as a Scots fan, sitting near her, yelled out that Bobby was a 'baldy c**t'. Gripped with maternal fury, Cissie lashed out at the abuser, cracking him across the side of the face. 'I was alone in the middle of that angry crowd,' she wrote, 'and for a moment it looked as though things were going to get very ugly. A woman, who had been with the man whose face I slapped, shouted: "You're no lady!" My fins were up and I yelled back, "If he's yours, then you can't be a lady either." Fortunately, Billy Bremner's father-in-law hauled Cissie out of the crowd before there could be any real trouble.

Jack could feel just as strongly, even 20 years later. Tony Cascarino told me of this incident when Ireland were on tour. 'We were playing cards in the room one day, about four of us. Jack came in and was watching us, as usual giving unwanted advice. The TV was on in the background and an advert came on for hair growth. The lads started laughing about it. And Jack suddenly said. 'My Bobby fucking lost his hair at 19 and all his fucking life he's fucking had to put up with people taking the piss out of him.' He really went mad, where we had just been having a laugh. We all knew that Bobby and Jackie are not that close, but I saw that day how fiercely proud and protective Jack is towards Bobby. He really took it personally. He was so angry that we were joking about hair loss. He kept going on about "our Bobby" and all he had to put up with. It just showed that, for all their differences, there is a real bond there.'

CHAPTER FOURTEEN

The Losers

At the time of the World Cup in Mexico in 1970, Jack was 35 and Bobby 32. Many observers felt the Charltons were too old to be taken on the trip, for neither could claim the same mastery they had possessed in the summer of 1966. In the Everton captain Brian Labone, Jack now had a serious rival for the position of centre-half, something he had not faced four years earlier.

Perhaps even more worrying from England's point of view was the fact that Bobby had suffered a loss of form in the previous two seasons. After more than a decade of non-stop, competitive football at the highest level, he often looked badly jaded. Typical of the criticism was a report by Hugh McIlvanney in the *Observer* in April 1969 following United's defeat in the European Cup by AC Milan in the San Siro stadium: 'Bobby Charlton was so much a non-influence that he might have been mistaken for a reserve disorientated by sudden inclusion in the side. It was, without question, one of the worst performances he has ever given for United, an amalgam of errors and neglected opportunities. His touch, pace, his very appetite appeared to have deserted him. We saw a fumbling, apprehensive parody of his real game and by the finish some of us were obliged to ask if the savage strain imposed on this sensitive man over the past few seasons is at last taking its ultimate toll, if we will ever again see the best of him.'

By continuing to pick Bobby, it was argued that Ramsey had fallen into the habit of indulging his favourite star. 'Charlton, it seems, had talismanic qualities for Ramsey,' wrote Max Marquis in 1970. 'For some time now – a season and a half or more – Charlton has been struggling as an international player. His courage and devotion are enormous; his prestige and influence unparalleled. If sentiment is to overrule grim necessity, then Charlton is the first player who deserves the benefit of it. But long since Charlton has looked physically and mentally tired to the very marrow of his being. Whether Ramsey realizes it or not, he makes allowances for him.'

Even his own captain, Bobby Moore, publicly expressed his concerns about Bobby's capacity for the campaign in the altitude of Mexico. 'He is so willing, so eager, that he tends to take more out of himself than he needs. He cannot help it. This is the part and the style he has played for both Manchester United and for England for the past five years, and it is difficult to get out of a habitual groove. Can he do this in this air? If only he were lazier, it might be better for him.' Moore also made the complaint, levelled by others including his own brother, that Bobby did not attack enough. 'It is lovely to see the way he can stroll and glide past opponents. But why do it in his own half of the field when there are so many younger men who can fill in behind him.'

Yet there was always a danger in writing off Bobby Charlton. As we have seen, it had also happened around 1963/64, when he was trying to make the transition from winger into midfielder. His own club manager thought there was no doubt that Bobby would overcome his problems: 'He is such a fantastic player and he is still so tremendously sound physically that I don't believe he won't start playing brilliantly again,' said Busby. 'I am confident that he'll do a great job for us again and that he can keep his place in the England team for Mexico.'

Ramsey felt the same way. Both Bobby and Jack were included in his England team which set out for Mexico on 4 May 1970. By now, Bobby had passed the milestone of a century of England caps, a target only reached previously by Billy Wright of Wolves, who won 105 caps. Bobby's 100th game had been against Northern Ireland at Wembley on 21 April 1970, when he was given the honour of the captaincy. He also scored that night, the 48th time he had hit the net for England, by far the highest tally in history. A genuine team man who preferred winning to goalscoring, Bobby had never shown much interest in personal statistics. But even for him, there was a certain appeal about trying to achieve the twin double of 50 goals and the highest-ever number of caps during the summer in Mexico.

England were one of the favourites for the Cup, because of their experience and balance – many of the heroes of 1966, such as Moore, Banks, Hurst and Peters, seemed to be at the peak of their careers. 'Most of us believed that England had a realistic chance of becoming the first European team to win in Latin America,' says Geoff Hurst. But it was to be a difficult – and ultimately depressing – tour. The extreme heat and altitude, over 7,000 feet above sea level, were partly to blame. During the pre-tournament training period, Bobby described in a BBC interview the experience of doing 50-yard sprints. 'You usually find you vomit if it's been really difficult.' Colin Bell gave a more graphic description of acclimatization in training in Colombia: 'It was amazing. You ran 10 yards and you'd stop and put your hands on your knees. You couldn't play a one-two, it was like having asthma.'

Perhaps more influential, in a negative way, was the siege mentality that Alf encouraged in the England party. Ramsey was an old-fashioned, highly conventional Englishman who was deeply suspicious of foreigners and foreign ways. Disliking the Mexican sun as much as the country's food, he had little time for either international diplomacy or the overseas press corps. 'Alf was a bit uptight when we were in Mexico,' wrote Jack Charlton. In a signal of the introspection that was to characterize his trip, Ramsey almost lost his temper at the first press conference. He also succeeded in alienating his hosts by importing not only a British bus to ferry the team around, but, even worse, British food supplies. This latter decision angered the Mexicans so much that meat intended for the England players was burnt on the quayside, which meant that they had to live off frozen fish fingers for a week. 'I was never able to touch a fish finger again in my life,' says Alan Mullery. One of the Mexican newspapers came up with a wittier riposte: 'If you're thinking of throwing tomatoes at the English team, always wash them first.'

Ramsey's sense of paranoia was only deepened when England were playing a pre-Cup friendly in Bogota. One night in the team hotel, the Tequendama, several of the players were milling around in the foyer when a trio of them, Bobby Moore, Peter Thompson and Bobby Charlton, decided to go into a jewellery store called the Green Fire, where the 21-year-old Clara Padilla was behind the counter. Bobby Charlton told his captain he was contemplating buying something for Norma. As Bobby Moore recorded, 'We were just browsing the way you do to kill time in any hotel with its own shops.' Bobby Charlton asked Ms Padilla if he could see a necklace that was locked away in a cabinet. 'It was priced at £6,000, enough to send me reeling to the door,' said Bobby. While they were there, some of the other England players drifted in and out of the shop. Eventually the two Bobbies left and sat down in the lobby. Suddenly they were approached by an elderly lady. 'She asked Bobby and me to go into the shop. We said yes, thinking they have found something for Bobby's wife,' said Moore. But it turned out that shop was alleging a bracelet had gone missing – and Bobby Moore was the prime suspect. Immediately, the police were on the scene and statements were taken from Moore and Charlton. 'I couldn't believe it. This couldn't be happening. Then I turned cold. What if they accused me? Why hadn't they accused me? I was sure they would admit it was a horrible mistake, but they didn't,' recalled Bobby Charlton. Peter Thompson also offered to say his piece but Alf Ramsey, who had gone to investigate, told him: 'They are not after you, Peter, it's a set-up. They are after the two most famous players in the world.'

Ramsey appeared to have sorted everything out with the hotel, police and shop once the statements were given and Moore thought the matter had been settled. The rest of the England team thought it was risible. 'Two straighter people you could not wish to meet in your life,' said Banks about Charlton and Moore. But Bobby Charlton, always the nervous type, could not relax, as Moore later recalled: 'Bobby was openly worried. Very edgy. I told him to put it out of his mind because it was finished. But I was not sure he believed that.' He was right. England played two successful friendlies against Colombia and Ecuador, but, almost a week later, when the team returned to Bogota to catch the return flight to Mexico, Moore was taken into police custody. The rest of the party left without him. News of the arrest had made Bobby Charlton more anxious than ever. He offered to stay behind to be with his captain but Ramsey ordered him on to the plane. In his apprehensive mood, he saw little of the humour behind his colleagues' mickey-taking. 'Our Bob was very nervous as we waited for the plane to take off. The other lads were playing tricks on him and I told them to lay off,' says Jack. After two days under house arrest, Bobby Moore was released, having effectively demolished Ms Padilla's evidence. It is a tribute to Moore's almost Zen-like inner calm that he was able to laugh off the whole episode as a farce, returning to the England camp as if nothing had happened.

It is unlikely Bobby Charlton could have handled himself with the same ease, as he himself admitted: 'To be honest, I wouldn't have weathered it as well as he did.' Peter Osgood said later, 'It was lucky it was Mooro and not Bobby Charlton, because Charlton would have come back like Yul Brynner by the time he'd got out of it; he was a worrier. But Mooro took it in his stride. He was so cool, so relaxed, it didn't seem so serious.' Bobby Charlton's sense of anxiety was confirmed by his wife Norma, who told the *Manchester Evening News*: 'Bobby telephoned me and said there had been some bother and he and Bobby Moore were involved. He sounded very upset about it. He said to me: "They are a right load of bandits and I wouldn't like to go again." But Norma, a much more confident personality than her husband, had no time for any of this Latin American nonsense.

'The whole thing is too farcical to be true. What a way of getting at the England team. It is ridiculous to think that Bobby Moore would have done such a thing and my Bobby would have shielded him. I am not worried because I know my husband would never be involved in anything shady. It is just ludicrous.'

This has always been the near-universal view of the 'Bogota incident' – and there is a great deal of evidence to show that the Colombian authorities were not beyond bringing trumped up charges against celebrities as a means of extorting money. But while it is absurd to suggest that Charlton or Moore did anything untoward, it is possible that the much-maligned Ms Padilla, who was sacked from her post after the affair, was not lying when she claimed that a bracelet had disappeared from the shop. Bobby Moore once confessed to his friend and biographer Jeff Powell, 'Perhaps one of the younger lads with the squad did something foolish, a prank with unfortunate consequences.' As Jeff Powell admits, 'Bobby would not have made such a remark lightly.'

The England team were relieved to get back to the business of football, though, as happened four years earlier, Ramsey imposed a rigorous discipline on the squad, with the same emphasis on physical fitness and abstaining from alcohol. Before the first match of the tournament, Alf Ramsey had the unfortunate task of naming the six players who would be left out of the final squad. Their number included Bobby's United team-mate David Sadler, who was furious that Alf had leaked the information to the press before he had been informed of the decision. But Sadler also says that the moment of his exclusion showed the good side of Jack Charlton: 'I was very, very disappointed. Within hours of being told, we were then given the option by the FA of flying home the next day – or we could stay with the team, though obviously not playing. I think, generally speaking, most of us just wanted to grab the next plane home and get out of there. But by then I had come to know Jack reasonably well. He sat me down and said, "Well, I understand your wanting to go back, but just think it out a bit. You're a professional, you can stay here and gain first-hand knowledge of a major tournament and work with England. If you go home, what are you going to do: sit on a beach somewhere for two weeks?" So I decided to stay. It was absolutely the right decision. He was instrumental. He was very straightforward.'

Another who got to know Jack Charlton well during that World Cup was Brian Labone, Jack's rival as England centre-half. He gave me these memories of the trip: 'Bobby was a great player, but he always looked a bit of a sad sack. Very quiet. I wouldn't call him aloof, just undemonstrative, you always felt you were intruding a bit with him. Jack, of course, was the opposite, a big brash Yorkshireman. He was probably the most outspoken member of the squad. You couldn't keep him quiet. Even physically they did not look alike – Jack was like a cactus.' On Jack as a centre-half, Labone says: 'There were about half-a-dozen decent centre-halves in the First Division then. Jack was no better or worse than the rest of us. I think I was more skilful than him, but Jack was very dominant and effective at what he did. He was hard, but he wasn't dirty – he'd kick you in the goolies or on the shin but nothing to threaten your career. We were portrayed as rivals but we always got on. When Jack was left out of some of the games in the World Cup, he said he was "resting". He never showed any jealousy towards me. He was dead straight.'

Bob McNab of Arsenal was another member of the original tour party to Mexico. He provided me with this candid assessment of Bobby from seeing him at both League and international levels: 'I found Bobby somewhat moody. He could be so amiable and friendly one day, and the next he would not speak to you. I was the only Arsenal player in the squad and I don't think Bobby had much time for Arsenal. He took exception to us because we were so much more tactical, whereas Manchester United were creative, free-flowing. As a footballer, he had two of the best feet I had ever seen. Some people could do the same things but they just looked awkward doing it. But Beckenbauer and Charlton had that gift of making everything look so beautiful.'

'One of his weaknesses was that he used to give the ball away. I didn't like it when he took the ball off my feet at left-back, tried to hit one of his long crossfield balls and then lost it. He didn't try to get it back. He would leave that to players like me and Nobby Stiles because Bobby couldn't tackle. He was a moaner on the field, a complete moaner. When we played United, he and George Best would always be moaning at each other. He would be moaning at George for dribbling too much instead of passing, and George would be moaning him for giving the ball away. It was very apparent that they didn't get on. Mind you, we're all flawed and to start picking holes in Bobby Charlton's game is really going to extremes. The football world is divided into soldiers and artists.'

Bob McNab is equally honest on the subject of Jack: 'We shared a room together during the 1969 tour to South America. He used to get on the bed and beat me up, telling me I was a "flash c**t". It was brilliant, all in good humour. He really picked on me but, because I liked him, I took it as a form of flattery. "Come here, ya little bugger," he would shout if I laughed at him during a five-a-side. He had a menswear shop at the time and at the end of the trip, he was pulling out from his suitcase all these plastic bags. They were full of clothes he could not sell in his shop. But you wouldn't have given them to the Salvation Army. Like he put a turtleneck on but he made it look like a T-shirt. I started to laugh and he caught me and started punching me, calling me names. We were like kids.' McNab has much more respect for Jack's football than his fashion sense. 'Jack had such judgement, intelligence about the game that it did not surprise me he went on to become a top manager. I have nothing but admiration for Jack. I thought he was an exceptional defender. He looked ungainly but he was very effective and had tremendous character. I tell you, you'd want him on your team. I had tremendous admiration for him. He was a hell of a man. Jack could be fierce. I could understand how he upset a lot of people. I remember on the England bus he and Peter Osgood had to be separated because they got into such an argument. That was a follow-on from the 1970 FA Cup Final [a bitterly fought, drawn-out contest which Chelsea won narrowly in extra-time of the replay].'

McNab also recalls the time when Jack was left out of one of the warm-up games and returned to his room in a fury. 'That's it. I won't be playing in this World Cup. I'm out.' McNab says: 'Jack was so angry that I went and locked myself in the bathroom. He is such a big man, his arms are bigger than my legs. I thought I'd better keep out of the way so I sat on the toilet, reading a book. I was in there quite a while and then there came a knock on the door.

"Eh, little man, I won't hurt you."

"Well, you won't if I keep this bloody door locked."'

Jack did not play in the first two England games of the World Cup, his place taken by Brian Labone. But Bobby was at the centre of the midfield in both encounters. The first, against Romania, was won 1–0 with a Geoff Hurst goal. The second was a classic match against Brazil, best remembered in England for Bobby Moore's awesome defending and Gordon Banks' miraculous save, when he dived full-length across his goal to keep out a perfectly placed Pele header. Pele himself said it was the greatest save he had ever seen. Brazil were 1–0 up on the hour, but England could have equalized had Jeff Astle not missed a sitter with what Bobby called a 'sloppy shot'. Afterwards, Bobby Charlton was in raptures about the contest: 'It really is what the game at the top level is all about. There was everything in it, all the skills and techniques, all the tactical control. There was some really special stuff played out there.'

Despite the defeat, England only needed a draw to qualify from their group. The next match against Czechoslovakia was Bobby's 105th for England, equalling Billy Wright's record. Billy Wright himself, who was commentating on ITV at the time, was full of compliments for Charlton, comparing him favourably to Tom Finney and Stanley Matthews. Equally complimentary was the international press, which talked of Charlton as a true English gentleman. To the Mexican public, Charlton became known as 'El Calvo Divino' – the Divine Baldy. One Mexican newspaper published a *World Cup Guide for Women*, which contained this entry on Charlton: 'A slight, wispy-haired Englishman who, off the field, looks as though a breeze would knock him over, but on the field becomes, in Latin eyes, a combination of Genghis Khan and Ivan the Terrible.'

The 'Divine Baldy' had his elder brother alongside him in the final qualifying game against Czechoslovakia, because Brian Labone had been so exhausted by his exertions against Brazil. This was one of the dullest games of the tournament, – 'you can see better on Hackney Marshes or Wimbledon Common' wrote Ralph Finn in *World Cup 1970* – with the result decided by an Allan Clarke penalty. Czechoslovakia nearly scored when Banks, troubled by the swerve of the ball in the thin air, saw a speculative shot go right through his hands and crash on to the bar. Having caught the rebound, he turned round to face Jack: 'Big Jack started to give me a rollocking and then grinned all over his face. "What are you going to do for your next trick, Banksie?" he asked.' Unfortunately Banks' next trick was to have disastrous consequences for England.

Jack admits that, due to lack of match practice, he played badly against Czechoslovakia. 'I found the game very hard and I must have looked a bit jaded.' He was dropped by Ramsey for the quarter-final in Leon against West Germany. Also missing was Gordon Banks, who had been taken violently ill the night before the game with a bout of food poisoning. As he had shown against Mexico, Banks was in the form of his life during the 1970 World Cup. 'Gordon was the best keeper in the world, by miles,' recalled Bobby Charlton. 'He was almost unbelievable. We used to practice shooting against him in Mexico, where the ball flies very fast, and he used to stagger us with his saves. Even hardened players, who had seen it all, could not believe his saves.' But Banks' absence did not worry the England camp too much, for his replacement, Peter 'The Cat' Bonetti, was reckoned to be one of the best keepers in Europe.

Again, in this crucial match, we can see the symmetry of Bobby's career. Once more he was to face Germany in the game that would decide his – and England's – destiny. Once more he was up against his old foe, Franz Beckenbauer. Just as happened four years earlier, both of them were told by the same managers, Ramsey and Schoen, to mark the other out of the contest. And after 90 minutes, the scoreline was exactly the same as the Wembley Final, 2–2, and the game had to go into extra-time.

For much of the contest, however, it had looked like England would triumph, with the team playing some of their best attacking football of the World Cup and Bobby Charlton full of running. Alan Mullery opened the scoring with a superb run and shot. Then, early in the second half, Martin Peters ghosted in for a typically deceptive strike. No Ramsey side had ever squandered a two-goal lead, and there appeared little chance of such an occurrence in this game, especially since Beckenbauer was so tightly restricted by his role of covering Charlton. 'When the second one went in I ran round the field shouting to the Germans, "Goodnight, God bless, see you in Munich,"' said Alan Ball.

Ball's celebrations were premature. With just 20 minutes to go, England suffered a dramatic, almost freakish, reversal in fortune. Beckenbauer, finally moving forward as Germany became desperate, was driven wide to the right by Mullery but managed to fire in a shot from the edge of the box. It was not struck with any power but somehow the ball managed to squirm under Bonetti's body. 2–1 and the Germans were back in the game. Bobby Moore later recalled: 'Franz's shot was nothing special. If Peter was going to be honest with himself, he had to be disappointed. Psychologically, it was a desperate goal to concede. It was the sort of goal which cut into your confidence from the back.' Jack Charlton could not bear to watch after this, as he explained in Jeff Dawson's history of the 1970 World Cup, *Back Home*: 'When it got to 2–1, I left the stadium, went down the road to a café and had a cup of coffee. Then I waited for the crowd to come out. They didn't. And I thought, oh shit, they must have scored.'

Before Beckenbauer had scored, Alf Ramsey had decided to take off Charlton, replacing him with Colin Bell of Manchester City. In fact, Bell was actually warming up on the touchline when the Germans scored, and he was on the field as soon as the game restarted. The reasoning behind Ramsey's move was obvious. Apparently assured of a win, he wanted to spare Bobby for the semi-final. As

Colin Bell explained later, 'The temperature and climate in Mexico took a lot out of you. The theme was fresh legs.' The captain Bobby Moore understood what Ramsey was doing: 'The semi-final was only three days away. Bobby was no youngster and it might have looked bad if such a key player had seemed jaded after playing on unnecessarily in the heat. Colin Bell was strong and powerful, just the man to run a beaten team into the ground.'

Bobby himself was surprised to be taken off. 'I saw Colin Bell warming up. I could hardly believe it was me who was to come off. I was only disappointed in that I felt fantastic. It was so hard playing in Mexico and when you did feel well you really wanted to enjoy it. I was full of running that day,' he said later. But like the good professional he always was, he did not show any dissent – there were no aggrieved gestures such as those displayed by Gary Lineker in the match against Sweden during the European Championships of 1992 when Graham Taylor substituted him. Soon afterwards, Norman Hunter came on for Martin Peters. Sitting on the bench beside Ramsey, Bobby watched in helpless anguish as England collapsed in front of the reinvigorated Germans. Beckenbauer, now freed from the Charlton millstone, led the counter-attack, while the German substitute Jurgen Grabowski tormented the shattered Terry Cooper at left-back. The inevitable happened in the 82nd minute, when a flick header from Uwe Seeler sailed over the head of Bonetti, who was stranded in no man's land. England were now going into extra-time. But, in contrast to four years earlier, they did not have the spirit or the strength for the battle, succumbing to a Gerd Muller volley after 10 minutes. England never looked like coming back after that. At the end, the dressing room was like a morgue. 'Players were speechless, shell shocked, numb with fatigue. Alan Ball was in tears. Bobby Charlton sat with his head in his hands,' said Bobby Moore.

Since that defeat on 14 June 1970 Ramsey's tactical substitution of Bobby Charlton has come to be seen as a disastrous turning point in the match. It was probably the second most controversial decision of his long reign as England manager, after the exclusion of Jimmy Greaves from the World Cup Final team in 1966, and many argued that it showed his powers of judgement were in decline. 'If I had been manager, I might not have done it,' says Jimmy Armfield. Bobby's own club manager, Matt Busby wrote: 'I believe that the withdrawal of Charlton was the chief reason why the Germans went on to equalize.' The journalist Frank Taylor, Bobby's fellow Munich survivor, was watching the match with his sons. 'When Bobby came off, I said to them, "We've just lost the match."'

"But why, Dad?"

"Because Beckenbauer has nothing to worry about now."

'I spoke to Matt Busby after the game and he said to me, "Of course, we all make mistakes, but you should never think of planning for the next game until you win the one you're playing."'

In taking Charlton from the field, Ramsey not only liberated Beckenbauer but also gave a vital psychological boost to the Germans, as Beckenbauer himself revealed: 'When England were leading 2–0, we were completely dead. After I scored what I thought was a rather soft goal, Alf Ramsey decided to substitute Bobby Charlton, who we felt was the heart of their game. Ramsey made such a mistake in taking him off.' By removing Charlton, Ramsey had altered the whole shape of the England midfield, a shape which had been crucial to their success over the last four years. 'Bobby Charlton had been brilliant, absolutely brilliant, he controlled that game till he went off,' Norman Hunter told me. Moreover Bobby, for all his advancing years, was much less exhausted than other members of the England side. Terry Cooper, for instance, admitted that he was 'dead on his feet' and should have been substituted. As the captain Bobby Moore said, 'Bobby was one of the fittest men in the squad. Always had been. Loved to play and could play all day in an oven if you asked him. As soon as he walked away it was like a ton weight had been lifted off Beckenbauer.'

But all this is said with hindsight. At the time, Ramsey's decision looked like a sensible one. He knew that the semi-final was only three days away and felt that, in the draining atmosphere of Mexico, he had to nurse his most valuable player. After all, Bobby had lost 10 pounds in the game against Brazil. Most of the England players felt

Ramsey was doing exactly the right thing. Alan Ball says: 'I remember thinking as Hunter and Bell came on, "Well done Alf." That's exactly what I would have done. It was tactically shrewd to give Bobby Charlton and Martin Peters a breather and send on Bell and Hunter who were both as strong as lions.' Francis Lee agrees: 'The effect of the substitutions has been overdone. Colin came on and played well and at that heat and altitude you needed to use the subs.' In truth, if Francis Lee had been more alert, the substitution might have looked inspired, for almost as soon as he came on Colin Bell burst down the right, and sent over a low cross, Hurst dived to head it, and if Lee had followed up, he could have tapped the ball in. Instead Hurst's header rolled inches wide of the post for a goal kick.

To blame the substitution for England's defeat is misguided, when the real fault lay with England's goalkeeper Peter Bonetti, whose howling errors led to both of Germany's first two goals. If Bonetti had reached anything like the standard of his normal play for Chelsea, England would have won 2–0 and no-one would be talking today about the removal of Charlton. This is the verdict that Bobby Charlton himself reached: 'I don't mean any disrespect to Bonetti but Banks was the best and I think his absence had more effect on the result than me being substituted. He was irreplaceable.' There have been complaints that Bonetti's mind was not sufficiently focused for the job, not only because of his lack of practice, but also because his wife Frances was in town, 'and Peter was a man who took his family responsibilities very seriously,' says Geoff Hurst. It was precisely the fear of such distraction that had made Bobby decide not to bring Norma to Mexico. 'I certainly didn't want to be exposed to the suggestion that my mind wasn't entirely on the World Cup,' he wrote. And Jack would not have dreamt of bringing Pat along – as he was to prove in his management of Ireland, he strongly disapproved of wives mixing with their husbands in major competitions.

The quarter-final defeat marked the beginning of England's drastic decline as a world force in soccer. It was to be 12 years before the country would again participate in the World Cup.

But it was the immediate end for both Jack and Bobby, who never played for England again after Mexico. Between them, they had played 141 games for England and been instrumental in their country's rise to the pinnacle. They deserved something better than the undignified exit at Leon.

CHAPTER FIFTEEN

The Outcast

It says much for the values of modern Britain that George Best should be regarded as a bigger hero than Bobby Charlton. Bobby achieved so much more as a footballer and a man than George Best, yet it is Best who is the cult celebrity, treated with a mixture of reverence and sympathy, his every move pored over by the media, his every utterance relayed to an excited public.

George Best's record pales beside Charlton's. He showed nothing like the same dedication, professionalism, loyalty, and dignity as Bobby. Best treated his club, colleagues and fans with contempt through his histrionic walk-outs and his self-indulgence. His defenders talk about the pressure he was under, as a shy working-class boy from Belfast suddenly having to handle fame. But Bobby was also a shy working-class boy from outside Manchester, and, at his peak in the mid-1960s he was just as big a superstar as Best. Furthermore, at Munich Bobby went through a personal and public trauma far deeper than anything Best experienced in his life. If anyone had the right to turn to drink, it was Bobby.

Bobby has diligently served Manchester United in a way that George Best could not begin to comprehend. Best was at Old Trafford for only 10, often troubled, years, yet Bobby has been there a lifetime, flying all over the globe in support of the institution he loves and respects. Bobby's detractors, including certain diehard United fans, say he is dull, unapproachable. But what could be more dull than George Best, continually replaying the same old cracked record about his life?

It is bizarre that Bobby should be criticized for his minor flaws, like his limited conversation or his difficult relationship with his family, when Best's vast defects – his drinking, unreliability, vulgarity – are celebrated. But we live in an age when Bobby's quiet virtues are out of fashion. Because he has always placed such importance on duty and restraint rather than excess and tawdriness, he is not a 'character' like George Best. In our laddish culture, the cheers are for the so-called 'bad boys', the sneers for the gentlemen. Best himself once summed it up when he described why he fell out so badly with Bobby: 'I thought he was too good to be true. I was dying for him to say "fuck" just once. I knew he didn't like me swearing, so I probably did it all the more.' As Bobby is a private person and does not go on the television hopelessly drunk, he finds himself condemned by the likes of Ron Atkinson, who says that when he was in charge of United, his players 'almost to a man regarded him as a dour, very distant individual. He has never been the most popular guy in the game.' Best has shown little interest in Old Trafford since his retirement, yet Bobby, who has given almost half a century of service to the club, is now attacked for being too wrapped up in the boardroom. United supporter Chris Robinson said to me: 'The fans love the other United players of the era, like Best and Law, much more. Bobby is seen as miserable. If you're at an away game in Europe and the singing starts, you will never hear a song dedicated to Bobby Charlton. But there will definitely be one to Bestie.'

In a piece of myth-making that is so typical of the warped attitudes to Best and Charlton, Best is often portrayed as the man who suffered at Old Trafford after 1968, while Bobby, because of his own dreary priggishness, refused to show him any compassion. 'Everyone got on with George,' says Pat Crerand, 'apart from Bobby. They fell out, and I can understand why. Bobby is a good, clean-living person who thinks every else should be perfect too.'

Dragged down by the burden of having to carry an unsuccessful team, Best was supposedly driven to the bottle and eventual escape from Old Trafford. But far from being the victim, Best was really part of the problem. He helped divide the club and set an appalling example to the young players. Bobby was unwilling to tolerate Best's abuse of Manchester United but, in taking his stand, he became an increasingly isolated figure in the dressing room.

Bobby's last four years at Old Trafford were to be the darkest of his time there. Though the waywardness of Best cast the largest shadow, Bobby's disillusion was compounded by the outlook of the club's management. In January 1969, after 34 years of unparalleled stability and success, Sir Matt Busby – knighted after the European Cup triumph – announced that he was to retire as full-time manager of United. Immediately, there was a frenzy of speculation over who would be his successor. Names touted in the press included Jock Stein of Celtic, Don Revie of Leeds and Dave Sexton of Chelsea. Fascinatingly, there was even a persistent rumour that Jack Charlton might be given the post, talk that Jack rightly dismissed as a 'load of rubbish', explaining that 'I have no intention of packing this game in for a long time yet. You can always be a manager but you can't always be a player.'

Busby, however, wanted to keep the appointment within the club. Noel Cantwell, who might have been the ideal choice, had taken over at Coventry, while Pat Crerand was ruled out by his lack of coaching experience. Like his brother, Bobby showed no desire to give up playing. So the only alternative was Wilf McGuinness, the 31-year-old youth team trainer. In his favour, Wilf had been highly successful in his work with the juniors at Old Trafford, bringing through the likes of Brian Kidd, George Best and John Aston. In addition, he had been one of England's four coaches during the 1966 World Cup. Passionate, knowledgeable, hard working, he was devoted to United. On the other hand, he was extremely young to be taking on a huge club. Perhaps more worryingly, in his role as trainer, he had always liked to be one of the lads, joining in the drinking sessions and the card schools. He therefore lacked the distance and authority required to be the boss. Through sheer charisma, Busby had inspired a degree of fear in his players – Bobby himself admits that he was 'frightened' of Sir Matt. But that quality was entirely missing with McGuinness.

Busby was all too aware of these deficiencies, so McGuinness was given only the title of 'chief coach', with Busby taking over as 'general manager' with responsibility for contracts, transfers and other administrative tasks. But this division of responsibility only emphasized how unsuited McGuinness was for his new role. Bobby himself had grave doubts about the appointment. Having joined the club at exactly the same time in 1953, Wilf had long been one of Bobby's closest friends, but that only made it more difficult to accept him as his boss. 'Wilf was given it too young,' Bobby once said, 'the best thing for him would have been to go somewhere else and prove himself in management, then maybe come back later. What the club did was to go from the absolute master, Matt Busby, to a schoolboy by comparison. Wilf was a bright lad and a good organizer, but Matt had the personality and presence and you can't learnt that on a coaching course.'

Wilf's response to such complaints was to try to impose his authority. 'Wilf was a cocky bastard. He came in with this attitude, "I don't like you or you. I'll have you, I'll nail you." He was like a man possessed, a complete arsehole. He was trying to establish himself but he did it completely the wrong way. He had the mind of a three year old,' Willie Morgan, one of Busby's last signings, told me. One dramatic way that McGuinness tried to show that he was in charge was by dropping two of his biggest stars, Denis Law and Bobby Charlton, within weeks of the start of the 1969/70 season. Wilf's justification was that they 'were getting a bit old, they were creaking'. The last time Bobby had been dropped by United was nine years earlier, and he was deeply upset by the move. As always, he was diplomatic at the time: 'It certainly came as a bit of a shock and I'm disappointed. But the coach has picked the team and that's his job. I'm just a professional and as such, I accept the boss's decisions,' he told the *Daily Mail*. Later, though, Bobby confessed that McGuinness' move had wounded him. 'Wilf's manner of telling players they were dropped rubbed them up the wrong way. The way he did it meant he lost their confidence, a thing a manager must not do.'

Another of Wilf's failings was his over-reliance on technical lectures. Unlike Sir Matt, McGuinness was very much a blackboard manager, obsessed with the idea of getting his players to adhere to complex systems. But, as Denis Law points out, this too, was counter-productive. 'Instead of going out to play football, as they had been accustomed to doing, players were going out with their minds stuffed with plans and tactics. United had never played football that way and the effect was to cause confusion.' Equally worrying – though he was hardly unique in this respect – was Wilf's inability to handle George Best. Best was still playing like a genius, but, off the field, his addictions to drink and sex were beginning to become all too apparent. 1969, he later admitted, was the year he really started to lose control.

The Best problem came to a head on 23 March 1970, when Manchester United were playing an FA Cup semi-final against Leeds at Villa Park. United were staying in a hotel in Worcester and at lunchtime, as was his wont, Best had picked up a businessman's wife at the bar and gone back to her room 'for a quickie' – to use Best's phrase. McGuinness had seen the couple together at the bar and knew that Best did not have the semi-final on his mind when he disappeared. Wanting to confirm his suspicions, he went upstairs, first to George's room, which he found to be empty, and then to Bobby's room, which happened to be next to the lady's. Bobby thought McGuinness had gone insane as he put his ear to the bedroom wall and told Bobby to be quiet. McGuinness went very still, then suddenly uttered a cry, 'the bastard'. He had heard all he needed. He went next door, confronted Best and threw him out of the room. McGuinness was so furious that he considered sending Best home, but Sir Matt persuaded him to let Best play. In the event, he had a nightmare game, even tripping over the ball when he had an open goal in front of him.

On their arrival at Villa Park, the Leeds players soon heard the gossip about Best's bedroom antics. Even some of the hard men of Elland Road were disgusted by what Best had done. As John Giles says, they felt he was letting down the game. 'That wasn't the way to behave before an important game, and I gave George a bit of a kicking for it. He complained afterwards that I'd called him un-professional about 10 times during the match, and kicked him each time, which was true.' During several of those kicks, Giles put to Best the question: 'Why can't you be like Bobby Charlton? He's a gentleman.'

Manchester United eventually lost the semi-final to Leeds, though their League form improved towards the end of the season and they finished in eighth place. Despite all his difficulties, McGuinness was appointed for another season and his title was changed to 'manager'. But the next season was even worse for Wilf, as he struggled to establish his authority. 'He was not strong,' says Alex Stepney. 'He could not stand up to administer the kind of discipline that would gain him respect – adult discipline. His powers of motivation were negligible.'

McGuinness' desperation to impose himself on the club led to an incident which is probably the most humiliating episode of Bobby Charlton's entire career. One Friday morning the players gathered, as usual, for a training session at The Cliff. With a match the following day, the workload was much lighter than in the rest of the week. Bobby had arranged to finish early so he could go into Manchester for a business appointment. While the rest of the team were completing their training, Bobby had a bath and changed into his suit. It was a damp, bitterly cold day, and The Cliff's pitch was thick mud. But in his wisdom, McGuinness decided to call a team meeting in the middle. So, just as Bobby Charlton was about to leave, he was told to come out and join his colleagues. 'As you can imagine, he was not very happy,' says Willie Morgan. Bobby had no coat and cut a miserable figure as he stood listening to McGuinness' lecture. According to the memory of some players, rain had started to fall.

'Come on, let's go under the stand,' said one.

'No, we're staying out here,' replied McGuinness.

In an attempt to stay warm, Bobby turned up his collar and put his hands in his pockets. Now, there was an informal rule at The Cliff that anyone caught with their hands in their tracksuit pockets had to do ten press-ups. 'It was a daft rule, really, just a joke,' says Willie Morgan. Even though Bobby was not wearing his tracksuit, McGuinness decided to stick to the letter of the law.

'Bobby Charlton, ten press-ups.'

'Don't be stupid.'

'Eh, the rule still stands.'

According to Alex Stepney: 'Wilf was completely out of order. But Bobby, new suit and all, got down and compounded the farce by doing his ten press-ups. He finished with his shoes and hands covered in mud. I felt that Wilf was completely in the wrong to ask Bobby, and that Bobby was equally foolish to carry out the instruction. Wilf was very fortunate that it was Bobby and not one of the less docile members of the team that he chose to pick on.' McGuinness told me that the whole thing was done in good spirit and conditions at The Cliff have been exaggerated. 'Bobby didn't resent me and I never set out to belittle him. It was all light-hearted. It is not true that it was raining. I would not have stood out there, in the rain and mud. I would have held the team talk indoors.' But that is not how it is remembered by the players who witnessed it. 'It was bloody childish of Wilf. He wanted to try and humiliate all the star players,' said Willie Morgan. And, revealingly, Wilf does admit that Bobby didn't laugh when he was ordered down on the ground, which undermines his claim that it was all a joke.

McGuinness' methods were achieving the opposite of what he wanted. By December 1970, United were fifth from bottom of the First Division. The United board decided to act and McGuinness was sacked. Looking back on his spell in charge, McGuinness says: 'It was awkward because you have to have a distance as manager, and that it is difficult when you have been best pals with some of the players. The hardest thing of all was dropping Bobby. But I learnt from that decision that it is no use dropping players if you have not got better ones to take their place and we had no-one better than Bobby at the time.'

Busby took over again and results improved immediately, with United eventually finishing eighth in the League. Bobby Charlton, who was captain of United, was so pleased at this change in fortunes that, after a pre-season tour of Austria and Switzerland, he approached Busby on the plane home.

'The boys and I have been having a long talk and we want you to know that we would all be very happy if you carried on.'

'Bobby, I'm very grateful, but I've had enough,' replied Busby.

Once more United began the search for a new manager. Almost every top name in English football, from Jock Stein to Bill Shankly, was linked to the job. And once more, the post went to a lesser star, Frank O'Farrell, the manager of Leicester City. A Catholic from County Cork, O'Farrell had been part of the famous 'West Ham Academy' as a wing-half in the 1950s, where, along with Noel Cantwell, Malcolm Allison, Dave Sexton and John Bond, he spent hours analysing and debating the latest thinking in European football. He began his management career with non-League Weymouth, before moving on to Torquay and then Leicester. Under his leadership, the East Midlands club reached the FA Cup Final in 1969 and took the Second Division title in 1971.

O'Farrell made a blazing start to the new season and by December 1971, United were top of the League. But O'Farrell rightly believed that this success was an 'illusion'. In the New Year, performances began to reflect the true reality of United: a badly divided club, riven by cliques and filled with players who were either too old or too cynical to be effective. Denis Law had never fully recovered from the knee problems that kept him out of the European Cup Final. Paddy Crerand was too slow. And Bobby was now showing signs of ageing, though Ian Storey-Moore, O'Farrell's £200,000 signing from Nottingham Forest, says: 'He was still a great player. I thought he was still good enough to be playing for England. Tell you what, for his age, he was very fit, very strong, strong as an ox. You could not fault his professionalism. You could never complain about his attitude. He could still score some spectacular goals.' It was not a verdict with which Frank O'Farrell agreed, believing Bobby was in severe decline. Yes, the flashes of magic, like the soaring pass or the thunderous shot, were still there occasionally, but with nothing like the same consistency as in the past. In April 1969, when he was already 31, Bobby spoke to *Reveille* of his possible retirement: 'I may settle for going out slowly and possibly losing a lot of face, or I may decide that it would be better for all concerned if I faded out quietly without prolonging the agony.' Three years later mutterings in the United dressing room, particularly from Best, suggested that he had chosen the first option. Best once said, 'Bobby never tried to disguise the weaknesses that come with age, the way some players did. He gave you his total commitment for the whole of the 90 minutes. But when a great player, any player, comes towards the end of his career, the timing starts to go. By the early 1970s, Bobby's passing ability was obviously not what it had been. The radar had gone wonky and the balls were going astray. But Bobby kept on and he shouldn't have done.'

Bobby's disappointment at his waning powers was exacerbated by his anger at what he saw as the failure of O'Farrell – and his fellow senior professionals – to bring George Best into line. At this stage, Best was still a brilliant performer on the field – indeed it was his goals which were keeping United afloat – but he was starting to miss training sessions with increasing frequency, while also capturing the headlines for his lurid nocturnal activities. When he did turn up for practice, he would often be a disruptive influence. Bobby despised such behaviour, regarding it as a betrayal of both profession and club. He demanded that O'Farrell take action. In turn, O'Farrell thought it was Bobby's job, as skipper, to apply the pressure. 'I didn't think Bobby was a good captain,' says O'Farrell. 'They'd be practising set-pieces and George would do something to cock everything up. And Bobby would come to me: "Why are we practising if he's screwing things up?"

"You're the captain with 100-odd England caps. If you can't

control the situation and work as planned don't come bloody moaning to me. Push George out of the way and get on with it."'

Like McGuinness, O'Farrell decided to drop Charlton, which only increased his depression. 'It was like the Wilf thing all over again,' says Bobby, 'they seemed to think if they dropped me it would prove something.' The United dressing room was plunged into more gloom, as Bobby withdrew further into himself. 'Bobby trained on his own for a while,' recalls O'Farrell, 'just running endless laps of the pitch, talking to nobody. As you can imagine, it was some club to try and manage.' Alex Stepney provides this graphic picture of the festering atmosphere of United at this time: 'The big three, Denis, Bobby and George were at loggerheads. There were long days when they simply did not speak to each other. I am sure it was George's complete lack of concern for the club that threw Bobby Charlton into the desperately black mood which seemed to envelop him every time he was at the club. Bobby was a sensitive person who idolized Manchester United. I do not think he could bear to see the way things were going. He would turn up in the dressing room and walk straight to his peg. Without as much as a nod to anyone, he would stare straight at the wall below his peg, change into his kit and leave the room. There was never any conversation. Often, behind his back, you would see Denis or George making gestures as if to say, "What's got into him?"'

Bobby became even more reluctant to socialize with his teammates than he had been in the past, as Willie Morgan says: 'When I joined the club in 1968, I didn't find Bobby too distant. He could be a laugh then, did very good impressions. He had an amazing one of Ben Turpin, that character from the Laurel and Hardy films. But he changed in his last few years at United. If we were playing away and were out on the belt, Bobby would not join us. He tended to hang around the hotel, staying in his own room. He became a strange cat. Very morose, awkward. He looked like he had the world on his shoulders.' David Sadler says that Bobby's unhappiness resulted from George's behaviour. 'When George started doing his disappearing act, it was totally alien to Bobby's code of conduct. I know he felt that George was showing disrespect to the rest of us. Bobby was the senior figure and constantly had people saying to him, "How can you allow George to upset the dressing room with his carrying on?" It was a difficult one for him to answer, because he was more pissed off by it than anyone.'

Ian Storey-Moore was appalled at the shambolic set-up: 'There was a lot of friction, players clashing,' he told me. 'It was not a particularly friendly club. Instead of integrating as a team, United was just a group of individuals. I had been used to everyone mixing at Forest but you could tell the atmosphere at Old Trafford was much more difficult. You could sense the dislike between Denis, Bobby and George. There were undoubtedly elements of jealousy in the club against him. Silly little things, like feeling annoyed at the amount of press coverage Bobby still got. A lot of it was because Bobby was so professional, kept himself so fit and disliked the way George conducted himself – and quite rightly so. Bobby was a bit of a loner, very quiet. He would come in, get stripped, go training, come back, have a shower, get dressed and leave, without saying a word. He was very intense, always wanted to do well. Not to say that he was not a nice person but he just went on his way. He kept to himself. I find Bobby a lot more approachable now than he was as a player.' John Aston recalls that 'When Bobby went straight out after training, without saying anything, there would be a snigger among some of the lads. It was like laughing at the elder statesman.'

It is interesting that the view of the Celtic gang of Law, Best, Morgan and Crerand – that Bobby was anti-social and unsympathetic – was not shared by another Scot, the greatest United player of the 1970s, the defender Martin Buchan. Buchan, who joined the club in 1972 under Frank O'Farrell, had those qualities of utter professionalism and quiet integrity which made Bobby so admirable. In fact, Buchan, because of his initial wariness of the Old Trafford cliques, was seen as a difficult character by some when he joined United. In the words of Alex Stepney: 'He rarely spoke. He went his own way and his manner was extremely cold. He quite openly did not want to mix with us' – just the criticism made of Bobby. Yet

Martin Buchan, as he explained to me, did not feel this way about Bobby at all: 'When I joined the club, he was very good to me. He took an interest in me. He tried to help me settle in. He took me to his home to show me the area, where I met his wife and daughters, and Norma was very pleasant. He was not the remote figure people will have you believe. He was a good impressionist – one of my memories was of the way he used to reel off an advert featuring chimpanzees. He also did a very funny little soft shoe shuffle. But he would only do that sort of thing when he felt comfortable with you. There are always a lot of people who want to get to know footballers, be their friends, so that's why so many top players are reserved, cautious.' Buchan says that one of the central problems at United was that the influence of Busby could still be felt: 'A lot of the players were living in the past. They would say, "Sir Matt did this" or "Sir Matt did that". They did not want to be organized. To his credit, Bobby was never like that. He was an eternal optimist. Even when things were not going well, he would come in at half-time and say, "Come on lads, keep going." Despite the negative mentality at the club, he never gave up, he always had his own pride. The word "great" is so hyped nowadays but Bobby was truly great. He was a wonderful example to any youngster coming into the game. I will always consider it a privilege to have played with him.'

But even the arrival of Buchan could not halt the slide of United under Frank O'Farrell, particularly with George Best more feckless than ever. Bobby became so frustrated that, after yet another Best escapade, he did something he had never done before: he went to see Sir Matt Busby at his home. As Bobby said to Eamon Dunphy, 'I complained about George. I told Sir Matt that the football world was laughing at us and asked him to do something about it.' Sir Matt's reply was magisterial: 'Bobby, to err is human, to forgive is divine.'

Bobby could not bring himself to be so tolerant. Nor could he understand how the great father figure of Old Trafford could grant Best such leeway, when he had dealt so ruthlessly in the past with those who had challenged him, like Johnny Giles in 1963 or the brilliant United goalscorer John Morris, transferred in 1949 after he had been seen to undermine the manager's authority. For Bobby, Busby's reluctance to tackle Best was all too indicative of the increasingly weak leadership at Old Trafford which had sent the club into decline. It was not the first time he had been disappointed by Sir Matt. Bobby had always been much closer to Jimmy Murphy than Sir Matt, and according to Dunphy, Bobby thought that when Murphy had retired, he had been treated badly by Sir Matt – particularly petty, he believed, was the decision to stop Murphy's taxi allowance though Murphy had never learnt to drive. Bobby was also aggrieved that Busby had broken a pledge to him in 1966 over his salary. Though he was never the greedy type – if he had been, he could have earned a fortune in Italy or Spain – he had been assured by Busby that no-one in the club would be paid more than him. Yet when Busby retired, it emerged that Denis Law was marginally the top earner. Bobby didn't really care about the money, but was upset that Busby appeared to have broken his word.

By the time he was appointed a director, in 1984, Bobby was again on good terms with Busby, and, on Busby's death in 1994, Bobby made a number of fulsome and genuine tributes. But the frostiness in their relationship was all too noticeable in the 1970s, and was another reason why some of the other players, who worshipped Sir Matt, sided against Bobby. Willie Morgan says, 'Almost all the United players were faithful to Busby, loved him to bits, including me. He was one of the nicest people I ever met in my life. But Bobby, after he had retired, put some of the blame on Sir Matt for the decline of United. When Bobby criticized him, that turned a lot of the old players against him. Nobody liked that. That is why there is a sense of unease towards Bobby.' Bobby's criticism of Sir Matt came when United were relegated in the 1973/74 season under Tommy Docherty. As usual, Bobby couched his attack in the most diplomatic language but the message was obvious. 'The present plight cannot be laid at Tommy Docherty's door or that of his predecessor Frank O'Farrell. It really hurts me but it's not a shock. I've seen it coming for the last five or six years,' he said. Harry Gregg has this memory of Bobby's relationship with Busby. 'I saw him destroy Matt Busby at a tribute dinner for Jimmy Murphy. I was in the company of other players and I was employed as a coach at Old Trafford. Bobby was not working then in football. I remember that evening well. Bob was a terribly bad speaker. I was sitting in the company of Denis Law, Pat Crerand and Tommy Smith. Eventually Bobby stood up and said, "Whatever I have accomplished in football, I owe to one man and one man only, Jimmy Murphy." Denis turned to Paddy Crerand and said, "I didn't think the bastard had the guts." But Bobby went on to glorify Jimmy and bury Matt. It was embarrassing, really. Poor Matt stood up and indicted himself. He was also a poor speaker and started to say things like, "Bobby was young and he would not understand that Jimmy knocked the rough edges off the diamonds and then they were passed on to me." But Bobby would have none of it.'

After his failure to persuade Sir Matt to do anything about Best, Bobby's relations with the Ulsterman plunged to rock bottom in the 1972/73 season. Best likes to paint himself in this period as battling against his demons without help from anyone. 'If someone from United had come and found me and spoken when I went missing, I would have listened. But no-one came,' he writes in the latest version of his oft-told autobiography. But this is patently nonsense. The entire club was bending over backwards to understand and assist him. Few players have been treated more leniently in the history of British soccer. Best was continually given chances to redeem himself, but was too recalcitrant ever to take them. Even Bobby, that stalwart professional, almost succumbed to this mood. 'Sometimes I'd see him looking as if he had been out all night and part of me would be outraged yet at the same time I often wanted to put my arm around his shoulder and offer him advice. But everyone was doing that and I just couldn't bring myself to make the gesture.'

But a professional football club is not a branch of social services. Training is not meant to be therapy. Instead of whining like a hurt teenager, Best should have grown up or got out. Sadly, neither of these outcomes happened, and Bobby was reduced to a state of impotent rage. In April 1973, Bobby said, 'I just don't understand him. What do you come into football for? It's your duty to give your best to the people who come to support you, but he didn't seem to see this.' Charlton's relationship with Best became so bad that they even refused to play properly together, never mind speak. 'For a long time,' recorded Best, 'I didn't want anything to do with Bobby and avoided talking to him, or even passing the ball to him. I thought, "If he wants to go for that crossfield stuff instead of giving it to me, why should I give it to him?" I can remember him looking up and deliberately not passing to me when I was open, and I know I did the same. It was all very childish.'

Even more childish were two other instances of Best's antipathy to Charlton. The first occurred when he was asked in a TV interview who was the biggest influence on his career. He replied, 'Cissie Charlton'. As he now admits, 'It was a deliberate dig and a bit of a cruel one, having a go at Bobby's mother.'

The second was just as cruel on a professional level. On the night of 18 September 1972, Bobby Charlton's testimonial match was played at Old Trafford between Manchester United and Celtic. It was the biggest-ever benefit game played in Britain, with a crowd of 60,000 turning out to pay tribute to Charlton. A fiercely competitive contest ended in a 0–0 draw, but the most emotional moment came after the final whistle. According to a report in the *Daily Telegraph*: 'As United's captain set off on a lap of the pitch on which he has played so significant a part in the club's post-war history, scores of excited schoolboys followed him. The crowd stood to applaud his every step until he disappeared in tears, through a guard of honour drawn up by the other 21 players, down the tunnel. Few sporting heroes can have received greater acclaim. None have deserved it more thoroughly.'

George Best refused to join in the applause. He was in the latest of his periodic sulks, claiming to have 'retired' from football. Instead of playing for United that night, he sat in his favourite pub in Manchester, The Brown Bull, drunkenly throwing beer and eggs at a poster of Bobby Charlton.

It was the sort of puerile, bumptious gesture that encapsulates the spirit of George Best at this time. But perhaps the final word on him should go to Jack Charlton, who never had to put up with half as much from Best as his brother did. Jack had agreed to play in Eusebio's testimonial in Lisbon, alongside Best. 'I walked out on to the hotel balcony and there was Tommy Docherty and George. I went and sat down with them, and I remember thinking that George was saying things that were way out of order – things like "there's no way I'm doing this" and "there's no way I'm doing that". I was so disgusted, I got up and walked away. He was just a fat little fellah who had been wasting his time.'

CHAPTER SIXTEEN

The Seniors

In Place of Strife was the title of the Labour Government's 1968 White Paper on solving trade union unrest. It is also an apt description of the contrast between Leeds and Manchester United at the time. Where United had chaos and feuding, Leeds had stability and unity. Old Trafford managed to get through four managers between 1969 and 1973 while Elland Road had Don Revie at the helm throughout this period. Where Manchester were constantly signing new players in the search for success, Leeds maintained essentially the same team.

Jack Charlton, for all his advancing years, remained a crucial member of the side. Every season from 1969 began with talk that this might be the year when Jack had to retire, but the speculation was always misplaced. In February 1970, for instance, Second Division Hull City wanted to recruit him as their new manager, but Jack turned them down because he wanted to carry on playing: 'I hope that somebody will think of me in this light in two or three years' time, for then I feel quite sure I shall be interested. But at this moment Don Revie believes I can still play on in top-class football for some years.'

Two years later, when he was 37 – older than the age at which Bobby retired from United – he dismissed any idea that he might be ready to go. 'Me retire? I haven't thought about it. That's just other people's talk.' As he continued to dominate the Leeds defence, organizing the back four like a military policeman, Jack seemed almost indestructible, playing with as much commitment and assurance as ever.

Revie's faith in his evergreen centre-half was rewarded by Jack's vital contribution to Leeds' run of success from 1968. Unlike United, Leeds were always challenging for honours at this time, even though too often the ultimate trophy seemed to elude their grasp. Having picked up the League Cup and the European Fairs Cup in 1967/68, Leeds went on to win the League for the first time in 1968/69, conceding the fewest number of goals and losing the fewest number of games in history, a reflection of the strength of the defence. It might also be pointed out that Leeds gained the title with the fewest number of goals scored. Like Jack, Leeds might not have been pretty to watch, but they were effective. The 1969/70 season was perhaps the most exasperating any British club has experienced. At one stage, they were in contention for a unique treble of League, FA Cup and European Cup, but ended up with nothing. The League fell away first, when Everton drew ahead of Leeds after Easter 1970. In the FA Cup, Leeds reached Wembley after their drawn out semi-final against Manchester United – one of the replays at Villa Park being the occasion when John Giles gave Best a thorough kicking for his trouser-dropping antics. But Leeds were becoming worn out by the demands of their fixture list; their third replay against Manchester United was their eighth game in 15 days. So drained did Jack feel that one night he booked into a hotel with Billy Bremner just to get drunk. 'I felt stretched like an elastic band,' he said.

The exhaustion exacted a heavy price, as Leeds stumbled at home in the first leg of their European Cup semi-final against Celtic at Elland Road, losing 1–0. Next they had to play the FA Cup Final against Chelsea, where Jack experienced almost the same kind of heartbreak he had been through against Germany four years earlier. Just as England had seemingly clinched victory in the World Cup with a goal deep into the second half, so Leeds were 2–1 up thanks to an 83rd minute strike from Mick Jones. But then, like Germany, Chelsea equalized in the dying moments of the game and again, as in 1966, the goal came from a disputed free-kick conceded by Jack Charlton. 'We should have beaten Chelsea and deserved to. It was 1–0 to us and then Gary Sprake made a dreadful mistake and let one go straight under him. It was infuriating, because when you work so hard to get ahead and then your keeper makes a howler, it's all for nothing. Gary was very talented but he was the weak link in our side. He let us down on a lot of occasions. He cost us some important games,' says John Giles, providing perhaps the best explanation as to why Leeds finished runners-up so often.

There were no further goals in extra-time and the match went to a replay at Old Trafford. Meanwhile, Leeds lost 2–1 in the second leg of their European Cup semi-final against Celtic in front of 135,826 spectators at Hampden, still the largest crowd ever to see an English club play in Britain. Leeds' hopes of any silverware vanished when they lost the FA Cup replay, again in extra-time. Jack blamed himself for the first Chelsea goal. He had been up in the Chelsea goalmouth for a corner, when he received a violent kick on the thigh. As he gave chase to the culprit – whom Jack has never named – the ball was knocked into the Leeds box and, with Jack out of position, Peter Osgood headed home. It was Chelsea's equalizer, and they went on to score the winner in extra-time with a scrappy David Webb header. 'The disappointment was incredible,' wrote Jack. 'I went straight to the dressing room and kicked open the door. I've never been more upset over losing a game, maybe because it was partly my fault. Nobody else came into the dressing room and I just sat there for ages.'

It is a tribute to the sense of togetherness which Revie inspired that Leeds did not fall apart after this triple setback – as might have happened to a less cohesive team. 'Don created this wonderful spirit,' says Giles. 'It's the thing I remember most about my time at the club. Whatever the disappointments we had, and there were a lot, we took it on the chin and we'd start again.' The next season, 1970/71, had more disappointments, as Leeds were just beaten to the title by Arsenal. Perhaps even worse was their early exit from the FA Cup at the hands of Fourth Division Colchester, who beat them 3–2 at Layer Road in one of the great upsets of all time. When the draw for the fifth round was announced, Billy Bremner had cheekily asked, 'Where's Colchester?' But the Essex team were soon 3–0 up, with the veteran former Ipswich and England striker Ray Crawford creating havoc in the Leeds defence. 'I had no idea Leeds would be so vulnerable. After all, Jack Charlton is four inches taller than me,' Crawford said after the game. Jack himself said later, 'We came home with a feeling of shame.' But Leeds had the huge consolation of winning the European Fairs Cup for the second time, when they beat Juventus on the away goals rule.

The next season Leeds again looked like they could win the Double. They beat Arsenal in a dull Cup Final at Wembley, with Jack brilliantly snuffing out the challenge of Arsenal striker Charlie George. In the League, Revie's team surprised their critics by playing more adventurous football than they had done previously, winning a string of pulsating victories, including 7–0 against Southampton and 5–1 against both Newcastle and Manchester United. Such was Leeds' superiority in the game against Southampton that at one stage 32 successive passes were made without a Southampton player being able to touch the ball. In fact, the only outfield Leeds player who was not involved in this remarkable display of possession was Jack Charlton. As Eddie Gray recalls: 'Jack was waving his arms around to attract the attention of the players on the ball but they pretended they had not seen him. Jack always fancied himself as a centre-half who could do more than defend and this was typical of the way we liked to tease him about it.' Afterwards, when Jack asked why no-one had given him the ball, John Giles said, 'Because we wanted to keep it, Jack.' After ten years, Revie was finally allowing his team to relax. But, as so often before, they failed in the match that really counted. Needing only a draw against Wolves at Molineux, they contrived to lose 2–1 and Derby County became champions.

Throughout these years, Jack was the senior professional. Though he was always a far more outspoken, gregarious figure than Bobby, he shared with his younger brother a sense of separateness from the rest of the team. This was partly because of his age and his interest in fishing and shooting rather than golf, but it also reflected his character. His volatility and occasional grumpiness made him the ideal target for the endless mickey-taking which is so much part of professional football. Whatever the practical joke, Jack would almost always rise to the bait. 'He would take a lot of stick from us, because he used to be the most miserable sod in the morning. We were always teasing him, trying to get him to snap,' says Peter Lorimer. 'I stripped beside him in the dressing room,' recalls John Giles, 'and in the morning, when he came in, I'd say: "Morning Jack."

"You little fuck."

"Are you not going to say good morning then?"

"I've other things on my mind."'

Jack's usual routine was to get in for training at 10am, strip, put a towel round his waist, pick up a copy of the *Sun* and then trudge across the corridor to read it on the toilet. One day Allan Clarke and John Giles decided to add to the excitement of the morning. So they went into the laundry room next to the toilets, got a large bucket, filled it with water and very quietly sneaked into the toilets. Allan Clarke takes up the story: 'We then stood on a laundry basket and leant over the wall of Jack's cubicle. What a sight it was: Big Jack sitting there, without much on, looking at Page Three. So Gilesy then let him have it, absolutely soaked him, and we ran out. When we got back to the dressing room, we told the other lads what we had done. We were killing ourselves. We were laughing so much we were crying.'

Then Jack walked in, still in his towel, 'looking like a drowned rat', according to David Harvey. The laughter stopped, as Jack looked around the dressing room. Allan Clarke continues: 'He's got this towel wrapped round him and he said, "Right, that's it. Anybody who goes to the loo while I'm at this club is unsafe." We just burst out laughing.

"Especially you." He pointed at me. He must have caught a glimpse of me over the top of the cubicle.

"Jack, I didn't do it. I didn't throw it."

"Well, you missed me."

That just made it even more funny. I mean, he was standing there absolutely soaked, his paper wringing wet. He hadn't got much hair but what he had was dripping. Incredible.'

David Harvey tells another story from his time on the Leeds ground staff: 'Jack lived only 250 yards from Elland Road. Yet he was so bone idle that rather than walk to the ground, he would get his car out of the garage and drive there. One day, it had been snowing very hard. We could not believe that, even in these conditions, Jack had actually jumped into his car. So while he was out training, a group of us pushed his car into the snowdrift at the bottom of the car park. All that was visible were two reflector lights. Then we piled more snow on to the car. After Jack had changed, he went outside, only to discover that his car no longer seemed to be there. He went back in to the club secretary and reported that it had been stolen. We were watching all this and laughing.'

The same mentality applied on the training ground. In Leeds, as at many other clubs, there was an informal tradition that the worst performer in the day's five-a-side match was awarded a yellow jersey. The decision was reached after a vote amongst the team and the name was recorded on a chart in the dressing room. In such practice games, Jack often liked to play up front. In the view of Alan Peacock, 'He just wanted to be like Bobby, he wanted to do something with the ball, but he couldn't.' It isn't much of a surprise that Jack regularly came bottom of the poll and was given the jersey, though, as John Giles admits, 'We sometimes did it just to gee him up.' But Jack became fed up with what he perceived to be the unfair judgement of his colleagues, as Allan Clarke recalls: 'One day, when he was given the yellow jersey, Jack went absolutely spare. He said, "You're all ganging up on me. I wasn't the worst player out there." He then tore the chart off the wall and kicked over a milk bottle. He was like a big, soft kid really. He had a bath, came out, was still raging, got his kit on and drove home. When he came in the next day, you would have thought nothing had happened. Unbelievable. He never bore grudges.'

There is an intriguing parallel here with Manchester United, in that Bobby – according to Willie Morgan – was also frequently given the five-a-side yellow jersey in much the same circumstances. 'It was just a joke that Bobby kept being given the jersey,' says Morgan. 'We did it because we knew we could get a reaction from him, whereas most other players couldn't care. And because he took exception, he was given it all the more.'

One of Jack's traits that has stood out all his life is that he has to have his own way. Now this sort of tunnel vision could be positive in that it enabled him, as a manager, to set out a clear vision for his teams. Everyone knew who was the boss if Jack was around. But it could also make him self-centred at times. 'In many ways, Jack could be very understanding, kind and helpful. But he could also be an absolute arse. It was just his attitude. It was a privilege to play with him, but he treated us all like shit. We were all subordinate to Jack Charlton,' says David Harvey. 'He had a very good side, was genuinely warm hearted, cared about people – that's why he was a big Labour supporter,' says Lorimer. 'Even his other side could be part of his charm. He's the only man I know who would charge you to babysit for him. He'd do it by borrowing a fiver and then, when you asked for it back and mentioned the babysitting, he'd say, "Well, you had the use of my couch all evening." He enjoyed winding people up like that.'

John Giles give this analysis. 'We had a saying for Jack in the dressing room: "He's not always right but he's never wrong." At Leeds, though he might not have been aware of it, he was always a bit apart, because he would always go his own way, have his own ideas. Jack could be totally insensitive to other people. Now I don't mean that I didn't like him. But that's just the way he was. We would be watching the television before the pre-match meal. Then Jack would come into the lounge and plonk his chair right down in front of the rest of us, obscuring our view.

"Eh, Jack."

"What?"

"We can't see the fucking TV. Fuck off out of the way."

"Ah for fuck's sake," he would sigh, making a big deal about having to move his chair, as if we were doing him a disservice. During Don Revie's bingo sessions, he would get mad if someone beat him on the last number. He would jump up as if the whole thing was a fix, saying "I'll never fucking win at this game." We would all laugh. But you could never be offended by him. There was no malice in him, no conniving. He would tell you straight what he thought of you. He would talk to anyone about anything, off the top of his head, even personal things. He would row with anyone, but never in a personal way. He was so honest, so open, it was endearing.'

It was Jack's almost brazen honesty that was to land him in the greatest controversy of his career. In October 1970, Tyne Tees Television conducted an in-depth interview with him about the realities of life as a top professional footballer. It was a far more thorough, interesting job than most of the dreary, cliché-ridden, 'boys-done-good' interviews that are served up today for public consumption. The first reaction to the programme was highly positive. In the Tyne Tees building, the studio audience watching the live filming of Charlton's performance laughed and applauded. Amongst their number were Cissie and Bob Charlton, who rose to his feet with pride and declared his brother to be 'a man's man'.

But, with characteristic forthrightness, Jack had used two sentences that would return to haunt him with a vengeance in the coming weeks. First, he said: 'I have a little book with players' names in it. If I get the chance to do them I will. I will make them suffer before I pack it in. If I can kick them four yards over the touchline I will.' The second went: 'If I was chasing a player in an international match and I could not catch him, I would flatten him.'

As usual with such sagas, it was not the interview itself which provoked the outrage, but the interpretation of it in the press. Several reporters, attending the Tyne Tees preview, picked up Jack's remarks and relayed them to their national offices. The moment they appeared in print, there was a national outcry. Macaulay famously wrote in 1843 that there is 'no spectacle so ridiculous as the British public in one of its periodical fits of morality' and it was exactly one such fit which now had Jack Charlton at its centre. 'These sickening comments,' ran the headline in the *Daily Express*, above an opinion piece by sports editor John Morgan which called for Charlton to be sacked by Leeds: 'The damage caused by the words Charlton used cannot be estimated in the effect it will have on hundreds of youngsters. The damage abroad will show in the inevitable reper-cussions years hence.' In the *Daily Mirror* Peter Wilson asked: 'Have these petulant, primping, over-paid, under-principled gladiators no responsibility?'

As he had always done on the football field, Jack displayed remarkable calm under pressure. He refused to retract any of his comments and rightly said he was only speaking the truth about what went on in professional football. He told the *Yorkshire Evening Post* on 5 October, 'I have no regrets. I stand by what I said during the interview. I have been in this game a long time and I am not a dirty player, but what I referred to in the interview does happen. Everyone knows what goes on but no-one has ever said it before. I was asked a question and I answered it honestly.' What particularly annoyed him was the way the journalists rushed to condemn him without actually having viewed the film. 'The press have knocked me terribly about something they know nothing about. It has been taken completely out of context. Everything I said was qualified.' With the loyalty that was his hallmark, manager Don Revie sup-ported him. Having viewed the film, he said he could not see what all the fuss was about.

Other, less feverish voices in the media put the row into some context. Ian Wooldridge in the *Daily Mail* praised Jack for break-ing 'a conspiracy of silence' over vendettas in professional sport. 'Vendettas did not start with Jack Charlton. They are as old as Dixie Dean.' Wooldridge then recounted the story of how the 16-year-old Dean had lost a testicle to a particularly vicious defender while play-ing for Tranmere. Dean had told Wooldridge, '17 years later, I saw him in a pub in Chester. I waited for him to leave, followed him down the road and then, in a quiet corner I beat the living daylights out of him.' Joe Mercer, the hugely respected manager of Manchester City, put forward the widely held view in the football world that Jack was not a dirty player: 'He is no soccer hard man. He's a good professional. He's a sportsman who loves to win. But he is not an assassin on the field who must win at all costs. I can tell you straight that none of my Manchester City players have any fear of Charlton.' For the Professional Footballers Association, Derek Dougan gave this balanced verdict: 'I have played against Jack at club and international level and have found him a very fair competitor. I wouldn't say he wasn't hard, but I don't think I have ever had any sort of injury when playing against him. He may be justified in saying this because in the past one or two players may have taken liberties against him.'

Football's administrators, however, felt they had to respond to the public mood and immediately imposed a temporary ban on Jack playing for England, a meaningless punishment given that Jack had told Ramsey on the plane back from Mexico that he wished to retire from international football. A special joint disciplinary committee was then organized by the Football League and FA to hear the charge against Jack of 'bringing the game into disrepute'. Ably supported by Revie, Jack persuasively argued his case and was, effectively, exonerated. There was to be no suspension or fine, and Jack was only required to make an apology for his remarks. This he did in the most adroit way, managing a not-too-subtle dig at the media: 'I apologize that, through me, the press were given an opportunity to knock football.'

It was ironic that Jack Charlton should be the focus of such a controversy over dirty play, given that, as we have seen, there were many in his own Leeds side who were far more guilty. Indeed, Jack strongly opposed the cynical, sour 'professionalism' of the Leeds approach as John Giles, confirmed to me. 'Jack would get stuck in, do his job and do it well, but that was it. Bobby Collins, for instance, was a great player, but he was also very aggressive and Jack didn't like that. Now in the sixties, football was a violent game. If you were a skilful player, other teams would try to put you out of the match. If you didn't give it back, you were a soft touch. My attitude was that I had to respond in order to play. So I responded, Bobby Collins responded and it could be very vicious. Jack knew what I was doing, and he never approved of that. So we had a few rows about it.' Alan Gowling, who played as a striker for Manchester United from 1968 before he joined Newcastle, gave me this perspective on facing Jack: 'I personally always found him always very fair. He was physically very strong, dominant in the air, tough to play against but he was not dirty. He could handle himself but he would not resort to the kind of off-the-ball tactics that a lot of Leeds players went for. I can always remember one occasion when we were at Elland Road. Jack had got the ball with his back to me. I tried to get past him and caught him on the leg. He turned round as if he was going to throw this great punch at me. And then he saw it was me and realized I was not someone who would normally kick him just for the sake of it. He said, "It's a good job it was you."'

The hypocrisy of the game in 1970 was that both officials and journalists whipped up a frenzy over Jack while doing little about far worse offenders. The idea that Jack was some sort of thug, working his way through a hit list, was just absurd, as John Giles says: 'The black book was just a joke in the Leeds dressing room. But Jack got in trouble because he never saw anything wrong in speaking his mind.' Later, Jack revealed the names of several of the players he particularly despised – Bertie Auld of Celtic, George Kirby of Southampton ('a player always liable to hurt you') and John Morrisey, the Everton winger. Brian Labone, Morrisey's Everton colleague, understands why Jack felt strongly about him: 'John was a dirty little bugger. He was about half the size of Jack and when he was around, you had to look out.'

Perhaps the most interesting aspect of this whole sorry business was the way it provided the first glimpse into the tensions within the Charlton family. Despite their distance, both the brothers had always been loyal to each other in their public pronouncements, but on this occasion, Bobby – who, coincidentally played his 500th game for United during the week of the broadcast – decided to go on the attack. In an article on 7 October 1970 in the *Daily Express*, under the headline 'Explain Yourself Brother Jack', Bobby said: 'The remarks on the record would not come well from a lad of 20 or 21 who had been in the game five minutes. But the effect is that much worse when they come from someone of Jack's experience and prestige. Jack must know what effect this business is having, that it is not doing the game any good. But he appears to be sticking to his guns. This is Jack all right. He is as stubborn as they come.' The New Zealand journalist Norman Harris was in Jack's house at the time of the crisis and, in a diary piece, described the reaction to Bobby's article: 'There is now some dissension in the family, and unpleasantness in a phone conversation between the two brothers.' Then Cissie took up the cudgels against Bobby, no longer the favourite son since his marriage to Norma: 'I am amazed at our Bobby,' she told the *Daily Mail*, 'he's in the same position as all of Jack's other critics. He hasn't seen the television programme.' And she added, in defence of Jack, 'Everyone knows Jack is not a dirty player. Where has everyone's sense of humour gone?'

As with so many press-inspired squalls, this one disappeared almost as soon as it had blown up. The lurid predictions of a collapse in the standing of the game never materialized. Nor was there any real long-term damage to Jack's reputation. Indeed, if anything, he was respected all the more for his plain speaking in the twilight of his career.

By the middle of the 1972/73 season, Jack realized that he was reaching the end of his time at Elland Road. He was now almost 38 and the club had signed the young Scot Gordon McQueen, who was soon regularly taking Jack's place in the side. Physically, Jack was still as strong as ever – Peter Lorimer says that 'he could have played on after 1973; he was as fit when he finished as when he started' – but mentally he could no longer motivate himself. He went to Don Revie and explained that he wanted to retire at the end of the 1973 season. Revie offered him a two-year contract, hoping that Jack might eventually join the Elland Road coaching staff, but Jack had made up his mind. 'I had seen it all as a player and frankly I didn't fancy the idea of soldiering on.'

Across the Pennines, Bobby had reached the same conclusion. Sickened by Best and the decline of United, he had become more disillusioned than ever, sometimes taking out his hostility on those around him. Ted MacDougall, one of Frank O'Farrell's signings, says: 'I once asked Bobby Charlton the best way to United's training ground. I'm still waiting for an answer. If he didn't feel like it, Bobby just wouldn't bother to reply.' MacDougall, who cost £200,000 from Third Division Bournemouth but scored just five goals in 18 games, was all too indicative of O'Farrell's poor judgement. By December 1972 O'Farrell had lost the support of the board and was sacked after United were thrashed 5–0 by Crystal Palace. To this day, he remains bitter about his dismissal, which Pat Crerand says Bobby was instrumental in securing: 'Bobby was the one who got Frank the sack. Bobby was running to Louis Edwards (the United chairman) all the time. If Frank wants to have the needle with anyone, it is Bobby Charlton.' This is going too far, for Bobby had nothing like the influence of Busby in such major decisions. But there is no doubt Bobby's disdain for O'Farrell had some effect, as he himself admits, 'I was as much to blame as anyone for Frank's dismissal.'

By the time O'Farrell's replacement, Tommy Docherty, arrived at Old Trafford, Bobby had decided to hang up his boots. Confirming Bobby's feelings about the decline of United, Docherty found it to be 'a club riddled with cancer. Old players, skivers, players who were more concerned with getting rid of the next manager, whoever he may be. Not all players had a bad attitude, I hasten to add. Just a section. They had virtually taken over. It was like a canker.' Bobby was one of those who could be exempted from this criticism, though Docherty says he was grateful for Bobby's decision to get out. 'Bobby did me a great favour when he decided to retire. I knew that was a decision I would have to make one day, I knew it wouldn't be a popular one.' During the season he admitted that it was Bobby's professionalism that would be missed more than his skills – 'I'll be able to replace him on the field but not off it.' To Eamon Dunphy, Bobby explained his reasoning. 'At the club we had really struggled for a couple of years and I began to feel mentally and physically drained. And the matches were getting hard, we nearly got relegated. I realized I was not looking forward to getting up on Saturday morning any more. So I said to Norma, I think I'll pack it in at the end of the season.'

In another indicator of the lack of closeness in the Charlton family, Bobby did not tell his brothers or parents about his retirement. The first they knew of it was when they read about it in the paper. 'It was a bolt out of the blue. My dad and I knew nothing about it. I never thought he would do it,' said Tommy Charlton, the youngest brother, who was working then in the Ashington Colliery. Jack echoed the same sentiments, 'I never thought our kid would give up playing of his own free will – I thought they would have to shoot him first.'

The last month of the 1972/73 season became the long farewell for Jack and Bobby. Jack held his testimonial match at Elland Road against Celtic, with exactly the same opponents, Celtic, as had turned out for Bobby. Tributes for the brothers poured from all corners of football. Typical was Frank Clough's in the *Sun* about Bobby, whom he described as the 'nicest man I know'. Warming to his theme, Clough wrote, 'I can say, hand on heart, that he is one of the most genuine, sincere and likeable men I have ever met.' Sir Matt joined in the chorus of approval, 'this wonderful footballer, this remarkable man who stands for the important values of both football and life'. Jack did not seem to suffer too much by comparison. Sir Alf, in Jack's testimonial brochure, called him 'one of the outstanding footballers of our time', while Don Revie wrote that 'I shall be forever grateful to him and Leeds United will too. No club could have had a greater servant.'

In this festival of flattery, one of the few discordant notes was sounded by the late and estimable Frank McGhee in the *Daily Mirror*: 'Bobby Charlton has had so much sentimental treacle poured over him recently it has become difficult to take a last honest look beneath all that goo at the player involved. For a couple of seasons now Bobby has edged dangerously close to the folly of going on just a bit too long. Everything that compelled the admiration of so many fans has still been there during that slow decline . . . the style, the stride, the swerve, the sweeping pass, the innate athleticism, even the shot of a man who was never a great goalscorer but always a scorer of great goals. But somehow it has all shrunk.' And, as McGhee pointed out, Denis Law, who was also leaving United at the end of the season after being given a free transfer by Tommy Docherty, had some reason to feel aggrieved at all the attention focused on Bobby. 'In comparison to the fuss made over Charlton, the belligerent Scot has been cold-shouldered by United.' To be fair to Bobby, he never wanted it this way and would rather have gone quietly. 'I would have rather liked just to have played my last game, collected my things and walked away,' he said on the day his plans for retirement were revealed. 'I feel a little embarrassed. But I wanted to say thank you.'

The Charlton recessional did not end in a blaze of glory. Jack pulled a hamstring and missed the last games of the season, including Leeds' shock defeat by Sunderland in the FA Cup Final. Meanwhile, Bobby's last game took place at Chelsea on 29 April 1973. The 21 other players formed a circle in the middle of the pitch, and then Bobby was presented with an inscribed cigarette box. At the final whistle, United had lost 1–0. It was symbolic of Bobby's last years with United.

CHAPTER SEVENTEEN

The Managers

Neither Bobby nor Jack wanted to leave football once they had retired as players in the summer of 1973. Club management was therefore the next obvious step. At first glance, they both seemed eminently suited to this role, given their playing record and the respect in which they were held by the football world. Jack, in particular, had long been seen as potential management material because of his coaching work and strong personality. In 1970, for instance, Bill Shankly predicted that Jack would become one of the top managers of the decade, citing these qualities: 'He gives you a straight answer to a straight question. He makes up his mind quickly and stands by it. That's important for a manager. You are no good if you allow yourself to be influenced by other people when your mind is made up. To be a good coach you must first have been a good player. And Jack is certainly that. He is the best English centre-half I have ever seen and one of the easiest coaches to understand.'

But others were more doubtful about the Charltons' managerial potential, including, interestingly, their own wives. Adopting her husband's brand of frankness, Pat Charlton said in 1972, 'I don't think Jack would make a good manager. He's too tactless, he's very outspoken.' Two years earlier, Norma had been equally concerned about Bobby. 'It wouldn't suit him being a manager. I think he would really like to be a coach. You've not got the same authority as a manager but then you haven't got the same worries.'

Such views were shared by some in the football world. David Harvey, the Leeds goalkeeper, told me: 'I must be a bad judge because I always thought Jack's man-management skills were next to nil. As a manager, you cannot treat everyone the same. Some players need a kick up the arse, some players need coaxing along. I could not for a minute imagine Jack having the patience to deal with someone who was not performing. When I heard at Leeds that Jack was becoming a manager, my first thoughts were, "Oh Christ". I thought both his patience was nil and that he lacked the skill in organizing people, not just on the pitch but off it.' John Giles, who knew him better than most, says: 'I never fancied Jack to make a good manager. I thought he would be too set in his ways and would not get a response from players or have any affection for them. I thought his view as a manager would be: "Fuck the players. They have nothing to do with our success."'

Over at Manchester United, John Aston had felt the same way about Bobby. 'I didn't think he would make a good manager. Footballers need to be barked at by sergeant-major types. Bobby wasn't like that.' Ian Greaves, who had played with Bobby in the 1950s, and, by 1973 was the successful manager of Huddersfield Town, argues that Bobby was 'never cut out for management. You've got to be able to give someone a right bollocking. You've got to be able to get everyone in the dressing room and give them the biggest lashing they've ever had in their lives. Football is not about loving each other, it is about winning bloody matches. It's about bringing them in for training on a Sunday morning if they've played badly the day before. It's about doing things that hurt. Bob couldn't have done that. He was too nice a guy.'

Jack himself had few reservations about this new career path, but Bobby was more circumspect. In April 1969, echoing Norma's words, he said, 'Whatever happens, I shall have to stay in the game in some capacity, but it is unlikely I shall ever become a manager.

It's the worst job with the best pay. There are easier jobs with much more satisfaction, like coaching, for instance.'

But, four years later, he had changed his mind. He had received a batch of job offers from public relations and marketing firms, and he had also flirted with the idea of going into journalism, the career he had first fixed upon as a child in Ashington. But, as he explained, 'Full-time journalism wouldn't satisfy me. I think as a journalist it would be frustrating to be connected with the game but not involved in it. Lots of friends say I should keep clear of being a manager, that there's too much back stabbing. I might not like it and I might not be any good but I'd hate to think that I hadn't given it a try if asked.'

Given their lack of hard management experience, there was little chance of either Bobby or Jack being offered a job at a top club, though in November 1972 Sunderland revealed a daring plan to lure the two brothers back to the north-east. The proposal, outlined by Sunderland's chairman Keith Collings, was to have Bobby and Jack as joint managers. The advantage, claimed Sunderland, was that Jack could be the 'tracksuited dynamo', while the quieter Bobby could provide the 'administrative and technical know-how'. Though Sunderland claimed to be '90 per cent confident' of pulling off this coup, the club had ignored the fundamental incompatibility of Bobby and Jack. The scheme therefore went nowhere and Bob Stokoe took over.

Less fantastic were the separate approaches of two other, smaller Second Division clubs, Middlesbrough for Jack and Preston North End for Bobby, which were accepted. Jack did indeed like the idea of going back to his native north-east, though not with his brother in tow. He was especially reassured when Boro agreed to his demand for full control over the club's affairs – 'I wanted to show I was the boss and had a say in everything.' Inevitably, Jack had to introduce a note of chaos into his appointment. When he was first approached about the job, over the phone, by his friend and England team doctor Neil Philips, who also happened to be a Middlesbrough director, he agreed to meet him to discuss it in more detail.

'Fine, Jack, you name the place,' said Philips.

So Jack chose a hotel he claimed to know, situated halfway between Leeds and Middlesbrough. When Philips turned up, however, he found that the nominated building had been demolished.

Bobby was pleased to take over at the Lancashire club, not only because Preston was not far from his family home but also because it had such a strong footballing tradition. 'When they offered me the job, my pride stopped me snatching the offer right away but I knew I was going to say yes. Me, manager of Preston! I thought about Tom Finney, Bill Shankly, Willie Cunningham and all those other great names that had made Preston famous and proud. I've always loved the place. Deepdale is one of those ground that reeks of football. You can smell the liniment, hear the crowd even when there is no-one there.' As so often before, the way Bobby handled his acceptance of the Preston offer caused some friction with his brother. Jack says that he had attended a Football Writers' Banquet in May 1973, just before the Cup Final and Bobby was also there. 'He'd already taken the Preston job, but he never mentioned it to me, which I found a little strange. The first I knew of it was when I read about it in the Sunday papers a few days later.' Bobby's excuse is that, at the time of the dinner, he had still not finalized the terms of the job. 'We hadn't talked about the contract, so I thought I would keep it close to my chest, in case it all fell through. Maybe I should have told him that Preston were interested in me, but I don't remember Jack ever phoning me up to ask for advice.'

When he started work at Preston, in July 1973, Bobby continued to make enthusiastic noises. 'Right now,' he told *Express* writer Jimmy Mossop, 'I'm loving every minute of it. When I was at Old Trafford and the team was struggling I used to wake up and toss and turn and wonder what the hell I could do about Manchester United. Now I wake up at 3am, have a little chuckle about me and Preston and go back to sleep again.' But once the season started, it became obvious that he had taken on a bigger challenge than he expected.

One of the endlessly fascinating aspects of football is no-one can ever predict with certainty which players will become good managers. Who would have thought that the elegant and religiously eccentric Glenn Hoddle would have become far more successful than the more earthy and aggressive Bryan Robson? If noise and passion were the key then Alan Ball would be the best of modern times, and David O'Leary the worst. If technical understanding is the answer, how does one explain the records of Brian Clough and Matt Busby, who both had little time for coaching? Shankly's rule, about the need to be a decent footballer, is utterly contradicted by the case of Sven-Goran Eriksson, who could not even make it in the Swedish Second Division, while probably the greatest English manager of all, Herbert Chapman, never played League football at all. Nor does age seem to matter. Stan Cullis, the great 'iron manager' of Wolves, took over the Black Country club when he was just 31, yet Bobby Robson is still performing wonders at St James' Park at almost 70. Bobby Charlton himself reflected on this point as he took charge at Preston. 'I don't know if I am management material. I wish I did. I feel like a kid at Christmas, just dying to open his parcels to see what's inside. I won't know till we start playing.'

Jack was not plagued with any such worries. He soon made his presence felt at Ayresome Park, ordering a new type of playing strip with a white band on red shirts, improving the television facilities, having the ground repainted, stepping up the marketing and public relations, transferring a couple of players he deemed to be trouble-makers, and buying Bobby Murdoch from Celtic, who turned out to be the pivot of the Boro defence in the first season. He also wore a tracksuit with the single four-letter word JACK emblazoned across the back – as if anyone could ever be in any doubt about his identity. But Jack did not throw his weight around mindlessly. Unlike so many managers who come into a club and feel they have to start a revolution, Jack retained most of the backroom staff, including the former England trainer Harold Shepherdson. The same was true of the playing staff – in fact, Bobby Murdoch was to be his only signing that first season. Jack felt his job was to improve his footballers, not acquire new ones. 'It is easy to fall into the trap of buying players who are no better than those already on your staff,' he once said.

The manner with which he went about his work was immediately striking to the players, as John Craggs told me: 'He was very confident, a big presence as soon as he arrived. He was like Brian Clough, knowing exactly what he wanted. I remember, right at the start, he took us to a local hotel and announced: "There are some good players here, some mediocre players here and some bad ones." And afterwards, privately, he pretty soon told us which category we fitted into. He was no-nonsense, very much a tracksuit manager, out on the pitch organizing things. He was very direct in telling us what he wanted.' The left-sided midfielder David Armstrong, whom Jack described as a 'key member of the team', has this memory of Jack's appointment: 'Because Jack was such a big name – World Cup winner and Leeds star – many of us were a little apprehensive about his arrival. We did not know what to expect. And I have to admit that, at first, I was a bit frightened by his imposing character. He could be pretty intimidating, especially to a young lad like me. When I wanted a pay rise, I was too nervous to ask for much because I was scared he might kick me straight out the door. But I soon saw how helpful he was. Like he felt I was a bit frail, needed building up, so he sent me to his parents' farm in Leyburn for a week, where I got proper home cooking, North Yorkshire air and long walks.' The visits to Cissie at Leyburn were to become a vital experience for many young Boro and Wednesday footballers over the next 10 years. 'He really nurtured me and was a vital part of my progression,' says Armstrong. 'In today's football, there aren't enough managers around like Jack, willing to develop youngsters.'

The gap in managerial confidence between Jack and Bobby soon became apparent once the 1973/74 season was underway. Like two swimmers, Jack had dived straight in and was already pulling away with powerful strokes, while Bobby was apprehensively feeling his way in the shallow end. In *The Sunday Times* on 19 August 1973, Rob Hughes wrote a profile, highlighting the contrast between the two novice managers. 'Big Jack's Middlesbrough is an open house. He may forget he invited you, but once you're there, he'll show you the works, unfold his mind. His players sweat under his boisterous command, but they laugh a lot too with the boss. Jack's learning to delegate. He'll have nothing of office work, has no named assistant and makes decisions after talking to his wife Pat, a good listener.' Of the younger brother, Hughes wrote: 'Bobby Charlton, by comparison, has begun managerial life as something of a recluse behind Preston's doors. Turning down a request for an interview, he said, "It may be interesting to you but it's hard work to me and I've no time to create unnecessary work by going into things in great detail."' Betraying his insecurity, Bobby then asked Hughes to 'appreciate I'm learning the business. I don't really know myself what my plans are. I don't really want to be observed while I'm finding out.' Again, unlike Jack, he had become involved in the administrative side: 'I try to do everything. I don't hate office work at all. Every aspect must be done and I'm trying to do it.'

In an attempt to make himself more at ease, Bobby surrounded himself with trusted former colleagues from Manchester United. He brought the veteran trainer, Jack Crompton, from Old Trafford and also imported Francis Burns and David Sadler. Most tellingly of all, in August he signed his former midfield partner Nobby Stiles, who had gone to Middlesbrough in May 1971. Nobby says there was nothing personal against Jack about the £20,000 move; it was just that he welcomed the return to his native Manchester: 'Middlesbrough was a bad experience family-wise. We just didn't settle. I'm a Manchester lad, a townie, a city person.' And he was also delighted to join up again with his old United captain, saying: 'I have great respect for Bobby. I have been a close friend and an admirer of his for years.'

With this kind of support, Preston made a solid start to the season. By November, they were just three points off a promotion place. Bobby claimed to be loving his new role: 'There is nothing better than a dressing room after a victory. Being a manager, the pleasure is 11 times better than it was as a player. Then, I suppose, victory was for myself. Now I see 11 lads completely happy.' David Sadler says that Bobby was greatly helped at this time by his reputation: 'He had no problem asserting his authority in the dressing room because he was so respected. He had earned that respect through all his efforts in the game. All of us looked up to him.' The winger Tony Morley, who went on to play for Aston Villa and England, gave me this concrete example of how Bobby assisted him: 'I have nothing but admiration for the man. He was always encouraging me. It was through him that I got into the England Under-23 team. He once taught me a lesson which was so valuable for my career. I was just 18, bit of a Jack the lad, a dribbler, could keep the ball all day. And he said to me, "That's great, but it's not what the game is all about." He brought over his old United team-mate Dennis Viollet (who was then coach at Crewe). Now Dennis was about 40 then, even older than Bobby. We all went out on the pitch for a practice match and Bobby told me to mark Dennis. I tell you, Dennis played one-touch football all afternoon, and I could not get near him. It really taught me about the game. Bobby was not trying to degrade me with that lesson. He just wanted to show that if I was to become a better player, I would have to add one-touch skills to my dribbling.'

Morley also points out that, for all his international reputation, Bobby retained his modesty. 'I have found during my life in sport that often the stars who truly touch greatness are the most humble – and I would certainly put Bobby in that category. I was in awe of him, yet he was just one of the lads. There was no sense of pride about him. Like he would be willing to carry the kit from the bus to the dressing room. He would have a drink, a game of cards.' Roy Tunks, the Preston goalkeeper, recalls an incident which demonstrates Bobby's lack of self-importance. 'We used to do silly things on the bus just to keep ourselves entertained, because there were no videos in those days. One time, we had some water pistols and I squirted the back of Bobby's head. He stood up and came storming up the bus. "Uh oh, we've gone a bit far here." But when he reached our aisle, the first thing he said was, "Can I have a go?" He was like a big kid at heart.'

But Preston's reasonable start was far surpassed by Jack Charlton's Middlesbrough, who went top of the table on 29 September 1973 and stayed there for the rest of the season. No other side looked remotely like catching Boro and promotion to the First Division was assured with seven matches still to play. It was a remarkable achievement, reflecting Jack's ability both to create a strong team spirit and impose an effective system of playing. 'He knew our limitations, our strengths and our weaknesses,' says David Armstrong. 'He made sure we performed to the best of our ability and we became a very difficult side to beat. He was not too bothered about the way the opposition played, to be honest. He concentrated on the good things we could do. Because of the respect for Jack, when he spoke, we listened. He could be pretty volatile at times, when we weren't doing what he expected. There were a few times when trays of tea were thrown around. A lot of that was because he was so keen to win, like the rest of us. So after the tea had gone splattering, then we got down to the business of putting it right. And most of the time, we did. That first season was marvellous. There was a real party atmosphere towards the end of the season. The older pros told me, "You've got to make the most of this, because these sorts of things don't happen all the time."'

'When you are a manager, the team is on your mind 24 hours a day,' says Ian Greaves. 'Jack was like that. He thought about the game all the time. He was mad for systems. He thought constantly about new patterns. He loved to do something no-one else was doing.' The system that Jack devised was essentially his own version of 4-4-2, with David Mills and John Hickton as the two strong men up front. Not surprisingly, given Jack's experience with Leeds and England, great emphasis was given to maintaining a powerful defence, with Stuart Boam and Willie Maddren at its centre. But the key to the pattern was Jack's idea of using a fast midfielder to latch on to long balls delivered behind the opposition back four. As a defender, Jack had always hated that kind of diagonal ball fired from a distance because it was so difficult to handle. Now, through his Boro team, he exploited that tactic to the full. 'Jack was a great believer in route one,' says Stan Cummins. 'He used to say that no-one likes being turned round, facing the wrong way, and one ball over the top can do that. Why mess around? That is what he was trying to drill into us all the time.' And in Alan Foggon, he discovered the ideal man to do the running job. Though Foggon was not a particularly skilful player, he was tremendously quick – as a schoolboy, he had been a local sprint champion. Fellow Boro player John Craggs describes him thus: 'Alan would trip over the ball nine times out of ten, but if you knocked it in front of him and let him gallop after it, he was brilliant. You could just put him on the field and he would motor all day.'

The virtue of Jack's formation was that it was almost watertight; the vice was that it failed to provide entertainment. Based on tough professionalism rather than attacking flair, it was a hard-nosed approach reminiscent of Revie's Leeds at their worst. John Craggs recalls how defending was Jack's priority: 'When I went to Boro, my game was built on attacking football. But Jack said to me, "First of all, do your job at the back. Do not, under any circumstances, just keep bombing up the right-hand side." If you did what Jack wanted, then he'd back you all the way. But if you tried to play football at the back and gave the ball away, then you were in for a real rollicking. His language could be 'unbelievable'. For all their success, Middlesbrough acquired the label of being a boring side as they won a string of games 1–0. Tommy Docherty once quipped that Jack took over a sleeping giant at Boro, then proceeded to put the fans to sleep, while Jack himself once admitted, ' I'm a negative thinker.' Barry Fry gives this affectionate appraisal of Jack's method: 'Jack has an entirely different philosophy to me. I believe in the Matt Busby approach: bugger the tactics, just get the best players you can and let them express themselves. That way, you'll win more than you lose and you will entertain at the same time. Jack is totally different. He is all tactics, stopping the opposition. He would always be happy with a 0–0 draw, I would sooner win 5–4. Jack's view was that if the opposition have a good player, you sit on him, kick the fuck out of him. I have never, in 28 years as a manager, said that to any of my players – but maybe that's why he was far more successful than me.' John Craggs confirms this: 'In those days you could get away with much more on the field. Before the kick-off, Jack would say to me about a certain opponent, "Give him a good dig in the first five minutes. Let him know you're there and he'll be watching you the rest of the game."'

Jack was to be tagged with the label of being a 'defensive' manager for the rest of his career, including during his spell in Ireland, and not without some justification. But no-one could dispute that he got results. Chairman of Middlesbrough Charles Aymer provided this picture of the club and the manager in January 1974 as Jack's team marched towards promotion: 'It's a wonderful, wonderful, happy atmosphere here. He always addresses me as "Mr Chairman" when we meet, which isn't very often because I never interfere with his job. Besides, I don't think anyone will ever be able to tell Jack Charlton what he's got to do.' Team captain and centre-half Stuart Boam gave another frank assessment: 'We didn't get on very well when he came. He didn't rate me as a player, he rather put me on a plate and chopped me up.' Another cause of friction was that Jack himself was still registered with the League as a player. It was only for use in case of an emergency but it made Boam suspicious that Jack might be after his job. They eventually established a better relationship, Boam saying, 'We still argue. I'm never frightened to put my case, and I think that's what Jack needs – someone who won't agree with him all the time.'

Jack may have been excellent on tactics, but he was hopeless about remembering his players' names – another trait that was to become legendary in his next 20 years of management. In team talks, for instance, Graeme Souness would end up being called Frank. 'Although most of us played with him for four years,' says David Armstrong, 'he could never remember our names. He'd say "You there" or "Thingy". He even got my own nickname, Spike, wrong.'

Over in Deepdale, Bobby had many more problems than just players' names. Having been in the top half of the table in November, his Preston team had a series of disastrous results and, by April had plunged into the relegation zone. For a while it seemed that Preston's fate might rest on the outcome of the final game of the season which, by a delicious irony, was to take place at Deepdale against Jack's already promoted Boro. If Jack had been responsible for kicking Bobby out of the Second Division, it would have been a telling metaphor for the fractiousness of their relationship. As it turned out, however, Preston, after being beaten 1–0 by Sheffield Wednesday on Easter Monday, were already relegated by the time Boro were due to play at Deepdale, though Jack's team did put the boot in by winning 4–2.

It was a humiliating beginning to Bobby's managerial career, made all the worse for him by the announcement, a few days later, that Jack had been named as Manager of the Year – the first Second Division boss to gain the award. In another indicator of their contrasting fortunes, Jack had managed to double Ayresome Park attendances from 10,000, while at Deepdale 1,500 season-ticket holders – 30 per cent of the total – refused to renew their subscriptions after relegation. The Preston North End board called a crisis meeting in April 1974, with private mutterings from three of the nine directors that unless there was a radical improvement, Bobby would face the sack.

There was to be no dramatic recovery the following year. Again Preston started well, and after 15 games were top of the Third Division, but they faded and could only finish in ninth place. In each of the two major Cup competitions they were equally dismal, knocked out in the third round in both. At the same time Jack's Middlesbrough, back in the top division for the first time in 20 years, continued their renaissance, ending up in sixth position, having climbed as high as second at Christmas after beating Sheffield United at home. Similarly, in contrast to Preston, they did well in both the League and the FA Cup, reaching the quarter-finals in both.

In an attempt to resurrect Preston's fortunes at the beginning of the 1974/75 season, Bobby made what seemed a rather desperate gamble. He decided to start playing again. Superficially, he could make a sound enough case for this move, arguing that that he could both provide guidance on the field and tackle one of Preston's biggest problems in the previous season, lack of goals. But the reality was that he was now almost 38 and had not played for a year. Both his great contemporaries, Pele and Beckenbauer, cautioned against a comeback. 'Why should anyone who has known such greatness want to finish his career at anything but the highest level? I could not do it. I could not end my days at a lower grade,' said Beckenbauer. More importantly, Charlton's decision to take to the field could do nothing to resolve the central problem of his management, that he still had failed to build a cohesive footballing unit. Nor, for all the talk in the media about his sacrifice on behalf of Preston, was it done for purely altruistic reasons. Throughout his life, there was nothing Bobby enjoyed more than playing – he was still turning out even on his 60th birthday. So, far from being a dutiful attempt to shoulder another burden, putting on his boots again was actually an excuse to break free from the routine of the manager's real job. Bobby virtually admitted this himself, saying, 'Basically I'm selfish. There is no substitute for playing and I want to play. That is the only reason I am coming back. I'm as fit as I've ever been and after a 12-month break from playing, I'm a new man, refreshed and dying to get started.'

In fact, by 1975 Bobby was arguing that he had retired too soon from Manchester United – the exact opposite of what Best claimed – and said he could have gone on at least two more years if he had not trained flat out. 'Stanley Matthews kept playing until he was 50 because he concentrated most of his training in later years on sprinting practice. I made the mistake of trying to train as hard at 35 as I did when I was 15. I left a lot of my fitness and stamina on the training field.' This was not just wishful thinking. His United colleague Alan Gowling feels the same way: 'Bobby was the complete professional. He was one of those players who always gave 100 per cent in everything, including training. He used to be up there, running with the young lads at the front. Having been through that myself, I now believe that had he taken it a little easier he could have played on for another two or three years.'

For all the forebodings from Pele and others, Bobby proved to be still a very effective performer in midfield. He appeared in 38 of Preston's 46 games in the 1974/75 season, scoring eight times, including his 200th League goal against Bury. When he scored with a rocketing free-kick against Carlisle, their goalkeeper Alan Ross reported, 'Our lads were still dreaming about the wall when the ball was past me.' Bobby himself said, with forgivable exaggeration, that a piledriver against Walsall had been 'the hardest shot I have ever hit'. Even though this was happening in the Third Division, Bobby still impressed his colleagues. 'There was no way he was finished,' says Francis Burns. 'He was still superb. I remember we went up to Glasgow for a pre-season friendly against Celtic reserves. Just the name of Bobby Charlton meant that thousands turned out. And when he scored, the whole place absolutely erupted. Kenny Dalglish was playing that night but the crowd had come to see Bobby.' Roy Tunks, who kept goal to him in training, says, 'He was still able to lash it in with either foot. Invariably he would hit the target, I always had to make a save. And in matches, he was a still a very clinical striker of the ball. It was very rarely that he would spill any Bovrils in the stands.' Ray Treacy, the Dublin-born Preston forward who played 42 times for Ireland, says, 'Bobby was still incredible. He was the best striker I have ever seen – better than Beckham or Lorimer.' But Tony Morley felt it was a bit more of a struggle for Bobby, perhaps, paradoxically, because he was competing at a lower standard. 'You could tell he was still a fine player. But the thing is, if you have played at the highest level, and then start dropping down the divisions, it can actually become harder because the game is so much more physical and lacking in style. Playing in front of a couple of thousand in a Cup tie at Halifax is a far cry from the World Cup in Mexico. But you would never once hear Bobby complain.'

But all Bobby's playing skills could not rescue his management career. After two years in charge, it was increasingly obvious he was not making an impact at Deepdale. So why did Bobby fail as a manager? The conventional wisdom is that he was too gentle, too 'nice a guy' – to quote Ian Greaves' phrase – for the hardened world of professional football. Supporters of this thesis could point to a story about his signing of Francis Burns, which appears to show his naivety. Under League regulations, when a manager is interested in buying a certain player, he is meant to approach the other's club board and management, not the player himself, though this rule has always 'been honoured in the breach than in the observance'. As Francis Burns, who was at Southampton before his move to Preston, recalls: 'Lawrie McMenemy took me into his office and told me Bobby wanted to sign me.

"He's probably been on to you already, hasn't he?"

"No."

"Come on, I'm sure he must have been speaking on the phone to you before us."

"No, honestly, he hasn't."

"Ah, well, I'll give him the benefit of the doubt. I don't think he's been in the game long enough to know how to do it properly."'

Yet this argument does not stand up. Innocence or integrity over transfer deals does not mean that Bobby was soft. Indeed, he was never an easy-going, laid-back 'nice guy'. There was a certain flintiness, a stubbornness about him. One invariable sign of male weakness is an eagerness to court popularity but Bobby was never like that. He was willing to risk ostracism in the United dressing room by showing open hostility to George Best. Similarly, he offended the rest of his family by attacking Jack over the 'black book', a move that must have required some courage. No man without a tough inner core could have come through Munich, three World Cup campaigns, and over 700 competitive games for Manchester United. On this point, Roy Tunks says: 'Bobby had a streak underneath. I mean he could cut people. If Bobby didn't like someone, he would let them know with a word or a look. I'm not saying he was an ogre or anything, but there was a bit of an edge to him that would occasionally come to the surface. Though he was diplomatic, he was not one to engage in idle chit-chat.' Despite his reputation for quietness, he was not afraid to raise his voice at his own players. 'I didn't see him throw a cup but I did see him rollick people, tell them they were not doing their jobs,' recalls Tony Morley.

The real reasons Bobby failed were twofold. First of all, unlike Jack, he had little technical grasp of the game, not only because he had never done any coaching, but also because, as an intuitive player, he had never had to analyse tactics too deeply. Therefore, when it came to developing systems, he was floundering. Ray Treacy says: 'Bobby never thought of a tactic in his life. He did things on a football field through sheer genius. When it came to assessing the game or judging ability or deciding how to get the best out of a player, that's where Bobby fell down and that's where Jack had it.' Treacy says that, because of Bobby's lack of tactical judgement, his team-talks at half-time would usually be about the very last incident that happened before the whistle rather than the overall pattern of the game. He recalls this example of Bobby's approach: 'I remember we were playing at Deepdale against Crystal Palace. Bobby was in the stand. And I made a mistake just before half-time. I got the ball in a right-half position. I could see their defence was very square so our outside left was wide open. One through ball of about 40 yards and he was clean through. But instead I passed the ball about 10 yards to my right. Bobby spent most of the half-time interval on my back as to why I did not pass the ball to the outside left.

"Did you see him?' he asked.

"Yes, I looked up and saw he was on."

"Well, why didn't you give it to him?"

I didn't want to start a row, so I just said that I decided to pass it right. 'That's ridiculous. If you said you didn't see it, fair enough. But you saw it was on, why didn't you do it?'

This went on for several minutes, so much so that I was starting to boil up.

"So why didn't you do it?" he asked again.

"Because I can't kick the fuckin' ball that far."

Which was not being cheeky but was the God's honest truth. Where Bobby would just have laid back and swept the ball in front of the guy, on a wet, heavy afternoon, I could not reach the lad. It was as simple as that.'

In direct contrast to Jack, Bobby paid little attention to the need for a strong defence but instead put his faith in continual attack. He had, of course, distilled this message from Busby, but then Busby was working with some of the finest players in the world and had carefully selected the right blend. 'Bobby still harked back to the days at United, when they used to win games 5–4,' says Francis Burns. 'That was his philosophy as a manager, a free spirit, always wanting to be on the offensive. If we came in at half-time 2–0 down, Bobby would say, "We've got to go forward", whereas Nobby and I would be thinking, "Hold on, let's make sure we don't concede another. It's no use piling forward and getting beat 6–0."' Roy Tunks recalls: 'His team talks were simplistic, motivational rather than technical, things like, "We've got to go forward together."' Tony Morley argues that Bobby was a bit like Kevin Keegan: 'He used to say to us, "Look, we're playing at home today. If we score three, they've got to score four, simple as that." Unfortunately we didn't have the best players at Preston, which didn't help that style of play.' Ray Treacy, who now runs a highly successful travel firm in Dublin, was surprised that Bobby was a poor speaker in the dressing room. 'I have travelled the world with Bobby and seen him talk brilliantly to audiences everywhere. Yet when he stood in that Preston dressing room in front of thirteen players, he struggled to say, "Do this," or "I want you to do that." When he was talking one-on-one with you, you almost had to finish his sentences. He knew what he wanted to say but found it difficult to do so. He was shy. He was just not a good communicator with hard-nosed pros. Again, that was where he was different to Jack. Jack was to communicating what Bobby was to playing.'

Bobby's other failing was that he found it difficult to work with players who did not have the same ability as, in Treacy's words, 'he had always done things so naturally that he never really came to grips those who were far less talented than him.' This is a common problem amongst truly great footballers who find it hard to relate to lesser lights – one major reason why, out of England's World Cup winning team, only Jack Charlton, perhaps the least innately talented of the XI, actually made it as a manager. Peters, Banks, Stiles, Moore, Hurst, Ball, along with Bobby, all tried but did not succeed. When Alan Ball was sacked by Blackpool in 1981, for instance, he was, according to Martin Tyler, 'criticized for being too demanding of lower division players'. Roy Tunks give this description of a Bobby coaching session, 'He would stop and say, "Now see him over there" and we would all need binoculars to pick out someone more than 60 yards away on the left wing. Bobby would then hit the ball right to his feet and we'd all stand there and go, "Bloody hell." Then he'd say, "Well, if that man's not on, there's also the fellow on the right wing" and he'd whack the ball right to him. And he'd expect us to do the same.'

Mark Lawrenson, who went on to such a distinguished career with Brighton, Liverpool and Ireland, began at Preston under Bobby. He gave me this recollection: 'In training, you would see him get so frustrated with other people. He would have a real moan. He himself was still performing brilliantly, he was unbelievable, but, as a player in matches, he had a funny effect on the team. For the good players, it was great. But for the average players, it made them nervous. Basically, if you did not pass the ball to him properly, you would get a bollocking. It was hard for him to accept that other people could not play at his level. He would be coming in every day thinking, "Oh God, I have to play with this lot, I can't replace them. What can I do with them?" He was not a great analyst of the game but, to be fair to him, he was the manager of a team that was basically in transition, going nowhere. The one very positive thing was that he loved the young players. He would join our five-a-sides. He was great with us and never got frustrated. I think he could relate to us better because we were all young, keen, trying. He did things more by example than by talking.'

David Sadler, who, apart from Nobby Stiles, knew him better than any other Preston player, gives this verdict: 'On the basis of that spell at Deepdale, you couldn't have said that Bobby had what it takes to be a manager. And he was not really an outstanding tactician. He obviously had enormous knowledge of international football, top club football and that is not the same when you are playing in the lower league. I think he had some difficulty in dealing with the reality of the situation. It was a bit of a culture shock for him, after playing so long at United. After all, Grimsby is not the Bernabeu. He found it difficult to accept that if he produced a good player, he would probably have to be sold to balance the books. Survival was on everyone's lips.'

After two years in the job, Bobby was coming to the end of his tether. He finally reached it at the beginning of the 1975/76 season when he had a severe clash with the board. The Preston directors had received an offer from Newcastle of £40,000 – plus one of two players, either Alex Bruce or Micky Burns – for the centre-half, John Bird, whom Bobby rated as one of the best defenders in the country. The board pointed out that the club was heading for a loss of £80,000 and had little choice but to reach a deal. Bobby would not accept this and, after a tense meeting on 21 August 1975, he resigned as Preston manager. Explaining his decision afterwards, Bobby said it had been 'a matter of principle. They pay a manager for his opinion and, if they won't take it, that's that. The directors had agreed to a transfer deal and I opposed it. When the crunch came, I refused to back down. I was determined I would not have players at Preston I did not want. Neither Alex Bruce nor Micky Burns would have got a place in my team. A manager has to stand firm on what he believes in.'

It is a tribute to the respect and affection which Bobby inspired, for all his managerial flaws, that so many of his Preston team expressed their outrage over the stance of the directors. The players passed a vote of censure against the board, saying that the 'manager should be allowed to manage', while Scottish midfielder Alex Spark immediately put in a transfer request. However, Ray Treacy felt that Bobby had made the right move, as he explains: 'Personally, when Bobby resigned, I was pleased for him, because anyone with an ounce of sense could see that management did not suit him. I am not saying that I was glad that he left Preston. I liked him and got on great with him – still do to this day. But I felt it was the best thing for him and Norma. And I sensed the other senior players – like Burns, Nobby, Sadler who were all very pro Bobby Charlton – thought the same way.'

There is little doubt that Bobby's confrontation with the Preston board had been inevitable. If it had not been over John Bird, it would have happened over another issue. Bobby was increasingly troubled at Preston as he admitted in an anguished interview with the *Sunday People* in August 1975, just days before his resignation. He said he had received 'very little reward' for his two years of toil, adding that when he came to Preston, 'I knew I had a lot to learn and was prepared to work at it. But the amount of effort needed has still come as a shock. I knew there would be pitfalls, but that didn't stop me falling into them. I probably listened to too much advice instead of being selective. I have been let down by people. And I think it was a mistake to start playing again last season.' Mark Lawrenson recalls how unhappy Bobby seemed: 'It was obvious to everyone that he did not enjoy being manager. He didn't really want to be there. He was a World Cup winner, a world-class player, so it was amazing to see how he would get so uptight, so nervous, before a match. He would bring the team sheet in and he would be shaking. He was never a picture of serenity.' If Bobby had proved a successful manager, then the Preston board might have fought to keep him, accepting his view of the Bird deal. But the truth was that after two years of failure, the directors saw no reason to do so. Little resistance was therefore made to Bobby's departure. Francis Burns recalls that when he, as one of the senior players, attended a meeting with the Board, he was surprised to learn that the deal with John Bird had not yet been finalized, yet at the same time the directors seemed all too willing to accept Bobby's resignation. 'How can we have lost a manager but still don't know whether John is going to Newcastle?' he asked. But the idea that Bobby was actually forced out was emphatically denied by the Preston Chairman Alan Jones: 'It has been a terribly unpleasant situation but we did nothing at all to force it. We have always found the money when he wanted players. This time we asked Bobby to see our point of view.'

No such problems afflicted Jack at Ayresome Park. The promotion triumph of his first year had been followed by three years of consolidation in the First Division, something that Middlesbrough had rarely experienced before in its history. In 1975/76 the team finished thirteenth, and of all the clubs in the First Division, conceded the fewest number of goals at home. That year also saw Boro win their first ever trophy as a professional club, when they beat Fulham in the final of the Anglo-Scottish Cup. Like a host of other second-rate competitions which have plagued modern European football, such as UEFA's Inter-toto Cup or the Zenith Data Systems Cup, this was hardly a major prize, for the only teams to compete in it were those which had not qualified for Europe. In fact, it was treated with so little seriousness by clubs that in 1981 it was abolished. Still, no one at Ayresome Park was complaining about finally seeing some silverware in the cabinet.

The current Blackburn manager, Graeme Souness, who began his career under Jack at Middlesbrough with a reputation for womanizing and drinking, has this verdict on Jack's skills as a manager: 'I must have been terrible to handle when I was young. Arrogant, thought I knew everything. Without a doubt, Jack was the man who sorted me out. When he talks to you, you listen. In my situation, he made it very obvious that there were two ways to go. There was the way out, never to get back in. Or I could show what I was really capable of. He worked me hard, and things worked out. I always found him to be fair. I couldn't criticize Jack on a personal level in any way. He is a pretty impressive man, aggressive and swears rather a lot. I have lot of time and respect for him.'

Stan Cummins, another who played his first top-class football under Jack, is revealing on Jack's charisma, and his – often unintentional – humour: 'He was a big man and could be blunt. He said what he thought and it came from the heart. He was very good in team talks, he knew what he wanted. And in drills, during training, he would regularly step in to show us how it should be done. He would irritate us with the way he would get it right every time. Every move always came off for him. Like to demonstrate the way he wanted the ball crossed, he would go out to the wing, then send over an inch-perfect ball for the striker to smack in the net. "Copy that," he would say. As a junior, I was obviously around the dressing room, and I would see Jack bawling players out. He was very demanding but he brought the best out of the team. The biggest bollocking I ever got from him was when I was going to America to play for Minnesota Kicks. I was just 18 at the time. Alan Willey was taking his wife and Ian Bailey was due to go with his fiancée. I decided that I should ask if I could take my girlfriend. So I knocked on the door of his office.

"Boss, can I see you?"

"Yeah, come in. What do you want?"

"Well, you know the trip to America. Alan is taking his wife and Ian's taking his fiancée. Can I take my girlfriend?"

He blew his top. "Get the fuck out of here. I'm not sending you over there to muck around. You're going there to learn about the fucking game. Get the fuck out of here."

"OK boss."'

Cummins gives other examples to show how Jack was very much his own man. 'In training Jack would sometimes set the dogs on us. He'd bring them to the ground in his Range Rover and then he'd let them out, saying, "Go get 'em." So there we were, being chased by his labradors. It was a bit of a laugh – for him. It certainly sharpened up your speed. IIe was a great character. We had a sauna at Ayresome Park. One time all the coaches were in there, sweating away, and Jack came in from his own changing room to join them. There he was, walking across the showers, naked as a jaybird. He told me to get a big bucket of icy cold water so he could throw it on the coaches.

"I'm not doing that," I said.

"You'd better, lad, you'd better. Or I'll fine you."

'So I got the bucket of water. He picked it up and then ordered me to crouch down and open the door. So he had the bucket in his hand; he said "Now." I opened the door. And then he threw the entire bucket all over me.

"That'll teach you to want to soak your coaches," he said.

'To be honest, I loved him. He was just a great character, a great manager. He's one of the best. You had to do it his way, and if you didn't, he'd find someone who did. I'm just glad I was around at Boro with him.'

John Craggs remembers one incident when he saw the ferocious side of Jack. 'We were on the training ground and the TV cameras were there. Jack set this five-a-side game up and then became involved in that, playing up to the cameras, trying to beat players. He went past me and I chased after him, just clipped his heel, and tripped him up. Jack was absolutely fuming. I have never seen him as mad. He chased me round the pitch and the cameras were following everywhere. I did not see him for three days after that. I just kept out of his way.' But he feels the same way about Jack as most of the Boro team. 'He was a typical Geordie. Spoke his mind. The players knew who was boss and there were not many who didn't do what he wanted. He was a colourful character but he was brilliant – the best manager I have ever experienced.'

Jack had proved that he had what it takes for management, something his brother could not claim. For the first time in their lives, Jack had outshone Bobby on the football field.

CHAPTER EIGHTEEN

The Eccentric

For most of his life until 1966, Jack had lived in the shadow of his younger brother. But, from the mid-1970s, the situation was reversed. In the football world, Jack was now the achiever, the top manager constantly in the headlines, while Bobby moved quietly off the centre stage.

After his resignation from Preston in August 1975, there had been talk of his taking over the vacant post at Stockport County, where his close friend Freddie Pye was joint chairman. Pye himself had been on Manchester United's books as a teenager, having been discovered, like Bobby, by the legendary scout Joe Armstrong. But he had nothing like Bobby's class. Having failed to progress beyond the reserves, he pursued his professional football career through a variety of lower division and non-League clubs, including Accrington Stanley, Rochdale and Congleton, before becoming the manager of Altrincham. He then went into business in the metal trade and travel. For all the difference in talent – Pye jokes that Bobby's life reads like a *Who's Who of Football*, whereas he is more *Who Cares* – he and Bobby struck up a rapport at Old Trafford when Bobby lodged with Pye and his wife. 'I used to cook him his bacon and eggs,' says Pye.

Bobby had seen too much of lower division management to think about taking the Stockport job. Instead, he became involved with a different concern of Freddie Pye's, and was appointed a sales director with Halba Limited, a travel agency with three outlets in the Cheshire area. Halba was an ambitious and expanding firm, owned by Pye and Ken Bates, now Chelsea chairman. Bobby's job at Halba was to organize tours abroad by top football clubs. Unlike Jack, Bobby, with his conscientious and orderly mind, was eminently suited to this kind of administrative role.

Bobby had not given up football altogether. One person who kept him in close touch with the game was Bill Shankly, who had unexpectedly resigned as manager of Liverpool in 1974. The years between his departure from Anfield and his death in 1981 were sad, lonely times for Shankly, as he came to realize that his retirement had been premature and he missed being involved with his beloved Anfield. To fill in the time, he would regularly turn up at Bobby's home in Cheshire, spending hours talking about football, his only topic of conversation. If Bobby was not there, he would be just as happy to chat to Norma and they became close friends – which undermines Jack's claims about Norma being difficult and aloof.

Bobby was also too addicted to the game to stop playing. He still trained with Manchester United and took part in charity games. Late in 1975, he turned out for Stockport County in a fundraising match against Manchester City. In 1976 he appeared four times for Waterford Football Club in the Bass Irish League, following in the footsteps of his adversary George Best, who had agreed to play a handful matches for Cork Celtic. Bobby had come to know the club through his old United friend, Shay Brennan, who had once been player-manager, and had taken part in a friendly match there in 1974 for an 'Old England' team. Brennan admitted that he was a hopeless manager, and particularly disliked dealing with the press. Whenever any journalist rang, the club had instructions to say that 'Mr Brennan is in the shower.' Once, at a sportswriters' dinner, a reporter came up to him and said, 'Mr Brennan, you may not be the best manager in the country, but you're certainly the cleanest.'

But if playing at Halifax for Preston had represented a step down from Wembley and Old Trafford, then going to the tiny Irish club must have seemed like a headlong plunge into near subterranean depths. In a poignant report in *The Guardian* Frank Keating wrote of Bobby's visit to Waterford: 'To many of us, at first thought anyway, the sadness was that he had come to this little corrugated greyhound stadium, two farmers' barns as "stands" on one side, a white block of housing estate on the other, sombrely overlooked by a hillocked quiff of elms. Not a place to end one's living days.' But, despite the grim surroundings, Bobby, as always, gave his full commitment to the club, playing his heart out and still displaying some of his old magic in those long crossfield balls and delicate chips. And the Waterford public showed their appreciation – when he turned out he more than quadrupled the average gate, taking it from 2,000 to 9,000. The one confrontation the Irish public would have loved to have seen, Bobby's Waterford against George Best's Cork Celtic, was avoided when Bobby diplomatically said that he wanted to concentrate on 'a little extra training'. Some of the local media were not so keen on Bobby's Irish odyssey. 'Our soccer circus of one-night stands,' thundered *The Press*, saying, 'The local players, the regulars who slop out the whole season have taken a cut in wages and must feel unhappy. How much will Best and Charlton contribute to raising the standards in this country? I venture to say nothing.'

While Bobby was causing a minor squall across the Irish Sea, Jack was creating a much bigger stir on Teesside with his continuing revival of Middlesbrough. In the 1976/77 the club again performed well in the League, finishing in 12th spot – a place higher than in the previous year – and also reached the quarter-finals of the FA Cup before falling to Liverpool. Their run had included a fifth round 4–1 thrashing of Arsenal. Yet for all these successes, Jack had decided to quit. It was a move which astonished fans and the press, since the unsought resignation is almost as rare in League football as it is in politics. But Jack had been disappointed with the lack of real progress and the failure to win a major trophy. During one slump, at Christmas time when Boro lost four games in a row, Jack's own morale evaporated: 'We have not faced problems like this since I came here. It is my job to give players confidence but how do you get it back into players who suddenly lose it like this?' he told the *Yorkshire Post*. The crisis only confirmed one of Jack's pet theories: that four years was the maximum period any manager should stay in his job. After that, thought Jack, he would become stale, unable to motivate himself or his players. There was also some aggravation over his devotion to fishing and shooting, because he was so often absent from the training ground. Jack saw no problem in this, as he believed his job was to mould a team, not put in office hours. But according to Neil Philips, the England team doctor and vice-chairman of Middlesbrough, some members of the board did object: 'Jack made it clear that he didn't intend to work more than three days a week. Eventually he fell out with a couple of directors and wouldn't show up for the board meetings. But he knew what he was doing and he did it well.' Ever since joining Boro in 1973, Jack had warned the club that he would not stay beyond four years. And Jack was usually a man who stuck to his guns. So despite the attempts of chairman Charlie Aymer to change his mind, Jack confirmed in February 1977 that he would resign at the end of the season.

Jack had achieved a great deal at the club, but, in retrospect, he thinks he could have done even more if he had been willing to buy some new players once he had reached the First Division. Allan Clarke describes Jack as 'one of the tightest fellows I have ever met in my life; he wouldn't give you a light'. Jack extended this frugality to his management, regarding the club's funds almost as if they were his own. Jack now admits this was an absurd view, adding that if he had been willing to deal more in the transfer market, Boro might have been able to mount a realistic bid for the title. Ken Prior, his old friend from Ashington, who had been recruited to work as a scout at Boro, recalls Jack's reluctance to buy. 'I went up to watch a game at Berwick against Dundee and there was a marvellous 19 year old. But Jack wasn't interested.

"But Jack, he's a great player. And he's only going to cost you £60,000."

"Nah, he hasn't played in First Division."

'Six weeks later this young lad went to Aston Villa for £100,000. His name was Andy Gray.'

In an unwarranted bout of self-criticism, Jack said, a year after leaving Ayresome Park, that he had 'done the club a disservice' with his parsimony. 'I should have spent the money we made at the club,' he commented. He admitted that he had even been told by the directors and colleagues to stop worrying about the finances. 'They told me that I would be judged on the team I produced and not on the profit or loss at the end of the year. But I have a bit of a conscience about that. I will never plunge a club into debt without a great deal of thought.' It was a philosophy that was to cause him serious trouble in the years to come.

By coincidence, in the summer of 1977 when he resigned, the job that he really wanted in football became vacant. A year after Jack had left Leeds, his former boss Don Revie had become England manager. But it rapidly became apparent that Revie could not handle the pressures of leading England. Paranoia and indecision characterized his reign, with an astonishing 60 players selected in just three years. As the campaign for World Cup qualification faltered badly and pressure for his sacking grew, Revie secretly negotiated a lucrative £340,000 contract to take over as soccer chief in the United Arab Emirates. News of his deceit caused outrage across English football, and right up to his death in 1989, Revie never lost his reputation as a money-grabbing traitor.

In his autobiography, Jack mounted a strong defence of his mentor, arguing that Revie, knowing he was about to be betrayed by the FA, had only been trying to do the best for his family. But 19 years earlier, Jack had viewed the affair very differently. Never was a friend more candid. Laying into Revie for destroying England's chances of World Cup qualification, he accused him of 'signing away his soul to the Arabs. He shouldn't have gone now. That he has is a scandal. He has angered people who respected him. Don needs to be told in plain language that he has got himself a bloody bad name.'

314

Though Jack was appalled by Revie's action, he felt that he might now have the chance to take over the management of England. Not only was he intensely patriotic, but he also believed he had exactly the right credentials. He had been an FA coach since 1957 and was highly respected by other managers for his technical ability. Uniquely amongst the possible candidates, he had played for the most successful England side of all time. His club management record, though brief, was impressive. So Jack wrote a letter stating his case to the FA's headquarters at Lancaster Gate, the only time in his life he had ever written a job application. But to his annoyance, the FA appeared to treat his submission with total indifference. Having failed to put him on the shortlist, the appointment panel did not even bother replying to his letter. While he was ignored, the FA interviewed five other candidates: Brian Clough, Bobby Robson, Lawrie McMenemy, Alan Wade, the director of coaching at the FA, and Ron Greenwood, who eventually got the job. Of this quintet, only Clough and Robson could seriously claim to be better qualified than Jack.

But Jack never stood a chance. Tainted by his long association with the now despised Revie at Leeds, he was regarded by the FA as far too explosive and undiplomatic for the sensitive post. His public avowal of socialism and his foul language did not go down well with the blazered mandarins of the FA. The incident of the 'black book' lived in the memory, while Jack's poor disciplinary record counted against him. For many at Lancaster Gate, he was still the rebel, ever willing to challenge authority. Not everyone had forgiven him for an incident in March 1968, when he became the first-ever player to contest a referee's booking. The appeal was successful, but he was condemned for setting a dangerous precedent. And his departure from Middlesbrough, though perfectly honourable, strengthened his reputation for impetuosity.

At the time, Jack described Ron Greenwood's appointment as a 'kick in the teeth'. Striking an unusually self-pitying tone, he told the *News of the World* that he had been 'sent into limbo and his life has been messed up in a way that it hasn't been messed up for 20 years'. To this day, Jack's treatment by the FA rankles, and not without justification. He was to show at Ireland that he was well suited to international management, and he would certainly have performed just as well as Ron Greenwood. Maurice Setters, who worked so successfully with Jack in Ireland, says that he would have made the ideal successor to Revie: 'He would have brought a revolution to English football. I know Brian Clough is cited as the people's champion. No disrespect to Cloughie, but Jack would have been a better choice. He would have also upset a lot of people with his honesty. That would have been a problem.' In a heartfelt interview six years after his rejection, he said that of all the positions in world football, manager of England was the only one that really mattered to him: 'There is no doubt in my mind that whatever else happened, that was the job. Deep down, that was the job I always wanted. And when I didn't get it or wasn't considered, it took something away from football for me because I couldn't see anyone else who had quite the same pedigree.'

The summer of 1977 was the first time for a quarter of a century that Jack had not been directly connected to professional football. Yet for all that he enjoyed his break, indulging in his favourite activity of fishing as well as taking his family to the Caribbean, Jack was itching to get back into football once autumn arrived. Several clubs had approached him since his departure from Middlesbrough, but the first offer to appeal came from Third Division Sheffield Wednesday, whose manager Len Ashurst had resigned after a disastrous start to the season had left them in the relegation zone.

Superficially, it might seem bizarre that Jack was willing to move from a First Division club to one that was heading for the Fourth. Yet it was precisely this challenge that attracted him. So low had the Sheffield club sunk, thought Jack, that the only direction it could now go was upwards. Moreover, Wednesday had even more potential than Middlesbrough. The fifth oldest club in England, they had a great tradition, having won the League four times and the FA Cup thrice. Whereas Boro had not played amongst the elite for 20 years when Jack took over, Wednesday had been in the First Division as recently as 1970. Even in the Third Division they still attracted a big following of around 15,000 a week, and in Hillsborough they had one of the most famous grounds in the country. 'I have always fancied them,' explained Jack on his appointment. 'They have a big set-up, a huge population surrounding them. There are not a lot of places you can go than can offer this kind of scope. And I like enthusiastic people. In Sheffield, there doesn't seem to be anything that distracts them from their football.'

As he had done at Middlesbrough, Jack refused to accept a contract. That way, he said, both he and the club had total freedom of action. 'If they don't like the way I'm working, they can get shot of me. And if I get fed up with them I can walk out. That's the way it should be,' said Jack, adding that contracts were for those who doubted their own ability to manage. Again, as at Middlesbrough, he did not immediately make sweeping changes in personnel, keeping John Harris, the former Chelsea captain, as his assistant and Tony Toms as the trainer, though he did bring in his own coach, Maurice Setters, who had been out of work since taking successful legal action against Doncaster Rovers for unfair dismissal as their manager in 1974. A craggy, tough, passionate character, Setters was built very much in Jack's own image, though he lacked Jack's vast presence and star quality. Setters recalls how Jack imposed himself on the club: 'Jack soon ruled the roost. He dominated the club once he had taken over. The chairman Bert McGee came into the dressing room one day and Jack said, "What do you want?"

"Oh I've just come to see . . ."

"No you haven't. Now get out. I won't have any directors or chairmen in here, none of you."'

Jack himself admits that once, 'with the help of a few expletives', he berated McGee outside a board meeting, telling him that he would tolerate no interference or McGee could 'stuff the job'.

Jack soon realized that he had his work cut out, for Wednesday were in poor shape. 'Before I joined Middlesbrough, I had a look at them and saw they had six good players. When I watched Wednesday, I didn't see any,' he told the *Sun*. During his first year, his main task was simply to ensure that the club avoided the drop to the Fourth Division. At the turn of the year, relegation had looked a real possibility, with Wednesday anchored to the bottom. They also suffered the humiliation of being knocked out of the FA Cup by non-League Wigan. But a long run of good results, including just one defeat in their last 12 games, meant that Wednesday reached the safety of mid-table by the end of the season. Jack also caught a glimpse of Sheffield's potential reservoir of support, when a crowd of 36,000 – unheard of for a Third Division club – turned out to watch a League Cup tie against Everton.

Jack knew that if he was to revive Wednesday, he would have to abandon his usual reluctance to spend money. Most of the players he had simply did not have the basic skills to develop. Mark Smith, one of Wednesday's central defenders, recalls an incident in training when Jack became utterly frustrated by the inability of another player, David Grant, to take a free-kick properly. 'There was about six inches of mud on the ground and Jack was standing watching, sheepskin coat, cloth cap, brogues. Jack wanted us to rehearse getting the free-kick round the wall but David Grant kept missing. Suddenly Jack called out, "Hold on a minute." He walked out on to the pitch, still in his brogues, the water and mud squelching over them. He put the ball down and then hit it straight into the top corner. "Now that's what I want," he said, and walked off the pitch.' Smith, one of the few on the staff who Jack rated, is full of admiration for the impact Jack immediately made at the club: 'We had been in serious decline, and Jack soon began to turn the place around with his knowledge and charisma. He was a maverick but in a different class as a coach. He did a lot for me, taught me to be a better player. I've worked with quite a few managers and I would rate Jack at the very top.' Purists of the game, however, might not be overjoyed at the example Mark Smith gives of Jack's coaching method. 'When I was first at Wednesday, I would indulge in a little bit of play, instead of just belting it into the crowd. I'd step over the ball, let it run a bit, then pass back to the keeper. Then Jack arrived and said to me: "You know, it's not a crime to hit the ball into the stands. You can't always play. A good old-fashioned boot is sometimes what is needed."'

But Jack did not have enough players of the calibre of Mark Smith. So though he never descended to anything like the levels of extravagance practised by Malcolm Allison at Manchester City, epitomized by the ludicrous £1 million signings in 1980 of Kevin Reeves and Steve Daley, he was still compelled to work the transfer market. After the first year, he imported a batch of new players, including the winger Terry Curran from Southampton, Brian Hornsby from Shrewsbury and the striker Andy McCulloch from Brentford, who was exactly the type of big, bustling competitor that Jack so admired. McCulloch feels the same way about Jack: 'He was his own man, like Brian Clough. A great judge of players, very single-minded, enormous self-confidence. He could be very quick-tempered. I remember once we were at Rotherham, where Emlyn Hughes was the player-manager. We lost narrowly in the last minute, after Emlyn had conned the ref into giving a penalty. I remember Jack and the trainer, Tony Toms, got Emlyn up against the wall. Tomsy literally lifted him in the air while Jack had a real go at him. Emlyn's voice was getting squeakier and squeakier.' Mike Pickering, Wednesday's centre-half says: 'Jack wore his heart on his sleeve. He was pure passion. He was not bothered about who he swore at. He could lose his temper. He had his views and was almost dictatorial. You couldn't really have an opinion with Jack. It had to be done the way Jack said.'

Another example of Jack's volatility occurred as a result of his stormy relationship with Curran, who was almost as fiery a personality as Jack. Their clashes came about partly because of different perceptions of Curran's job. Terry wanted to play as a traditional out-and-out striker, but Jack wanted him to adopt a more unorthodox role, effectively acting like a winger in a central position, wrong-footing defenders with his darting runs. It was an example of Jack's originality, developing a creative new way to use a talented player. But he also told Curran that he had to take on wider responsibilities as well, tracking back in defence when the opposition had the ball, whereas Curran wanted to stay up front. So bitterly did they row that they once even got into a fight in front of the other players. Brian Hornsby, Jack's first signing at Wednesday, gave me this description of the incident: 'We were lining up in the gym, ready for a practice match, when suddenly the doors burst open and in came Jack, followed by Terry. They were shouting their heads off at each other. As they moved into the gym, Jack told Terry to get out. Terry refused. Then Jack took off his jacket and handed it to his assistant, John Harris. Instead of John saying, "Come on Jack", he just took the jacket and Jack got into a scuffle with Terry. There weren't any real blows. It was quite funny, really. Jack's hair was going everywhere. But Tony Toms and a few of the players stepped in and calmed it down. That's Jack.' Curran left the club in 1982, rubbing salt into the wound by joining arch-rivals Sheffield United.

On the more positive side, Bob Bolder, whom Jack elevated to the first team on the departure of Chris Turner to Sunderland, remembers how Jack galvanized the players after his arrival. 'Perhaps, under Len Ashurst, the players had become a bit complacent. When Jack took over, we quickly realized who was in charge. He was a much bigger figure than Len. He was great at building camaraderie in the team from the start. One of his first acts was to take us all up to his parents' place in Northumberland. Half of us stayed with his mum and dad, the other half in a local pub. It was a fantastic experience. We played five-a-side in a local field, spending most of our time dodging cowpats. That sort of thing got the lads together. He had this great passion for the game and he could communicate it to the players. I got my fair share of bollockings off him, but he was great for my career. I was around 19 when he arrived and I was quite naïve. He hardened me up, really pressurized me into becoming a better keeper. He would bully me to come off my line. In training, he kept putting me under pressure to come for crosses, always talking and shouting at me. Basically he set me up and I played the next six years in the first team.'

As well as building the team he wanted, Jack imposed his own system on Wednesday. Essentially, it was a less sophisticated version of the one he had used at Middlesbrough, getting the ball as quickly and directly as possible into the opposition box. But now, instead of using a fast midfielder to run behind the defence, he aimed to fire long balls upfield to the big target man, Andy McCulloch. It was an effective but bludgeoning approach, which, for many critics, made Wednesday a dreary side to watch – just as Watford and Wimbledon, who later used much the same long-ball method, were heavily attacked for their thumping inelegance. Even one of the club's own histories, *One Hundred Years at Hillsborough* written by Jason Dickinson, admits that though Jack's Wednesday became 'a difficult side to beat' in the Third Division, the matches 'did not always register high in the entertainment stakes'. 'Jack liked to put it into the dangerous areas instead of passing it around, but I think we may have overdone it at times. I sometimes felt under a bit of pressure, particularly when the ball was just hit at me and I didn't have much chance,' says the player who was the key to the system, Andy McCulloch.

Any improvement in Wednesday was not immediately felt in Jack's second season, as they again finished in 14th place, though the finances were boosted by a marathon third round FA Cup tie with Arsenal, which went to no less than four replays. The first match, which ended in a 1–1 draw, was played in freezing conditions in January at Hillsborough, so freezing that the pitch was covered in snow before the start and Jack recruited an army of local volunteers to clear it. Mark Smith recalls, 'Jack was determined that the game should go ahead, so he was out there at nine o'clock in the morning, supervising the operation. He was like a foreman, shouting "Come on, let's show 'em we can do it."' In the replay at Highbury, Wednesday looked like causing a huge upset, as they led until the last minute when Liam Brady equalized. The next three matches were played at Filbert Street, because Leicester City's ground had a vast covering to keep its pitch playable, with Wednesday eventually losing 2 0. Though it had been an exhausting saga, Jack was pleased with his side's spirit: 'We've proved that on our day we can be a match for anybody.'

Managers are always expected to achieve immediate results. After two years languishing in the middle reaches of the Third Division, questions were asked about Jack Charlton. In a colourful passage in the *Daily Express* in August 1979, James Lawton wrote of Wednesday as that 'great shell of a football club lying in a hollow in the Pennines. The club remains inert, bloated on potential, starved of achievement.' But Jack did break that cycle in the 1979/80 season, finally winning promotion into the Second Division. Almost as satisfying for Wednesday fans was the 'Boxing Day Massacre', when Wednesday beat Sheffield United 4–0, in front of a crowd of 43,309, the biggest-ever gate in Third Division history.

Just as he had done at Ayresome Park, Jack kept faith with his squad on arrival from the Third. He wrote in his autobiography, 'I believe in giving the players who've won promotion the opportunity to show how they'll perform in a more competitive environment.' He did, however, make one big summer signing. Having agreed terms with Nottingham Forest to sign Stan Bowles for £110,000, he saw the deal fall through when Bowles refused to move to Sheffield. So instead, he went for the little-known Yugoslav, Ante Mirocevic, whom he believed would add some quality to the Wednesday midfield. The Eastern European performed well enough, though he was not worth the £200,000 Jack paid for him. Perhaps he had been too traumatized by Wednesday's pre-season routine. The trainer, Tony Toms, who had served in the Marines, took the team to the commando base at Lympstone on the south coast, where the Wednesday players had to go through the assault course wearing full military equipment. Brian Hornsby takes up the story: 'We had all the gear for the course, backpacks, helmets and rifles. Ante at the time spoke very little English. We came to this lake and you had to go through an S-bend pipe. One guy, standing up to his waist in water, would push you into the pipe and, at the far end, another would haul you out. When it came to Ante's turn, he just said, in broken English, "No, no, no, where's the ball?"' Andy McCulloch continues: 'The funniest sight I ever saw was this Yugoslav running away, with Jack shouting at him as he disappeared over the hill.'

Tony Toms was, according to Jack, a 'real character', a strong, good-looking man with an eye for the ladies – even the wives of directors from other clubs were not immune to his charm. Jack loves to tell the story of the night he and Toms went out in Swansea. They had such a late night that when they returned to their hotel it was locked up and they were unable to rouse anyone. So Jack and Tony went round to the back of the hotel, where they found a ladder. They then saw a window which was slightly open. Tony placed the ladder against the wall, while Jack climbed up. When he reached the top and crawled in through the open window, Jack found to his disbelief that he was in his own room. 'Tomsy was wonderful entertainment, but he could lead Jack astray. On some of our away trips, they would go out on a Friday night and Jack would look a bit dishevelled on a Saturday morning,' says one Wednesday player.

On the first season back in Division Two, Wednesday had a promising but hardly dramatic season, finishing in 10th place. Off the field, Jack's cautious methods had proved more successful, for the club's annual accounts showed that, to the end of the financial year in 1981, it had produced a surplus of £219,000. Yet for all the healthy balances, Jack was not able to establish a promotion-winning side, and again, as at Middlesbrough, this highlighted a failing of his management. Former club captain Mike Pickering points out: 'Jack showed his weakness by not being prepared to buy new players. I think Jack was very confident in his own ability to make average players better. And he succeeded in that, but maybe not by enough for the level they were playing at. Sometimes you just need better quality. But the transfer fees and wages paid in those days were dead against Jack's philosophy. He never threw his own money about, and he had the same attitude towards the club's.'

Eccentricity was becoming the hallmark of Jack's reign. He was the manager who kept fish in the ice machine in the treatment room and used his apprentices as beaters for grouse shooting. This was the manager who could analyse every move on the field and yet forget the names of his own players. This was the manager who once called a priest to the ground to establish whether a player was lying over a disputed goal in a five-a-side practice game. Ian Mellor, one of Jack's signings, remembers playing an evening game away in Cardiff. 'Less than 20 minutes to go before the kick-off, we still did not know the team. Then the physio walks in with some names written on the back of a cigarette packet and reads it out. Incredible.' Ian St John, who worked with him for a year at Sheffield, gave me this similar example of Jack's disorganization: 'Wednesday were playing Villa in a League Cup game and we stopped halfway between Sheffield and Birmingham so Jack could announce the team. He ran down the list, and then he gave a team talk, explaining what he wanted. We got back on the coach, fired up for the game. Then Roger Wylde tapped me on the shoulder and asked: "Am I playing?"

"Well, did Jack say you were playing?"

"Yes he did, but he also named another guy in my position."

'I summoned Jack, and explained the problem, that he had named two players for the same position. Jack, casually as anything, gave Roger a tap on the arm and said, "You're not playing." I was laughing.'

Ian St John has a similar memory of a home game: 'Jack once came into the dressing room one night at Hillsborough. Tony Toms and I were there. He turned to Tomsy and said, "Right, Tomsy, get the lads in, we'll give them a bit of a wind-up."

"That would be a bit difficult, Jack."

"Eh?"

"Well, we're kicking off in a minute."

'It turned out that Jack thought the match was starting at 7.45 rather than 7.30. But how, if you were the manager, would you not know the time of the kick-off?''

But Ian St John, like so many others, is a big fan of Jack's. 'I liked him as a coach. He made great football decisions. He was simple, yes, but he could get his players to work. His man-management was excellent. He made people play to a system. He noticed things on the field that so many others missed. He was great to work with. I had so many laughs with him at Wednesday.' The striker John Pearson, who first played for Wednesday in 1980, agrees: 'I thought

Jack was brilliant, an absolutely fantastic bloke. His bark could be pretty fearsome and, occasionally, if we were beaten, the players were frightened to go into the dressing room afterwards, even the senior pros. But once he had said his piece, he never held a grudge. Deep down, you knew he cared passionately for Wednesday and the players he had with him.'

Ian Mellor says that when he signed for Wednesday, he turned up at the ground as arranged, only to find that Jack had gone fishing. So the assistant manager, John Harris, drove him deep into the Pennine countryside, where Jack was tracked down to a pub. 'Then we go into the pub to start talking about contracts. The place was absolutely packed and I am trying to keep my voice down as we discuss my earnings. But Jack was talking as loud as he wanted, telling me what I could and could not have. Anyone who wanted could listen to our conversation, but Jack didn't give a toss. I did, because I didn't want everyone knowing my pay. Considering how successful he has been, it is amazing how laid back he was. I remember once we were playing Gillingham on New Year's Day. The night before, New Year's Eve, we were all in bed by 11pm at the hotel. Then, just before midnight, all the phones went off and we had to go down to the bar and have two pints with Jack. Just to see in the New Year. But he was a superb manager, one of the best, when he really switched on, when it really mattered. Sheffield Wednesday were in a mess when he arrived and he turned them round. He was so down to earth. He could have a cup of tea with the laundry girls or a glass of wine with the directors.'

There are two, less obvious traits that emerge from these years at Hillsborough. One was his sense of kindness. He was always more warm-hearted than his public image; putting up Ian St John in the family home when he came to help at Wednesday was just one example. Similarly he did a benefit dinner for Bob Bolder, refusing to accept any fee and telling Bolder afterwards, 'That was for all you did for me.' Brian Hornsby provides another example: 'When my wife was carrying our second daughter, it was a difficult pregnancy and she was in and out of hospital for the whole nine months. She collapsed after one game at Hillsborough. On the Sunday, Jack called me in and said, "Right, you and Anne can clear off to Scarborough for a few days. I've booked you in to a decent hotel, all paid for by the club. We don't have a game for a week so just take the time off." That was Jack all over. There was no side to him.'

Interestingly, for all his bombast, some players say he was not an inspiring talker. 'He was not the best motivator in the world. I thought he was too negative,' says Andy McCulloch. 'He would just snap sometimes, or pick on one or two players, which was no good for the rest of the side, especially if one of them was Terry Curran, who would have a go back at Jack.' Ian Mellor reinforces this point: 'Jack was not a motivator. He did not believe in motivating players. He would give a team talk, tell you what was expected of you and that was it. He was not like Kevin Keegan or Malcolm Allison, who at Manchester City was the greatest motivator of my generation. Don't get me wrong. He would go bananas if you weren't doing what he wanted. He would rant and rave and all the rest of it. His language at such times would be pretty ripe. But pre-match, not a motivator.'

Jack's most terrifying outburst at Sheffield Wednesday came at the end of the 1981/82 season, when his team missed out on promotion by one point. Wednesday had visited Bolton in a match they had to win, but had been beaten 3–1. Jack could hardly have been more disappointed, as Bob Bolder recalls: 'We played really poorly, a pathetic performance, and Jack just came in and hit the roof. He took off his cap and sheepskin coat, just threw them aside and steamed into the players. There was no hiding place, no excuses. It made you realize how much he wanted to win and how much he believed that things were possible.'

The next season, Jack suffered almost as much agony, when Wednesday reached the semi-final of the FA Cup, only to lose to Brighton at Highbury. There was a typical Charlton incident before the game, when the team bus left from the London hotel without two of the players, Pat Heard and David Mills, who had to make their own way to the ground by taxi. 'Jack was hopeless with arrangements like that,' says Ian St John, who happened to be on the bus that day, in an unofficial capacity. 'Sometimes, when we got on the coach, I would ask him, "Are we stopping anywhere, Jack?" Now you would think the manager would know what's happening. But Jack was always the first one to be playing cards. "Ask the driver," he said. For the semi-final, Jack had climbed onto the coach and got straight into the card school, without checking who was on the bus.' Wednesday never got going that Saturday in London: 'I think our mistake was in treating it as just another game, when, in reality, it was a massive occasion,' said Wednesday's Gary Megson, now manager of West Bromwich Albion. 'In the dressing room afterwards we were all upset but Jack was absolutely gutted. He'd got tears in his eyes. But he was crying, not for himself, but for the players. That's the sort of man he was.'

The failure to win promotion or reach Wembley in successive seasons ensured that Jack called it a day in May 1983. Having already stayed two years longer than he had originally planned, he decided he could do no more at Hillsborough. Months before, in January, he had confessed to the *Guardian*: 'People who used to smile at me when I came to Sheffield don't any more. I can feel a change in attitudes towards me.' Once more, he recognized that some of the blame lay with his perceived miserliness, saying, 'Maybe I should be more like Brian Clough and splash some money around.' By April he had decided to leave whether Wednesday reached the Cup Final or not, and told the chairman of his decision. Jack dismissed as a 'load of rubbish' the claim that the majority of the board wanted his resignation and, in his autobiography, revealed that he had received visits from several directors begging him to stay.

Jack could look back on his time at Hillsborough with mixed feelings. He had left the club in better shape than he had found it, but progress had been slow. And it hardly reflected well on Jack that his successor Howard Wilkinson won promotion in his first season in charge. Mark Smith, the Wednesday centre-half, might now be full of nostalgic praise for Jack, but back in 1983, he revealed that he would have 'moved on to another club' if Jack had stayed. 'I thought it best for Sheffield Wednesday that Jack left when he did,' said Smith in the *Daily Mail* in August 1983. 'There is a different atmosphere here now. The new boss has been a breath of fresh air.' And Smith also had an indirect snipe at Jack's legendary love of fishing and shooting, which was said to have frequently kept him away from the training ground. 'While the new manager is putting in long hours and showing he is dedicated, it tends to make the players feel more like dedicating themselves as well.'

At least Jack, for all such criticism, could say that he had not been forced out of the club. That experience was still to come.

CHAPTER NINETEEN

The Failure

Newcastle United should have been the ideal club for Jack to manage. He had been devoted to the place since his boyhood in Ashington, which lies just 15 miles north of the city. The first League result he turned to was Newcastle's. His cousin and friend, Ashington-born Jackie Milburn, was the club's greatest hero. In a sense, Jack would be 'coming home' if he went to Newcastle.

During most of his playing days, Jack dreamt of taking over St James' Park one day. His close friend, the journalist Jimmy Mossop, wrote this telling passage in a profile of Jack in November 1972, when Jack's career with Leeds was drawing to a close: 'He nurses private fantasies about the club he watched as a boy. He can lie on his pillow at night and see himself as a manager of a team full of Geordie players. There would be so many supporters, he says, that it would need a season ticket even to get near the ground.'

The problem for Jack was that the offer to run the club came at the wrong time for him. When he was approached by Newcastle in July 1984, he had been out of football for more than a year – apart from one short spell – and had enjoyed the break, pursuing his favourite activities of fishing and shooting, as well as making money through after-dinner speaking, advertising, and commentary work for ITV. He claimed not to miss the pressures of management at all, describing the process of watching his team play on a Saturday afternoon as 'agony'.

Jack did make a brief return to management in the 1983/84 season, when the chairman of Middlesbrough, Mike McCullagh, an old friend, implored him to help out at his former club. In the spring of 1984 Middlesbrough were in crisis, lying near the relegation zone in the Second Division and gripped by financial problems because of falling attendances. Malcolm Allison had refused to sell players and, as a result, had been sacked. So Jack, who did not have any of Allison's qualms about ditching players, stepped into the breach. He had retained a fondness for Ayresome Park and often admitted to friends that he had made a mistake in leaving in 1977 – 'we had some good players who were going to become better', he said in 1983. But Jack only took the post on the condition that he would leave once he had guaranteed Boro safety. This he achieved comfortably. In June 1984 he resigned from Middlesbrough for the second time.

In one of those twists that litter the intertwined story of the Charlton brothers, Bobby had also made a temporary resumption of his management career in very similar circumstances. In 1980, in a move very rare for a former professional, Bobby became a director of a football club, joining the board of Fourth Division Wigan Athletic at the instigation of his friend and Halba Travel boss, Freddie Pye. Pye, who had resigned as chairman of Stockport County, had recently acquired a controlling interest in the club. Two years after Bobby's arrival, the club, which had only been elected to the League in 1978, won promotion to the Third Division. But, like Middlesbrough, Wigan had been over-ambitious and by the spring of 1983, were in major financial difficulties, weighed down by a £250,000 overdraft. Moreover, results had been poor and in April manager Larry Lloyd was sacked. The board turned to Bobby, despite his record at Preston. This time he was more effective, pulling the club to safety. Once that objective was achieved, he resigned both as manager and director, along with chairman Freddie Pye. It was to be the last time he would be involved as manager at any football club.

Jack thought he had escaped from management too. But in the summer of 1984, he began to be pestered by his relative, Jackie Milburn, about the manager's post at Newcastle, which had just been vacated by Arthur Cox. Cox had taken Newcastle into the First Division with an exciting brand of attacking football, utilizing the talents of two young stars, Chris Waddle and Peter Beardsley, and one veteran, Kevin Keegan. In that 1983/84 season, these three strikers had scored 65 goals between them. Yet the prospects of success in the First Division were not as healthy as the exhilarating promotion drive suggested. Keegan had retired in a blaze of theatrical glory, airlifted from St James' Park by helicopter after the final game of the season in front of 36,000 adoring fans. Arthur Cox soon followed him, unhappy at both the terms of his proposed contract and the limited sum he was offered to spend on new players.

In such circumstances, Jack was understandably reluctant to accept the post, for all that he had been brought up 'black-and-white eyed' as a fan of Newcastle and was the club's first choice as new manager. He told Jackie Milburn, 'I don't want the job. I'm OK. I'm doing very well as it is.' But Milburn would not give up so easily. Shamelessly exploiting his blood connection, he kept telling Jack that he had a duty to his birthplace and to his family. This was the absolute reverse of Jackie Milburn's stance with Bobby 30 years earlier, when he warned the younger Charlton that he would be making a great mistake to join Newcastle because it was such a badly run club.

Worn down by this barrage of sentiment, Jack Charlton eventually agreed to talk to the directors when he was up in the north-east opening a double-glazing factory in Consett, just the sort of celebrity appearance from which Jack has been making a fortune for more than 40 years. They met at a golf club in Durham, where, for one of the few times in his life, he was persuaded to change his mind. 'To be honest,' said Jack later in an interview with Ashington historian Mike Kirkup, who wrote the definitive biography of Jackie Milburn, 'I got the impression that they were desperate for someone to do the job, because they wanted to stay in the First Division. And with Keegan leaving, they did not feel strong enough to stay up. I don't think I would have even considered the job if Jackie Milburn hadn't approached me. So I said, "OK, I'll do the job for a year, and then I'll see how I feel."' As always Jack refused a contract – the very source of Arthur Cox's aggravation – but agreed to a salary of £35,000, more than he had been receiving at Wednesday. True to his management style, he pledged that the jobs of his coaches, Colin Suggett and Willie McFaul, were safe, while also demanding total control over the running of the club: 'I must be completely in charge of everything. If the secretary and me have a row, then I will win or I'll leave.'

On taking up his appointment in June 1984, Jack could not have presented a more optimistic face, talking about giving the people of Newcastle 'the team they deserve. I know Geordies and they know me. Together we might be able to bring the glory days back to Tyneside.' In the *Newcastle Journal*, he spoke of his passion for the area: 'This job is the one for me. Even when I was with Leeds and managing Middlesbrough and Sheffield Wednesday, I never told people I was from those places. I always said I was from Newcastle.' And then he made what turned out to be a disastrous prediction. 'Now I want to stay here and make it my last managerial job. I want to stay here for 10 years. If I can do that, I will have been wildly successful.' Behind the scenes, however, Jack was disturbed by the impoverishment and lack of ambition he found at the club. Newcastle were £700,000 in debt and he was to be allowed only £200,000 to spend on new staff, though such a sum would barely purchase a single quality First Division player in the mid-1980s. Having witnessed some dismal performances in the opening months of the season, including a 5–0 drubbing by Manchester United, Jack knew he needed a higher standard of professional in key areas, especially defence. But he was trapped in the classic bind of the manager at a club in debt: he had little money to buy new players; but without new players he could not bring in the fans to raise the money he needed.

More aggravation came in the form of widespread sniping at his

Happier times for Bobby,
Jack and their mother
in 1966.

The proud father Bobby
with his wife Norma and
young Suzanne Charlton.

Brothers reunited in grief. The Charltons at St John's Church, Ashington, for their mother's funeral.

The greatest forward line in history? George Best, Bobby and Denis Law at Old Trafford, August 2000.

Mutual admirers: Sir Bobby and Sir Alex Ferguson.

The ambassador. Bobby at a children's summer camp, promoting England's bid for the 2006 World Cup.

habit of disappearing every week to shoot and fish. Ever since he had gone into management, Jack had been subjected to the criticism that he was only a part-time boss, more interested in being on the river than the training ground. At Newcastle, the problem became even worse because he was in the heart of the Northumberland country-side he had so adored since childhood, thereby making the temp-tation to don his wellingtons or waders all the stronger. At the time Jack was extremely defensive on this point. 'Listen,' he growled to the *Sunday Express* in June 1984, 'there's endless rubbish talked about my hunting, shooting and fishing image. Football's my first love – that's the game that has given me the chance to do other things and I've never lost sight of that. I'm not some glamour boy type – the one thing I've always done is to work at this game. And when I'm not working and coaching I'll take a day off and go fish-ing or shooting. Some folk play golf. I fish and shoot. That's it. Understand?'

If Jack had been able to work more successfully with his Newcastle players, his time away from St James' Park would probably not have been the cause of such insidious gossip. Yet the truth was that he was not able to establish the personal authority and rapport which had been a hallmark of his spells at Boro and Wednesday. This was partly because the Newcastle team, reared on Keegan and Cox's spirit of adventure, had little time for Jack's defence-minded, long-ball approach. 'Arthur's idea of a perfect game would be a 5–4 victory,' said Peter Beardsley. Jack himself admitted that his style was much more workmanlike: 'I'm not a spectacular manager. I'm a plodder. I'm a good pro.'

Plodding professionalism was despised by the more skilful members of the side, such as Chris Waddle who remembers being shocked at a Jack Charlton intervention in a five-a-side match. Terry McDermott and Chris Waddle had played a one-two when Jack stopped the game and came striding over to them.

'I don't want you playing one-twos on goal. I want you play-ing one-twos with God.' Waddle says that the players looked at Jack, 'as if he had taken leave of his senses or was having some kind of religious experience'. According to Waddle, Jack then told him and McDermott to stand on benches at the end of the gym while the rest of the players chipped balls into their hands.

'That's what I mean,' Jack said, 'you can't get hurt as long as the ball's up in the clouds.'

Waddle also recounts the time when Jack sent the whole team on a cross-country run, and was furious when he and another player, Steve Carney, trailed in far behind the rest. Jack then ordered the pair to undertake a lap of the Benwell training ground, following them on a child's bicycle, cap on head, coat flapping in the wind. Waddle says he was glad when Jack subsequently left most of the coaching in the hands of Willie McFaul: 'As long as Willie took the sessions and Jack, with his eccentric ideas, stayed away, then life was tolerable. The team generally felt much happier when Jack was not around.'

It was with Terry McDermott that Jack had his first major clash. McDermott had already been in dispute with Arthur Cox over his contract, and when Jack offered him the same terms, he angrily rejected them. Unwilling to improve his offer, Jack let him go. McDermott was only too pleased to have the chance to walk out: 'I knew within half an hour of meeting him that I could never play for him,' said McDermott after his resignation. 'Charlton's ideas on football are completely different to mine. He even had the cheek to tell me that he might want to change my style of play. I'm sad for the fans. They deserve better.'

The mood at Newcastle worsened as the season progressed. On 22 September, in a match on the controversial astroturf at QPR, United were leading 4–0 at half-time, only to end up drawing 5–5, a spendthrift performance that went wholly against Jack's instincts. After the final whistle, he kicked the advertising boards in his fury and then, according to Waddle's account, in the dressing room 'he completely lost it. He was like a man demented, swearing and ranting, apparently close to hitting somebody. He even had the goal-keeper, Kevin Carr, by the throat.' To fulfil Jack's long-ball strategy, he bought two tall strikers, Tony Cunningham from Sheffield

Wednesday and George Reilly from Watford, both more distinguished by their height than their ball skill. He then despatched Waddle out to the left wing and Beardsley to the right, from where they were meant to send over a barrage of crosses. But Waddle complains that the service was 'non-existent', with the result that he spent much of his time wandering up and down the touchline. Peter Beardsley was equally disenchanted, becoming bored with Jack's long ball game: 'I didn't enjoy the way we played and I am certain that the fans didn't like it either. I needed to be involved with the play. I did my best but I was not happy and the boss knew how I felt.' Jack admits that his relationship with Beardsley was 'very tindery'. In one game against Luton, Jack was vexed to see Beardsley disobeying his specific instruction to keep possession in the final minutes by taking the ball out to the corner flag and holding it there. Instead, said Jack, 'He sets off straight down the middle of the pitch. He overruns the ball, the goalkeeper collects it and but for a goal-line clearance by John Anderson, we would have dropped two points.' Jack decided to give Beardsley a piece of his mind the moment he came off the pitch, despite the pleas of coach Willie McFaul to hold his tongue. 'No bloody way, Willie, that silly bugger almost cost us the game and I'm going to let him know it,' replied Jack.

In Jack's own words, he gave Beardsley 'the bollocking of a lifetime. I put my arm round his neck and he shrugs me off.'

"I nearly scored," he protested.

"You nearly cost us the fucking game. Why don't you ever listen?"'

Beardsley says that he was so amazed at the ferocity of Jack's outburst that 'I thought for a brief moment he might have been taking the mickey.' According to Beardsley, Jack carried on ranting even in front of the press, before storming off with the words 'to hell with the lot of you.' There was more of the same the following week in a game against Watford, when Newcastle, leading 2–1, had a free-kick in the dying minutes. From a well-flighted ball delivered into the box by Beardsley, the big centre-forward George Reilly scored with a header to see Newcastle into a 3–1. But instead of congratulating

Beardsley, Jack turned on him again. 'What did I tell you last week?' Beardsley says that at this moment, 'I just thought this bloke is not for real.'

By the turn of the year, with results still not improving, the fans were becoming almost as restless as the players. Few had been impressed by Jack's signings, the biggest of which was £120,000 midfielder Gary Megson from his old club Sheffield Wednesday. Compelled to defend his policy, Jack denied that he was a 'miserly manager'. 'I would spend the money if I had it,' he said, 'but we have an overdraft of £500,000. If I buy two players, that would make it a million. I know the club can't stand that.' But it was the approach on the field that caused the real discontent. As Roger Hutchinson wrote in his *Complete History of Newcastle Football Club*, 'Most of the fans were bored and confused by the manager's instructions to the full-backs to lob the ball over the forwards for them to chase and not to pass to feet. Obsessively defensive, insistent upon stopping the opposition rather than starting Newcastle, loud and persistent in his criticism of players, Jack Charlton was not overly popular in some areas of St James' Park.' In January 1985, Jack was barracked by a section of the crowd who chanted 'Charlton must go' during the home game against Everton. This kind of abuse had never happened during his time at Middlesbrough or Sheffield Wednesday, but then neither of those teams had descended into the kind of relegation battle which now gripped Newcastle.

Amidst this crisis, there was one positive sign for the future in the chubby form of a curly-haired 16 year old. He had a cheeky grin, a love of cream cakes and an astonishing gift for football. His name was Paul Gascoigne. He only played a couple of times for Jack's Newcastle United, but he credits Charlton with starting him on the path to soccer glory. According to Gascoigne, the first time Jack hauled him into his office, he said: 'I hear that you're a cheeky chappie. There's a lot of fat there but I'm told underneath you've got a bit of skill. I'm giving you two weeks to get yourself fit. If you've not made it by then, I'll show you the door.' Just to make sure that Gascoigne obeyed these instructions, Jack instructed the tearoom beside the training ground – where Gascoigne would regularly enjoy a carbohydrate-fest – to serve him only high-protein steaks and salads. So shaken was Gascoigne by this twin-pronged attack on his corpulent lifestyle that he shed the necessary weight and was soon captain of the youth team.

Pleased with Gascoigne's progress, Jack promoted him to be one of the first-team substitutes towards the end of the 1984/85 season. It was in this role that Gascoigne first encountered Jack's legendary inability to remember names. In one game, Chris Waddle was injured and Neil McDonald was to take his place. But Jack had once worked with a player called Gary McDonald. So in his pre-match talk, he kept calling Neil 'Gary' when he was telling McDonald to go wide on the right. Unfortunately, to deepen the confusion, Gascoigne thought Jack was calling out his own nickname 'Gazza' every time he said 'Gary'. At last, it seemed his chance of a debut in the first team had finally arrived and he duly went to put on the number seven shirt.

'What are you doing?' asked Jack, turning in his direction.

'Well, boss, you told me to play wide on the right. I don't think it's my best position but I'll give it a go.'

'You idiot. I was talking to Gary, not you.' By this time, Neil McDonald didn't have a clue what he was meant to be doing.

Gazza did soon have his debut, playing at home against QPR in April 1985. 'It was like having sex for the first time. You never forget that either,' says Gascoigne. Jack always cites one moment, in a Youth Cup Final against Watford, when he realized that Gascoigne was a truly special player. In *The Sunday Times* in September 1993 he described it thus: '30 yards out he checks, sees the goalie of his line and instantly digs the ball out with his right foot and it sails clean over the top into the goal and the keeper ends up flat on his arse. I turned to my assistant Maurice Setters and said, "You'll have to wait a thousand years to see that again."'

But Gascoigne's emergence could not compensate for the fact that Newcastle's leading player, Chris Waddle, was leaving the club at the end of the 1985/86 season in a £590,000 move to Spurs.

Waddle, rather piously, says that he found the initial offer from Newcastle to stay at the club 'insulting', but the fact is Newcastle could not compete with the much richer clubs. And Waddle was already disillusioned enough with Jack to want to leave anyway, whatever promises Newcastle made. In the words of his agent Mel Stein: 'Chris never actually disliked Jack as a person. Indeed, he was the sort of man he'd be happy to sit down with for hours and talk football. It was just his tactics with which he could not agree. Those tactics were not working out for Newcastle or Chris.'

Nor were they working for the fans. Such was the growing mood against him that at the end of the year, Jack was ready to quit. 'Looking back over my first season on Tyneside, I can say that this has been the most difficult I have ever experienced as a manager,' he said in May 1985. Now in his fifties, Jack was increasingly exhausted by the amount of travelling he had to do in the job. On one occasion, he almost had a frightening accident: 'I was coming back from some bloody match in Manchester. I'd been driving along the motorway for six hours and was knackered. Suddenly I realised I was falling asleep at the wheel and I thought, 'What am I doing this for?' What actually kept him at the club was not football or money, but the fact that he had just bought a large converted farmhouse in Northumberland, having sold the family home in Barnsley, and Pat was not prepared to go through another move. So he decided to plough on for another season.

But during the summer, the clamour against him from the diehard fans intensified. What enraged them was not just the departure of Waddle, but the failure to use the £590,000 fee to buy any quality replacements. His only purchases were Ian Stewart, a little-known winger from QPR and Alan Davies, a striker who had failed to make the grade at Old Trafford and who later committed suicide, unable to handle the emotional pressure of his broken ambitions. Jack succeeded in increasing the fans' anger when he tried to sign the Ipswich player Eric Gates. A fee had been agreed between the clubs, but then Jack baulked at Gates' own financial demands and the deal was off. Gates subsequently moved to arch-rivals Sunderland, where Jack's old friend Lawrie McMenemy was in charge.

The announcement that Gates had been snatched by Sunderland was made on the day that Newcastle were playing a pre-season friendly at St James' Park. What happened next was the lowest point of Jack's career in British football. As he made his way to the dugout, he was greeted by a wave of abuse from the Newcastle fans. Cries of 'Charlton out', 'We hate Charlton' and 'Sack Jack', echoed across the largely deserted ground. When the match got underway, the crowd of 5,000 cheered every time Sheffield United touched the ball and then continued with their protests. A meaningless friendly had suddenly become a rally against Jack Charlton. Shaken by this demonstration of public hostility, Jack turned to his assistant Willie McFaul and said, 'I don't fancy this one bit. I don't need it.'

On taking the Newcastle job in June 1984, Jack had said, 'The minute they find out they don't want me, I'll be out the door.' And that is exactly what Jack now did. Straight after the final whistle, he marched into the directors' room and handed in his resignation to chairman Stan Seymour. 'I'm off. I'm not going to tolerate that. As far as I'm concerned you can stick the Newcastle job,' he said, fuming. Seymour tried to persuade him to change his mind. 'Don't let the hooligans drive you out,' he said. But Jack was having none of it.

Over the weekend, more efforts were made to encourage Jack to stay but to no avail. It was as his brother Bobby said, 'He's very strong-willed when he's reached a decision.' Jack sensed that there was no point in going on, even if he had wanted to, because his continued presence would have only split the club. He was particularly struck by the view of the Newcastle chief scout, Joe Harvey, captain of the great Cup-winning side of the 1950s and the club's manager between 1962 and 1975, who told him, 'Once they get on to you here, there's a certain section that will never let go.' On a personal level, Jack was deeply hurt by the way, for the first time in his life, he seemed to have lost the respect of football followers. And he was also angered at the way his own family was made to suffer by his very public humiliation. His son John, visiting from Australia, was sitting beside Pat during the match: 'It was sickening. My mother was almost in tears. My dad doesn't have to take that sort of thing.'

Jack's resignation showed that he was a much more sensitive man than his hard image suggested. Other managers, perhaps most notably Howard Kendall at Everton, had been through a similar experience at the hands of impatient fans, but had ultimately emerged triumphant. But for all his extraordinary honesty and rudeness, there has always been a side of Jack that wants to be loved by the public. He simply could not stomach being hated by any group of fans from the club he worshipped. The affair also showed his impetuosity and determination. He might have made up his mind in the heat of the moment, but nothing was going to change it. More negatively, it also revealed his egocentricity, that thoughtlessness which the ex-Leeds players still talk about. Jack did what he wanted and ignored the needs of his colleagues. Maurice Setters, who had loyally served him for eight years, tells the story of going home after checking on a player for Jack, switching on the television and hearing the news that Jack had quit. 'Eventually I managed to track him down. I asked him what was going on and you know what he said, "Oh, I forgot all about you."'

There appeared to be few regrets amongst supporters about his resignation. The view of the Newcastle supporters' club secretary John Mullen, was typical: 'He never had any rapport with the fans. All we want is someone who can give us entertaining football and a bit of excitement. When Keegan left the stage was set. But since then, the atmosphere has changed.' Season-ticket holder John Brunton gave this thoughtful summary of Jack's weaknesses: 'His buying and selling was poor, he was too quick to criticize the fans and he failed to build on the springboard created by promotion. I think he also failed to have any feel for the job, something that is surprising for someone from this area.'

Many of the players felt the same way. 'I think Jack bottled it,' said Peter Beardsley. 'He thought he was above criticism. If he said it, we did it. Geordie fans never took to him and there are no better

judges than our supporters. I am convinced that Jack's way of playing the game helped Waddle make his decision about moving. And
he never did me any favours. It didn't take me long to become
disenchanted. I'm no hypocrite and I shed no crocodile tears when
Jack announced he was quitting. The truth is that if Jack had stayed
I would almost certainly have left.'

The Newcastle fiasco, especially his failure to exploit the Waddle
sale – the biggest in the club's history – exposed Jack's worst idio-
syncrasy as a club manager: his reluctance to buy new players,. Jack
could not stomach the modern League football transfer market,
with its paraphernalia of agents, bloated fees and excessive demands
and so he was not able to operate effectively in this world. He admitted that 'I don't enjoy wheeling and dealing.' Yet all the rest of his
faults – his dictatorial approach, his simplistic tactical approach,
his refusal to give up his interests outside football – might yet be
turned to his advantage if he could be provided with the right
managerial environment.

That environment was about to appear, in the strangest of
circumstances. As the old Sinatra song goes, 'The best is yet to
come'.

CHAPTER TWENTY

The Director

In the summer that Jack took charge of Newcastle, Bobby had also gone back to the club he had been devoted to since his boyhood, Manchester United. But he was returning in a very different capacity, not as a manager but as a director. On 27 June 1984, Bobby and the solicitor Maurice Watkins came on to the board in place of vice-chairman Alan Gibson and Bill Young, who had been directors since 1960 but now became vice-presidents. This was no corporate revolution, merely a move by United's chairman Martin Edwards to refresh the club's image at the top. Maurice Watkins confirms how smooth the reshuffle was: 'It was a very amicable, friendly transaction. Alan proposed Bobby, and Bill myself. I had not known Bobby before that, though I had obviously seen him play. But immediately I found him approachable, shrewd, willing to speak his mind, good to work with.'

When Bobby began his career with United, the idea of an ex-professional being appointed to a club's board of directors would have seemed utterly laughable. Reared in the public school tradition of the glorious amateur, most club chairmen had, at best, a benign social contempt for those who were forced to earn their living from sport. Never was the Marxist term 'wage slave' more appropriately used than when describing the lives of professional footballers before the 1960s, when they were without rights, had their pay capped and could be retained against their will by the club. None of them could have possessed anything like the personal wealth needed to take them to the boardroom. Even the most distinguished players, such as Stanley Matthews and Billy Wright, were given precious little status off the field. No matter what they achieved, footballers generally remained part of the working class in reality as well as spirit. Ivor Allchurch, for instance, the brilliant Welsh forward who, like Bobby was universally regarded as a gentleman on and off the field, ended his working life as a storeman. A glimpse into the hardship of life as a professional in the 1950s was provided to me by Bobby's United colleague Ray Wood: 'Footballers were very badly paid. We had 12-month contracts but, in reality, we were bound for life because the club held your registration. So you would wait, at the end of the season, for the letter saying, "you've been retained" or "you've got a free transfer". Even if you had been in the first team you still would worry about this letter, wondering if you still had a job next year. It was ruthless, the way football was run. You were only as good as your last game.'

But Bobby was lucky to reach his peak in the mid-1960s, when there was a profound change in the position of players in football's hierarchy. Freed from the chains of the maximum wage and restrictive contracts, they could no longer be treated as serfs. It was not so easy to sneer at men who were earning more than most of those in the boardroom. This change in attitudes was helped by the great managers of the time, Busby, Revie, Ramsey, and Shankly, all once top professionals themselves, who treated their players with a genuine respect and equality that had rarely been seen before in soccer. But the speed of this change should not be exaggerated, as snobbery continued well into the 1970s. When Don Revie was appointed England manager in 1974, he had this exchange with the chairman of the FA Sir Harold Thompson:

'When I get to know you better, Revie, I shall call you Don.'

'And when I get to know you better, Thompson, I shall call you Sir Harold.'

The fact that Bobby could so easily become a director without causing an outcry was not just a reflection of new social realities, but was also a tribute to Bobby's own famous qualities of decency, caution, good manners and diplomacy. There was never any danger of his being an embarrassment to the boardroom, something that could not be said of other senior footballers, including his own elder brother. And he was much more suited to a football directorship than to a managerial job. With his huge international reputation, his contacts throughout the game and his passion for the club, Bobby was seen by Martin Edwards as a potentially huge asset to the club, even if his business experience was limited. Unlike all other directors appointed since the controversial rights issue of 1978 – when Louis Edwards, Martin's father, raised money by selling new shares to existing investors – Bobby did not have to purchase a large shareholding through the Edwards family, though even as a player he had bought some shares in United, such was his attachment to Old Trafford.

When he was still playing, Bobby had developed an interest in working as a football ambassador. An article in the *Manchester Evening News* in June 1971 had this snapshot of Bobby's luxurious but hectic lifestyle during the close season, when he was jetting round the continent in support of the Ford youth programme in European football: 'Bobby Charlton, dapper in a grey suit and carrying an executive briefcase, strode through oppressive heat 1,000 miles from home to follow a multi-millionaire's trail to Europe's top soccer kids. It was a flight of fancy for the world's most respected footballer – with a £500,000 air cab at his disposal. Sitting in motor mogul Henry Ford's private twin-engined jet, Captain John Wilson watched Bobby's approach across the tarmac and switched on the power.' In 36 hours, he flew over 5,000 miles – 'it was a matter of breakfast in Portugal, lunch in Switzerland and dinner in Holland,' wrote reporter Ted Macauley. As well as showing the impressive resilience of the Munich survivor, the trip also dispelled the idea – so widespread in the United dressing room at the time – that Bobby was aloof. 'He spent four hours in the sultry, depressing heat of a Zurich stadium, with his smile never faltering, encouraging the boys and posing for endless pictures with them as proud parents pushed their sons to his side. In Holland Bobby stayed up until dawn talking football with friends on the beautiful canal-side terrace of his hotel and was out of bed only hours later, clear eyed and ready to get to work making some of Europe's soccer kids glow with happiness.'

By 1984, having proved himself a success in business with Halba Travel and gained the experience of the boardroom at Wigan Athletic, Bobby was ready for United. But yet again, his elevation became a source of friction with some of his ex-Manchester colleagues, who saw his move as another example of his willingness to betray the legend of Sir Matt Busby. The fact was that after his retirement, the ageing Busby had become an increasingly disgruntled figure at Old Trafford. He had once harboured hopes of becoming United chairman himself but these had been disappointed by the continued hold of the Edwards family on control of United. More seriously, he was aggrieved that his own son Sandy had never been appointed to the board, in direct contravention of a private deal he thought he had reached with Martin Edwards' father, Louis. He had also opposed a rights issue organized by Louis to raise money for the club – and his own faltering business. It was Busby's opposition which stirred *World in Action* researchers to investigate the running of Old Trafford by the Edwards family, ultimately resulting in the 1980 documentary 'The Man Who Bought United', the screening of which was soon followed by Louis Edwards' fatal heart attack. 'If Matt had gone along with the rights issue at the time, *World in Action* would probably not have had a story. But the publicity from Matt opposing it got people interested and they started to dig,' comments Martin Edwards with a degree of filial bitterness.

Given this sorry history, some ex-players who still worshipped Busby bore a grudge against Bobby for accepting a directorship of Edwards' United. He had, in effect, chosen the other side. He was seen as a front man for the board that had disdained United's greatest figure. But, as Bobby pointed out to Eamon Dunphy, he was a pragmatist, not a sentimentalist. He thought his critics were dwelling in the past: 'You have to be realistic in this day and age. Oh, it's not the same game as it used to be, much as you might like to go back to the good old days. The only way you can have the same sort of feeling is to try and have the same kind of success.'

Bobby may have been a gentleman, but he was never without his inner toughness. Harry Gregg recalls talking to Bobby's younger brother in about 1980, when Gordon was concerned about the way Bobby was handling his absence from professional football. 'I remember Gordon saying, "Our Jack was always going to do all right because he's got a big mouth but I worry about our Bob." And I replied, "Your Bob's got far more steel in him than people realize." I was 100 per cent right.' Indeed Gregg was, for Bobby was soon taking on the manager of United, 'Big Ron' Atkinson, who had been in charge of Old Trafford since 1981. Atkinson might have sneered at the quiet, self-effacing figure who arrived in 1984, but, he soon learnt that Bobby could be a 'relentless boardroom adversary', to quote his own phrase.

Their first clash arose on a relatively trivial issue: the deployment of coaches at Old Trafford. Since 1979, Bobby had run a number of Easter and summer schools in Manchester for children from all over the country. They had become major operations, backed by the FA and handling over 4,000 children in the holidays. Atkinson's objection was that some of Bobby's coaches were supposedly interfering with the training at Manchester United's own school of excellence for youngsters. 'I was not prepared to tolerate that and made my view directly and very forcibly clear. I might, I now accept, have trodden on Bobby's toes when I made it transparently clear that I didn't want his men around. I had Eric Harrison, now proven as arguably the most successful youth coach of all time with the development of Beckham, Butt, Scholes and the Nevilles. I was very confident in Eric's ability to educate the kids in the craft of the game and I didn't want him being bothered by a bunch of schoolteachers with big ideas, whether they were under Bobby's patronage or not.'

What Atkinson ignores is that Beckham was actually a product of one of the Bobby Charlton schools, winning his first ever football prize in a national skills contest there in 1986. Indeed, when Bobby watched Beckham performing, he said he was 'the best 11-year-old I've seen in the years I've been running my school.' Beckham's success established a bond with Bobby which lasts to this day. Alec McGivan remembers sitting in the stands with Sir Bobby watching the England v Argentina game in the 1998 World Cup in France, when Beckham was sent off: 'Bobby could not speak for the rest of the game. He did not say a thing he was so upset. After the match he said to me, "I've got to try to speak to David." Bobby ran over to the players' area, went in and put his arms around David. He was there for at least ten minutes. Bobby was terribly concerned, he was like a father figure to David, saying that this was "a terrible experience for David." I did not pry too much but you could tell there was a huge amount of feeling about it.'

But two former England players, David Sadler and Stan Anderson, who both worked at the Bobby Charlton summer schools, think it is a nonsense to see Bobby as some sort of empire builder. On the contrary, they say, he was totally relaxed, just happy to be still involving children in the game he loved. Far from throwing his weight around, he displayed his customary shyness. 'He was so good with kids, but he was also so modest about it,' says Anderson, who worked there in the early 1980s. 'Although he was in charge, he might come along to one of my coaching sessions and say, "Do you mind if I join you?" "Of course not. Come on, Bob, show them how to do it." So I would be throwing spin balls to him and he was cracking them into the net from all angles. I wanted to show the kids that they could not expect the ball to come easily every time. Bobby loved this sort of thing. He showed the lads exactly what could be achieved. And you could see the kids, with their eyes wide open, looking at this fella who had retired but still had so much talent. He was anxious about usurping my authority so he would ask. He was so polite that way. We had kids from the age of seven upwards and we put them in groups each day. It was wonderful. He was a natural with children, an absolute natural. He is such a nice fella and kids enjoyed being in his company because he has got this nice soft voice. He likes children, and he gets a lot of pleasure from working with them.' David Sadler echoes this view, describing him as a 'bit like the Pied Piper'. Sadler was involved on the administrative side of the schools. 'Before I went there, I had thought that Bobby would not be directly involved. I had thought he was really just lending his name to the organization. But when I arrived, I could see that he was really hands on, so involved with the kids. He really did love getting out there and playing for hours with them during the summer months. It was terrific to see. He was so at ease in the middle of hundreds of screaming 10 year olds. I wouldn't have thought that would be his cup of tea, but he obviously just loved working with them.'

Bobby's delight in this work was shown by his memory of work-ing with one young boy who was feeling desperately homesick on joining the school. 'One day he sat on my knee in the dressing room, crying his eyes out. He said he was missing his dad. At the end of the week, his dad came to pick him up. I waited with him until his dad arrived. When Tommy saw him, he raced towards him in floods of tears, crying "Dad, Dad, it's been the greatest week of my life."'

To the cynical, perma-tanned Ron Atkinson, that sort of moment would have meant little. With his love of expensive cars, vintage champagne, designer jewellery and sharp wisecracks, he and Bobby had almost nothing in common except that they were at the same club, something that Bobby was determined would not be the case for much longer. He was depressed by United's failure to challenge effectively for the highest honour, the League Championship, and when he joined the board in 1984 – after a season when United had again finished fourth – he had a dig at Atkinson's record: 'I'm young and experienced enough to help Manchester United. The lesser trophies like the UEFA are all right but they're a bit Third Divisionish. I'd like to see United winning the European Cup again and that means they would be champions of England.' Bobby was equally dismayed by some of the disastrous signings of the Atkinson reign. Alan Brazil, for instance, was bought from Tottenham for

£700,000 but played only 18 games, just four more than Terry Gibson who cost £630,000 from Coventry. Nor could the £600,000 forked out for Peter Davenport be deemed a bargain, while he bought Peter Beardsley from Vancouver Whitecaps, only to let him go back to Canada after a single game. In fact during Atkinson's five years in charge United lost £2.2 million on transfer dealings, without much silverware to show for it.

For his part, Atkinson deemed himself to be a success – two FA Cups, never finishing below fourth place in the League, a campaign in Europe every season. He had little time for Bobby's complaints, and instead revelled in the sort of verbal bullying that had been inflicted on Bobby in the past by the likes of Pat Crerand and George Best. Atkinson gleefully recounts how his senior players 'were never all that close to him. At times, they were quite disparaging in the mickey-taking way that is the favourite pastime of most footballers. Coming back from a game at Wembley, I remember them taunting Bobby as he sat at the front of the team bus with the other directors. "Bobb-ee, Bobb-ee, give us a smile", they sang out until it was almost embarrassing.' But Atkinson was not quite the popular figure he imagined amongst the Old Trafford faithful. 'He's big, he's round, he's worth a million pounds,' they would sing in derision.

The simmering feud between Atkinson and Charlton came to a head in 1986 over Atkinson's desire to buy the defender Terry Butcher from Ipswich, using the money from the £2 million move of Mark Hughes to Barcelona. By this time, Bobby was becoming an increasingly influential figure on the board and chairman Martin Edwards regularly deferred to him on football matters. Having lost faith in Atkinson's judgement, Bobby now argued strongly against Butcher, saying the £700,000 price tag would not be a wise investment and that Butcher was no better than the other United backs already in the squad. Atkinson's reply was dripping with sarcasm: 'I don't care who you have as the manager of this football club, whether it's Terry Venables, Graham Taylor, Alex Ferguson or me, I don't think any of us would be too unhappy to have Butcher alongside Paul McGrath for the next five years at the heart of this defence.' He then added, 'He might just have been good enough, Bobby, to have kept Preston up when you were briefly there as manager.' Atkinson admitted later, 'It was not the most diplomatic comment. The words ricocheted around the room like a sniper's bullet.'

What angered Bobby about Atkinson was not just the poor results and foolish transfers, but also his failure to tackle the drinking culture which had gripped United by the mid-1980s, led by Paul McGrath, Norman Whiteside and Bryan Robson. Bobby feared that he was seeing a re-run of the bad old days at Old Trafford in the early 1970s, when a succession of managers had indulged the lurid excesses of George Best, with disastrous consequences for the team's morale. The growing indiscipline at the club was highlighted at the beginning of the 1986/87 season, when seven players were fined after a heavy drinking session in Holland. Then Remi Moses was involved in such a serious fight with Jesper Olsen that the Dane needed 11 stitches.

Bobby and the rest of the board had seen quite enough of Atkinson. When United plunged to second from bottom of the table and were beaten in the League Cup 4–1 by Southampton in November 1986, Atkinson was sacked. Though he says it came as a shock to him, few others in the football world were surprised. The board now had to find a manager who could restore the glory days to Old Trafford. And the directors were pretty sure they knew who they wanted: Alex Ferguson of Aberdeen.

Atkinson believes that, before the 1986/87 season started, United were already lining up Ferguson as replacement, with Bobby Charlton playing the key role in this subterfuge. Bobby is said to have tapped Ferguson about the job during the 1986 World Cup in Mexico, where Bobby was working as a BBC commentator and Ferguson as the caretaker-manager of Scotland. 'I had my suspicions then, and I have not had any reason to change my opinion, that the approach was made by Bobby,' wrote Atkinson, who claims these suspicions were confirmed early in the season when he bumped into Ferguson at a European game. The normally sociable Ferguson 'could hardly bear to say hello. He was very sheepish, more distant than I had ever known him,' because, according to Atkinson, he was embarrassed at facing the man whose job he had secretly agreed to take.

But this is conjecture and Atkinson has produced nothing tangible to support his case. In fact, all the evidence points the other way. In his own autobiography, Sir Alex Ferguson is adamant that the United job offer came as a surprise in November 1986, since he had received no approaches before that and certainly not one from Bobby during the World Cup. 'Although Bobby did speak to me at the side of the pitch before Scotland's fiasco of a game with Uruguay, the furthest he went was to ask that if ever I decided to move to England I should let him know. I don't think that can be considered an offer and it did not send any signals to me that I was bound for United. Apart from that brief contact with Bobby, there was nothing but rumour to link me with Old Trafford.'

Bobby himself maintains that he essentially just 'said hello' to Ferguson during the Uruguay game. He does not deny that he was always sure Ferguson was the right man for the job and argued the case strongly with the other directors. But he disputes that he played any unique part in bringing Ferguson from Aberdeen. 'Yes, I wanted him to come, but it was the board's decision, not mine.' And that is the memory of the other directors as well. 'In retrospect, we'd all like to claim that we were personally responsible for the idea – yes, it was definitely mine,' jokes Maurice Watkins. 'But the truth is that the directors played a very unified role in that appointment. There were just four of us on the board at the time, Martin Edwards, Mike Edelson, Bobby and myself, so it was very easy to get together and have a meeting. We all were agreed on going for Alex.' Mike Edelson, in an interview for the book *Manchester Unlimited*, describes flying back from the disastrous Southampton game with Martin Edwards, when they discussed 'what we should do about Atkinson'. The next day, according to Edelson, Bobby and Maurice were quickly summoned. 'We discussed it again and narrowed it down to two options: Terry Venables and Alex Ferguson. Terry

Venables wasn't really available because he was at Barcelona. They were still in the European Cup and they wouldn't release him, we thought. We decided it wouldn't be worth considering Terry. Alex was obviously the first option.' It was then agreed that Edelson should make the call to Ferguson, who, it turned out, was only too eager to discuss the job. The four directors then flew up to Scotland where, after some tough negotiations, the deal was concluded.

During the next three years, there were times when the faith of Bobby and the other directors in Ferguson was severely tested, as United failed to make the progress they had hoped for. By December 1989 there was talk of a deepening crisis at the club, as United went a month without a victory and were thrashed 5–1 by Manchester City at Maine Road. When the team played Forest on 17 January 1990 in the third round of the FA Cup, it was widely predicted that if United lost, Ferguson would be sacked. Thanks to a Mark Robbins goal, scored against the run of play, United scraped through to the fourth round. It was to be the vital turning point in Ferguson's reign, for Manchester went on to win the Cup, and from then on the trophies came in thick and fast.

But the belief that Ferguson was facing the axe at the Nottingham Forest game is wrong. Bobby, whose voice on football matters was the strongest on the board, has stated that there was no such possibility. 'Personally, I never had any doubts about what Alex could achieve with us. By the time we won at Wembley in 1990, I reckon he was bang on course. I knew people had been calling for his head but as a board we decided that when we appointed Alex we were going to give him the time he needed. What happened with Ferguson should be a good example to others. Too many clubs don't give their managers the backing they deserve,' he said in 2001. Maurice Watkins confirms this: 'We were never going to sack Alex. We were not a board that was forever nitpicking. It was a very cohesive unit and we had a genuinely strong belief in the club and what it stood for. We thought Alex was taking us in the right direction. We were very supportive of him. People keep saying he was about to be shot before that game against Forest. Well, the answer is that the matter was never discussed.' And this is not just said with the warm glow of hindsight. The journalist Ken Montgomery gave me this memory: 'I clearly remember phoning up Bobby for the *Sunday Mirror*, on the day before a crucial FA Cup tie with Nottingham Forest in 1990 and he told me "Whatever the result tomorrow, Ken, win, lose or draw, Alex will be staying. He's got an excellent managerial record and we need him. Once he has put one trophy in the cabinet, he'll then put a whole lot of them in there." And he was absolutely spot on.'

The courage of Charlton, Edwards and the board in sticking to their long-term strategy puts in perspective the constant bleating from a hardcore of United fans about Bobby Charlton. To those of us outside Old Trafford, it is incomprehensible that one of the greatest footballers ever seen, who has led an exemplary life both on and off the field, should be treated with such circumspection by a certain element of the club's following. The main reasons for this are partly political, in that he is seen as a 'creature of the board' – and directors are rarely the most popular figures among the supporters – and partly in Bobby's shy, downbeat character. Richard Kurt, the author of several books about Manchester United, told me, 'The Man United fans don't always like him because he's seen as a bit of a cold fish. Fans thought that an ex-player on the board might have been sympathetic, but he's such an establishment figure. He seems suspicious of the real fans. Like in a hotel, he'll see a group at the bar and say, "How did you lot get in here?" It is hard to find anyone who knows the club who actually likes him. To be one of the least popular directors at a club like United is a remarkable achievement, a bit like being the least humorous man in a group of Germans.' Michael Crick, the brilliant biographer and himself a United follower, says, 'Charlton has a saintly image but many of the fans think he has a miserable attitude. He never seems to have anything to do with the fans' forum and doesn't seem to believe that fans should be listened to at board level.' Crick admits, though, that Bobby played a crucial role in protecting Ferguson at the height of his unpopularity. 'Most fans wanted Fergie sacked but Bobby protected him. If Bobby had not been around, Fergie might have gone then.'

There is also the traditional British eagerness to pull down someone who has been placed on a pedestal. People like Best or Cantona can get away with anything. With Bobby, because of his gentlemanly image, every tiny flaw is blown up out of all proportion. As United fan Chris Robinson admitted to me, 'He is portrayed as a saint and I think that's why people are a bit envious towards him. Maybe we take an overly critical view of him. I mean there are people at Old Trafford who have done far, far worse than even his strongest critics have accused him of, people who have abused their positions, but somehow, because of Bobby's image, there is more resentment.'

One of the more frivolous accusations against Bobby is that he is not always ready to sign autographs. Well, this may happen very occasionally, though there cannot be a celebrity who has never had to endure this claim. And Bobby, as probably the second most famous footballer in the world after Pele, has to put up with more exhausting demands from the public than most. Sometimes, he can resent the invasion of his privacy, and, as a player, he intensely disliked being pestered before a game. Once this trait led to an argument between Bobby and Jack, as the Sunderland footballer Ron Routledge recalls. 'It was before a Leeds v Manchester game at Elland Road, and as Bobby and Jack walked to the ground, the kids were asking for their autographs. Bobby refused, saying, "Later on, I'm busy now."

Jack just stood and said, "Kid, what the hell's the matter with you?"

"I want to get to the ground."

"Give the kids their autographs. The day that they stop asking for your autograph, there's something wrong. Never refuse them."'

But, in most circumstances, Bobby has taken this responsibility seriously. According to the promoter Mike Newlin, Bobby is 'marvellous at signing autographs. Wherever he goes, he is always in the spotlight, people always want to stop him, and I am sure it can get exhausting. Yet nothing ever seems too much trouble.' The late Frank Clough of the *Sun* once watched in amazement as Bobby, taking part in a charity cricket match at Cheadle Hulme, made all the arrangements for an autograph-signing session and then systematically wrote out his name more than 1,000 times for the children, then 'He slipped off without even waiting for the thank you he had earned from the organizers.' Alec McGivan also saw him in action during the 2006 World Cup bid: 'Wherever he goes, people want both his autograph and a photograph with him. He must be the most photographed Englishman in the world. I have never yet been to an airport lounge with him where someone has not asked for his autograph – I have even been there when he has been asked to sign a piece of toilet paper. And he did. I have never seen him refuse an autograph. Sometimes he would say, "I haven't got time," and then he would turn and quickly sign it. He never got ratty and never got difficult. There was a great moment when we went to Malta. Someone on the airport staff came up to Bobby and said, "Would you sign my book?" and so he did. After he signed it, she turned back the page and said, "Can I show you this? This is the same autograph book and on the previous page, you signed this for my father 30 years ago." It was a lovely moment. I realized that, over the decades, so many different people had been coming up to him.'

'A prophet is not without honour save in his own country,' says *St Matthew's Gospel*. The lack of acclaim for Bobby shown by certain fans also extended to his fellow directors at other League clubs. Despite his vast experience and his worldwide fame, the Football League decided twice in the 1980s that he was not a suitable candidate to win a place on their management committee. The idea that some blazered nobody was more worthy of elevation than Bobby Charlton now seems grotesque, but the mood in League circles then was that he lacked the political clout and independence to serve as a committee member. A specific fear amongst the chairmen of the League's smaller clubs was that Charlton would be a mouthpiece for Manchester United and would thereby increase the domination of the Big Five – United, Liverpool, Everton, Spurs and Arsenal. 'There is a feeling among most of the First Division that the big clubs' influence should be kept in check,' said one chairman. So in June 1988, when he stood for election, he trailed in fifth place, well behind the winning four candidates, prompting Patrick Collins in the *Mail on Sunday* to write this acerbic analysis of the Football League's attitude to Bobby: 'It may well be that Charlton wouldn't have been terribly good at helping run the Football League, since his instincts are for the establishment and his preference is for the status quo. But that is scarcely the point. In every other major football nation, Charlton's glowing image would have been flaunted and exploited at the very peak of the game. In England he gets nine votes.' Four months later, when two more vacancies on the committee arose with the departure of David Dein of Arsenal and Philip Carter of Everton, Charlton was again snubbed, the places being taken by John Smith of Liverpool and Robert Chase of Norwich. Bobby could not hide his disappointment. 'I don't agree with being against people because they are the big clubs' candidates. If they are the right people it doesn't matter where they come from. It's a pity because I think I have something to offer. I feel disappointed. The game is struggling and needs a bit of a boost.' Some might argue that Bobby had shown little understanding of the realpolitik of League football, but, as a fault, his naivety was more attractive than his chairmen's blinkers.

Following his rejection by the League, Bobby was forced to concentrate on his work with United. Within barely a year of his second failed election bid, he was involved in his first major boardroom struggle at Old Trafford, caused by the decision of chairman Martin Edwards to sell his 50.2 per cent controlling stake in Manchester United to entrepreneur Michael Knighton for £10 million. More than ten years later, it might seem bizarre that control of Old Trafford could be bought for such a tiny sum, but at the end of the 1980s, United was nothing like the club it is today. Failure on the pitch was matched by cash shortages, while the stadium itself was in urgent need of redevelopment following the Taylor report on the Hillsborough tragedy. The bill for that work was estimated at over £12 million yet the club had made a loss of £3 million in 1989.

But Bobby and the other directors were doubtful as to whether the Knighton takeover would be in the club's interest. They were particularly suspicious – rightly as it turned out – as to whether Knighton actually had the money to buy Edwards' option. Mike Edelson led the campaign to undermine Knighton, getting all the information he could on him and using every legal weapon against him. This sort of business tussle was entirely new to Bobby, but, as Edelson recalls, he entered it with relish. 'We used to be at Old Trafford every day sitting round gorging on food, trying to find out what Knighton was up to. It was a campaign. We used to get calls from waiters to say Knighton was in a certain restaurant. So Bobby and I went and sat outside waiting for him to come out, to see who he was with.' At one stage in the campaign, the media baron Eddie Shah, who had rebuffed an approach from Knighton, offered to pass on a confidential report to Charlton and Edelson: 'Eddie was straight up front and offered to help. He phoned once about two o'clock in the morning. I remember going to his house to get the report he wanted to give us. Bobby came with me. Eddie has three of those great big dogs, Dobermans, and when we got there, these dogs came from nowhere. Bobby was very good because he's got dogs and he just stood there. I dived back into the car and wouldn't get out.'

Thanks to the efforts of Edelson, Charlton and the other directors, the Knighton bid evaporated under this intense scrutiny, as the backing for his audacious takeover plan turned out to be a chimera. After his initial enthusiasm, Bobby grew weary of the whole affair, as he later confessed to the BBC: 'It was a very uncomfortable period. It set off a chain of events where all that mattered for nearly a whole year was the ownership of the club. I hope that we've put that behind us because football is about scoring goals, not squabbles in the boardroom.' But in one respect Knighton had been very useful, in that he had opened the eyes of the board to the real business potential of Old Trafford. Following the end of the Knighton bid, Martin Edwards was then involved in talks in the summer of 1990 with fellow United director Amir Al Midani, the son of a Lebanese millionaire who had joined the board in 1987. With Bobby Charlton part of his consortium – and lined up as a possible chairman – Al Midani was hoping to buy out Edwards. But he baulked at the £30 million price tag demanded by Edwards. Negotiations soon broke down and Bobby's brief glimpse of power quickly faded. But the central theme of Al Midani's buy-out offer, that the club should be floated on the stock market, gained ground. Plans were now drawn up to turn United into a public limited company, and in 1991, the flotation went ahead successfully. Such a move, copied by many other major clubs, was part of the structural revolution in British soccer which, whatever the critics say, was to leave the game infinitely wealthier and healthier than it had been a decade earlier.

Without a legal or financial background Bobby played little direct role in the flotation, which required the administration of the club to be split in two, with the main plc board overseeing the running of the club, and a secondary board overseeing football matters. The decision as to who would go on the plc board was made by United's City of London advisers, the merchant bank Henry Ansbacher. In effect, Glen Cooper of Ansbacher was a one-man selection committee and he felt that Bobby, without any major corporate experience, did not meet the right City criteria. In the words of Jeff Randall of *The Sunday Times*, the City was determined 'to market the club to private and institutional investors as a proper business rather than a soccer novelty'. Bobby was deeply hurt by the decision to leave him off the plc board and almost contemplated leaving Old Trafford, as Cooper later explained: 'There was a lot of manoeuvring from the existing board of the football club. Mike Edelson lobbied me hard, really out of an inexperienced belief that he was important. Charlton was the most grumpy. He threatened to resign at one point if he did not go on the plc board. He realized later that he was much better off sitting where he was on the football club board. But he didn't feel that at the time.'

Since he has not been on the main Manchester United board since 1991, Bobby has not been directly involved with the major business decisions of the club, such as the Sky takeover bid in July

1998, which provoked such political controversy. Indeed, Bobby's main objection at the time was that he had not been consulted before the bid became public knowledge. The United plc directors said, that, with confidentiality of the utmost importance, they could not discuss the takeover too widely. The communication problems were made all the more difficult because Bobby was away in Thailand working on England's campaign to host the 2006 World Cup finals. But this did not wash with Bobby. According to Tim Bell, who was working on the public relations for United, 'He was furious he had not known about it.'

Yet Bobby did not oppose the bid itself and his failure to do so was a source of great antagonism to a group of fans, led by Andy Walsh, who thought that Sky would destroy the soul of United. For these supporters, Bobby's behaviour was typical of the elitist, establishment stance that Bobby had adopted since he became a director. Walsh claims that when some of the anti-Sky campaigners wrote to him, 'He just ignored their letters. I bumped into him in central Manchester and tried to tell him of my concerns, but he was quite dismissive, saying, "Do you not think I've thought of all that? I'll make sure the club is all right." He does not seem to like talking to supporters, though people say that at public meetings he can be very charming.'

The way Bobby was seen as an establishment figure also led to a degree of awkwardness with some of the survivors of the Munich disaster. 1998 was the 40th anniversary of the crash, but in the years since the horror, many of the families of the victims felt that they had been poorly treated by the club. Though the survivors had been given compensation of £5,000 at the time – paid for by the club's insurance, much of this had been taken away in tax, while some of the relatives received far less – the mother of Tommy Taylor, for instance, only received £1,800 because it was said she was not dependent on him. There were other slights, like the way the club removed Jackie Blanchflower's season ticket because they said he was not using it enough, or the way Johnny Berry lost his club accommodation when he was still recovering from his injuries.

United goalkeeper Ray Wood, who lost his form and confidence after suffering terrible injuries in the crash and was subsequently sold to Huddersfield, says: 'I didn't want to leave Old Trafford. I thought to myself, "they have to look after me" but they didn't. I actually took my own transfer forms to Huddersfield. The PFA did more than the club. We had lost everything, all our suits, watches, belongings, kit and yet there was even haggling over compensation for that. I learnt a lesson about how much people really cared. We were just a commodity that no longer served a purpose.'

In a gesture of goodwill that most felt had never been shown to them by the club, the survivors were invited by UEFA to attend a reunion and the European Cup Final in Munich in 1998, with first-class accommodation and all expenses provided. Harry Gregg recalls that when he received the invitation he spoke to Ray Wood, who said, 'We've got to shaft those bastards, they've never done anything for us.'

Gregg replied, 'Woody, they're too big, and I'm not going to go stirring up shit.'

Having arrived in Munich, the former players held a meeting at their hotel to discuss how they would take forward the campaign to win more compensation. Gregg takes up the account: 'There was Ray Wood, Jackie Blanchflower, Albert Scanlon, Billy Foulkes, Kenny Morgans and me. Dennis Viollet hadn't appeared and Bobby Charlton wasn't there. As promised, I gave my opinion, thus: "They're too big a club. If you've got a brain you will involve the PFA and the United Former Players Association."

Jackie Blanchflower was next, moaning that he didn't go to Old Trafford any more "because they insult me". Kenny Morgans said, "I'm very bitter. The club promised that if I went to Swansea, I would be taken care of. So I went to Swansea, but I got nothing. A few games, then Newport, then I'm finished."' Gregg, always the most voluble of the survivors, says that his suggestion of turning to the PFA was agreed, but there were some mutterings against involving Charlton, the complaint being that, as a director, he should have been more supportive. Gregg continues: 'So I said, "Hold on, whether you like him or you don't, he's one of us. He's one of nine of us."

"He'll be out here with the fucking directors and he won't even speak to us," replied one of the others.

"When I see him, I'll tell him what's going on. I'm not having that."

The following day I met Charlie (one of Bobby's nicknames) at the desk. I told him about the meeting and that some of the lads didn't want to tell him because of his position as director. I asked, "Are you going with us?"

"I'm in a cleft stick. I'm a director and an ex-player."

"I'm asking you a direct question."

"Yeah, I'll go with you."'

On the return to England, meetings were arranged with the PFA and eventually £47,000 was won, but again there was a feeling that Charlton could have done more. 'Remember, he was a director at Man U. He never took the side of the players who played with him and died, or their relatives. He never stood up and was willing to be counted,' argues Gregg.

Whatever the fans or campaigners might think, Bobby never had a magic wand to deal with all their problems, even had he felt so inclined. Frequently, whether it be over Sky or Munich, he was unfairly made the scapegoat for the wider resentment of others. And no-one could ever dispute that he felt the agony of Munich just as strongly as anyone else. Indeed, David Beckham has said Bobby's speech at the memorial service in Manchester Cathedral on the 40th anniversary of the crash, was 'one of the most emotional experiences of my life. It was hard to believe looking at him that he had survived the accident and gone on to become such an ambassador for Manchester United and England.'

Where Bobby could make a real contribution as a director was on the football side, where his knowledge and judgement were invaluable. Sir Alex Ferguson, in his autobiography, writes of the inspiration Bobby is still providing to the players with his 'passionate' speeches. Fellow director Maurice Watkins gave me this verdict on Bobby's influence in the boardroom: 'He does speak his mind in meetings. He's never hesitant about that. He's extremely knowledgeable on the subject of football, though you don't always have to agree with everything he says. And he is never dogmatic. There are some people in business or football who think they have the answer to everything, but Bobby has never portrayed himself as a know-all. He is now an eloquent performer with an easy manner, a charming, confident style of talking, backed up by a fund of stories. And he can be self-deprecating. He gets on very well with Sir Alex. In a way that goes back to the 1980s, when Bobby was one of his sponsors and always supported him so strongly. Alex attends the football board, but Bobby will also go and talk to Sir Alex quietly. If the team is away, Bobby will have a meal with them beforehand. Bobby has views and if he feels strongly about something, he will sit down with the manager. Bobby has a balanced approach, as he showed after Cantona kicked that Crystal Palace fan in 1995. Bobby was firmly of the view that we should give him a very strong suspension of four months but that we should also support the player, ensuring that he was not cast adrift. We were all sorry when the FA doubled the punishment, something that had never happened before.'

Les Olive, who had a spell on the board from 1988 following his retirement after 30 years as United secretary, has nothing but praise for Bobby's contribution to the club. 'Despite his fame, he is never full of himself, never throws his weight around. For instance, he likes to have a laugh and a chat with the laundry ladies. When I was at board meetings, I always found him sensible and pragmatic, coming at problems from a player's point of view. He was a very good speaker in that setting, able to put his ideas across. He has a phenomenal knowledge of the game. And I always thought him very shrewd in his judgements. Once when we were in the USA in the late 1970s, when there was a lot of excitement over the new soccer league there, Bobby just said there was no way it would work because there were not enough home-grown players. He turned out to be absolutely right.'

Bobby's beneficial influence is felt almost as strongly abroad, in his ambassadorial role, as another fellow director, Peter Kenyon, has described: 'I think Manchester United's success was built on the 1950s and 1960s, the heritage, the style of play, the imagery. We go to China, we go to South Africa. We say we've come from England. They know Manchester and they know Bobby Charlton. Bobby Charlton is the second biggest name in the world next to Pele. If you have ever travelled anywhere with Bobby or Pele, internationally they are superstars. It transcends generations. Kids who have never seen Pele play just revere him and it's the same with Bobby. Those are the things that make Manchester United. Players come, players go. Boards come, boards go, but United goes on.'

CHAPTER TWENTY-ONE

The Irishman

The relationship between Jack Charlton and the Republic of Ireland was to be one of the most extraordinary in modern football. Jack fell in love with the country, and its people welcomed him with open arms. At the peak of his reign in Eire, Jack's popularity was exceeded only by the Pope. Hardened Irish nationalists and Gaelic fans were swept along by the adulation for this patriotic Englishman; he drew bigger crowds than Nelson Mandela in Dublin; his presence in any Irish village would bring thousands on to the street; pubs would keep his signed cheques as autographed souvenirs rather than cashing them; even his cigarette butts were collected like holy relics.

Yet perhaps the strangest aspect of Jack's love affair with the Irish was the way it began. Jack became the manager of the Ireland in the most unusual of circumstances. At the outset of the selection process, he was not very interested in the job – and the Irish were certainly not very interested in him.

After his resignation from Newcastle, Jack had no intention of ever going back into club management. His first instinct, to reject the job at St James', had been proved correct. Moreover, as a wealthy man with a host of commercial and leisure interests, he had no need to look for work in that area. Within months of leaving Newcastle, he had turned down an offer from tycoon Robert

Maxwell to take over at Oxford United. The only post that might have attracted him would have been a part-time one without all the aggravation of club administration, contracts and transfers.

The vacancy at Ireland arose at the end of 1985, after a doomed World Cup qualification campaign had ended in a 1–4 home defeat to Denmark and the subsequent departure of manager Eoin Hand. This failure had been all too characteristic of Ireland's efforts in international football ever since 1923, when the fledgling Irish Free State had first joined FIFA. The country had produced a number of excellent players over the years, such as Johnny Carey, Charley Hurley and John Giles, but had never managed to qualify for a major tournament. In the mid-1980s, they looked stronger than ever on paper, their ranks filled with stars like Mark Lawrenson, Liam Brady, Frank Stapleton, Kevin Moran, David O'Leary and Ronnie Whelan, yet they never appeared to gel as a fighting unit.

One of the key problems for Irish soccer was that it was frowned upon as a 'foreign' sport, and therefore attracted little official support or public following. In terms of popularity, it came a poor fifth in Ireland behind Gaelic, horse racing, rugby union and hurling. One home game against Mexico at Lansdowne Road in 1985 had attracted a crowd of just 6000. The lack of interest left the Football Association of Ireland in dire financial straits, a problem compounded by the shambolic nature of the organization. For instance, the Spurs player Chris Hughton was picked for a 1982 Irish tour of South America, but when he turned up at Heathrow he received a message from the FAI saying that he was not required to travel. The Secretary of the FAI, Peadar O'Driscoll, exemplified the body's amateurishness, regularly failing to secure manager Eoin Hand's accreditation for major championships – at the 1982 World Cup Hand was reduced to begging for tickets off Ron Greenwood. Jack himself was not too impressed when he first starting working with O'Driscoll: 'I wasn't very inclined to go to Peadar for my business because he didn't do it. I'd give him a list of players for a match and then find that he had added a couple of players to the fucking list whom he fancied.' In this climate of chaos, it is no wonder that several of the players regarded international duty as something of a joke, treating their trips to Ireland or abroad as little more than holidays. Nor was Eoin Hand, a former Portsmouth centre-half, the man to impose his authority on the big stars of the team: 'Eoin was probably not forceful enough. I think he kind of felt a little bit overawed,' said Frank Stapleton.

After the disaster of the 1986 World Cup qualification campaign, Des Casey, the President of the FAI, was determined to have a professional manager from Britain, rather than the usual ex-Ireland player. So he and Tony O'Neill, his dynamic ally on the FAI executive, travelled to England in December 1985 and embarked on an exhaustive series of discussions with potential candidates. Jack, whom they interviewed at an airport hotel near Manchester, was one of the nine they met. The talk lasted around an hour, with Jack his usual blunt self, warning that he had no intention of taking up permanent residence in Ireland if he got the job, because the future of the team lay in England. He also took offence when Casey asked if he 'might do a Newcastle on them' and stated, in the clearest terms, that he had 'never been a quitter.'

Others interviewed included John Giles, who had managed Ireland between 1973 and 1980, Billy McNeill, Noel Cantwell, Terry Neill the ex-Arsenal boss, Gordon Lee and Pat Crerand, whose fanatical devotion to the Irish cause could not mask the fact that he had little club management experience. With some reluctance, Casey and O'Neill also talked to several home-based candidates, the most impressive of whom was Liam Tuohy, the manager of the Irish youth team. For Casey, McNeill (then manager of Manchester City) was the leading contender, especially when John Giles decided to withdraw his application. But, amongst the Irish footballing public, Liam Tuohy was the overwhelming favourite. The newsletter of the Irish Supporters Club claimed: 'It is highly unlikely that a foreign man will be appointed. With many people not exactly ecstatic with the present squad containing too many English-born players, imagine the outcry if an Englishman is appointed.'

The final shortlist, drawn up by the FAI, read: McNeill, Tuohy,

Charlton. To the delight of these Irish fans – and the despair of Casey – Tuohy's position became all the stronger when Manchester City refused to release McNeill for any international duties, despite the offer of compensation. It now seemed the battle would be down to Charlton against Tuohy, English v Irish, and, in such a contest, Tuohy would almost certainly emerge the winner. Casey could not tolerate this outcome, so pressure was put on Giles to re-enter the race. At the same time, he secretly had talks with Bob Paisley, the former boss of Liverpool. One of the most successful club managers ever with a far better record than Jack or John Giles, Paisley expressed his willingness to take on the job. But Casey, perhaps too clever for his own good, decided he would not introduce his name until the last minute.

The crucial meeting of the FAI Executive Committee was held on the 7 February 1986 at the association's headquarters in 80 Merrion Square, Dublin. At the start, the shortlist comprised only Jack Charlton and Liam Tuohy. Casey then suggested that the committee allow the list to be opened again, so that John Giles could be re-admitted. This led to an hour-long debate, at the end of which it was agreed to re-open the shortlist. Suddenly, to the surprise of many of those present, Casey introduced his new favoured candidate, Bob Paisley. If Casey had handled it better, Paisley should have had a walkover. But the way his name was sprung on the 18-strong committee incurred the hostility of several members, depriving Paisley of the absolute majority he needed. In the first ballot, he received nine votes, with Charlton, Giles and Tuohy all on three. Tuohy was then eliminated in a vote between this trailing trio. In the second full ballot, Paisley again received nine votes, Charlton five and Giles four. Amidst growing confusion and hostility towards Paisley's candidature, Jack then emerged the winner on the third ballot by 10 votes to eight.

It had been a bizarre turnaround for Jack. He had won, not because he was the most wanted candidate but because he had the fewest enemies, just like the victor of the 1990 Tory leadership contest, John Major. As with Heseltine, Hurd and Thatcher, the other three in the 1986 FAI vote all had strong lobbies against them: Paisley because his candidature had been too precipitous; Giles, because he had been tried before; and Tuohy, because he was not based in Britain.

Jack's indifference to the job was reflected in the fact that the FAI could not even contact him after the meeting, for he was away shooting in north Yorkshire. Eventually he was tracked down by his old England team-mate turned journalist, Jimmy Armfield.

'Congratulations, Jack, you've got the job.'

'What job?'

'Managing Ireland,' said Armfield.

'I'd forgotten all about it.'

'What do you know about them, Jack?'

'Nothing. Absolutely nothing.'

Many in Ireland were appalled at Jack's appointment. The former Northern Irish star, George Best, was probably the most outspoken: 'Why football keeps pulling Jack Charlton back, I will never understand. He keeps running away from jobs and the game drags him back again. The Eire officials would have been impressed that he is a big name and appears regularly on TV. Well, if appearing a lot on TV is important, Terry Wogan should have got the job and would have probably done it better.' Some of the English press were equally scathing. The fans' magazine *When Saturday Comes* commented: 'The Republic of Ireland have made one of the worst decisions of the season by appointing Jack Charlton as manager. The numbing dullness of the sides he has managed before doesn't exactly promise to inject the pride and cohesion which have been lacking in Irish football for so long.' Intriguingly, the only voice raised on Jack's behalf was that of Eamon Dunphy, now writing in the *Sunday Times* who wrote that 'leadership, a sense of purpose, has been restored to Irish football at an international level.'

Jack was as surprised as the newspapers. 'My initial reaction was one of astonishment,' he wrote later. 'I'm an Englishman, not an Irishman.' But Jack was never a man to be easily intimidated. At his first press conference in Dublin, when Eamon Dunphy started asking him about the Paisley affair, Jack turned on him: 'I know you. You're a fucking troublemaker. I'm not going to argue with you. I'm bigger than you. If you want to step outside, I'm ready now.' It was not the way Eoin Hand had usually dealt with the press.

Jack's customary eagerness to impose his will was next felt by Liam Tuohy, who was still the manager of the Irish youth team when Jack took over. On 25 February, his side was playing a game against the England Juniors at Elland Road. Jack came along to watch and called in on the dressing room before the start to wish the players good luck. But he was not so genial at half-time, when the Irish were 2–0 down. According to Liam Tuohy, he was just about to speak to the boys when 'in comes Jack, walks directly in front of me, not a 'by your leave' or 'excuse me Liam'. He just ignored me as if I wasn't there. I couldn't believe he had the bad manners to do a thing like that. He was quite forceful in his comments and some of the things he said were quite negative. He undermined my position in front of the players.' After this experience, Tuohy felt he had no option but to resign as youth coach. Out of loyalty to their former boss, Tuohy's assistants Brian Kerr and Tony O'Reilly also resigned.

It was the first time in his managerial career that Jack had fallen out so quickly with one of his technical staff. At all his three clubs, he had managed to work successfully with the incumbents. In his gripping book about Irish soccer published in 1994, *The Team That Jack Built*, the author Paul Rowan records Jack's verdict about Tuohy: 'He caused me more aggravation when I took over the job than anyone else.' Jack claims that he had given his half-time talk at the request of Tuohy, and had, in his usual way, emphasized the need to be tighter and for the midfield to push forward when the long ball was hit into the opponents' last third of the field. Jack admits that he 'might have gone on too long', but was amazed that Tuohy could use this as a cause for resignation: 'I was left with bloody international sides all over the place. I didn't know anybody in Ireland. Tuohy just dropped me on my head.' But Jack believed he got his revenge: 'Hey, Liam made a bloody big mistake. He could have been on the inside and now he's on the outside. Now, with everything I have achieved, the one thing that gives me great pleasure is that I stuffed it up his arse. That gives me great pleasure.'

Charlton's first game in charge was against Wales at home. Still feeling inexperienced in his new role, he told the physiotherapist Mick Byrne – soon to be a stalwart of the Charlton regime – to pick the team. 'You've been with this lot seven or eight years. You know the form. I'll just sit back and watch and take it from there,' he said. It was a poor 0–1 defeat for Ireland, prompting Con Houlihan to write in the *Evening Press*: 'Jack Charlton talks a great game. Yesterday he produced a stinker. This was the pits, and in a decent country, the spectators would be entitled to a refund. I am tempted to sell my property in Spain and give the proceeds to the FAI. Then they could pay off the manager who never should have been appointed. We have the players. The pity is that Brian Clough has so little interest in fishing.'

Houlihan was not to know that Jack himself was pretty much a spectator, and had been just as upset by what he had seen. One player in particular had disappointed him: David O'Leary, the Arsenal defender who had always been talked of as a world-class player. But Jack had little time for O'Leary's cultured, ball-playing style, which was so different to his own vision of what a stopper should be. 'He didn't believe in getting tight on an opponent,' wrote Jack, 'preferring instead to rely on his pace to pick up the bits and pieces. To be brutally frank, that didn't fit my game plan. I needed centre backs who would compete with the players in front of them, push them out, deny them time and space to turn with the ball. Davie O'Leary didn't do that.'

Jack's suspicion of the Arsenal player was further confirmed when Ireland went on a tour of Iceland to play in a tournament against the host nation and Czechoslovakia. O'Leary was not named in the original party, but when several players withdrew, Jack rang him up to see if he would come. O'Leary refused, explaining that, after he had been left out, he had booked a family holiday.

'Well, this is a bit more important than your holidays. You can take them any bloody time.'

'The arrangements have been made.'

'OK then, forget it.'

O'Leary would not play again for Ireland for three years. Though Jack has always denied that he held a grudge, his attitude certainly made players realize who was in charge. As Mick McCarthy puts it: 'Before Jack came in, the players were the top dogs. It turned around when Dave all of a sudden was left out. All new managers have a look at things like that. They do it at every club. It's like walking into a bar and picking on the bully and sorting them out. Dave's not like that but it was a psychological thing – if you don't do it my way you won't do it at all. The fact that one of the stars of the team could be left out encouraged the rest of us to toe the line – if anyone had any doubts about messing with Jack.' O'Leary has never forgiven Jack for his attitude. 'You learn sooner rather than later that there is only one way – Jack's way. Deviate an inch, try to inflict your own ideas on the game and you're gone. The way he treated me for three years was disgraceful. He was the only man I had a problem with in Irish football. I was a fall guy in Big Jack's game,' he has said.

But many other players were far more receptive to Jack, including McCarthy, who took O'Leary's place and went on to become Jack's captain at Eire. 'When Jack turned up with his flat cap, kicking the ball around in his shoes and with no memory for names, a lot of players wondered what had happened. But he soon turned it around. He was terrific, fantastic at man management. He was personally very supportive of me. I remember one incident when he came to see me playing at Manchester City. I was getting a bit of stick because I was not doing particularly well and Jack talked to me after the game. He was a huge encouragement. Instead of just criticising me, he gave me pointers on how to put right my technical problems. It was all very positive. Jack knew his job, knew how to motivate people. He was not into bawling at people but he certainly let you know where you stood. We had a couple of ding-dongs but we came out of them even firmer friends. There were never any grudges with him, no brooding. I love the guy. I would have done anything for him.' Mark Lawrenson, the Liverpool centre half, known for his assurance on the ball, told me: 'I have tremendous respect for Jack. He deserves all the credit he gets for turning around Ireland. The best thing for me about Jack was that he realized there might be complications with me over the way I played as an attacking defender. When he had taken over the team, I had been away in the first few games because of Liverpool commitments, but Jack had told the back four: "Right, you lot can't play. If I see someone passing across the back, I'll have you off." Then we had a get-together at Lilleshall, and the other lads were saying to me, "Eh, this should be fun. You're in for it. He says defenders can't play." Then Jack arrived. As he started to talk, they were all nudging each other, especially when he said, "Don't forget your instructions from the last game. I'm telling you defenders, no messing around." Then, as the others were looking at me, he said, "And I want you to play in midfield." Jack was very clever that way, seeing a potential problem and dealing with it.' Lawrenson is unique in football in that he is the only person who was managed by both Jack and Bobby. 'Jack was just completely different. He is one of the most bloody-minded people you could ever meet, in a nice way. He was far more engaging than Bobby. Tactically, Jack was very strong. He never left any team member in two minds as to how he should be playing.'

Paul McGrath, who was to become the lynchpin of Jack's Irish team, was equally taken with him: 'My first meeting with him was impressive. He laid it on the line. He was going to do things his way. Nobody was bigger than his team. The senior pros, who had influenced Eoin towards the end of his reign were put back in their place. Things like going home to your parents in Dublin the Monday night before a game were over and done with. This was to be serious. The squad were in it together.' Like Lawrenson, McGrath was moved from centre-half to a more forward, midfield position in the Irish formation: 'He said he was doing this because I was too good a player to waste at the back. That remark won a special place in my heart.' Before the first meeting at Lilleshall, though, McGrath also learnt of the eccentric side of Jack, who had driven down from Northumberland to Shropshire with the Newcastle and Ireland right-back John Anderson. According to McGrath, 'Jack got into the car in Newcastle, stuck on a tape about fishing into the cassette player and never said a word to John for the rest of the journey.'

As soon as he took over, Jack was developing the aggressive, hard-running, long ball system which was to make Ireland so famous and controversial throughout the football world over the next ten years. At the height of his powers with Eire, Jack was playing his own unique system of 4-5-1, getting large numbers of players behind the ball in defence or attack, ensuring that the opposition could never easily settle on the ball and constantly aiming to hit the ball into their box. It was the exact opposite of the pattern John Giles had adopted when he was in charge of Ireland in the 1970s. His emphasis had been on keeping possession and building up from the back. The contrast between Giles and Charlton as Irish manager precisely replicated their difference as players at Leeds in the 1960s, when Jack used to harangue Giles for coming back to pick up the ball. Giles himself has mixed feelings about Jack's approach: 'I thought when Ireland did not have the ball, they were the best team in the world, because they were so tight on people. But I thought that when they had the ball, they were limited in expression, because Jack wanted them to be limited. He never wanted them to take any chances, or play at the back. So I don't think he got the full potential out of his players. For instance, I don't think he ever fancied David O'Leary because he saw Mick McCarthy as the stronger player. I did not agree with that. I thought David was better.'

Tony Cascarino tells this story about the debut of John Sheridan, a midfield play-maker, in 1998. 'Jack had said to John before the game: "If you play a one-two, I'll bring you straight off." In the dressing room, John was shitting himself, saying to me, "One-twos, one-twos, that's my whole game." Andy Townsend recalls a similar experience on his first game with Ireland a year later. 'At Norwich, we had the reputation of being a really good footballing team that played short, one-touch passes. Cass (Tony Cascarino) warned me, however, that Jack's philosophy was different: "I know what you do at Norwich looks good and all that, but for God's sake don't do none of that with us." So I looked at him and laughed, thinking he was trying to wind me up. "What do you mean, Cass?"

"I'm serious, Andy, don't mess about with him. If you're in any danger, have any doubts, just lump it forward. And I mean that literally. Jack's a serious fella. Don't fuck him about." And as he said it, there was a look of fear in his eyes that left me in no doubt.'

Using examples like that, purist critics often sneered that Ireland, under Jack, became 'Wimbledon in green,' but John Aldridge, who was the key target man up front, defends the system. 'Yes, it was exhausting for me up front,' Aldridge told me, 'but it was very effective and made it hard for other teams to play. We aimed to play in their half most of the time, putting balls behind their defence. People often complained that we were only playing the long ball, but that's not true. When we had the chance to play in midfield, we did so. Far from being outdated, I think Jack's system was ahead of its time. You look at how Liverpool play now, one up front and one coming back into midfield – that's exactly the same as Jack's formula, with me as the runner up front, and Frank Stapleton going back into a five-strong midfield.' Like Mark Lawrenson, John Aldridge is a huge admirer of Jack. 'It is nonsense to say Jack was lucky. Before he arrived, Ireland had very good players but had used the wrong system, whereas Jack knew how to stop the best teams in the world. He came up with the ideas. He was very warm-hearted, very loyal. He was decent, cared about his players and always talked commonsense. People can be a bit intimidated by Jack, but when you get to know him he is very likeable.'

'Jack's style suited me down to the ground,' says McCarthy. 'I wasn't a good footballer but I was a good defender' – exactly the words that Jack used about his own career as a player. For all the talk about Watford and Wimbledon, however, it was not these two clubs which were the inspiration behind Jack's Irish style but rather a much more lowly side, Northampton Town, who were then residing in the Fourth Division. In *Action Replay* magazine in 1997, Jack himself explained the little known influence of the Cobblers on international football: 'Someone told me to go and have a look at how Northampton played when they were top of the Fourth Division. It was so simple. When the goalkeeper had the ball, the rest of the Northampton team had five seconds to get into the other team's half. The goalkeeper kicked it long and if it was headed back, the opposition would be offside. Northampton put teams under pressure by getting the ball quickly into areas behind defenders and making them turn. They don't like that, at any level of the game. It was a simple way of playing that brought the Irish success for nine out of 10 years.'

In other interviews, Jack expanded on the philosophy he used at Ireland: 'When I took over,' he told the *Sunday Telegraph* in 1990, 'I thought there was no way we could expect to be successful playing the way the rest of the world play. So we invented a new way of playing. Instead of retreating, we go forward. We play the ball behind people and we play in their half of the field as much as possible. If we do have to retreat, we do it under protest. We contest the ball all the way back.' Jack was dismissive of his critics: 'We have been accused of playing a hump-up game. People say we just knock the ball forward and run. But that's not true. What we do is to play the ball behind people, whether it's from five or 50 yards.' To Frank Keating in the *Guardian*, he summed up his approach thus: 'Get the buggers, turning, turning, turning. When you've got the ball behind them enough times, holes are going to open up.'

It could be asked why this system worked so well with Ireland, when more primitive variations of it had achieved nothing like the same results at Sheffield Wednesday or Newcastle. The primary reason was that he was now working with far better players, who could hit passes more accurately, move with more pace and intelligence, hold the ball better, and use the openings more clinically. And because they were of a higher calibre, they understood immediately what Jack was trying to achieve. At a lower standard, the professionals had to have the message constantly drummed into them. John Aldridge, who used Jack's system when he was manager, says: 'At Tranmere, I had to tell the lads what I wanted week in, week out. But

Jack only had to tell us once. We were clever players and that's why his formula worked so well. We were all astute.'

One way that Jack was able to acquire better players for his Irish team was by exploiting to the full FIFA's generous qualification rules on eligibility for national teams. Ireland's population of only 3.5 million and soccer's state as a minor sport within the country meant that the pool of Irish-born players was simply not large enough to compete effectively on the international stage. So the Republic frequently recruited players of Irish stock who were born in the United Kingdom. It is a common misconception that Jack was the first Irish manager to do this. In fact, the first English-born player given an Irish cap was Bobby's Manchester United friend, Shay Brennan, whose selection in 1965 was, according to the author Adam Ward, 'one of the most controversial and momentous occasions in Irish history', especially because Brennan had almost been picked for the England World Cup campaign in 1962. After Brennan's pioneering debut, the appearance of the 'Anglos' – as they were labelled by cynics – became more common, until by the early 1980s around only half of the Eire team had actually been born in Ireland.

Eire particularly benefited from a FIFA ruling which, in practice, allowed players to represent a nation where one of their grand-parents had been born – the so-called 'granny rule'. Though the FIFA constitution never made any direct reference to the heritage of parents or grand-parents, it stated, in Article 18, that 'Any person who is a naturalised citizen of a country in view of that country's laws shall be eligible to play for a national or representative team of that country.' Eire's own nationality law, passed in 1956 and per-haps the most liberal in the world, stated that anyone could become an Irish citizen who was the child or grandchild of an Irish citizen. The steady waves of emigration that had occurred since the Great Famine of the 1840s, meant that there were far more potential Irish citizens living in Britain than in Ireland.

There had been objections to the growing number of 'Anglos' who were playing under Eoin Hand, especially because they brought little improvement to results. But Jack Charlton, the ultimate English import into Irish soccer, had no concerns about tapping into this source of talent, so much so that it was joked that during his reign FAI stood for 'Find Another Irishman'. One of the first he selected was John Aldridge, whose avalanche of goals for First Division Oxford United had, to his frustration, failed to win a call-up to the England team. With a grandmother from County Athlone, Aldridge was eligible and keen to play for Ireland. On a cold March night in 1986, Jack Charlton came to see him play in the League Cup semi-final at Villa Park. Aldridge later recorded.: 'Happy with what he saw, Jack approached me in the players' lounge after the match.

"How do you fancy playing for Ireland?" Jack asked me.

"I'd love to, Jack,' I said, 'By the way, you know about Ray Houghton, don't you?"

"No."

"He's more Irish than I am. His parents are from Donegal."

"Is that right?"

'In one memorable evening, Jack Charlton acquired the services of us both.' Jack himself once said, 'That night, getting Aldo and Ray, was the best bit of business I've done.' A stream of others followed in the next 10 years of Jack's reign, among them: John Sheridan, born in Manchester; Chris Morris, from Newquay; Andy Townsend from Maidstone; Phil Babb, born in Lambeth; and Jason McAteer from Birkenhead. And he also recruited Devonian Maurice Setters as his assistant, despite political arguments within the FAI that the job should go to an Irishman.

It might be thought that the introduction of a stream of British-born players could have undermined the team spirit of the Irish squad. In his book, *The Men in Green,* the award-winning Irish writer Sean Ryan argues that Jack's management did see a split between English and Irish: 'When the crunch came, Jack tended to place more faith in his English-born players. All the principal rows were with the natives.' The cases of Tuohy and O'Leary are cited by Ryan as examples. Frank Stapleton, never a fan of Jack, made the same point: 'Jack seems to see the home-born Irish as a threat to him,' he once said. But this view is strongly rejected by most of the other players, who argue that one of Jack's greatest qualities, along with his strong tactical awareness, was his ability to create a powerful team spirit. And there is no real evidence of any such Anglo-Irish split. Liam Brady, born in Dublin, argues: 'Irish born players like me did not feel any anxiety at all. In fact we welcomed the change because it meant we could compete better. The idea that Jack had any bias is absolute rubbish, just rubbish. If you did a job for Jack, he didn't care where you were from. Sean Ryan's view is typical of someone who is based in Ireland and reads the situation in the wrong way.' If anything, says Preston-born Mark Lawrenson, the British players helped to unify the side. 'They had an extra-incentive to perform, in that if they did not play particularly well, then they would be told, "Why don't you lot just bugger off back to England?"' Besides, many of the imports, despite their birthplace, had been reared in Irish emigrant households which still celebrated their Celtic culture. John Aldridge, for instance, says that he was brought up in a home that always supported Ireland.

Like his mentor Alf Ramsey, Jack succeeded in that most difficult of goals, building a club atmosphere in a national side. One of the first ways he achieved this was by ensuring that the team focused together on football. Before he arrived, many of the players would treat Irish duty as a chance to see their relatives or friends, with the result that the squad became fragmented. The FAI, with characteristic foolishness, supported this sort of behaviour by actually laying on cars so they could speed off to their home towns as soon as they arrived at Dublin Airport. Those without families in Ireland, such as Mick McCarthy, were left on their own in their hotels with little to do. It was impossible to establish any camaraderie in this way. Jack called the players together at a meeting and said: 'Look, when you come in to play for us, you're here to represent Ireland to play and win an international match and you're here to prepare for two days for that game and we're going to do it properly. You don't go out of the bloody doors of this place without me knowing where you are. Because I tell you, it has got to be something really important before you're allowed to bloody well go. I've cancelled the cars. There's none of that any more. While you're here, you're mine.'

The impression should not be given, though, that Jack was some sort of curfew-obsessed ultra puritan, for he was, in reality, almost the opposite. All he was trying to do in that meeting was to bring some sense of unity to the Irish squad. He was actually well-known for his relaxed approach to discipline. He treated the Irish players as men rather than wayward children, and saw the benefits of a communal drinking session. He was also fiercely loyal to those players who were doing a job for him, maintaining his loyalty in public even when they under the most intense media pressure, as he showed with his sensitive treatment of Paul McGrath, who suffered from a drink problem – though without all the attendant petulance of that other Irish alcoholic George Best. In his autobiography, McGrath wrote: 'Jack has treated me better than I ever deserved to be treated. He has covered for me, dug holes for himself by making excuses for me. He has always defended me no matter what the weight of evidence against me. He's been like an old mongrel; no matter how many times you kick him, he will always come back on side.' McGrath drew an interesting contrast between Jack, the laid-back Geordie and the far less tolerant Alex Ferguson, the Scottish Protestant, who was 'never able to understand the spirit of the Celtic Irish soul that drove me on in the thirst for life and my hunger for a good time.' Their relationship deteriorated so much that in 1989, Ferguson sold McGrath to Villa for a cut-price £450,000.

Tony Cascarino is convinced that it was Jack's relaxed attitude that made the Irish so formidable. 'Jack was easily the best manager I have ever known,' he told me. 'He always made you feel like a man. He was a very strong character and had a natural air of command. He was so confident in himself that he never had to impose petty rules on the team. Like if you said, "Jack, can I have some wine with my dinner?" he'd just say "Yeah, fine." He trusted his players, sometimes at the risk of cutting his own throat, as with Paul McGrath. I'll always remember before the World Cup in 1998, when Teddy Sheringham was caught drinking in a nightclub. The England manager Glenn Hoddle forced him to read out a public letter of apology. When I saw this on the TV news, I thought to myself that Jack would have done the complete opposite. He would have said to the press, "Of course Teddy had a drink. I told him to. He's been training non-stop and it's nine days before the game. What's the problem?" Then, in private, he would have given him a right bollocking. Jack felt that the team was your family, and you don't expose your family.'

The striker Dave Kelly, who won 26 caps for Ireland, says, 'Jack treated us all fantastically, like real people, and because of that, no-one overstepped the line. There was a brilliant spirit, no cliques at all. He always made you feel wanted, part of the set-up, even for those on the periphery of the first team.' Kelly maintains that because Jack made the squad so happy, hardly anyone wanted to pull out, even if they were injured. He cites the case of Kevin Sheedy who went on a tour of the USA even after tearing a calf muscle, because he was 'so desperate to be with the lads.' He gives another example of the warmth that Jack generated, when, just before Italia 90, the Irish team were returning from a day at the races. 'All the lads were as pissed as farts, in all honesty. Jack had won himself a good sum and was in a pretty good mood. A bit of a sing-song started up, led by John Sheridan: *"Jackie, Jackie, buy us a drink."* We were in the middle of nowhere when we pulled over beside a country pub. Jack said, "Right Sheridan, you buy the first fucker, then I'll buy one." So John steams into the pub, followed by the rest of us. There were only about four other people in the pub, but soon the word got around, and within minutes, it was absolutely crammed. John bought the drinks for the whole of the squad, then we started on Jack, asking him to get the drink. It was so clever of him. He ordered everyone a drink, including the staff behind the bar. Then he wrote a little cheque out. Of course, the pub would never cash it, but would just stick it up behind the bar. So Jack never needed to buy a drink in Ireland. That's why he was a millionaire.'

Jack's first big test was the campaign for qualification in the 1988 European championships in Germany. Ireland opened with a creditable draw away to Belgium, the team that had finished fourth in the last World Cup. Then against Scotland at Hampden, they had finest game of the campaign away from Dublin, winning 1–0 thanks to a Mark Lawrenson strike. The goalscorer recalls: 'That was the result that turned Ireland's fortunes. Jack came on the pitch, walked right over to me and people thought he was congratulating me. But he wasn't. He said: "Tell me this."

"What Jack?"

"Why, when you took the ball in the corner so late in the game, did you try and cross it? Why did you not keep it there?"

"I thought we had a chance of scoring. 2–0."

"Right." Then he paused. "By the way, well done."

But Ireland stumbled in several of their other games, losing to Bulgaria away and scraping an unconvincing 2–1 victory at home against tiny Luxembourg. In their final game of the programme, they had to win against Bulgaria to keep any hopes of qualification alive, while Bulgaria just needed a single point to go through. 'This was the day when quality and passion came together in an unbeatable formula,' wrote Jack later, as Ireland won 2–0 at Lansdowne Road. Liam Brady was outstanding, playing in the kind of forward mode that Jack had always been demanding of him. During the Euro 88 campaign Jack had commented on the reluctance of Brady, who had played for Juventus and Inter Milan, to stick to the new system: 'The players have been instructed to run further and harder, dwell less on the ball and put opponents under pressure by attacking them quickly. Some of the players have accepted readily. Others, like Liam, have had problems. He is used to the slow build up of Italian football. It has been difficult with him.'

Brady himself gave me this opinion of Jack's method: 'When he arrived, he laid out in no uncertain terms how he wanted the game to be played. I was not particularly happy with his approach. What I didn't like were his instructions that we were not going to play through midfield any longer. The midfield would be by-passed and it was up to us to support the ball going forward and get in the game from there. That was very different to what I was used to, where I looked to take the ball from the back. There was absolutely no talking to Jack about it. If you wanted to play for Ireland, you just had to accept it. That is the sort of guy he was. So I just got on with it.' Brady slightly marred his brilliant performance against Bulgaria by being sent off with only two minutes left, after retaliating for a foul. But Jack, remembering his own hot-headed moments as a Leeds player, only empathised with him. Nor did Brady's subsequent suspension look like it would matter too much. Despite the win, Bulgaria still only needed one point to qualify, and their final game was at home in Sofia to Scotland. It was such a formality that, rather than watch the Bulgarian game live, Jack went duck shooting with a friend in Shropshire. But then the miracle happened. With only minutes to go, Bulgaria were drawing 0–0, just the scoreline they wanted. Then suddenly, Gary Mackay was fed the ball by Gordon Durie and put it in the back of the net. Ireland were through to their first ever major tournament.

'For the want of a nail the kingdom was lost.' Luck plays a bigger part in football than any other major sport. One match, one kick, can be a turning point for a team or a manager. Careers can be decided by the slimmest margins of woodwork and time. The history of the game is littered with strange twists of fortune, the 'if only's' that make it so compelling. What would have happened if Gordon Banks had not been ill that fateful day in Leon in 1970? What if Beckham had not scored against Greece in the last seconds? The story of Jack Charlton's career could have been different if Scotland had not won in Sofia. Instead of being looked upon as a wise leader, he would have been just another failed Irish manager. The pressure on him would have become intense. The differences with O'Leary and Brady would have been blown up into huge stories, cited as examples of his poor judgement. His well-known traits, like his poor memory for names and his enthusiasm for fishing, would become the material for vicious satire. He might easily have become a grotesque caricature, the loud-mouthed Englishman whose cloth cap was as outdated as his tactics. But now Jack had achieved something hitherto unknown in Irish soccer history. Whatever happened now, Jack's reign could be deemed a success.

Before Ireland went to the European Championships in Germany, they suffered two major setbacks in injuries to two of their star players, Mark Lawrenson and Liam Brady. The former had snapped his Achilles' tendon in 1988 and was never to play top-class football again. The latter pulled ligaments in his knee and was out for 10 months. But even without this pair, Ireland performed well in the competition. The highlight was the first game, against England in Stuttgart. It was a match with tremendous significance for the Irish public, given the complex political and emotional relationship between England and its former colony. Ireland had only beaten England once before, in a game at Anfield in 1949, but they had never triumphed in a competitive meeting. All that changed when Ray Houghton scored in the opening five minutes with a header, and Ireland never relinquished their lead, thanks partly to the brilliance of Packie Bonner in goal and the unusually poor finishing of Gary Lineker. The 1–0 result confirmed that Ireland at last were becoming a major force in international football. Messages of congratulations came in from the Taoiseach and the Irish President. Paul McGrath recalls the celebrations afterwards: 'We let our hair down with Jack's blessing. He told us to have a few pints and a sing-song. There were fiddles and guitars all over the place. Even Liam Brady got up on a chair with a guitar he couldn't play and started singing. There were bodies swaying and dancing all over the place.'

The other two games did not have such happy outcomes, as Eire drew with the Soviet Union in a game they should have won, and then narrowly lost to Holland. But the fact that the Dutch were the eventual winners only reinforced the remarkable progress of the Irish under Jack. Football was no longer the poor relation of the Republic as a crowd of some 200,000 turned out to greet the team on its return from Germany. Only three years earlier a villain in his own native region, Jack was now a national hero. Jack was bemused by the response. 'We haven't won anything yet,' he kept saying to those around him. After years of enduring a national football team which was widely regarded as a joke, they could hold their heads high. Peter Byrne of the *Irish Times* said that the reception 'demonstrated how hungry the Irish people were for recognition in international competition.' And it had taken an Englishman to defeat the English, a lovely contradiction that appealed to the Irish sense of humour.

Jack had no time to dwell on his achievements. Almost immediately, Ireland was plunged into the Italia 90 World Cup qualification campaign. Their group consisted of Spain, Northern Ireland, Hungary and Malta, and Jack arranged for Ireland's first three games to be played away from home against the toughest teams. It was a strategy that could have backfired disastrously, but Jack was now confident that Ireland could hold their own against any opposition. It worked to an extent, with Ireland gaining draws in Belfast and Budapest, though they were badly beaten by Spain in Seville. But in the spring of 1989, successive home wins over the Spanish, Hungarians and Maltese put Ireland top of the group, and they were to stay there.

The victory over Spain had been the crucial moment of the campaign, but after the game, there was a serious row between Jack and certain members of the team. The cause of the bust-up was ostensibly a petty one, but it illuminated some of the tensions and insecurities brought about by Jack's management style. Ireland's increasing success meant the FAI was attracting more lucrative sponsorship deals than it had experienced in the past. Opel Cars, part of the General Motors conglomerate, had signed a four-year deal for IR£400,000, while Adidas paid £100,000 for the exclusive rights to provide the Irish kit. Moreover, the FAI's finances had never been healthier because of the dramatic rise in attendances. After years of crisis, in 1989 the Association reported a profit of IR£700,000. What annoyed the players was that they had seen very little of this new bounty. This was not Jack's fault. Following his experiences in club management, he had refused any involvement in the team's financial affairs.

Yet still he was to bear the brunt of the players' anger over their perceived neglect. It was the usual practice, after home games, for the team to go to the Opel sponsors' tent at Lansdowne Road and mingle with the corporate guests. But in the dressing room, the players agreed to hold a boycott of the reception. 'We felt that we were being exploited by the sponsors and that they had failed to come up with a satisfactory arrangement in terms of money. Jack was not happy about it, but we just got on our bus and went straight back to our hotel,' said Frank Stapleton, who acted as the shop steward in this dispute. Indeed, Jack was not happy, for he had taken part in Opel's advertising campaign and was embarrassed by the players' public snub of the company.

There was also a more personal undercurrent to his annoyance, in that he felt that his authority had never been truly accepted by the old guard of Stapleton, O'Leary and Brady. In the Dublin airport hotel that night, Jack directly confronted Stapleton. According to Stapleton's account, 'He accused Liam Brady, David O'Leary and myself of having an influence on the team and that the boycott had not been a decision taken by all the players. I told him he was talking nonsense, that no-one could influence an experienced group of players like that and that the vote had been unanimous. It was obvious that Jack had been drinking.' Stapleton claims that the row, which took place in a public area, was so heated that even Jack's wife tried to 'get him into the restaurant.' But tellingly, the team captain Mick McCarthy refused to intervene, despite the pleading of Stapleton's wife, who was sitting beside him. 'I never felt the same way about Mick McCarthy after that,' said Frank Stapleton. Nor did Jack feel the same way about Stapleton. Though the Opel sponsorship row was soon settled when the company contributed £20,000 to the players' pool, Stapleton's days with Ireland were numbered.

Liam Brady's time was almost up as well. He had made a brave recovery from his injury the previous year, but his return to international football was to end in humiliation. Against his better judgement, Jack picked Brady for a friendly against West Germany in September 1989, partly in response to the public clamour for his inclusion in the side. Jack was perplexed by what he saw. When

Germany equalized, he felt that Brady was simply unable to cope with the pace of the game. 'We were getting run to death across the midfield. It was obvious that Liam had had his day. He wasn't tackling anybody. He wasn't getting away from anybody like he used to. He just wasn't the fucking Liam we knew and loved.' After 32 minutes, Jack decided to pull him off, much to Brady's indignation, as he explains: 'I thought it was completely unfair after all I had done for him and all I had done for Ireland. I never agreed with what he did. That substitution brought everything to a head. I realized that I was not part of his plans for the World Cup. He did not sit down and talk through the decision with me. We had a bit of a row in the dressing room at half-time. I think anyone would who was substituted well before the end of the first half. I think I was owed more respect than Jack showed me, given my long service for my country stretching back to 1974.'

Brady, like Jack, is not one to bear grudges. Having been in management himself, he understands that Jack had to make tough decisions. 'Jack, to be fair, never shied away from them. If you make your mind up, you have to stick to it. But I think Jack could have handled it better than he did.' At the conclusion of the West Germany game, Brady announced his retirement from international football.

For the rest of the Irish team, the real adventure was about to begin. In November 1989, after defeating Northern Ireland at home and Malta away, Ireland had qualified for the World Cup for the first time. Around 15,000 Irish fans followed Jack to Malta, where the celebrations in the capital Valetta went on into the early hours of the morning. Joe Melling, of the *Mail on Sunday* gave this description of the way Jack was greeted by the Irish fans when he arrived in a Maltese bar at 2am. 'They poured out of the bars in their hundreds, bottles in hand, bedecked in green and white. The tall, angular figure was engulfed within seconds. "Quiet!!" boomed out the Geordie command. Silence fell in an instant. "They wouldn't let you into the hotel so I've come out to join you. It's too posh for me in there anyway." It would be impossible to imagine any other football manager being so happy and at home with his public.'

CHAPTER TWENTY-TWO

The Saint

The concept of papal infallibility has always been a source of theological controversy. But no-one could dispute the truth of the pontifical announcement which was made when the Holy Father was introduced to Jack Charlton during Italia 90: 'I know you who you are – you're the boss.'

By the end of the tournament, everyone knew who the boss was. For the first time in his life, Jack's fame around the world was equal to his younger brother's, thanks to Ireland's remarkable campaign in Italy.

It is a reflection of Jack's enormous self-confidence that he did not want to change anything about the way the Irish played in Italia 90, despite moving up to a higher plane. The direct system had served Ireland well enough over the last four years, he said, and if anything he relished the chance to prove that it could work against the best. Unlike some blackboard managers who aim to conceal their plans from the enemy, Jack was all too keen for other nations to know what he was up to, as he told Hugh McIlvanney in the *Observer* in February 1990: 'I want the managers of other countries to know how we play, because there is bugger all they can do about it. And the more they try to cater for what we are doing, the more likely they are to interfere with their basic approach and misuse their strengths. That gives us a real chance of putting them in trouble.'

Nor did Jack show any change in his own personality, becoming neither nervous nor arrogant over his move into the world's elite. Essentially, he remained the same unaffected, unself-conscious, undiplomatic character. 'He was always a very honest, basic man,' says Tony Cascarino, 'simple in his football, simple in his approach to life. Always had the cloth cap. Never cared what other people thought of him. His success never went to his head. He didn't enjoy the trappings of wealth, like flash cars. He certainly never spent his money on anything, except fishing.'

Jack is not a man to confess easily to his mistakes, but he admits that he made one in his selection for Italia 90 by picking Frank Stapleton in front of Gary Waddock. Stapleton was in the twilight of his long career up front, and held the record as Ireland's leading marksman, though his strike rate – 20 goals in 71 games – was disappointing for a player of his class. A battling midfielder with Millwall, Gary Waddock had shown impressive resilience in the way he had fought his way back from a serious knee injury which would have finished off most other players. Impressed with his recovery, Jack picked Waddock for two of the pre-World Cup friendlies. Understandably, Waddock now thought he had a chance of making the squad, but, to his anguish, he was omitted. In his place was Frank Stapleton

It was at Malta airport that Jack broke the news. 'I don't think that was necessarily the right place to be told, waiting in the terminal with the bags going round the carousel,' says Waddock. 'I did have an idea that this was going to happen. Things just did not feel right to me before then but it was still a devastating blow. Back at the hotel in his room, I got what I wanted off my chest. He told me his reasons for leaving me out but that did not make any difference to the anger that I felt. It was just as bad when I got back. It was the hardest thing in the world trying to get away from reminders of Italia 90. You pick up a bottle of Coke and the advertising for the World Cup is splashed all over it.' On his return to England,

Waddock was made huge offers by the press to sell his story, but he refused to do so. 'I was bitterly upset but I was not going to slag off Jack because it was his job to select the team. That's not the sort of man I am. Life is about how you cope with setbacks. Though I have bittersweet memories of my time with Jack, I have great respect for him. There are no hard feelings. It's all water under the bridge now.'

The same can hardly be said of Jack's relationship with Frank Stapleton. Already sour before the World Cup, it broke down completely during the campaign. Jack thought Stapleton made little effort in training and was incensed that he regularly disobeyed instructions, as when he left the hotel without permission to take a boat ride while the other players were cooped up in the rooms. Nor had Stapleton taken any precautions against the baking Sicilian sun. 'He knew the rule that you wear your hat in the sun. I should have said to Frank, "Get your fucking passport and fuck off home," Jack later told the author Paul Rowan. Jack was just as annoyed when Stapleton ignored the regulations about bringing wives back to the team hotel. Regarding women as a distraction during a major tournament, Jack had arranged for wives to be put up by the FAI in a separate hotel. They were occasionally allowed to see their husbands, like after big games, but had to be out of the team hotel by 12.30am. It might sound petty, but Jack's experience of England's failed Mexico campaign in 1970 encouraged his belief that too much female company could undermine the focus of the team. That is not the way Stapleton looked at it: 'It was like being back at school again and we were being treated like children.' On one occasion, Frank Stapleton was still with his wife more than an hour after the stipulated curfew, provoking yet another confrontation with Jack. 'It was aggravation that I could do without,' he wrote later.

The question arises as to why Jack chose Stapleton at all, when he felt he had so little to contribute. The answer reveals a rare weakness in Jack's management. The truth was that Jack thought Stapleton was too popular, especially with the Irish media, to be left out. Any decision to exclude him would, he feared, have provoked uproar in Ireland, thereby undermining the morale of the team before the players had even left. So rather than having 'knocking stories' in the press, he picked a man he never wanted. 'The biggest fucking mistake I ever made,' said Charlton to Paul Rowan in a savage attack on Stapleton. 'I should have sent him home in Malta because he was miserable. He didn't help for one minute, he never stopped moaning and grousing. He could have helped with the training, instead of which he carried on like a spoilt kid. You can never do anything right for Frank. He's a begrudger.' Stapleton himself says of Jack: 'I felt bitter about the way I was treated. I always felt that Jack had something about Liam Brady, David O'Leary and myself when you consider he tried to humiliate us at one time or another. Jack seems to feel he is above criticism. He never liked anybody standing up to him.'

A completely different, much more generous, view of Jack's personality is provided by another Irishman, the Belfast-born commentator Alan Green, who calls Jack 'a wonderful man'. He cites an example of Jack's behaviour which show both his decency and his laid-back eccentricity. This occurred in Dublin in 1990, when Green was due to interview Jack at the Irish team's hotel prior to a friendly against Finland at Lansdowne Road. Unfortunately, Green's flight from England was delayed so he arrived late at the hotel, less than four hours before the 5pm kick-off. 'Friendly or not, you don't mess around a manager or his players so close to a game,' says Green. Full of apologies, he rang Jack's room to see if he could still do the interview, only to find that Jack, true to form, was in his bed, having forgotten all about it. Once his memory had been stirred, Jack agreed to see Green at 3pm. He then proceeded to talk so profusely that Green became increasingly worried about the time. 'Ah, that's all right. The bus can wait. It won't go without me – I'm the manager.' They did not finish until 4 pm, just an hour before the kick-off, and still had to travel right across Dublin in the rush hour. Green did not see how they could make it, yet Jack remained totally relaxed. When Green explained that, because of his late arrival in Dublin, he had been unable to pick up his ticket from the FAI's headquarters, Jack said, 'Stuff that. Come on the bus with the boys.'

Green continues his account: 'I can't tell you how embarrassed I was climbing on to the coach behind Jack. All the players were laughing and gently teasing him. They had been sitting around for half an hour. "Shut up, you lot. Right! Off we go." The police motorcyclists performed a miracle and somehow we got to the ground in time for the game. Jack walked me in with the players, so typical of the man.'

In the campaign itself, Ireland experienced wildly fluctuating fortunes. Their first game, against England at Cagliari in Sardinia, ended in a 1–1 draw, after Kevin Sheedy equalized in the second half. With most of the participants based in England, the game took on the appearance of a dull, mid-table First Division clash, the players more anxious about closing down their opponents than displaying their skill. The endless back-passing to Packie Bonner, followed by long boots up the field, captured the dreary essence of the spectacle. Jack might have felt satisfied with this solid result, but the Italian media were appalled at the match, rating it the worst of all the opening first-round games.

Ireland then moved on to Sicily for their next two games. On their arrival on the island, many of the players were shocked at the poor standard of their hotel after the comparative luxury of Sardinia. Lack of air conditioning and tiny rooms were just two of the faults, while some of the players were expected to sleep on camp beds. One player joked that the IRA had been out to bomb the place, then found that it had already been done. For Tony Cascarino, such poor accommodation was an indicator of Jack's attitude. 'He was always very basic about everything. No other team would have stayed in that place, but there was Jack, saying, "What are you moaning for? You've got a bed haven't you?"'

And Jack was, of course, famously indifferent to his surroundings, as his assistant manager, Maurice Setters, recalls: 'Jack was hopeless to room with when we were away. I would go into our room and say, "Look at that, why can't you tidy up for once in your life."

"Here we go again," he'd say. I'd like to see things put away but Jack was the opposite. The socks would be in the sink and other clothes would be all over the place.

"Why don't you send them to the laundry and let them do it?" I would ask.

"Ah stop bothering me." He was not the greatest organizer in the world. But it was a laugh. As soon as he would see me, he'd say, "Here he comes, Mr Organizer."'

Jack's great journalistic friend, Jimmy Mossop, visited him at a hotel in Bilbao in the 1982 World Cup when he was working there as a commentator. 'Jack was leaning out of his window hanging socks and underpants over a makeshift clothesline. He explained that he had sprinkled soap powder on to his clothes and literally danced on them as he showered. The hotel's prices had offended him, even though ITV was picking up the tab.'

There were later to be similar complaints from the players about the standard of their hotel in Rome, described by Paul McGrath as 'a joke'. But for all Jack's apparent carelessness, there may have been a deliberate policy behind his choice of hotels. Ian St John gave me this insight: 'When I was working on the television in the 1990 World Cup, and I was with Jack at this great hotel, lovely views, everything you wanted, meals, swimming pools. So I said to Jack, "It's great here, isn't it?"

"Too comfortable. I'm getting them out of here."

I would always argue Jack's corner on this. He made great football decisions. He thought about things that others missed, like his determination to get his players in a more Spartan environment. A lot of other managers would have been quite happy to stay there, saying, "Here we are in the World Cup, lovely, we deserve it, let's enjoy it and relax." But Jack always wanted his players to focus completely on the job.'

If the first game against England had been dull, the next, against Egypt in Palermo, plumbed new depths of tedium. The Egyptians, massed in defence, had no intention of playing open football, and the Irish resorted to a desperate aerial bombardment which never looked like achieving a breakthrough. It was excruciatingly turgid stuff. Afterwards Jack attacked the negative tactics of the Egyptians, yet his own Irish team, ruthlessly drilled to play one system, failed to show any imagination. Back in Ireland, Eamon Dunphy, analysing the game for RTE, Ireland's national broadcaster, threw his pen on his desk in anger and said: 'Anyone who sends a team out to play like that should be ashamed of themselves. When we got the ball we were cowardly, ducking out of responsibility. I feel embarrassed for soccer, embarrassed for my country, embarrassed for all the good players, for our great tradition of soccer. I feel embarrassed and ashamed of that performance, and we should be.'

Dunphy's outburst caused howls of outrage across Ireland. The RTE switchboard was jammed with callers protesting against him, while an instant opinion poll conducted for one paper showed that 97 per cent of the Irish public disagreed with him. 'Eamon Dunphy's been forced to share a flat with Salman Rushdie,' was one joke doing the rounds in Dublin. The row only intensified when Dunphy flew over to Palermo to report for the Irish *Sunday Independent* on the final group game against Holland. Dunphy was already disliked by Jack for his criticism of the Irish team, especially the continual attacks on Mick McCarthy, who was a particular bête noire of Dunphy's. After one such article, Charlton called Dunphy 'a little cunt', adding 'I want fuck all to do with you.' At the press conference just 24 hours before the Dutch game, Dunphy began to ask a question about Ireland's style of playing. Then Jack, who had received news of the RTE rumpus, interrupted him: 'You are not allowed to ask a question. You are not a proper journalist. People here are interested in football. You are not. End of story.' To the astonishment of the media, Jack then stormed out and decided to hold a conference in his own room, restricted only to five senior football writers.

No football manager, of course, has a duty to report to the press. He is not an elected figure or a public servant. And whatever journalists might think, public relations skills are nothing compared to the ability to building a winning team. Ramsey was not in the same league as Keegan when it came to media friendliness, but who had the better record? Jack himself had rightly grown fed up at Newcastle when he was expected to hold a press conference almost every other morning, even when he had nothing to report. When he failed to do so, he would soon have to read the snide comments about his love of fishing.

Yet Jack's behaviour at the press conference was ludicrous. To decide that Dunphy was not allowed to ask a question was bad enough, but then to describe one of the greatest of all football writers, responsible for two classics of sporting literature, as 'not a proper journalist' was absurd. Some of the English reporters, who had witnessed the bizarre scene, thought that Jack was now losing his grip. In the *Daily Mirror*, Tony Stenson wrote: 'Charlton's uncharacteristic snub highlights the growing pressure he is feeling in this World Cup as his team's Stone-Age style and tactics are attacked from all sides. That, added to the fact that the Irish have so far only managed two well below par performances against England and Egypt, has got many wondering "Has Jack had enough?"'

One of the interesting aspects of this row was that Dunphy was one of Jack's few supporters on his appointment in 1986. When Jack first came to Ireland, he and Eamon would have a drink or a meal together. Like Jack, Dunphy is a strong-minded, self-confident individual – a 'cocky little devil' in the words of one of his ex-Manchester United colleagues – and, as his seminal book *Only a Game* reveals, he was a great believer, like Jack, in the importance of strength of character in professional football. But, having been reared at Old Trafford under Busby, he had a completely different philosophy to Jack's. Results were not everything. Looking back on his relationship with Jack, Eamon told me: 'Jack was the quintessential Lilleshall product as a coach, like Graham Taylor. His basic outlook was that what really mattered was the system, and the players with talent could not be trusted. Initially he was great at Ireland because he organized what was a rabble. He imposed discipline, which was welcome. For the first time an Irish side had a coherent look about it. I felt, on balance, he was doing a good job. But then I took a harder look at it and started to write critically about the style of play. I wrote tough stuff about his selection and the way he played. I argued that a team with players of that quality should do better. Now most Irish people believed it was a miracle that we were at a major championships. In fact, that was not the truth. He had a very gifted side, but his tactics were bonkers. Far from being a tactical genius, he was a one-trick pony. They were playing like Watford, pushing up, getting stuck in, pretty basic stuff. He messed around people like O'Leary and Brady. When I criticized Jack, he could not understand that I had a job to do and there was a natural conflict there. He felt betrayed because we had been having the odd meal and drink together.' But, unlike many others, Eamon had not succumbed to Jack's charm: 'Jack was not objectionable. He was a decent, unaffected man, who stayed close to his roots. But I did not greatly enjoy our meals together, because I didn't find him easy company. He lived in a world of his own. He did not have much interesting conversation. He was like the boring man in the snug of the bar.'

Where Dunphy went wrong was in suggesting that Jack Charlton had somehow betrayed 'the great tradition' of Irish football. That tradition was failing to qualify for any major tournament for the previous 50 years. That tradition had seen Ireland lose 2–1 to Trinidad and Tobago as recently as 1982. That tradition had seen crowds fall to below 10,000 for home games. Now, for the first time in Irish history, Jack had given the public the chance to see top games. It is also too easy to exaggerate the depth of quality that Jack had to choose from. Whatever is thought about the way that Jack treated Stapleton and Brady, there is no doubt that they were well past their peak by 1990. Of the core team in Italia 90, it is doubtful that Aldridge, Morris, Cascarino, Quinn, McCarthy and Townsend would have been selected for Robson's England. In terms of talent, Eoin Hand's side which so badly failed to gain World Cup qualification in 1986 was just as strong, containing Mark Lawrenson, Chris Hughton, Kevin Moran, Ronnie Whelan, as well as Stapleton, Brady, and O'Leary, who were all at their peak. Mick McCarthy sums up the view of most Irish players: 'Why can the critics not congratulate Jack on his success? There is this horrible, jealous streak against him. Look, other people had the same players but got nowhere. We needed someone at the helm to steer us in the right direction. I find it amazing, staggering that people criticize Jack. They just need to take a look at his record.'

The bust-up with Dunphy was put into perspective by Ireland's qualification for the next round, though there was to be no dramatic improvement in entertainment. Against Holland, Ireland fell behind to a Ruud Gullit strike but then equalized through Niall Quinn, who had come in after a disappointing performance by Cascarino against Egypt. A draw would be enough to take Ireland through, and for once, rather than belting the ball up the field, the back four kept possession by passing the ball to each other. So slow did the game become that the referee implored the Irish to move forward.

'This is the World Cup. You must start playing football.'

'But we are playing football and it's the first bloody time in four years we have been allowed to play football,' replied captain Mick McCarthy. And Paul McGrath, who had started his career under Eoin Hand, thought the way that Ireland came back to equalize against the Dutch showed the new spirit which Jack had engendered: 'Five years earlier an Irish team in that position would have thrown in the towel. Jack's arrival changed all that. We replied to Gullit's shock with the determination of a team fighting for survival.'

Ireland now moved into the unknown territory of the last 16 of the World Cup finals, playing against Romania at Genoa for a place in the quarter-finals. Once more, Ireland found it difficult to score, so the match went to extra-time and then penalties. It was the first time there had ever been a shoot-out in the competition and Jack had given no thought as to who would be the penalty takers, which meant there had to be five volunteers. Kevin Sheedy, Andy Townsend, Ray Houghton and David O'Leary, now restored to the Irish colours, all put up their hands. One more was needed.

'What about it Cass? Are you a man or a fucking mouse?' Ray Houghton asked of Cascarino.

'Mouse,' whispered Townsend.

'Yeah, all right, I'll have one,' said Tony, rising to the challenge.

Jack tried to relieve the pressure by telling his players: 'If anyone misses, sod it, we've had a good tournament.' The score on penalties was 4–3 to Romania when Cascarino walked up to the spot. 'My legs felt like rubber sticks as I ran towards the ball. I choked over the shot and stubbed my toe in the turf on contact and almost fainted with relief as the ball followed the divot under the keeper's arm and into the back of the net. It was a terrible penalty but Lady Luck had been kind to me.' As Mick McCarthy later remarked, 'I think the keeper went for the sod of grass.'

It was now 4–4. Daniel Timofte for Romania struck the ball to the right of Bonner, who dived the correct way and made a heroic save. Now Ireland just had to score to go through. Who should have the responsibility for the next kick but David O'Leary, the man that Jack had ignored for the previous three years? What is more, O'Leary had never taken a penalty before in his life. Jack could hardly bear to watch, and admits that he covered his face with his hands until the last fraction of a second, when he viewed the cliffhanging moment on the big screen. But with the cool assurance that was the hallmark of his career with Arsenal, O'Leary slotted the ball into the left-hand corner. Ireland were in the quarter-finals of the World Cup. Sneered at, written off, described as prehistoric, Jack Charlton had turned Ireland into one of the best, if not the most attractive, sides in the world. No-one was expressing any shame at this performance. As the Irish contingent sang, 'You'll never walk alone,' Jack said it was the greatest moment of his career: '1966 was a wonderful day, but this is an even more wonderful day.'

Ireland were now due to see the hosts, Italy, in the quarter-final. Before the match, Jack arranged for his team to attend one of the Pope's audiences in the Vatican. Hardly the most devout of individuals, Jack had thought an audience meant a private meeting and was surprised to find more than 7,000 people of a vast array of nationalities present in the auditorium. With the proceedings so drawn out, Jack, admits that he almost fell asleep during the endless translations of the lesson. Struggling to keep his eyes open, he suddenly found the Pope turned in his direction and apparently waving at him. 'So I half stood up and waved back at him,' said Jack, not realizing that he was the recipient of the papal blessing. Moments later, on his way to being introduced to the Holy Father, he nearly stumbled over the physiotherapist Mick Byrne, who was kneeling on the floor to kiss the papal ring. It was then that the pontiff made his famous declaration that he recognized Jack as 'the boss'.

The boss demonstrated his unorthodoxy shortly before the game. Facing a World Cup quarter-final against Italy in Rome, most other managers would be whipping their team into a frenzy of heightened anticipation. Jack did the exact opposite. Just two days before the game, Jack walked over to John Aldridge carrying a pint from the temporary Guinness bar erected in the hotel foyer.

'How would you like one of these? You haven't had a pint for five days, have you? Tell you what, Aldo, get all the lads together and you can all have a pint of Guinness.' The other players, inevitably, relished this instruction. And they did not stop at one pint; within a couple of hours, a full-blown session was underway, with most of the team ending up with four each. As Aldridge put it to me, 'There were Italian police around and they could not believe that we were preparing for a World Cup quarter-final in this way. But it was great man management by Jack. He said to us, "There is far more good in a Guinness than in a bloody Coke." And he succeeded in defusing the whole situation. Everybody was anxious and worried about the game against Italy. So he took it off all our minds. It was a bloody good night.' The next morning, according to Cascarino, 'We had a good walk and sweated off the night before. We felt great.' Jack further defused the situation when, the day of the game, he said, 'Don't worry lads. You're playing against the Italians in Rome. You'll soon be on your way home.' Strange as it may sound, Cascarino feels such language helped: 'It was a clever way of removing our fear, encouraging us to just go out and play.'

Ireland did indeed play well that night, losing to a single goal from Schillaci, the hero of the tournament. At the final whistle, the Celtic dream was over, but it had lasted longer than anyone dared to think was possible. Jack's team returned to Dublin a few days later amidst scenes of unprecedented popular acclaim. It was estimated that more than half a million people turned out on the streets of the capital that day to welcome the Irish footballers home. Such was the throng that it took more than four hours for the bus to drive from the airport to the city centre, a journey that should take less than hour. 'I'd never seen anything like it,' wrote Jack, 'there were masses and masses of people everywhere, clinging to window ledges, hanging out of trees, doing anything for a glimpse of the squad on an open-topped coach in O'Connell Street.' Not everyone was happy to be at Jack's side, according to Eamon Dunphy. 'David O'Leary told me afterwards that Jack never spoke to him following the game, never said, "Well done, great," never acknowledged his existence, until they were coming home in triumph to Dublin. The crowd were cheering for David. Jack appeared at David's side, put his arms around David's shoulders and gave him a big hug. Pure PR. David told me that he wanted to throw up all over Jack, but he didn't say a word and went along with it. That was Jack, there was a lot of native cunning there.'

And others were only too glad to see the back of Charlton's Irish. Jeff Powell, the *Daily Mail* columnist, referred to the 'caveman attrition and crass long balls', a 'primitive philosophy gaining ground after ground in England for its capacity to destroy rather than delight, stifle, not surprise, diminish instead of decorate the greatest game of all'. It could be pointed out, in support of such an argument, that Ireland scored just two goals in their five games. But then no other side in the tournament did much better. Italia 90 was perhaps the most boring of all World Cup finals, where every team – apart from Cameroon – put a premium on avoiding defeat rather than gaining victory. For all the rich glamour of the Italian settings, this tournament represented the nadir of modern international football. So disgusted were FIFA by what happened that they made two crucial – and wholly beneficial – changes to the law, banning both the back pass and the tackle from behind. Jack Charlton's Irish may have epitomized the negative mood of Italia 90, but to blame them entirely for its creation is unfair.

There was nothing negative about the reaction back home. Despite the attacks of a small number of critics, Jack was greeted as a messiah in the Republic. He was, in the words of one ironic commentator 'the most popular Englishman in Ireland since Parnell'; Parnell, though born in County Wicklow, was the Cambridge-educated, land-owning, cricket-loving Protestant who became the leader of radical Irish nationalism in the 1880s. Jack was so loved because, for the first time since Irish independence in 1921, he had given Eire the chance to break free from its inferiority complex. He had brought to Ireland a sense of genuine pride that it had never experienced before, the feeling that it was a nation in its own right, no longer the poor relation within the British Isles. Few cared about the style. 'He created a labouring team for a labouring nation. There's no problem with that. He's made us proud to be Irish,' said one supporter in a Dublin bar after the Romania game.

Jack's personality was part of the appeal. The only English figures of authority that the Irish encountered were politicians like Margaret Thatcher, who tended to make them feel patronized. But Jack, with his gruff Geordie accent and raw honesty, could speak to them in their own language. He did speaking engagements all over the country, sometimes getting attendances of over 1,500 for an evening in a village hall. Len Dunne, of the Harp Brewery which helped to organize his speaking tours, said, 'We get enormous crowds and enormous goodwill everywhere we go. In some of the small country towns you literally get people coming out of the mountains to see Jack Charlton. He is the biggest hero in Ireland.' He never tried to spin or deceive or flatter, but just told it as he saw it and they loved him all the more for it. Once when he was doing a meeting in Galway, the heartland of Gaelic football in Ireland, he was asked by a boy: 'What do you think of Gaelic, Jack?'

'Who?'

It took some moments for the laughter to subside.

Feminist campaigner and writer Nell McCafferty summed up the affection in which he was held: 'Jack Charlton was smashing. He was truthful, honest. And that voice. I think I could listen to that man forever. We could adopt an Englishman and say, "Isn't he gorgeous?" We could show that it is not the English people we don't like, but the British regime. Jack Charlton reminded us of all the best things that the British can do. It just makes you long for what could be, when the British are our neighbours, and we've more in common with them than we have with most people.' Jack admitted to being surprised at his female following in Ireland. At a meeting in Rathfarnham he was asked:

'My wife regards you as a sex symbol. How do you cope with that?'

'I'm absolutely delighted. 54 years of age, married with three kids, going bald and I'm a sex symbol. I'll have to tell my wife . . .' The pub duly collapsed in uproar.

Perhaps only with the Irish could Jack have behaved as he did as manager. Anywhere, else, his eccentricities and disorganization would have counted against him. His forgetfulness with names had become worse than ever, calling Paul McGrath 'John', Liam Brady 'Ian' and Tony Cascarino 'Ice Cream Man'. He called the Austrians the 'Australians' and before the 1994 World Cup said that the team would leave early for North America so they could become 'alcoholized' rather than acclimatized. In Jack's case, though, that might have been a Freudian slip – he is the only man known to have bought duty-free whisky on an internal flight between Cork and Dublin. One another occasion, in talking about Brazil, he referred to the 'the Marijuana' stadium rather than 'the Maracana'. Before one Northern Ireland game, he went up to Alan McLoughlin and said, 'Now listen, you've got to watch that Alan McLoughlin', when he was referring to Alan McDonald. On another occasion, when McLoughlin turned up in Dublin, Jack asked, 'What are you doing here?'

'You picked me.'

According to David Kelly, 'If we were playing anybody with a foreign name there was no chance that Jack would go through the team. In 1993 we were playing Wales and Malcolm Allen was in their side. During the team talk, for some strange reason he picked up the programme. 'These lot can't be any fucking good. They're Welsh for a start.' Then he looked down the list, where the surnames were printed first, as in Southall, Neville. Suddenly he stopped, "Who the fuck's this Allen Malcolm? Never heard of him. He can't be any fucking good."'

David Kelly, whom Jack occasionally called 'Eddie', tells another story which illustrates this difficulty with names: 'When I was playing for Newcastle, I was with my wife in the Metro Centre. We had just had our first boy, called Zack. Suddenly I see Jack and Pat are just walking towards us.

Jack says, "Ah David, how are you?" Then he looked down at the baby and said, "What's this littl'un called?"

"Zack!"

"Jack! That's absolutely fantastic, what a great name. You've named him after me. That's brilliant."

Pat had obviously heard me say "Zack", so she turned to her husband and said, "No, Jack, it's Zack."

"I know it's bloody Jack. It's a fantastic name." Then he put a pound into my son's hand. I could hardly tell him then that it was Zack, not Jack. Jack walked off and I could see Pat giggling away. It was so typical of Jack, both to think that I would name my son after him, and to get the name wrong.'

When Ireland were playing their crucial World Cup qualifier in 1995, Jack gathered the team to watch a video of Holland playing. Immediately, the Irish team felt there was something wrong, as the footage showed unfamiliar players in a minor stadium. Soon they realized they were viewing a tape of the Dutch Under-21s. But Jack carried on regardless. 'Now look at Bergkamp, the way he's dropping off.' The Irish players started sniggering, and soon the laughter became so loud that Jack demanded to know what was going on.

'Look, Jack, there's been a mistake, this ain't the Dutch side,' said Andy Townsend.

'No way.' But once it had been proved that Dennis Bergkamp was nowhere to be found, Jack resorted to claiming he was the victim of a conspiracy by the Dutch FA, which had deliberately sent him the wrong tape.

Alan McLoughlin recalls the preparations for a game against Latvia: 'Jack got us all together. From his jacket he pulled a fag packet. We were saying to ourselves, "What's going on here?" Jack explained, "What you've got to watch . . ." Then he seemed at a loss for words. He was looking down at this packet but it obviously did not make any sense to him. Suddenly he said, "I've brought the wrong bloody fags." It turned out he'd been to Latvia and he had written the notes to the game on a different packet. So he then he said, "Oh balls, don't worry about them. Just this lad with the long hair. If you stop him, you'll win easily. Right, on the bus."'

Despite his elevation to an international managerial role, Jack's language always remained industrial, according to Tony Cascarino, who recalls a game of Trivial Pursuit in a hotel: 'It was basically the staff against the players. Jack, of course, was captain of the staff. We were going through the questions and then this one arose: "In which city in the world is Portuguese the most widely spoken language?" Jack said Rio, but Andy Townsend, with a smile on his face and the card in his hand, said, "No Jack, it's Sao Paolo." Jack then went berserk, saying: "I was about to fucking say that. It was going through my head. Now you've given me the fucking answer." We were all in creases laughing. Then another question arose: "Which city is known as Little Venice?" Jack would never take advice from anyone. When Mick Byrne, the physio, said he thought it was Brussels, Jack replied, "Fucking Brussels? Fucking Brussels? No fucking way. The fucking Belgians hate the French." We were all laughing while Jack opted for another city. Then the answer came: "Brussels."

Mick Byrne said to Jack, "I told you."

Jack: "Well you fucking should have stood up and been a fucking man."

We were now in tears of laughter. A wrong answer about the US presidency saw the staff defeated. Jack picked up all the chips and threw them across the room. Because we were playing for a fiver.

"What a fucking crap team I had to play with. Didn't answer a single fucking question," he said as we went off to bed.'

Cascarino remembers another such occasion: 'Andy and I were playing an international game in Dublin and, the day before the match, Jack said to me and Andy, "I've left me fucking cap at home. Will you get me one when you go into town?"

"All right, Jack."

It cost £12.99 and the ticket was still on it when we got back to the hotel. Jack took one look at it and said: "Fucking hell, £12.99. You should never have paid that. I never spend more than a fiver on me caps, you fucking idiots."

"Yeah, but Jack, even so, are you not going to give us our money back?"

"Fuck off. I bloody made you millionaires. You were shit, fucking nobodies before I knew you." We could not believe it. But that was Jack. He just walked away.

He was a card. He was so funny. Like before big international games in Dublin, the atmosphere would sometimes be a bit nervous. Then Jack would say, "Come on you lot, get out there warming up. Get the applause from the crowd. I'll let you go first because I'll get the bigger cheer when I go out." Then he'd come out behind us, and the fans would be going "Jackie, Jackie" and he would say, "I told you fuckers who was the most popular." It was hilarious, because he was both half-serious and half-joking.'

It was precisely Jack's laid-back attitude that helped to breed such a strong team spirit in Ireland. There is no better way to unify a group than through communal laughter, and there was never any danger that Jack, with his natural air of total authority, would ever become the object of their contempt. The opposite was true. The more they laughed, the more endearing they found him. 'He was just such a fantastic man. He doesn't care what anyone else thinks of him. He had a brash exterior, but underneath, he was very decent, honest,' says Alan McLoughlin. The present Irish manager, Mick McCarthy, argues that the very fact that Jack was such a character in Ireland helped the rest of the players: 'Unusually for an international team, the manager was the star. Big Jack was the icon and in many ways that took a lot of the pressure off us. All the attention was on him and we could just get on with our game.' McCarthy also believes that Jack's absent-mindedness had no bearing on the team: 'Yes, he forgot names, but so what? The coach's job is to get the best out of the players and that is exactly what Jack did. All the rest was irrelevant.' It was an outlook that Jack says he had learnt from the single-minded Alf Ramsey: 'Alf didn't give a toss for anybody who was not directly involved. Only the team – and I mean the team, not the individuals, mattered to him. I liked that because in football you are always coming up against some smart-arse who thinks he knows better.'

Jack's way did not always achieve results. In the campaign for a place in the 1992 European Championship finals, Ireland, though not losing a game, failed to qualify after squandering a deluge of chances in their home games, particularly against England in Dublin when Sheedy and Houghton both missed sitters. The battle for the final place was, as in 1988, a very close run thing, for if England had failed to get a draw in their game, away to Poland, then Ireland, having beaten Turkey 3–1 in Istanbul would have gone through. Deep into the second half of that England game in Poznan, Poland were leading 1–0, but then, with 19 minutes left, Gary Lineker equalized and Ireland were out. Standing in the Irish dressing room after victory over the Turks, Jack was shattered by the result, especially because he had been told, only moments earlier, that Poland had won. It was Mick McCarthy who informed him of the Lineker strike. 'In the space of perhaps no more than 90 seconds, I had gone from the summit all the way down to the valley.' Jack said that the experience was even worse than losing to West Germany in the 1970 World Cup quarter-final. 'For half an hour, nobody moved in the dressing room. They refused to dress, just sat there with their heads buried in their hands, trying to come to terms with it all. I tried to do the jollying bit, but deep down, I hurt as much as any of them.'

One of the difficulties Jack faced early this European campaign was Paul McGrath's continuing drink problem. McGrath was perhaps the key man in Jack's Irish side. 'His natural talent was such that he could play in any one of three or four positions. No matter where you posted him, he read the game perfectly,' wrote Jack. As he was so important to the team, there was usually a player or official posted to keep an eye on him. It is a tribute to the cohesion that Jack built in his side that his colleagues were so willing to protect him. 'Don't worry Boss, we'll take care of him, because we're a better team when he's with us,' the Eire players would say. And he was never a nasty drunk, like George Best; in fact, Maurice Setters describes McGrath as 'the most amiable lad you could ever meet, so soft-hearted that he would give away his last shilling'. Yet McGrath's drinking gradually became more serious, and by 1992, he was, for the first time, becoming unreliable. He missed the home qualifier against Turkey because he was suffering from a crippling hangover: 'This time I had gone overboard. I had disgraced myself. I had let my family down. I had betrayed Jack Charlton. I had put alcohol before the Irish team,' he wrote in his autobiography. But Jack, whom McGrath called his 'guardian angel', showed nothing but understanding and later booked him into a drying-out clinic in Edgbaston. McGrath had gone missing on a binge during the week-end before the Turkey game, but Jack covered up for him by saying he was visiting his mother. McGarth admits that during those few days he was 'drowning in a sea of alcohol', yet when he finally showed up at the team hotel, 'Jack treated me like the prodigal son. He welcomed me back with open arms.' Though McGrath recovered to provide sterling service for Ireland for another five years, he did miss a further game in Tirana against Albania. But 'Jack was as forgiving as ever. I would not have been surprised if he'd told me to take a hike, but to be honest, he's been nothing but brilliant to me.' It could, of course, be argued that Jack was demonstrating favouritism; after all, he had never been nearly so tolerant of Brady, O'Leary and Stapleton. But then Jack was always a pragmatist rather than a moralist. He considered McGrath indispensable, an opinion he did not hold of the other three.

After the disappointment of the European failure, qualification for the 1994 World Cup looked to be more straightforward. Ireland had drawn Denmark, Spain, Albania, Northern Ireland, Latvia and Lithuania in their group. Excellent results home and away meant that Ireland were top of the group before the penultimate match at home to Spain in Dublin, where victory would ensure automatic qualification without having to worry about the last fixture against Northern Ireland. But, for once under Jack, the fortress of Lansdowne Road was breached, with Ireland conceding three goals in the first 25 minutes in front of a shell-shocked Irish public. John Sheridan managed to pull one back in the second half but Ireland would now have to travel to Belfast for their final game still needing points if they were to go through.

There could hardly be a more awkward fixture, not just because of the traditional rivalry between north and south, but also because the long-running Ulster troubles were going through a particularly violent phase. A wave of brutal sectarian killings swept across the province in October 1993, making it the worst month for terrorist casualties in 17 years. Particularly gruesome was the cold-blooded bombing by the IRA of a shop in the Protestant Shankill Road, killing nine civilians. The inevitable loyalist response was just as vicious, as a group of UDA gunmen burst into a bar in the village of Greysteel and assassinated seven Catholics.

In such circumstances, there was a great deal of apprehension about the match between Northern Ireland and the Republic due to take place on 17 November. Some advocated postponing the game or switching it to another venue, but the police, British and Irish governments and the two Irish Football Associations feared this would only inflame the situation. Their strategy was to ring Windsor Park in Belfast with the highest possible security. The same approach was used at the Irish training camp in Monaghan, which was surrounded by heavily armed soldiers and police.

Religious and political sensitivities have long been acute in Ireland, especially in Ulster. In this bitterly divided land, it might have been feared that Jack Charlton's legendary lack of diplomacy could lead to disaster. But he handled himself with aplomb, steering clear of any controversy. For once, Big Jack's mouth stayed shut. Whenever he was asked about current affairs at any meeting, he just said, 'Oh I don't get involved with politics.' The only time he landed in difficulty was when it emerged that the Irish team frequently played a tape of traditional Irish rebel songs on their way to matches. One of the numbers was *Sean South from Garryowen* about an IRA volunteer who led an attack on an army barracks during the Anglo-Irish War of the early 1920s. The news of the team's pre-match routine led to a predictable media-orchestrated row. The Ulster Unionists reacted with their usual outrage, the MP for Mid-Ulster, William McCrea, claiming that Charlton's behaviour was 'despicable', while in England MP Teddy Taylor said that 'Jack Charlton should hang his head in shame.' But the controversy soon died a death when Jack refused to react.

But there was another, less manufactured, dispute on the eve of the game when the Northern Ireland manager the usually courteous Billy Bingham made a powerful attack on Jack's Irish team, calling them a band of 'football mercenaries'. 'I take a totally cynical view of the entire business, although it is for others to judge whether the Republic are devaluing the World Cup.' Stung by the words, Jack replied, 'What am I to do, ignore a damn good player with Irish parents just because he happens to have been born in the UK?' John Aldridge joined in, saying that Bingham's statement was 'nothing short of scandalous, a disgrace'.

The exchange of words only added to the pressure of the night in Windsor Park, where the hostility of the Belfast crowd was obvious from the moment Jack's team stepped on to the field. 'Fuck off back to Dublin you Fenian bastard,' Niall Quinn was politely told, while racial abuse poured down on Paul McGrath. The tension in the air was almost palpable. 'I have never played in a game like that, it was just so nerve-wracking,' says McGrath. But Eire held Northern Ireland at bay until the 73rd minute, when Jimmy Quinn, out of the blue, hit a superb volley into Bonner's net. 1–0 to Northern Ireland and America now looked like a fading dream for the Republic. Quinn's goal re-ignited the flare-up between the Bingham and

Charlton camps. As the ball flashed in, one of Bingham's assistants turned to Maurice Setters and said, 'Up yours.' 'You'd better keep your mouth shut, pal,' replied Setters, before telling Jack what had happened.

Just as Ireland were giving up hope, another Charlton miracle happened, when he sent on Alan McLoughlin for Ray Houghton. Almost immediately, he latched on to a free-kick from Dennis Irwin, chested the ball down and then put it past the keeper with his left foot. 1–1 and Ireland were through to USA 94. McLoughlin recalls that moment: 'Jack was never a big one for lavishing praise or giving instructions. When he sent me on, his words were, "Get out there and score a fucking goal." There were no tactics. After the final whistle, there were lot of interviews and photos, but I don't think Jack said anything to me like "Well done." It did not bother me in the slightest. We flew back to Dublin, did a big press conference and, with me sitting beside him, he said, "The little bugger managed to do something right for once." That in itself meant more to me than if he had stuck his hands around me and given me a big hug.'

Amidst all the celebrations, there was another unfortunate run-in with Billy Bingham. When the Northern Irish manager proffered his hand at the end, Jack refused to take it, telling him 'Up yours too, Billy.' It was a typical example of Jack's volatility, and he says he regretted the words as soon as he uttered them. That night, in another bizarre twist to a strange day, Jack had the chance to make it up when he was invited to a reception at Belfast's Linfield Football Club to present Billy with an award on his retirement as international manager. After all the animosity of recent days, Jack was astonished to be greeted by rapturous applause as he entered the hall. It turned out the people of the north, now their own team had been knocked out, were delighted that an Irish side was on its way to the USA.

And Big Jack had done it again. The miser's touch of Newcastle had become the Midas touch in Ireland. When Jack was appointed manager of Ireland in 1986, Bert Millichip, the chairman of the FA, reflecting the received wisdom of the football establishment, said to Des Casey, the president of the FAI: 'You've made a mistake appointing that man.'

Several years later, when Ireland met England at Wembley, Casey turned to Millichip.

'Quite a good mistake we made there, wasn't it?'

CHAPTER TWENTY-THREE

The Sons

'We don't live in each other's pockets,' has been the phrase regularly employed by both Bobby and Jack to describe their relationship. 'Down the years people have been fond of saying that we aren't close but that's not the case. We went our own way, had our own football clubs, led our own lives. Every now and then we would meet on the pitch. We are still quite close, we speak regularly and get together now and then. We don't phone each other for permission to do something every day. No, there was never much jealousy. I'm very proud of him and I think he's proud of me. That's more than you can ask, eh?' said Bobby in an interview in 1989.

But this was something of a rose-tinted exaggeration. In reality, by this time the distance between Jack and Bobby was now wider than ever. When Bobby made one of his very rare phonecalls to Jack in Italy to wish him good luck before the game against England, Jack could not bring himself to be gracious: 'You've never made contact to wish me well before. Why now?' The rift between them was also highlighted that summer when Eamon Dunphy, who, as we have seen, had been through a volcanic fallout with Jack during the World Cup, rang Bobby for information for his 1991 biography of Matt Busby. Dunphy recalls that Bobby's wife disliked having Jack in the house because she thought him boorish, the opposite of her own husband. 'When I rang Bobby to discuss my book, it was just at the time of my worst period with Jack. I called his home, and his wife said, "Eamon, how are you? Certainly, I'll get Bobby now. It was a pleasure to talk."'

Jack's major grievance against his younger brother was that, though Bobby had been Cissie's favourite when they had been growing up, he had allegedly neglected their parents once he had married. Jack himself was immensely proud of the way he had looked after Cissie and Bob ever since he had made some money as a professional footballer. His first – and probably best-known – act of generosity towards them was just after the World Cup in 1966, when he bought them a home on a newly built estate in Ashington. Jack made the announcement of the purchase on the day after the civic reception for the two World Cup-winning brothers. According to Cissie, Jack turned up when she was hanging out the washing.

'I've bought you a house, Mam.'

'You haven't.'

'I have. Do you want it?'

'Oh yes.'

It turned out that Jack, having performed the opening ceremony at this estate in College Road, was so taken with the properties that he decided to purchase one for his parents. It was widely reported in the press that Jack had used his bonus from winning the World Cup to pay for the home, but this was not the case, for World Cup winnings came to less than £1,000, whereas the College Road house cost £2,700. However, Jack was only too delighted to give his parents what he felt they deserved, as he later wrote: 'My mother and father had lived in two-up, two-down coal houses all their lives. They had never had a bathroom. They'd always had to make do with an outside toilet, coal fires, washing and cooking in the pantry. Now they had a new three-bedroom house with a proper bathroom and kitchen. They called it Jules Rimet, after the World Cup trophy.'

The gesture did not turn out to be quite as successful as Jack had hoped. Despite the modern luxury, Cissie missed the sense of community of Beatrice Street and felt she was looked down upon by her more middle-class neighbours. 'I never succeeded in settling down there. I found that I had exchanged the sharing happiness of a working-class atmosphere for middle-class estate snobbery.'

Apart from the usual media interest in Cissie, the World Cup of 1966 also threw the spotlight of publicity on Bob Charlton. The nation was fascinated by the story of how Mr Charlton Senior, rather than watching his own sons in the semi-final against Portugal, chose to work his shift underground. The BBC's star commentator David Coleman was so amazed that he arranged with the Coal Board's management for Bob to be given a special screening, in the Linton colliery office, of a TV recording of the game; not that this was any great pleasure for Bob, given his indifference to football. But even if he personally had not felt any real sacrifice was involved, Bob Charlton's example was said to be an inspiration to a nation in the throes of economic crisis: 'Today the *Sunday Mirror* salutes Mr Robert Charlton. On Tuesday night, as his sons Bobby and Jackie helped take England into the final by a brilliant victory over Portugal, where was their father? In the stands at Wembley? In front of his TV at home? No, he was at work, two miles below ground. England certainly needed the Charlton brothers last Tuesday. But how much more in these days of grave national crisis does the country need men like their father.'

The third son, Gordon, was also at work, serving as an engineer on board the merchant ship The Glengyle. One of his shifts coincided with the World Cup Final itself, and he only knew that England had won when he climbed on to the upper deck to see the ship's captain dancing wildly. Later, Cissie gave this romantic account of her son's celebrations at sea: 'Gordon told me that a new sound filled the warm air of the Oriental ocean that night. One by one, British ships began to sound their sirens until all were chorusing their congratulations.'

Gordon Charlton had started his working life, not at sea, but, like Jack, as an apprentice at Leeds, serving on the ground staff – a job that was deemed to be below Bobby. But he did not last long at

Leeds, because he lacked the application to become a professional. 'Time after time, the people at Elland Road would come to me with complaints that Gordon wasn't doing this or that,' wrote Jack, 'that he wasn't showing up in the mornings to do the little odds and ends which were required of ground staff. They let him go after a year – and that was a terrible waste of talent.' Rob Storey, an old Ashington friend of the Charltons, says, 'Gordon was sometimes compared to Bobby, but I know he got sick of those sorts of comparisons. That's why he packed it in.' Having abandoned football, Gordon then worked as a colliery fitter, before going to sea and then ending up a sales director of a plant hire firm. Despite his experience at Elland Road, he also did some football coaching in the Sunday League in Leeds. It is sometimes said that Tommy was the most talented of all the four Charlton brothers. Evan Martin, Bobby's schoolfriend from Bedlington Grammar, says: 'Bobby once surprised me by saying that Tommy was an even better player than him. I just could not believe that. Tommy had hardly any interest in football at all.' Indeed, unlike the other three, Tommy was never involved in professional football. Instead, he went briefly into the merchant navy before following his father down the colliery, first as a fitter and then as a mines rescue brigadesman. Jack maintained that Tommy, who now lives in Lancashire, had the stature to become a top union official 'but he chose the quieter life'.

When Bob retired from his job as a miner, Jack continued to be the dutiful son, asking his parents to live on a farm he had bought in Carleton in the Yorkshire Dales. Bob was suffering from pneumoconiosis, a disease caused by coal dust which left him with congested lungs. He was therefore grateful for the fresh air of the moors after 43 years of working underground, while Cissie was delighted to cater for the stream of visitors – including tourists – who came through the farm. Jack and Pat were among the regular visitors, as Cissie recalled: 'Jack and Bob argued as they always had, but Pat and I had learned long before that it was just their way together.'

By settling his parents in the Dales, Jack felt he had finally earned the real love of his parents that was missing from his wandering childhood. Showing the emotion that was often close below the surface with Jack, he once explained, 'I remember one New Year's Eve my dad saying to me, "I've never been happier in my life, son, and it's all down to you."' Sadly, he was not able to enjoy this tranquillity for much longer. In April 1982, he died from cancer. Now a widow, Cissie moved back to Northumberland where she felt among friends, first living in a council flat in Ashington and then, as she became more frail, in a nursing home in Newbiggin-by-the-sea. Even in her late life, she retained her love of soccer – in her seventies she was still giving coaching classes in one of the local primary schools.

It was when Cissie was in the nursing home that the chasm between Bobby and Jack became more apparent, because Jack was furious at his younger brother's reluctance to visit his ageing mother. Jack says that Cissie had been hurt for years by her son's reluctance to make any contact. 'I tried to get him to go and see her, even phone her, send a card. And he just said, "I'll do it when I think the time is right. I'll run my life the way I see it and I'll do what I want to." But of course I still hoped I could persuade him to go and see our mother. I caught hold of him finally at a hotel one night in London, took him to one side and tried to lay it on the line as urgently as I could. "Listen, I'm bloody sick of arguing with you about going to see our mother. I don't want to mention it again. It's down to your conscience."' Cissie desperately wanted him to go and see her. But he never did. Harry Gregg, the United goalkeeper, remembers Jack once speaking vehemently about the issue: 'That bastard has been in Ashington and never gone near her. Don't let him kid ya, HG. He never bothered with her.' Gregg also recalls another, much earlier indicator of the sourness between Bobby, Jack and their mother. 'I was at Carlisle as manager in the mid-1980s and Cissie and Jack came over.

"How's Bob?" I asked.

Jack turned to his mother: "Cissie, did you get a fucking Christmas card?"

"No."

I think Bobby was her favourite, that's why she was so upset about it.'

There were other examples of Bobby's alienation from his family, like the time Bobby's parents turned up at Old Trafford, at the invitation of Jimmy Murphy, prompting a tirade from Bobby: 'What are you doing here? Don't ever come here again unless I tell you.' Jack said later, 'Mum recalled this to me. It was very cruel.' Jack says that on another occasion, Bobby would not even have his own father to stay at his Cheshire house, claiming to have the decorators in.

The main reason for the animosity between Cissie and Bobby was simple: Bobby's wife and Cissie could not stand each other. Since Bobby's wedding in 1961, Norma and Cissie had barely been on speaking terms; Cissie had hardly ever seen her grandchildren, Suzanne and Andrea, and was not invited to Suzanne's wedding. In 1992, four years before Cissie's death, Norma revealed how much she loathed her mother-in-law: 'People think the Charltons are a close family but we are not at all. I was never accepted into the family by my mother-in-law. She has never acknowledged me or our children. She is very domineering and has a strong personality. It used to worry Bobby but he no longer bothers. He is very, very proud of his girls. They have never received birthday cards from her – not once.' In response, Cissie openly admitted to the 30-year feud: 'I do not accept my daughter-in-law. There is a rift and it's up to her to come to me. But I don't want to make up. It has gone on too long.'

Cissie was hugely admired, not just by Jack, but by large numbers who knew her in Ashington. Vince Gledhill, the Newcastle journalist who co-wrote her autobiography, told me: 'I was very fond of her. She was a very loving lady and when I was writing the book I wanted that to shine through, that she was a special person in her own right, not just because she was the mother of Jack and Bobby. She was very outgoing, very much a people person.' But though others were fond of her, they also admit that she could, to quote Norma's phrase, be 'very domineering'. Evan Martin, who liked her immensely and confirms that 'Cissie blamed Norma for the fallout with Bobby', recalls Cissie's brother Stan Milburn (Jack and Bobby's uncle) telling him that: 'she liked too much of the Charlton limelight, that she played too much on the Charlton name, and that she should not have pushed herself forward so readily. I totally disagreed, because I knew Cissie was so outgoing, she couldn't help it. It was just her nature. And the complaint about playing on the Charlton name, well, she did all those things like opening fetes and coaching for free.'

Rob Storey, another who admires Cissie, calling her 'a very caring person, the mainstay of the family', recalls being with Jack at the unveiling of the statue in Ashington to Jackie Milburn: 'Cissie was at the front of the official party, in her wheelchair, greeting everyone and waving at them. Jack turned to me and said: "You know, she just laps that up. She's sitting there waving like the Queen."

"As far as I am concerned, she is."

In an indicator of her regal outlook, Cissie once said in a BBC interview that 'I think I have been one of God's chosen people. Really I do.' Another time she admitted that her personality was closest to Jack's: 'He is very straight talking and doesn't soft-pedal if he thinks I am wrong. By the same token, I like to have my say too, especially on football.' In such circumstances, it is easy to see why Norma, a strong-willed woman herself, would have clashed with Cissie. And Bobby was always going to take the side of his wife. For all his antipathy to Bobby, Jack accepted that his younger brother had little choice: 'Norma thought my mother didn't like her and my mother thought she didn't like her and it was never solved. Bobby virtually came down on the side of his wife, which was correct. I mean what other way is there to come down? So where he used to come home as often as I did, suddenly he stopped visiting as much. In the later years, he didn't visit her as often as I would have liked him to, which caused a split and we have the same argument to this day. That was all there was about it, nothing serious, purely and simply family. But my mother was hurt by it. She was hurt right till the day she died,' Jack said in the *London Evening Standard* in 1997.

The *Mirror* writer Clive Crickmer was one of the first to break the story of the rift between the brothers, after Cissie's death in 1996. As he explained to me, he had actually talked to Cissie three years earlier about it, but at Cissie's request, had not run the story. Interestingly, he suggests that, before Cissie's final decline, Bobby's avoidance of his mother may not always have been as absolute as Jack sometimes suggests: 'I had gone over there at the behest of the features editor, just to sound her out about one of our female writers doing a piece on her. She was very friendly, made me a cup of tea. She was pretty self-sufficient. She said that she did not want to see another female reporter. "I'm past all that now. I'm getting too old for that sort of thing." We then started chatting. She then volunteered the information that she and Bobby's wife did not get on at all. The only time she saw Bobby, she said, was when he came north on business. He would then pop in and see her, for a fairly brief visit. She said that there was no rift with Bobby. She still loved him. But she suspected that Bobby probably did not tell his wife that he had been to see his mother. I asked her what caused the rift. She said, "I don't know. We got off to a bad start. I just think we rubbed each other up the wrong way. We didn't get on." She continued, "I am very sorry about it all. I look at Suzanne, giving the forecasts. And just like any other grandmother I try to see who she looks like. I can see both mother and father in her. I'm very proud of the fact that she's my granddaughter, although I have hardly ever seen her.' It was a sad, touching moment. She was obviously talking from the heart. She was certainly sombre. There were no tears, she was too strong a lady for that. But you could tell there was great sadness there.

'This had never really come out before. There had only been hints at the rift, but never from the lips of the family. I was thinking to myself, "This is a great story." Then Cissie stopped and said, "Oh dear, I should not have told you all this. I have said far too much. Please, please do not publish it." She was quite impassioned when she made this plea. I'm glad I didn't run it. And I'm not sure, given her objections, the *Mirror* would have used it. I liked her and I didn't want to hurt her.'

But when Cissie died, the disunity in the Charlton family came out in the open. It was not actually the national press that broke the story, but North News freelance agency, which spoke to the matron of the Beachville nursing home, Alma Charlton (no relation) who told them, 'Sir Bobby has never been to Beachville. He was informed last week that she had taken a turn for the worse by his brother. Cissie has wanted to see him for the last few years. It upset her a great deal that she didn't see him. She talked about him all the time. Seeing Bobby meant more to Cissie than anything else as she realized she was about to die. It's very sad she didn't get her last wish.'

It is a sign of how low relations had sunk between Jack and Bobby that it was the press, not his family, which informed Bobby of the loss of his mother. Bobby was out in Tunisia on business when Cissie died, but in the 24 hours after her death, no messages were left at the hotel by his relatives. It was a journalist from the *Mirror* who was the first to tell him: 'I had no idea. You are breaking news to me. I have only just walked in. Please forgive me.' Bobby flew straight home, of course, for the funeral, though Noel Cantwell says that sometimes in the past, Jack had been so angered by Bobby's neglect of his mother that he thought Bobby would be a hypocrite to turn up. 'I remember Jack once telling me, "You know, I hope that when anything happens to her, he won't be running up there, just when she's passed away and all that business."'

But there was no way Sir Bobby – and Lady Norma – would have not been there. And, despite all that had passed between them, Jack says he was grateful for their coming. 'I was pleased about that. I thanked Norma, too, for I didn't want anything to happen that would take away from my mother's funeral,' he wrote. Inevitably Jack was shattered by the loss of his mother, the pain all the greater because they had grown so close in her last years. 'She was a great lady and I'm going to miss her very much,' he said. Vince Gledhill, who gave the oration at her funeral, had this interesting description of how Jack was physically affected by her death. 'He came round to see me to ask me to do the oration. It was a great honour for me. But it was very strange the day of the funeral. You know how tall Jack is, 6' 2" and I am only 5'5", yet that night, I swear I could have looked him straight in the eye, he was so diminished by her death. He seemed almost to have shrunk. He was very quiet.'

Since the passing of Cissie, Jack's mood towards Bobby has fluctuated. In the epilogue to his autobiography, he made a powerful attack on Bobby, and in one of his articles publicizing the book, he said, 'I'll never forgive him. We've never been further apart than we are now. I just don't want to know him.' Bobby, of course, has maintained his usual silence, apart from to say that 'Jack's book won't change anything.' But at other times Jack has expressed puzzlement and regret rather than anger.

There is nothing unique about the Charlton brothers. Family quarrels are as old as mankind. One very famous footballer told me that he has not spoken to his own brother for 30 years, while in his recent autobiography *1966 And All That*, Sir Geoff Hurst revealed a major split with his parents. 'My relationship with my mum and dad was profoundly changed by England's World Cup victory. They found my new fame hard to handle, I don't know why. Their change in attitude towards me and my family became a source of great sadness.' Just as in the Charlton family, he admitted that his own daughters 'hardly knew' their Hurst grandparents.

When all the sad business of the feud with Cissie is washed away, what remains is a fundamental clash of personalities that can never be bridged, as Jack himself recognizes. 'To be honest, me and our kid were never the best of friends. Brothers don't have to be friends. Everything I like in life he didn't have anything to do with, and everything he likes in life, I don't want to know about.'

CHAPTER TWENTY-FOUR

The Millionaires

Throughout their careers in football, Bobby and Jack had a complex, even contradictory, attitude towards finance. Neither of them could be described as greedy. Neither exploited their stature in the game in a crudely mercenary way. Bobby turned down numerous offers to leave Manchester United, especially those from Italy and Spain, which could have made him an extremely rich man in his early twenties. In the same way, unlike almost every modern League manager, Jack always refused to have a contract, which meant he never received any compensation when he left a club. When he went to work for Ireland, he did so for a salary of just £20,000 a year, an astonishingly small sum for an international coach.

Both have done an impressive amount of charity work, particularly in the football field, and, as we have seen, had a sense of kindness towards colleagues. Ex-United player Nobby Lawton told me this tale which contradicts a lot of the nonsense spoken about Bobby's miserable nature at Old Trafford. In 1972 Lawton was having a testimonial with Lincoln City and had mentioned the event to Bobby. 'The night of my testimonial, United were preparing for the sixth round of the Cup at the Norbeck Hydro Hotel in Blackpool. And he came over from Blackpool to Lincoln, arrived about 5pm, met some of the staff and fans, and left about 11pm to go back to Blackpool, driving right through the night. He shook me by the hand and said "Well done," before he left. He did not take money, nothing at all. He signed autographs for everybody. It was a tremendous gesture, but typical of the man.'

Frank Taylor, the distinguished football writer who has known Bobby well since Munich, views him as 'a very genuine guy. In the late 1970s, I went to the British Army of the Rhine with Bobby Charlton and Bobby Moore to boost the morale of the troops. The very first thing he did on arriving was to say, "Where's the children's hospital?" That has always stuck in my mind.'

In a similar vein Alan McLoughlin told me this story about Jack's willingness to help out: 'When I was at Southampton, I was moving house and some legal problems had arisen. I had been speaking to my wife on the phone while I was at a hotel on Irish duty, and neither of us were sure about what to do. I was walking to the dining room, thinking about these legal difficulties, when I ran into Jack.

"Jack, I need your advice on something." That showed how comfortable I felt with him.

I explained to him the legal problems over my mortgage.

"So how much do you need?"

"No, it's not money, I'm only looking for some property advice."

"Listen, whatever you need to borrow . . ."

"Jack, it's not about money."

"Look, I'll lend you what you need. I'll write you a cheque right now and then you can pay me back next June."

Jack was completely off the point but he had offered to lend a relative stranger a substantial sum. That was remarkable, that he would have been prepared to do that for one of his players. Not that I had even asked for it, but I was genuinely touched by his attitude.'

Unlike so many sportsmen, neither Jack nor Bobby ever revelled in the money they had made. Jack, it is true, owns four properties, but he could hardly be described as a magnate. His main home is the converted farmhouse in Northumberland, then he also has holiday retreats in County Mayo, Altea in Spain, and Filey in Yorkshire. For Jack, clothes and cars are purely utilitarian. Meanwhile, Bobby has his substantial home in Cheshire, but, again, he hates showing off. 'Even if I won the lottery,' he once said, showing a creditable degree of self-awareness, 'I would never buy anything flash like a Rolls Royce or a Lamborghini. It's not my style. I did once have a Mustang. Norma loved it but it had to go. It was a bit of a poser's car. With the best will in the world, I cannot look like a poser.'

Both are inherently cautious. Jack boasts that he has never had a mortgage since he first became a manager, while fellow Manchester United director Maurice Watkins says of Bobby, 'When it comes to money, he is well known to be careful – like he still has that case of port he was presented with from 1966. But he is very shrewd and has made a success of all that he has done in business, whether it be the travel or the soccer schools or United. Shrewd, smart, cautious, understands business.'

Yet for all their generosity and modesty, neither had ever shown any reluctance about making money. Both of them have developed a vast range of lucrative interests, always showing enthusiasm for what Jack calls 'the earner'. The way some of Bobby's ventures have been interwoven with Manchester United has occasionally raised a few eyebrows. And in Ireland Jack became legendary for the way he raked in a fortune from speaking engagements and endorsements.

Jack's first business was started at Leeds when he and Pat ran the souvenir stall at Elland Road, hardly an arrangement that would be countenanced by any player today – can you imagine Nigel Martyn or Rio Ferdinand selling scarves at Leeds? Indeed, the club's officials did eventually decide that the arrangement was too bizarre to continue, closing Jack down and taking over the operation themselves. Another of his interests as a Leeds player was selling Yorkshire cloth for bespoke menswear, something that always amused his colleagues given his famous lack of sartorial elegance. Travelling all over the country with the material, Jack claims that at one stage he was making more money from suits than from soccer. The journalist Brian James, former chief football writer of the *Daily Mail*, says that 'Jack was, obliquely, one of the reasons why many footballers were so well dressed in the late 1960s. He used to come down to London with his boot full of the finest cloth from Yorkshire. He would then arrange to meet you and sell you some of this material. Personally, I had no less than four suits from him. The cloth cost just about £20, while the suit could be made up for only about £50, so the result was that you had a very expensive suit for only about £70.' Alan Peacock, his fellow Leeds player, often worked with him on this sideline: 'We used to get suit lengths from the mill and then sell to other players. Like after a game against West Ham, you might find us in the opposition dressing room showing some fine mohair to Bobby Moore. Jack was in with the mills at Bradford where he got the stuff for about £5 for a suit length' – which, given Brian James' figures, shows how Jack was making a good profit on every transaction. After this experience, Jack went properly into the menswear business in Yorkshire when he was coming to the end of his Leeds career, becoming a sales executive of Maple Clothes. On his retirement in 1973, he was promoted to the rank of full director – two years before Bobby had his first directorship at Halba Travel. But this business failed badly and within four years, Maple had called in the receiver. Fortunately for Jack, with the success of his managerial career, his role was purely a titular one by then. 'I have not attended any board meetings and I cannot see the situation affecting me. My name is used on official notepaper but I have not had a great deal to do with the company,' he told the *Yorkshire Evening Post*.

Throughout the 1970s and 1980s, Jack continued to do well from broadcasting and after-dinner speaking, but it was when he had real success with Ireland from 1988 that he started to make serious money. It is difficult to calculate exactly how much money Jack made during his time as the Republic's boss, but some estimates have put the figure at around £5 million. Those figures are not entirely denied by Jack, who used to joke – using his stump of a third finger – about how much he was earning. Tony Cascarino recalls: 'After the first World Cup, he raised one finger to represent the million that he had earned. Then, after USA 94, he raised a second finger to show he now had £2 million. It was, as always, a bit tongue in cheek. Then, in the run-up to the European Championships in 1996, he said, "If we get there, we'll have that" and he raised half a finger. We all laughed and he said, "Well, it's not as big as the World Cup, is it?"' After the success of qualifying for Italia 90, the cash turned into a flood. His numerous public appearances were bringing in least £3,500 a time, while he also earned £250,000 a year from advertising Guinness, the Bank of Ireland, Mitsubushi Televisions, and Shredded Wheat, £30,000 from his newspaper column, and £25,000 a time for lending his name to a variety of organizations such the Irish Milk Marketing Board and the Irish Permanent Building Society. On top of this, he was thought to have taken a £100,000 share of the commercial jackpot arising from Italia 90 and another £250,000 as a bonus for the USA 94 qualification. And when he stood down as Ireland's manager, his pay-off was said to be around £500,000.

No-one in Ireland was begrudging Jack a penny. After Italia 90, Fran Fields, Des Casey's successor as president of the FAI said, 'When I took office two-and-a-half years ago, I could never have dreamt that anything like this was possible. But who can blame the public or the sponsors for wanting to share in this great success. And I certainly don't blame Jack or the players for cashing in. Without them, it would have never happened.' By 1994, he had turned football into one of Ireland's richest exports, boosting the economy by over IR£100 million. Getting through to USA 94 was especially beneficial to Irish companies because of the vast size of the Irish American market – one fifth of all US citizens are of Irish stock. 'He was certainly Saint Jack to me,' says Ray Treacy, whose Dublin travel agency boomed after Ireland's football success. 'In my business, Jack was a godsend, absolutely brilliant. Before he arrived, we'd have 15 people travelling to an away game. But for Italia 90, we took 1500 people to Italy and four years later another 1900 to the USA.'

As he had such a big name in world football, Jack's proposed autobiography, to be published just after his retirement as manager, became one of the most sought after books in British publishing. After an intensive negotiating battle, Transworld finally secured the rights to the story for £500,000, by far the largest advance ever paid to a British sporting figure at that time, doubling the record held jointly by the cricketer Ian Botham and the former Arsenal boss George Graham. Ghosted by the Irish writer Peter Byrne, the subsequent book lived up to the marketing hype and became an international bestseller, though unlike much of the public, Jack with his usual brazen honesty admitted that he had hardly read any of it, never mind written it. During a publicity tour for the book in 1997, he said, 'I haven't even had time to read it yet. I've got a copy in my bag and have read the first five chapters. To be honest, I've quite enjoyed it. It's not complicated. No big words.' Jack was not quite the literary ignoramus he pretended. Just as his love of fishing runs counter to his general restlessness, so too he has often been a keen reader. Allan Clarke says one of his chief memories of Jack on away trips to Europe was that he usually had his head in a book during the plane journey. 'I'm reading *The Steel Bonnets* by George MacDonald Fraser at the moment. I like books of historical interest like that. I also read a lot of fishing and wildlife books,' he told the *Guardian* in May 1994.

In view of Jack's bonanza in Ireland, he might have been sur-prised to learn that in 1994, at the peak of his Celtic earning power, he was supposedly far outstripped in personal wealth by his younger brother. In April of that year, the highly respected *Business Age* magazine reported that Bobby was worth £6.5 million, while putting Jack's attributed assets at just £2 million.

The claims of a vast difference reflected the fact that Bobby's main business involvement was in publicly listed firms, while Jack's income – especially his huge array of endorsements and appear-ances – was essentially private, so private that Jack admits that he was once visited by the Inland Revenue wanting to ask him about his accounts. Apart from his support for youth soccer programmes, Bobby did not become involved in business until he teamed up with Freddie Pye at Halba in 1975. Four years later, inspired by what he had seen during the World Cup in Argentina in 1978, he set up the Bobby Charlton Summer Schools, investing £30,000 of his own money. 'It was the BBC who asked me to join a group of

Argentinian boys in the 1978 World Cup. We knocked the ball about together and the response was terrific. Other countries also screened the film and I thought, on my return to England, "Why not do that sort of thing here?"' Thus the schools were born and, by 1990, more than 120,000 young people had graduated from its coaching sessions. Beginning at Old Trafford, the schools had within a decade reached out across the world, extending into the USA, the Soviet, Union, Scandinavia and Saudi Arabia. 'I've created a monster,' he once said, 'a nice one, but it does consume my life.'

Due to their success, the soccer schools enjoyed heavy corporate sponsorship. In 1991, for example, the school in Manchester attracted £250,000 of support from British Gas. In another development that year, a deal with Pepsi-Cola to take the school to 25 Arab countries was said to pull in £2.5 million. The schools were a central part of Bobby's footballing empire, which then went under the trading name of 'Bobby Charlton Enterprises', with Bobby, his wife Norma and the PFA as the main stakeholders. Other interests included corporate entertainment, security, and consultancy. In December 1990, Bobby proclaimed the virtues of the celebrity 'lunches with legends' which he was organizing, attracting stars like Ian Botham, Henry Cooper and Gareth Edwards and making around £23,000 a time. This venture, however, aroused some animosity from the promoter Mike Newlin, who felt that Bobby was treading on his turf. 'The circuit is really quite small. We nearly fell out because we were doing the same sorts of lunches in the same area and also because Dave Sadler, who went to work for him, used to work for me. But I never closed the door on him. Life is too short. The problem eventually resolved itself.'

In 1991 Bobby Charlton Enterprises was bought by the textile firm Conrad International for £3.5 million. Conrad wanted to expand into the leisure industry and saw Bobby's company as the ideal vehicle for this, especially as Conrad was intimately involved with Old Trafford. Bobby's business partners Mike Edelson and Nigel Burrows were on the board of Conrad, while United plc director Amir Al Midani owned 12 per cent of the company. It was this sort of close relationship which has led to some complaints, how-ever unfair, against Bobby and some of his Manchester critics. They cite the fact that, at the time of the flotation of Manchester United, Conrad supplied goods to Old Trafford worth £100,000, while, in turn, United provided business to Conrad worth £60,000. Also that year, Halba Travel, of which Bobby was still a director, supplied rail and air tickets worth £15,000 to United.

Yet such links were hardly a matter of real concern in a football world riddled with vast bungs and managerial corruption. Once more, a far higher standard of ethical behaviour was being de-manded of Bobby, simply because of his good name, than was applied to many other leading figures in the football world. In terms of sharp practice, he could not begin to compare with the likes of George Graham, Brian Clough or Terry Venables.

If anything, Bobby was naïve rather than unsavoury. Unlike some of his more sophisticated, politicized detractors, he could not see a conflict between his various roles in the football business. If his soccer school was based at Old Trafford, which happened to be the club of which he was a director, then so what? The only time he knew that the critics did have a genuine case was when it was revealed, in March 1989, that he had passed on a Cup Final ticket which had ended up on the black market. The revelation occurred after a major 10-month FA investigation into touting after widespread anxiety over the misappropriation of tickets during the 1988 Liverpool-Wimbledon Cup Final. There was some speculation that he might be banned from ever receiving Cup Final tickets again, but he escaped with a reprimand, having made a formal apology and said he was the victim of a misunderstanding. Bobby, who as a director of United was entitled to 30 tickets, said, 'It's my own fault. I'm very em-barrassed by this. It is true I gave a couple of tickets to friends and have been badly let down. This will make me more careful in future. I'm no tout myself, that's for certain.' But it was not the last time he was to be in trouble over prestige football tickets. In July 1990, he was caught up in a multi-million pound wrangle over the sale of World Cup tickets. The Cheshire-based travel firm Mundicorp, in which he had a 20 per cent stake, was accused of flogging cut-price seats at the expense of Novantour, the World Cup's official ticket agency. Novantour made a £12 million loss, while the Italian authorities were said to be 'furious that 600,000 of their tickets for overseas fans went unsold, as supporters grabbed cheap travel firm deals'. Bobby denied any involvement in the row: 'I have had no problems with Novantour, although I know Mundicorp has.'

As the Mundicorp row highlighted, Bobby Charlton had developed a bewildering array of different business interests during these years. He was involved not only with his soccer schools and the board of Manchester United, but he also served as a director of such diverse companies as Marketing Manchester, Matchwinner Sports, Twenty/Twenty Systems, Sports Ventures and the public relations and lobbying firm Citigate. Furthermore he was he official spokesman for Eurocard-Mastercard's football sponsorship programme and he endorsed Admiral sportswear. 'You don't get much better than Bobby. You can go anywhere in the world and people know who he is,' explained Lance Yates of Admiral when he announced the decision to recruit Bobby. With becoming modesty, however, Bobby did not feel compelled to follow the example of another Admiral backer, Ruud Gullit, who launched his own range of Ruud underwear and jackets.

In the mid-1990s Bobby began to wind down his many business dealings. In 1997 he bowed out of his soccer schools and consultancy business, now known as Bobby Charlton International after his company had incurred losses of some £200,000 the previous year. Not only was he approaching retirement age, but there was also an additional difficulty in that Conrad had now bought Sheffield United in a £10 million deal. His ferocious loyalty to Old Trafford meant that he did not feel comfortable with the new set-up. He did not, however, give up his business interests completely. Apart from remaining on the football board of Old Trafford, he was also a director of MSS Stockholders, a north-eastern metal company with a turnover of around £60 million, according to the latest accounts at Companies House.

Whatever is said about the two brothers' business careers, no-one could dispute that the two sons of Ashington had done extremely well for themselves. Indeed, it may be the very fact that they were from a coalmining background that drove them to be so concerned about seeking financial security. Having seen their own father struggle all his life, having shared a bed until they were 15, there is little doubt that they were haunted by the fear of poverty. All their 'earners' and deals were a way of ensuring they would never have to endure what Old Bob experienced.

Throughout their post-playing careers, Bobby and Jack were in constant demand by broadcasters, and were regular participants in the panel discussion at major games. But as always, the difference between the brothers was all too apparent. Jack, with his outspoken views and deep tactical awareness, was the far better analyst, while Bobby was constantly inhibited by his natural diplomacy. Ian St John, one of TV football's great figures, says of the pair: 'Bobby did some commentary for the BBC but he was murder at it because he did not want to criticize players, whereas Jack would be totally honest. I mean, Bobby had been one of the greats and he must have looked at some performances and thought, "That's useless." But he could not come out and say it. He is that kind of guy. He is a nice guy. He was worried about the feelings of others. But if Jack thought something was crap he would say so.' Kenneth Wolstenholme, the man whose commentary on the 1966 World Cup Final was immortalized by the phrase 'they think it's all over', told me: 'Bobby was not always used as a commentator because he was too bland. He would not attack anybody. But Jack always gave forthright answers.' None were more forthright than when he was discussing the Holland v Germany game on ITV during the 1990 World Cup, when Frank Rijkaard and Rudi Voller had a go at each and Rijkaard spat at his opponent.

'What about that Jack? What would you have done if Rijkaard had done that to you?'

'I'd have chinned him.'

Brian Moore paid this tribute to Jack's work as a commentator:

'ITV got great value out of Jack over many years as an opinionated panel member. His views were never less than forthright and positive, even if his tongue and brain found it impossible to get in tune when it came to dealing with players' names.' Ian St John remembers a few technical difficulties with Jack: 'As a commentator, Jack was outspoken, intelligent. But he simply did not understand that timing is everything in television. He did not seem to realize that you have only a very limited time to put your points across and then you have to shut up. The floor manager would tell him that there are 20 seconds to go, and yet he would still be rambling away. Once we were commentating during the European Championships in Sweden in 1992, and Elton Wellsby was the presenter. Jack was on about a player who always had a hard shot at free-kicks. And, typically, he could not remember the name. He kept clicking his fingers, saying, "It's the guy . . . you know . . . at Forest . . . you know him . . . that boy." Out of desperation I said, "Stuart Pearce." "That's him, that's the one." Then we were counted out. As soon as we were off the air, he said angrily "It wasn't Pearce, it was Johnny Metgod." But I had just said a name to get out.'

In his autobiography, published not long before his sad death, Brian Moore wrote, 'Jack Charlton is a champion of many parts, but he is not an advertisement for self-organization. He once almost missed the live ITV Coca-Cola Cup seni-final at Birmingham when he fell asleep behind the wheel of his car in the St Andrews car park. We found him, with five minutes to spare.' Moore also recalled how Jack had rung him in panic from Stockholm airport during the 1992 European Championships, explaining that he had lost his contact book and tournament accreditation. Moore suggested that Jack try lost property.

'Yes Brian, they had it. Can't tell you how relieved I am. Now, shouldn't we be getting along to the match?'

'Jack, the match is tomorrow.'

Moore later said that at the end of the championship, he received a call from the manager of Jack's hotel. 'Your friend, Mr Charlton, has checked out. But he has left a number of things in his room.

Could you collect them?' According to Moore's account, 'Jack had somehow managed to leave his room without a couple of shirts, some socks, a pullover, a collection of toiletries, a packet of small cigars and some papers.' Soon afterwards Brian Moore rang his producer in Stockholm, to check that Jack had arrived safely for the final edition of the programme. 'Don't talk to me about Jack Charlton,' she hissed, 'at the moment, we are scouring the whole of Stockholm looking for the taxi that brought him from the airport. He left his fishing rod in it.'

Bobby turned down offers of commentary work for the 1994 World Cup because he was tired, in his own words of being 'pulled around' by the broadcasters. But soon he had found a niche more suited to his talent for charm and courtesy, in Sky TV's long-running nostalgic programme *Bobby Charlton's Football Scrapbook*, which he co-presented with Dickie Davies, though the original idea had been for Michael Parkinson to front the show. It began in 1996 and in total 86 editions of the programme were made. Producer Mark Pierman gave me these memories of working with him. 'At our first meeting, he was very straightforward, very businesslike. And he was always like that, very punctual and professional. It was in my interests to look after him, make sure he had everything – as I would with any guest – but there was a wonderful humility about Bobby. On a couple of occasions, the taxi meant to meet him at the airport had not turned up and he would just make his own way to the studio. He would never complain about it. And he was very good about requests from other Sky programmes. I hated any feeling that the channel was taking advantage of him but he was always very straight if I put a request to him. "Yeah, I'll do it," he would say. He didn't want to let anyone down for any reason. Even when his mother died he was like that. I rang him up and said, "Look, we can easily cancel."

"No, no, no, I'll be absolutely fine. We'll get the programmes out of the way."

He was incredibly kind to me. Like one time he took me to a Manchester United game at Crystal Palace and throughout he would be saying: "Mark, are you all right? Do you want a drink? Something to eat?" It was those little touches that made him so special.'

Despite his advancing years, Bobby impressed Pierman with his vitality. 'Sometimes we did six shows in three days. His energy was quite incredible. For instance, he would fly down from Manchester at six in the morning, get to the studios at half-past eight, and then, after a bit of breakfast, he would be performing in front of the camera. He was incredibly well-organised. Another thing was his dignity. Occasionally, in the canteen, he would be telling a colourful story, and another footballer, in such circumstances, would have started effing, but Bobby wouldn't lower himself to that level in front of us.'

Pierman particularly remembers going with Dickie Davies and Bobby for an edition of the programme with Franz Beckenbauer, about the 1966 World Cup Final: 'I have never seen anyone with more respect for an individual than Franz had for Bobby. We recorded the pair of them together watching the 1966 Final and they had obviously never seen the game together before. There would be little incidents that cropped up, like Beckenbauer's annoyance at the way Hurst crashed into the German keeper Tilkowski in the first 10 minutes.

"We were very angry at the time," said Beckenbauer.

"Well," replied Bobby, "that's the way we play."

"Yes, but Tilkowski had badly hurt his ribs in training. Didn't you know that?"

"No," said Bobby.

Things like that emerged during the conversation. It was fascinating. Then Franz laid on this great meal for us in the Munich boardroom. He and Bobby obviously admired each other so much. It was just a brilliant day.'

According to Pierman, another player Bobby adored was Stanley Matthews, who was also a guest on the show. 'He loved listening to Stan talking about his fitness regime, how he used to starve himself during the season. There was a side to him that would just love to switch off and listen to the old stories of his great colleagues, great friends. He loved reminiscing, and Dickie Davies was very good at creating the right environment for him.' Interestingly, Bobby also enjoyed having on some of the more colourful characters of his era, such as Stan Bowles, Frank Worthington and Tony Currie, while Pierman says he also got on well with his old adversaries from Old Trafford, George Best and Denis Law, when they were on the show. The old animosity appeared to have faded. 'I know all the stories about George and Bobby but on our show, they got on very well,' says Pierman. 'They seemed to appreciate each other as individuals. George and Denis were obviously totally different characters to Bobby, but he had a fantastic sense of humour. He had a great laugh with them, especially when Stan Bowles said that he was always late out on to the field because he was listening to the result of the 2.45. Sir Alex Ferguson also came on, and Dickie asked him if he would swap his managerial career for Bobby's playing career and he instantly said yes. We were too embarrassed to ask the question in reverse of Bobby.' Pierman says the shows were unscripted, though he would provide Bobby with a few notes about the guest and the teams in the League at the time. But because the programme related to football, he was comfortable and relaxed. 'It was a simple format but it worked extremely well. And everyone we approached loved coming on the show. There was never any problem there.' Such words destroy Ron Atkinson's claims about Bobby's unpopularity in the football world. Interestingly, though, one of the few footballers Bobby would not have on the show was his own brother Jack, saying he would not 'feel comfortable' about it.

By the time Bobby began his *Football Scrapbook*, Jack had retired as Ireland manager. Qualification for USA had reinforced his image as Ireland's most popular figure and in May 1994, he was given the freedom of Dublin, an extremely rare honour for an Englishman. 'It would be impossible to overestimate the extent of Jack Charlton's popularity in Ireland. Today he will be made a freeman of Dublin, but already he is a freeman of every city, town, village and hamlet in the Republic,' wrote Con Houlihan of the *Dublin Evening Press*.

Houlihan then recounted a story of Charlton visiting a little village on the Cork-Kerry border late at night, long after licensing hours. A discreet knock on the pub door and Jack and his chauffeur were let in. 'Within five minutes the bar was more than full; a crowd had gathered outside. There were men, women and children who had got out of bed to see the Pied Piper. It was a famous night in that village. There was a Garda (Irish police) barracks nearby. If they had closed the pub that night, there would not have been blood on the streets, because there is only one street. But there would have been a lot of ill will.'

According to Maurice Setters, Jack had said that if the Republic lost to Northern Ireland in Belfast, then he would have resigned, and not without some relief. Now almost 60, Jack was feeling increasingly exhausted by the pressures of being an international manager. In January 1994, he suffered a rare bout of ill health brought on by a combination of stress and an ear infection. He had been driving himself too hard, both through his managerial work and all his speaking engagements.

It was time to wind down. The USA 94 campaign would be Jack's last on the world stage. It started in glorious style, as Ireland took on Italy at the Giants Stadium in New York in probably the most memorable game in the FAI's history. Before the match, the Irish players had been worried that their supporters would be far out-numbered by the vast number of Italian-Americans. But the moment they walked out on to the field amidst deafening roars from the crowd, they were embraced by a sea of green, white and gold tricolours. 'I don't think I have ever seen so many Irish shirts in my life,' says John Aldridge. Alan McLoughlin recalls: 'The game against Italy was amazing. We had trained the day before in the Giants stadium, and we found it a strange place because it was really on top of you. But the next day, when we went out to warm up, we just could not believe it. I had never seen anything like it. The hairs on the back of my neck stood up as we came out. It was just unbelievable. There were obviously thousands more Irish than Italians.' To the delight of the crowd, the result matched the Irish enthusiasm, as a Ray Houghton strike in the 12th minute secured a 1–0 victory. Maurice Setters remembers Jack being remarkably phlegmatic at probably the biggest triumph of his career. 'At the final whistle it was just phenomenal, one of the greatest moments of my footballing life. But the surprising thing was that Jack did not change much at all. He was quite quiet afterwards. He was often like that. He rarely went over the top, even when we had a fantastic victory like that.'

Roy Keane, fast emerging as a truly world-class footballer, was one of the stars of that victory – interestingly it was Jack Charlton who suggested to Sir Alex Ferguson that he purchase Keane from Forest – while Paul McGrath, despite his increasingly dodgy knees, was a Trojan in midfield. But perhaps the real hero of the evening was the unheralded Tommy Coyne of Celtic who played as a lone striker up front and ran till he dropped. As always, Jack had been confident of winning before the game, despite the Italians' awesome World Cup reputation. Prime Minister Albert Reynolds had met him at dinner the night before the match: 'I said to him, "What do you think the result will be?" I suggested that a draw would be a good Irish performance but Jack would have none of it. He said he thought we would do better and win.'

Sadly, the rest of the tournament did not match this high point. In their next group match against Mexico, in the boiling cauldron of Orlando, Ireland lost 2–1. With his temperature raised by the heat, Jack became involved in a serious row with FIFA, after becoming infuriated by a delay in allowing John Aldridge to come on to the field as a substitute. The row was caused by a communication problem between the Egyptian FIFA official and the Irish bench over whether Aldridge was legally registered to play. His temper as high as Jack's, Aldridge yelled as the official, 'You're a cheat, a fucking cheat.' As Jack intervened, he was physically shoved by the official and fired back some choice Geordie words. This altercation led to his being fined £10,000 by FIFA and banned from the touchline, while Aldridge was given a penalty of £1,500. FIFA's animosity towards Jack had already been roused when he had demanded the right, against World Cup regulations, to be able to throw bottles of water on to the pitch for his players in order to combat dehydration. The move was sensible, in view of the stifling conditions, but Jack's hectoring manner did not endear him to the World Cup hierarchy. 'FIFA cannot tolerate officials being insulted. Jack Charlton will have to sit in the stand. It is only a one-match ban, but there is no appeal against this decision.' The FIFA representative added: 'Jack Charlton is a funny man,' words that have been echoed by many down the decades. It was a tribute to Jack's huge following in Ireland that, when a public collection was held for him to pay off the fine, more than £100,000 was raised. Again, reflecting his generous heart, Jack decided that the money should go to the family of Andres Escobar, the Colombian player murdered on his return home, on the alleged grounds that he had scored the own goal which put his country out of the tournament.

As Maurice Setters recalls, Jack's touchline ban for the Norway game did not worry him too much, as arrangements had been made for him to communicate from the stand by telephone with the Irish dugout. 'The first time he got through to me, I asked him, "What's it like up there, Jack?"

"Bloody great, air conditioning, gin and tonic. No need to throw bottles around up here."'

Ireland's result was pretty good as well, a typically Charltonesque 0–0 draw ensuring Ireland's qualification for the next phase. But there, the World Cup dream ended, as poor mistakes by Terry Phelan and Packie Bonner saw Holland win 1–0. 'Jack was not too downcast,' says Setters. 'He was proud of what we had achieved. That's what was great about Jack. He'd built up such fantastic team spirit.' That spirit was reflected the night of the Dutch defeat, as the Irish players celebrated with their fans. Andy Townsend recorded in his World Cup diary the reaction of Teddy Sheringham, who was in the USA at the time, to the sight of the Ireland squad in full party mood. 'Teddy can't get over the singing of the Irish supporters and the way they are mingling with the players as if they are the best of pals. "This is special all right," he says. "Can you imagine standing here amongst English fans after we had just gone out of the World Cup? They would probably want to have a go."'

Until 1994 Jack had been a master of timing his departures. He always knew when he might be in danger of outstaying his welcome. Looking back, he should have left on a high note after the US campaign, basking in the warm glow of another strong campaign. Even Jack himself said in his column in the *Sunday Press*: 'I don't know if I want to go through all this again. Maybe I'm getting a bit weary over the whole business, maybe my thoughts are not as clear as they should be, maybe I'm not as sharp as I was.' But he decided to stay on for the next European Championship programme. The result was a dismal anticlimax, as Ireland failed to qualify after some uncharacteristically poor results, including, most notably, a shameful 0–0 draw in Liechtenstein, one of the tiniest footballing nations in Europe, and a narrow 2–1 win against Latvia. As John Aldridge admits, the squad was in decline: 'Towards the end of Jack's reign, it began to go wrong, but that was because the team was getting old. We were probably past our sell-by date on the international scene, myself included.' There was also a sense of Jack losing his grip on the discipline and focus of the squad. During the week-long preparations for the match against Austria, Jack disappeared, and with Maurice Setters on duty with the Under-21s, Jack's own son was left in charge of a friendly against a local team. Little wonder there was talk that week of late-night drinking in Limerick's nightclubs.

Despite the poor results, Ireland managed to get a play-off spot against Holland, the match played at Anfield. Right to the end, Jack was displaying his unique character, as the Dutch coach, Guus Hiddink revealed: 'I couldn't believe it. There were 10 minutes to go before the kick-off and there was Jack Charlton talking to me about fishing and golf. I will take that memory with me always.' Sadly, Jack could take no happy memories from this game, as the Irish went down 2–0. But the Republic's fans, recognizing that they were probably about to lose their greatest-ever manager, stood cheering him at the Kop long after the teams had departed. Again, Jack should have probably announced his resignation that night but, clinging to office, he dragged out his exit for more than a month, eventually being summoned to Dublin to meet the FAI executive, where he was told point blank by the five-member committee that they wanted him to go. It was a sorry, undignified end to what had been a glorious reign.

But almost immediately the sourness passed, to be replaced by a heartfelt appreciation of what Jack had achieved in Ireland. Thanks to his success, football in Ireland was enjoying an unprecedented boom. The numbers playing the sport had trebled over ten years from 65,000 in 1986 to 175,000 in 1996. During the same period, the number of registered teams had gone up from 4,000 to 10,000. As Mick McCarthy, his successor as manager, put it, 'It seemed an incredible fairytale to be part of Jack's glory days as a player but the spin-offs for the game in Ireland have been immense.' And Jack's influence had been felt far beyond football. He had given the Irish nation a new sense of pride, unity and identity. As a tribute to all he had done, he was made an honorary citizen of Ireland, and a statue – complete with fishing rod – was erected to him in Cork airport. Albert Reynolds, the former Taoiseach, perhaps put it best: 'Jack's the man who has done for Ireland what none of us politicians could possibly achieve.'

While Jack was being showered with honours from the Irish, Bobby had received the ultimate award from his native land, when in 1994, he was made a knight of the realm. As usual, Jack, who was training with the Irish team in the US World Cup, was publicly diplomatic about his brother's elevation: 'When I see Bobby over here, I shall shake his hand and say, "Hello, Sir Robert Charlton." Bobby has been a great ambassador for his country since he finished playing in the 1970s and, deep down, I always suspected it might happen to him.' Similarly, Bobby wrote several articles giving balanced praise to Jack's record in Ireland, naming his motivational talent, his experience of coaching and his single-mindedness as his qualities. In one piece, however, in the *Sunday Telegraph* in June 1994 there was a barb towards the end: 'I must be honest, though, Jack is not perfect, you know. Because he is abrasive, he falls out with people left, right and centre. He has never changed over the years. You could easily light his fuse. I think, because of that, he was intensely competitive when he became a manager.'

If Jack had never changed since he was a child, Bobby had certainly been transformed, growing up from the shy Busby Babe of the 1950s into the elder statesman of world soccer by the 1990s. On this journey, Bobby had shown the courage to overcome two of the greatest fears of his Manchester United youth: his dislike of public speaking and his immediate post-Munich fear of flying. Ironically, those are the two areas which have taken up so much of his working time in recent years.

By the end of the last decade, Sir Bobby had become an old hand as an ambassador and campaigner. His soccer coaching took him all over the world, particularly to Africa and the Far East. In 1994, for instance, John Major brought him to Johannesburg on a mission to boost the sports development programme for black South Africans. When he went to Beijing in 1996 to assist the Chinese Under-18 squad, his arrival in the country was watched by more than 300 million people on television. As one Chinese official discreetly remarked, this was far more than used to tune in for Chairman Mao's speeches. So Jimmy Hill was not far wrong when he once described Sir Bobby as 'the most famous Englishman in the world'.

His long association with Manchester made Bobby the obvious front man for the city's bid for the Olympic Games in 2000. Though that venture failed, it did pave the wave for the city's successful bid to host the Commonwealth Games in 2002. And Bobby's talent as an ambassador became all the more obvious. A speech in support of Manchester in the intellectually rarefied surroundings of the Oxford Union – just the sort of place that would have intimidated Bobby in his playing days – was described thus in the *Mail on Sunday*: 'He walked to the despatch box, slipped on his thin-rimmed spectacles, thrust his hands into his pockets and spoke, virtually without the benefit of note, for some 20 minutes. There were no oratorical tricks, no catchpenny gimmicks, just the gentle vowels of Ashington, tinged with the tones of his adopted city, drifting around the hall.' After he sat down, one undergraduate turned to a neighbour and said, "That Bobby Charlton is some performer, isn't he?"'

With all this experience he was also an obvious figurehead for England's ultimately humiliating attempt to win the right to stage the 2006 World Cup. 'He was top of everyone's list,' says Alec McGivan. In retrospect, that bid was doomed from the start because of the English FA's lack of political influence in UEFA and FIFA, and, perhaps more importantly, because of the perceived notion that England was breaking the 'gentleman's agreement' with Germany, whereby Germany agreed to support England's bid for Euro 96 in return for England's backing for the 2006 World Cup. Though former FA chairman Sir Bert Millichip denied that he had ever concluded such a deal with Germany, his statement was never seen as convincing, with the result that the 'gentleman's agreement' became a sticking point for England's bid. Throughout the campaign England's representatives had to put up with the charge that they were acting dishonourably in breaking their word to Germany, something that Bobby, with his keen sense of his own reputation for integrity, found hard to take. Alec McGivan, who as the chief executive of the 2006 bid had 'long conversations' with Bobby about this issue, says that Bobby's view of the 'gentleman's agreement' was this: 'Bobby is an honourable man. If he felt there had definitely been an agreement that everyone knew about and it had all been above board, then Bobby would not have done the bid. Bobby, like me, felt that Sir Bert Millichip must have had some sort of cosy chat with the Germans, but Sir Bert was never able to articulate exactly what had happened. Bobby felt that unless anyone could tell him exactly what this was all about, he had to assume it was a pig's dinner and a muddle, and so England had just as much right to bid as the Germans. We talked about it endlessly. We had thought that the issue would just slip away over the four years of campaigning because people would probably get used to our bidding. But that never happened. The Germans were very clever, everywhere they went they kept saying, "What about the gentleman's agreement?"

And we never got away from the issue.' Graham Kelly, former chief executive of the FA, told me that the fault for this mess lay with Millichip. 'Sir Bert has denied that the agreement ever existed. But the problem was created by Millichip being too buddy, buddy with the Germans. He wanted to keep in with his German friends and with UEFA. Millichip was an old man and wanted to stay involved with UEFA.' The international businessman and sports promoter, Jarvis Astaire, goes even further, claiming that he was present in December 1993 in Las Vegas at the time of the draw for the 1994 World Cup, 'when it was made clear to me by Bert Millichip that the FA would be supporting the German bid for 2006 in return for Germany supporting us as hosts in 1996.' In his memoirs, Astaire says that later he spelt this out in an awkward conversation with Bobby, who had explained to Astaire that he was unsure about the status of the so-called agreement. 'Bobby pointed out to me that the agreement between Millichip and the Germans had never been minuted, but, as Millichip told me recently, there were many arrangements he made during the time of his chairmanship which were never minuted yet the FA acted upon them.'

After FIFA decided to award the World Cup to Germany, the FA was attacked, with some justification, for wasting £10 million on a bid that was certain to fail. 'It's a complete nonsense, a scandalous waste of money,' said one FA official after the flop. Bobby, who was paid £250,000 plus lucrative expenses for his role as President of the English bid, was also criticised by some for his lack of both charisma and judgement. 'When you put the footballing knight with thunder in his boots into his a lounge suit, he's as dour as porridge,' wrote Martin Kelner of the *Guardian* during the campaign. Martin Lipton, now chief football writer of the *Mirror,* makes this interesting comparison between Bobby and his old rival Beckenbauer, who was fronting the German bid. "Franz is a brilliant operator. As soon as he comes into a room, he picks his target, cruises across to them, does the business and then returns to base. He is magnificent at it, a master room-worker. Bobby is not instinctively like that. He does not quite have that same awesome, ultra-confident presence and bearing.' Lipton says that, at the start of the campaign, Bobby could be a stumbling performer: 'The worst speech I saw him give was the night before the 1998 World Cup at the British Embassy in Paris. He gave his speech, sat down, then suddenly stood up and said, "Oh, I forgot to say, we're backing England for the World Cup in 2006." He forget to mention it because he was not very good. Later he got better because he gave so many speeches.' But Lipton's most persistent charge against Bobby is that he showed a 'stunning degree of naivety' during the campaign. 'He never realized how the game of politics is played. He was too honourable, decent. Because he is a very nice chap, he thought when people said they would support him, they actually meant it. Because he himself is genuine, he had the mistaken belief that others would not lie to him. And, having committed himself to the bid, he was desperate to win it. He took any opposition to England's bid very personally. At times, he and I were not even talking because he felt I was not being supportive enough.' In an example of the way Bobby personalised the issue, he even fell out with his old England team mate, the Southampton winger Terry Paine, who had emigrated to South Africa and was working on their bid. According to Lipton, Bobby sometimes refused even to acknowledge Paine's presence when they ran into each other, while Paine admits there was 'a bit of frostiness in their relationship.'

But these were all the failings of a passionately loyal, patriotic man. Even if he was perhaps naïve at times in ignoring the hard realities of sporting politics, he threw himself into the campaign with total dedication, travelling over 500,000 miles in his quest to bring the World Cup finals to England. In a sense Bobby's behaviour was similar to the way he played at Manchester United, perhaps lacking in cunning, perhaps too intense, but never less than wholehearted in its commitment. Almost 50 years earlier, Jimmy Murphy had used the phrase 'get stuck in' with his young charges and that is exactly what Bobby had done for the FA. Just as he had done with Manchester United, Bobby felt a personal loyalty to the bid, which cynics sometimes laughed at. When a FIFA committee, after visiting

England's facilities, rated them behind those of Germany and South Africa, Bobby's sense of passionate injustice was palpable. He told the House of Commons Culture Select Committee on 8 March 2001: 'We had taken great lengths over a period of time and put a lot of effort into taking people to see what we had to offer.' He continued, 'I felt, like everyone else on our committee, a sense of outrage, that we had been insulted. I was really insulted for the young people at Sunderland, the young people at Derby, who were waiting out in the rain for those people (the FIFA team) waving flags.'

But Bobby was no histrionic, oversensitive celebrity, as Alec McGivan remembers: 'Everywhere he goes he gets feted by the rich and famous. He gets well looked after and he is used to staying in five-star hotels. But he did not ever complain if things were a bit awry. Sometimes when we were travelling the places were not all that great. During the World Cup in France in 1998, we were staying in an absolute dump because trying to get rooms in France at the last minute had proved very difficult. I felt really embarrassed to see Sir Bobby Charlton in it, but he put me at my ease, saying, "Don't worry about it."' The *Daily Telegraph* sports columnist Sue Mott, who travelled with him on a trip to Malta, wrote: 'His vim is astonishing.' And she, like McGivan, was impressed by his lack of self-importance, for he had been forced to wear the same clothes for three days after British Airways lost his luggage. 'Anyone else, especially at 61 and ever more especially a global superstar, might have been tempted to shriek prima donna-ly at minions, demanding help, sleep, spoiling and a lay-over in a five-star hotel. As it was, he climbed aboard KM601 to Malta with his modest parcels and demeanour to fulfil his obligations to our nation.'

Graham Kelly has this analysis of Bobby's contribution. 'We had two great assets on our side, Sir Bobby and Wembley stadium. Unfortunately Wembley fell by the wayside pretty quickly but Bobby kept going. He was the human face of our bid, able to charm presidents and street kids alike. He had that magical touch throughout the campaign, whether it be walking into senior boardrooms or coaching kids in the middle of Africa. We felt very guilty about the schedule that was imposed on Bobby, not just the flying, but all the duties he had to perform in every venue. So, even if he arrived late at night, there would be a press conference the next morning at 7.30am with Sir Bobby. The demands on his time were almost never-ending wherever we were. It didn't really matter what the rest of us did, if Bobby Charlton was on the trip, it was a success.'

Contrary to the view of some of Bobby's critics, Kelly maintains that Bobby 'had this astonishing charisma, derived from both his stature and from his innate dignity. It is something I personally have only ever seen in one other person, Pele. He is far bigger than anyone else in British soccer. Bobby had this tremendous love of football; that is the essential heartbeat of the man. I went on several of the trips with him to Africa and South America. Though a very private man, he was easy company, modest and engaging. But what was so impressive was the way he handled himself. I remember when we went to Bolivia, we were ushered into this massive reception room, where there were 55 TV cameras. Now when I spoke, they were, of course, switched off. But as soon as Bobby got up, on they went. And he was brilliant in front of this audience, really speaking from the heart and getting all the right points across. He might speak in a homespun, down-to-earth way, but he was magnificent then.'

Alec McGivan, the man who saw him even more closely, sharing most of those 500,000 miles, says: 'Being with Bobby is rather like being with royalty. I was with him several times with John Major and Tony Blair, and both prime ministers were obviously in awe of the guy. He is very modest, very gracious about it, but everyone is excited about meeting Bobby Charlton. When we went to Argentina, two interesting things happened. The president of Argentina, Carlos Menem, invited us to the Presidential Palace. The first thing he did there was to start kicking a ball around with Bobby in the reception area. Now Menem is actually quite a skilful ball player so they were doing ball juggling. The other fascinating thing that happened was we went to a big lunch at the British Embassy for various Argentinian dignitaries, and one of the people there was

Rattin, who had been sent off in 1966. Rattin came across the room and Bobby got up from his table. They looked at each other. Then there was this huge smile and they went up and gave each other the biggest bear hug I have ever seen. And the whole room applauded. It was such a fantastic moment. It brought a lump to the throat. They had not seen each other for decades but they came together like long-lost friends.'

'Wherever we went, he would also insist that we did things with local kids, we would do street children's programmes, coaching. The British Embassy would set all this up before we got there. Throughout the bid he never lost his enthusiasm for kicking a ball about. He was fantastic with kids. In Bangkok he was asked to sponsor a street kids' football tournament. When we went to Mali, one of the poorest countries in the world, he did a superb training programme with kids there. He was excellent at all that. He loves Africa and Asia. He genuinely likes meeting people wherever they come from. He is naturally quite a shy person, but over the years his fame has made him more comfortable in public arenas. He has a very engaging smile when he walks into a room. He is very professional as a lobbyist. He would always say to me, "Is there anyone I haven't spoken to?" or "I haven't been over there, I'd better speak to them."'

McGivan is interesting on the last days of the campaign, when it was obvious that England did not have the votes, yet Bobby's fighting spirit shone through. 'I had a private meeting with Bobby and Tony Banks at the House of Commons. I said to Tony, "We've got to see the FA board tomorrow, and I think we should recommend pulling out because we cannot win and the last week is going to be hell for everyone. We are just going to get attacked by the British press right, left and centre." Tony said, "On balance, I think you're right." But we agreed we could not do anything until we talked to Bobby. I knew that Bobby would absolutely hate this idea, not because he thought we could win but because Bobby believes that you should never give up, that there is always a chance. But after a long discussion, we agreed that we would go to the FA board and recommend that we withdraw.' But the FA rejected this advice, and told McGivan and the team to press ahead. 'We went back to my office, and Bobby said, "That's it, that's what I wanted. I know we can't win but I want to see this through." I got all the staff together. A lot of them were a lot younger than me, and they thought it was fantastic working with Bobby. I said, "You know we are not going to win this. We are going to have an awful week. There will be media everywhere. We have to put a brave face on it." A few of them were in tears. Bobby was there, and he gave a talk and he made them feel a million dollars. He said, "Come on, we're going to see this through." It was real Dunkirk spirit. I was quite choked by it. You could tell that the last thing he wanted to do was give up. In that sense he was such a great guy. You have to admire him.'

But, unlike 1966, the Charlton fighting spirit was not enough. FIFA awarded the tournament to Germany, with South Africa their closest challengers. England finished nowhere. 'Before I die, if there is one thing I really, really want, it is to bring back the World Cup to my homeland,' said Bobby in one of his speeches. As Britain's sports administration stumbles from one crisis to another, that dream looks more distant than ever.

Epilogue

Now in their mid-sixties and almost forty years after their World Cup triumph, the Charlton brothers remain household names across the country. Even in semi-retirement, they are rarely out of the spotlight. Jack continues to be in huge demand as a pundit and performer, his distinctive Geordie tones echoing through car finance advertisements or commentaries on Channel 5. Typical of the grip he still has on the public imagination was an appearance he made in 2001 at Belfast's new Waterfront Hall, a vast auditorium which he sold out weeks in advance, something that few other English sporting celebrities could achieve. Meanwhile, Bobby Charlton remains the ambassadorial figurehead for Manchester United and England, continuing to attract the headlines with his pronouncements. He was embroiled in controversy, for instance, when, true to his patriotic traditionalism, he strongly opposed the appointment of a foreigner as England's manager and came under fire from George Best, who told him he was 'so wrong'. On a less disputed note, he was the front man for Manchester United's business and merchandising link up with the US baseball team the New York Yankees. Like Jack, his services are always wanted by event organisers, so – just to choose some examples from his multifarious activities – he can be found backing road safety campaigners in

Cheshire, presenting the trophy in the National Health Service football competition 'The Hospital Cup', lending his support to the National Football Museum in Preston, helping the charity Football Aid raise funds for diabetes research, and organising soccer coaching for youngsters in Great Yarmouth.

The compelling and contrasting personalities of the Charlton brothers obviously explain part of their appeal: Jack, the hilarious individualist who says what he likes and likes what he says; Bobby, the self-effacing embodiment of those values of decency and service which seem all too absent from modern Britain. But the appeal also rests in their remarkable contribution to British and Irish football as both players and managers. And this prompts the question: just how good were the Charlton brothers?

As a centre-half, Jack must be in the top-ten list of all-time England defenders. Though not in the same class as his colleague Bobby Moore or Billy Wright of an earlier generation, he could match most of the subsequent stars of the England defence, such as Terry Butcher or Tony Adams. At his peak in the mid-1960s, he was certainly the second best in the country after Moore, while there has probably never been a better defensive header of a ball than Jack. And he still remains the most capped English player at Leeds, a remarkable record for a man who did not get the international call-up until his late twenties.

Bobby, though, has a justifiable claim to be regarded as the greatest English footballer of all time. As a goalscorer, despite still holding the record for the highest total of strikes, his ratio of goals to games is not quite as impressive as Jimmy Greaves or Gary Lineker. Further down the scale, he is not in the same category as the likes of Tommy Lawton (23 in 22 games) or his Manchester United colleague Tommy Taylor (16 in 19 games). In the league, his ratio is even more disappointing, sliding down to one in three, which is far exceeded by contemporaries such as Roger Hunt, Jimmy Greaves and Geoff Hurst and by more recent stars such as Ian Rush, Alan Shearer and Michael Owen.

Yet it has to be remembered that, apart from his first brief spell at

Manchester before 1960, Bobby Charlton was never and an out-and-out striker. Rather, he played as a winger and then, more creatively and successfully, as an attacking midfielder. In this context, it is unfair to judge him alongside the pure goalscorers. Again, on the wing, he could not be bracketed with the two greatest practitioners of that art, Stanley Matthews and Tom Finney, whom Bill Shankly famously said 'could have played in a concrete overcoat.' But in his deep-lying forward role, there has probably never been an England player to match Bobby Charlton for skill, pace, vision, and explosive shooting. Only Beckham today comes near, but, for all his huge influence over the present England team, he cannot begin to compare with Charlton for goals scored. And he has a long way to go before he can equal Charlton's twelve years as an international. The charismatic footballer and TV analyst, Rodney Marsh, argues: Bobby Charlton was the greatest midfield player that Britain has ever produced, without a shadow of a doubt. Not only that, he was probably the best naturally two-footed player in the history of the game. Talented as Beckham is, he could never do what Bobby did in the centre of the park. He could run with and off the ball, his movement was supreme and he could find spaces where none existed.'

The crucial point about Bobby Charlton – and to an extent Jack – is that they did their best on the highest stage when it really mattered. It is all very well for the nostalgia brigade to wax lyrical about Lawton, Matthews, Wright and Finney, but it should be noted that English football went through its darkest period when these players were the heart of the national side, being beaten 1–0 by the USA in the 1950 World Cup, thrashed twice by Hungary in 1953 and 1954 and doing nothing in international tournaments through the 1950s. In contrast, it is surely no coincidence that when the Charltons were at their peak, England won the greatest prize in football.

As a club manager, Bobby was a disaster and Jack nothing more than average. Though Jack achieved promotion with both Middlesbrough and Sheffield Wednesday, he never looked like winning a major title and his sorry performance at Newcastle, when he alienated both fans and players, is undoubtedly a blot on his career. As to his league record, he cannot be mentioned in the same breath as club giants such as Alex Ferguson, Brian Clough or Bob Paisley. Yet, thanks to his decade in charge of the Republic of Ireland, he deserves to be named as probably the second best international manager the British Isles have ever seen. Two World Cup qualifications, a World Cup quarter-final and a European championship quarter-final far exceeds the achievements of Glenn Hoddle, Sir Walter Winterbottom, Craig Brown, Ron Greenwood or John Giles. Some say that Jack had a good pool of Irish players to choose from but that has always been true of the Irish. Jack was the first to organise them into a proper team. Indeed, according to commentator Alan Green, Johan Cruyff thought Jack Charlton was 'one of the very best of international managers.'

There can be no dispute that Sir Alf Ramsey has to be named as the greatest for winning the World Cup, but there are two others who could challenge Jack to the title Best British Isles manager. One is Bobby Robson, who took England to both a quarter-final in the World Cup in 1986 and a semi-final in 1990, and, with a fraction of luck, could have won the trophy in either of those years. But I would put him slightly behind Jack, not only because he had a much greater number of players to choose from, but also because there was often an air of crisis and panic about his reign, something that could never be said about Jack's Irish years. Apart from Ramsey, the one manager who might deserve to rank higher than Jack is Billy Bingham, who took tiny Northern Ireland to two successive World Cup finals in 1982 and 1986 with less talented players than Jack had at his disposal. Interestingly, as with Jack, Bingham's club record with Everton, Linfield, Plymouth, Southport and Mansfield gave no indication of the heroics he would achieve on the international stage.

Whatever the merits and controversies of the lives of Jack and Bobby Charlton, the British Isles owes them both a deep debt of gratitude. Without them, the sporting history of these islands would have been much poorer.

Career Appendix

SIR BOBBY CHARLTON

- Born Ashington, Northumberland, 11 October 1937.
- Started playing at East Northumberland Schools.
- Represented England at Schoolboy Level (scored on his debut) before signing for Manchester United as an amateur in January 1953.
- Manchester United won the Youth Cup three years running with Bobby in the team 1953–4, 1954–5 and 1955–6.
- Signed professional forms at Manchester United on his 17th birthday (11 October 1954).
- Made his Manchester United debut on the 6 October 1956 at Old Trafford against Charlton Athletic in place of the injured Tommy Taylor. Manchester United won 4–2 with Bobby scoring two goals.
- Played as an inside left/outside left/centre forward.
- Was one of the survivors of the Munich Air Disaster in 1958.
- Retired from playing for Manchester United on the 28 April 1973 at Stamford Bridge against Chelsea.
- Playing record with Manchester United:

Competition	Appearances (as sub)	Goals scored
League	604 (2)	199
FA Cup	79	19
League Cup	24	7

Europe	45	22
FA Charity Shield	3	2
Totals	755 (2)	249

- Came out of retirement to play for one season at Preston North End in 1974–75 re-registering in May 1974.

Competition	Appearances	Goals scored
League	38	8
FA Cup	4	1
League Cup	3	1
Totals	45	10

- Made his Full England debut on 19 April 1958 at Hampden Park against Scotland in the Home Championship. England won 4–0 with Bobby scoring England's third goal.
- Made England Captain for the first time on 6 November 1968 when England played Romania in Bucharest.
- Retired from International football after defeat on 14 June 1970 in the World Cup Quarter-Final defeat by West Germany in Leon 3–2. (He was substituted when England were winning.)

Sir Bobby Charlton Managerial Record
- Appointed manager of Preston North End on 4 May 1973.
- Re-registered as a player in May 1974 becoming Player–Manager.
- Resigned after one match of the 1975–76 season after a dispute with the club's Directors over the transfer of John Bird to Newcastle United.
- Record as Manager of Preston North End:

Season 1973–74	P	W	D	L	F	A
Division 2	42	9	14	19	40	42
FA Cup	1	0	0	1	0	1
League Cup	2	0	1	1	1	3

Season 1974–75	P	W	D	L	F	A
Division 3	46	19	11	16	63	56
FA Cup	4	2	1	1	8	3
League Cup	3	2	0	1	3	1

Season 1975–76	P	W	D	L	F	A
Division 3	1	1	0	0	2	1

Complete Record	P	W	D	L	F	A
League Matches	89	29	25	35	105	99
FA Cup Matches	5	2	1	2	8	4
League Cup Matches	5	2	1	2	4	4

- Was appointed Caretaker Manager of Wigan Athletic on 4 April 1983 after the departure of Larry Lloyd. He stayed in the post until the season ended.
- Record as Caretaker Manager of Wigan Athletic:

Season 1983–84	P	W	D	L	F	A
Division 3	9	2	3	4	10	11

Playing records held by Sir Bobby Charlton:
- Most appearances in total for Manchester United – 752 (2)
- Most goals in total for Manchester United – 247
- Most League appearances for Manchester United – 604 (2)
- Most League goals for Manchester United – 199
- Most FA Cup appearances for Manchester United – 79
- Most capped Manchester United player – 106
- Most goals in total for England – 49

Honours won by Sir Bobby Charlton:
- Schoolboy and Youth International for England
- Under-23 England Caps – 6
- Full England Caps – 106
- Footballer of the Year 1966
- European Footballer of the Year 1966
- League Championship Winner 1957, 1965 and 1967
- FA Cup Winner 1963
- FA Cup Runner Up 1957
- European Cup Winner 1968
- Awarded OBE in 1969
- Awarded CBE in 1974
- Knighted in 1994

JACK CHARLTON

- Born Ashington, Northumberland, 8 May 1935.
- Started playing at Ashington YMCA and for Ashington Welfare.
- Joined Leeds United as youth player (ground staff) in 1950.
- Signed professional forms at Leeds United on 17th birthday (8 May 1952).
- Made his Leeds United debut on 25 April 1953 at Doncaster Rovers in a 1–1 draw.
- Missed large parts of the next two seasons as he was on national service with the Horse Guards Regiment.
- Played as a centre forward (early career)/centre half.
- Retired from playing career on 28 April 1973 at the Dell against Southampton.
- Playing record with Leeds United:

Competition	Appearances	Goals scored
League	629	70
FA Cup	52	8
League Cup	35	7
Europe	56	10
FA Charity Shield	1	1
Totals	**773**	**96**

- Made full England debut on 10 April 1965 at Wembley against Scotland in the Home Championship. England drew 2–2 but Jack's brother Bobby scored one of England's goals.
- Scored his first England goal on 26 June 1966 against Finland in Helsinki in a 3–0 win.
- Retired from International football after a 1–0 win against Czechoslovakia on 11 June 1970.

Jack Charlton Managerial Record
- Appointed as manager of Middlesbrough on 7 May 1973.
- Resigned as manager on 21 April 1977.
- Record as Manager of Middlesbrough:

Season 1973–74	P	W	D	L	F	A
Division 2	42	27	11	4	77	30
FA Cup	2	1	0	1	2	1
League Cup	3	1	1	1	3	3

Season 1974–75	P	W	D	L	F	A
Division 1	42	18	12	12	54	40
FA Cup	6	3	2	1	7	3
League Cup	5	3	1	1	6	3

Season 1975–76	P	W	D	L	F	A
Division 1	42	15	10	17	46	45
FA Cup Matches	2	0	1	1	2	3
League Cup Matches	5	4	0	1	8	5

Season 1976–77	P	W	D	L	F	A
Division 1	37	12	10	15	34	43
FA Cup Matches	1	0	0	1	1	2
League Cup Matches	4	2	1	1	5	2

Complete Record	P	W	D	L	F	A
League Matches	163	72	48	43	211	158
FA Cup Matches	14	6	4	4	16	9
League Cup Matches	14	8	2	4	18	13

- Appointed as manager of Sheffield Wednesday on 8 October 1977.
- Resigned on 27 May 1983
- Record as Manager of Sheffield Wednesday:

Season 1977–78	P	W	D	L	F	A
Division 3	36	15	11	10	44	39
FA Cup	2	1	0	1	3	4
League Cup	2	1	0	1	1	1

Season 1978–79	P	W	D	L	F	A
Division 3	46	13	19	14	53	53
FA Cup	9	2	6	1	14	11
League Cup	4	2	0	2	2	2

Season 1979–80	P	W	D	L	F	A
Division 3	46	21	16	9	81	47
FA Cup Matches	2	1	0	1	3	3
League Cup Matches	2	1	0	1	5	4

Season 1980–81	P	W	D	L	F	A
Division 2	42	17	8	17	53	51
FA Cup Matches	1	0	0	1	1	2
League Cup Matches	4	2	1	1	7	4

Season 1981–82	P	W	D	L	F	A
Division 2	42	20	10	12	55	51
FA Cup Matches	1	0	0	1	1	3
League Cup Matches	14	2	0	1	2	3

Season 1982–83	P	W	D	L	F	A
Division 2	42	16	15	11	60	47
FA Cup Matches	8	4	3	1	16	19
League Cup Matches	5	3	1	1	6	4

Complete Record	P	W	D	L	F	A
League Matches	254	102	79	73	346	288
FA Cup Matches	23	8	9	6	36	29
League Cup Matches	21	9	5	7	23	21

- Appointed as caretaker manager of Middlesbrough on 28 March 1984 until the end of the season.
- Record as Caretaker Manager of Middlesbrough:

Complete Record	P	W	D	L	F	A
League Matches	9	3	3	3	9	10

- Appointed as manager of Newcastle United in May 1984.
- Resigned on 10 August 1985.
- Record as Manager of Newcastle United:

Complete Record	P	W	D	L	F	A
League Matches	42	15	13	16	55	70
FA Cup Matches	4	2	1	1	6	5
League Cup Matches	2	0	1	1	2	4

- Appointed as manager of the Republic of Ireland in February 1986.
- Resigned as manager of the Republic of Ireland in December 1995.
- Record as Manager of Republic of Ireland:

Year	Venue	Opponents	Score	Competition
1986	Dublin	Wales	0–1	
	Dublin	Uruguay	1–1	
	Reykjavik	Iceland	2–1	
	Reykjavik	Czechoslovakia	1–0	
	Brussels	Belgium	2–2	European Championship Qual
	Dublin	Scotland	0–0	European Championship Qual
	Warsaw	Poland	0–1	
1987	Glasgow	Scotland	1–0	European Championship Qual
	Sofia	Bulgaria	1–2	World Cup Qualifier
	Dublin	Belgium	0–0	European Championship Qual
	Dublin	Brazil	1–0	
	Luxembourg	Luxembourg	2–0	European Championship Qual
	Dublin	Luxembourg	2–1	European Championship Qual
	Dublin	Bulgaria	2–0	World Cup Qualifier
	Dublin	Israel	5–0	
1988	Dublin	Romania	2–0	
	Dublin	Yugoslavia	2–0	
	Dublin	Poland	3–1	
	Oslo	Norway	0–0	
	Stuttgart	England	1–0	European Championship
	Hanover	Soviet Union	1–1	European Championship
	Gelsenkirchen	Netherlands	0–1	European Championship
	Belfast	Northern Ireland	0–0	World Cup Qualifier
	Dublin	Tunisia	4–0	
	Seville	Spain	0–2	World Cup Qualifier
1989	Dublin	France	0–0	
	Budapest	Hungary	0–0	World Cup Qualifier
	Dublin	Spain	1–0	World Cup Qualifier
	Dublin	Malta	2–0	World Cup Qualifier
	Dublin	Hungary	2–0	World Cup Qualifier
	Dublin	West Germany	1–1	
	Dublin	Northern Ireland	3–0	World Cup Qualifier
	Valletta	Malta	2–0	World Cup Qualifier
1990	Dublin	Wales	1–0	
	Dublin	Soviet Union	1–0	
	Dublin	Finland	1–1	
	Izmir	Turkey	0–0	
	Valletta	Malta	3–0	

	Cagliari	England	1–1	World Cup Finals
	Palermo	Egypt	0–0	World Cup Finals
	Palermo	Netherlands	1–1	World Cup Finals
	Genoa	Romania	0–0	World Cup Finals
				(Ireland win 5–4 on penalties)
	Rome	Italy	0–1	World Cup Finals
	Dublin	Morocco	1–0	
	Dublin	Turkey	5–0	European Championship Qual
	Dublin	England	1–1	European Championship Qual
1991	Wrexham	Wales	3–0	
	London	England	1–1	European Championship Qual
	Dublin	Poland	0–0	European Championship Qual
	Dublin	Chile	1–1	
	Boston	United States	1–1	
	Gyor	Hungary	2–1	
	Poznan	Poland	3–3	European Championship Qual
	Istanbul	Turkey	3–1	European Championship Qual
1992	Dublin	Wales	0–1	
	Dublin	Switzerland	2–1	
	Dublin	United States	4–1	
	Dublin	Albania	2–0	World Cup Qualifier
	Washington	United States	1–3	
	Boston	Italy	0–2	
	Boston	Portugal	2–0	
	Dublin	Latvia	4–0	World Cup Qualifier
	Copenhagen	Denmark	0–0	World Cup Qualifier
	Seville	Spain	0–0	World Cup Qualifier
1993	Dublin	Wales	2–1	
	Dublin	Northern Ireland	3–0	World Cup Qualifier
	Dublin	Denmark	1–1	World Cup Qualifier
	Tirana	Albania	2–1	World Cup Qualifier
	Riga	Latvia	2–0	World Cup Qualifier
	Vilnius	Lithuania	1–0	World Cup Qualifier
	Dublin	Lithuania	2–0	World Cup Qualifier
	Dublin	Spain	1–3	World Cup Qualifier
	Belfast	Northern Ireland	1–1	World Cup Qualifier
1994	Dublin	Russia	0–0	
	Tilburg	Netherlands	1–0	

	Dublin	Bolivia	1–0	
	Hanover	Germany	2–0	
	Dublin	Czech Republic	1–3	
	New Jersey	Italy	1–0	World Cup Finals
	Orlando	Mexico	1–2	World Cup Finals
	New Jersey	Norway	0–0	World Cup Finals
	Orlando	Netherlands	0–2	World Cup Finals
	Riga	Latvia	3–0	European Championship Qual
	Dublin	Liechtenstein	4–0	European Championship Qual
	Belfast	Northern Ireland	4–0	European Championship Qual
1995	Dublin	England	1–0	abandoned
	Dublin	Northern Ireland	1–1	European Championship Qual
	Dublin	Portugal	1–0	European Championship Qual
	Eschen	Liechtenstein	0–0	European Championship Qual
	Dublin	Austria	1–3	European Championship Qual
	Vienna	Austria	1–3	European Championship Qual
	Dublin	Latvia	2–1	European Championship Qual
	Lisbon	Portugal	0–3	European Championship Qual
	Liverpool	Netherlands	0–2	European Championship Qual

Playing records held by Jack Charlton:
- Most appearances for Leeds United – 773
- Most League appearances for Leeds United – 629
- Most capped player while playing for Leeds – 35

Honours won by Jack Charlton:
- England B International Cap – 1
- Football League representative – 6
- Full England Caps – 35
- Footballer of the Year 1967
- Division Two Championship Winner 1964
- FA Cup Winner 1972
- FA Cup Runner Up 1965 and 1970
- Football League Cup Winner 1968
- Inter City Fairs Cup Winner 1968
- Inter City Fairs Cup Runner Up 1967 and 1971
- Manager of the Year 1974
- Championship & Promotion from Division Two (Middlesbrough 1974)

- Promotion from Division Three (Sheffield Wednesday 1980)
- Awarded OBE in 1974
- Made Freeman of Dublin in 1994

BOBBY V JACK: HEAD TO HEAD

League:

1958–59	Division One	Manchester United 4–0 Leeds United (Bobby Charlton goal)
		Leeds United 1–2 Manchester United
1959–60		Leeds United 2–2 Manchester United (Bobby Charlton goal)
		Manchester United 6–0 Leeds United (Bobby Charlton 2 goals)
1964–65		Leeds United 0–1 Manchester United
		Manchester United 0–1 Leeds United
1965–66		Leeds United 1–1 Manchester United
1967–68		Manchester United 1–0 Leeds United (Bobby Charlton goal)
		Leeds United 1–0 Manchester United
1968–69		Leeds United 2–1 Manchester United (Bobby Charlton goal)
		Manchester United 0–0 Leeds United
		Manchester United 2–2 Leeds United
		Leeds United 2–2 Manchester United
1970–71		Leeds United 2–2 Manchester United (Bobby and Jack Charlton goals)
		Manchester United 0–1 Leeds United
1971–72		Leeds United 5–1 Manchester United
		Manchester United 0–1 Leeds United
		Manchester United 1–1 Leeds United

FA Cup:

1964–65	FA Cup(SF)	Manchester United 0–0 Leeds United (Hillsborough)
	Replay	Leeds United 1–1 Manchester United (City Ground)
1969–70	FA Cup(SF)	Manchester United 0–0 Leeds United (Hillsborough)

Replay	Leeds United 0–0 Manchester United (Villa Park)
2nd Replay	Leeds United 1–0 Manchester United (Burnden Park)

Facts and dates:

- Both turned professional on their 17th birthday.
- Both hold appearance records for their clubs.
- Both had testimonial matches against the same team – Glasgow Celtic.
- Both scored for England in the same match on 16 November 1966 against Wales.
- Both scored in the Leeds United v Manchester United game on the 17 October 1970.
- Both retired from International football in 1970 after the Mexico World Cup Finals.
- Both retired from football after the matches on 28 April 1973.
- Jack never lost to Bobby in the FA Cup.
- They never met in Europe or the League Cup.
- Jack was never a substitute and Bobby was only on the bench twice (both in his last season).

BOBBY AND JACK: IN SAME TEAM

Matches	Won	Draw	Lost	Winning percentage
28	20	6	2	71.4%

INTERNATIONAL RECORDS SEASON-BY-SEASON

Sir Bobby Charlton's England Career
Matches marked as(*) are those played *with* brother Jack in the team

Year	Venue	Opponent	Score	Competition	Goals
1958	Glasgow	Scotland	4–0	British Championship	1
	London	Portugal	2–1		2
	Belgrade	Yugoslavia	0–5		
	Belfast	N. Ireland	3–3	British Championship	2
	London	Soviet Union	5–0		1

	London	Scotland	1–0	British Championship	
1959	London	Italy	2–2		
	Rio de Janeiro	Brazil	0–2		
	Lima	Peru	1–4		
	México	Mexico	1–2		
	Los Angeles	United States	8–1		3
	Cardiff	Wales	1–1	British Championship	
	London	Sweden	2–3		1
1960	Glasgow	Scotland	1–1	British Championship	1
	London	Yugoslavia	3–3		
	Madrid	Spain	0–3		
	Budapest	Hungary	0–2		
	Belfast	N. Ireland	5–2	British Championship	1
	Luxembourg	Luxembourg	9–0	World Cup Qualifier	3
	London	Spain	4–2		
	London	Wales	5–1	British Championship	1
1961	London	Scotland	9–3	British Championship	
	London	Mexico	8–0		3
	Lisbon	Portugal	1–1	World Cup Qualifier	
	Roma	Italy	3–2		
	Vienna	Austria	1–3		
	London	Luxembourg	4–1	World Cup Qualifier	2
	Cardiff	Wales	1–1	British Championship	
	London	Portugal	2–0	World Cup Qualifier	
	London	N. Ireland	1–1	British Championship	1
1962	London	Austria	3–1		
	Glasgow	Scotland	0–2	British Championship	
	London	Switzerland	3–1		
	Lima	Peru	4–0		
	Rancagua	Hungary	1–2	World Cup	
	Rancagua	Argentina	3–1	World Cup	1
	Rancagua	Bulgaria	0–0	World Cup	
	Viña del Mar	Brazil	1–3	World Cup	
1963	Paris	France	2–5	European Championship Qual	
	London	Scotland	1–2	British Championship	
	London	Brazil	1–1		
	Bratislava	Czechoslovakia	4–2		1
	Leipzig	East Germany	2–1		1

	Basle	Switzerland	8–1		3
	Cardiff	Wales	4–0	British Championship	1
	London	FIFA	2–1		
	London	N. Ireland	8–3	British Championship	
	Glasgow	Scotland	0–1	British Championship	
1964	London	Uruguay	2–1		
	Lisbon	Portugal	4–3		1
	Dublin	Ireland	3–1		
	New York	United States	10–0		1
	Rio de Janeiro	Brazil	1–5	Nations Cup	
	Rio de Janeiro	Argentina	0–1	Nations Cup	
	Belfast	N. Ireland	4–3	British Championship	
	Amsterdam	Netherlands	1–1		
1965	London	Scotland(*)	2–2	British Championship	1
	Cardiff	Wales(*)	0–0	British Championship	
	London	Austria(*)	2–3		
	London	N. Ireland(*)	2–1	British Championship	
	Madrid	Spain(*)	2–0		
1966	London	West Germany(*)	1–0		
	Glasgow	Scotland(*)	4–3	British Championship	1
	London	Yugoslavia(*)	2–0		1
	Helsinki	Finland(*)	3–0		
	Oslo	Norway	6–1		
	Chorzów	Poland(*)	1–0		
	London	Uruguay(*)	0–0	World Cup	
	London	Mexico(*)	2–0	World Cup	1
	London	France(*)	2–0	World Cup	
	London	Argentina(*)	1–0	World Cup	
	London	Portugal(*)	2–1	World Cup	1
	London	West Germany(*)	4–2	World Cup	
	Belfast	N. Ireland(*)	2–0	European Championship Qual	
	London	Czechoslovakia(*)	0–0		
	London	Wales(*)	5–1	European Championship Qual	1
1967	London	Scotland(*)	2–3	European Championship Qual	
	Cardiff	Wales(*)	3–0	European Championship Qual	1

	London	N. Ireland	2–0	European Championship Qual	1
	London	Soviet Union	2–2		
1968	Glasgow	Scotland	1–1	European Championship Qual	
	London	Spain(*)	1–0	European Championship Qual	1
	Madrid	Spain	2–1	European Championship Qual	
	London	Sweden	3–1		1
	Firenze	Yugoslavia	0–1	European Championship	
	Rome	Soviet Union	2–0	European Championship	1
	Bucharest	Romania	0–0		
	London	Bulgaria	1–1		
1969	London	Romania(*)	1–1		
	Belfast	N. Ireland	3–1	British Championship	
	London	Wales(*)	2–1	British Championship	1
	London	Scotland	4–1	British Championship	
	México	Mexico	0–0		
	Montevideo	Uruguay	2–1		
	Rio de Janeiro	Brazil	1–2		
	Amsterdam	Netherlands(*)	1–0		
	London	Portugal(*)	1–0		
1970	London	Netherlands(*)	0–0		
	Cardiff	Wales	1–1	British Championship	
	London	N. Ireland	3–1	British Championship	1
	Bogotá	Colombia	4–0		1
	Quito	Ecuador	2–0		
	Guadalajara	Romania	1–0	World Cup	
	Guadalajara	Brazil	0–1	World Cup	
	Guadalajara	Czechoslovakia(*)	1–0	World Cup	
	León	West Germany	2–3	World Cup	

Matches	Won	Draw	Lost	Winning percentage
106	60	23	23	56.6%

Types of Matches

Friendlies – 50

World Cup Qualifiers – 4

World Cup – 14
European Championship Qualifiers – 9
European Championship – 2
British Championship – 25
Other Tournaments – 2
Total – 106

Jack Charlton's England Career
Matches marked(*) are those *without* brother Bobby in the team

Year	Venue	Opponent	Score	Competition	Goals
1965	London	Scotland	2–2	British Championship	
	London	Hungary(*)	1–0		
	Belgrade	Yugoslavia(*)	1–1		
	Nuremburg	West Germany(*)	0–1		
	Gothenburg	Sweden(*)	2–1		
	Cardiff	Wales	0–0	British Championship	
	London	Austria	2–3		
	London	N. Ireland	2–1	British Championship	
	Madrid	Spain	2–0		
1966	Liverpool	Poland(*)	1–1		
	London	West Germany	1–0		
	Glasgow	Scotland	4–3	British Championship	
	London	Yugoslavia	2–0		
	Helsinki	Finland	3–0		1
	Copenhagen	Denmark(*)	2–0		1
	Chorzów	Poland	1–0		
	London	Uruguay	0–0	World Cup	
	London	Mexico	2–0	World Cup	
	London	France	2–0	World Cup	
	London	Argentina	1–0	World Cup	
	London	Portugal	2–1	World Cup	
	London	West Germany	4–2	World Cup	
	Belfast	N. Ireland	2–0	European Championship Qual	
	London	Czechoslovakia	0–0		
	London	Wales	5–1	European Championship Qual	

1967	London	Scotland	2–3	European Championship Qual	1
	Cardiff	Wales	3–0	European Championship Qual	
1968	London	Spain	1–0	European Championship Qual	
1969	London	Romania	1–1		1
	London	France(*)	5–0		
	London	Wales	2–1	British Championship	
	Amsterdam	Netherlands	1–0		
	London	Portugal	1–0		1
1970	London	Netherlands	0–0		
	Guadalajara	Czechoslovakia	1–0	World Cup	

Matches	Won	Draw	Lost	Winning percentage
35	24	8	3	68.6%

Types of Matches

Friendlies – 18
World Cup Qualifiers – 0
World Cup – 7
European Championship Qualifiers – 5
European Championship – 0
British Championship – 5
Other Tournaments – 0
Total – 35

ENGLAND SCORERS' RECORDS

Player	Appearances (Goals)	Goals per game
Bobby Charlton	106 (49)	0.46
Gary Lineker	80 (48)	0.60
Jimmy Greaves	57 (44)	0.77
Nat Lofthouse	33 (30)	0.90
Alan Shearer	63 (30)	0.50
Tom Finney	76 (30)	0.39

Bibliography

Aldridge, John: *My Story* (Hodder & Stoughton, 1999)

Allan, Dave (editor): *The Boro Alphabet* (Middlesbrough FC, 1998)

Allen, Matt: *Jimmy Greaves* (Virgin, 2001)

Allsop, Derek: *Reliving The Dream* (Mainstream, 1998)

Astaire, Jarvis: *Encounters* (Robson, 1999)

Atkinson, Ron: *Big Ron – A Football Memoir* (Andre Deutch, 1998)

Bale, Bernard: *The Legend of Billy Bremner* (Andre Deutch, 1998)

Banks, Gordon: *Banks of England* (Arthur Barker, 1980)

Banks, Gordon: *Gordon Banks Soccer Book* (Pelham, 1973)

Ball, Alan: *It's All About A Ball* (W.H.Allen, 1978)

Beardsley, Peter: *My Life Story* (Collins Willow, 1995)

Beckham, David: *My Story* (Andre Deutch, 1998)

Best, George: *The Good, The Bad And The Bubbly* (Simon and Schuster, 1990)

Best, George: *The Best of Times* (Simon and Schuster, 1994)

Best, George: *Blessed – The Autobiography* (Ebury Press, 2001)

Busby, Matt: *Soccer At The Top* (Weidenfeld & Nicholson, 1973)

Bose, Mihir: *Manchester Unlimited* (Orion, 1999)

Bowler, Dave: *Three Lions on the Shirt* (Gollancz,1999)

Bowler, Dave: *Winning Isn't Everything – A Biography of Sir Alf Ramsey* (Gollancz, 1998)

Bowler, Dave: *Danny Blanchflower – Biography of a Visionary* (Gollancz, 1997)

Broadbent, Rick: *Looking for Eric – The Search for the Leeds Greats* (Mainstream, 2000)

Bremner, Billy: *You Get Nowt for Being Second* (Souvenir Press, 1969)

Cascarino, Tony & Paul Kimmage: *The Secret Life of Tony Cascarino* (Simon & Schuster, 2000)

Charlton, Bobby (with Ken Jones): *My Most Memorable Matches* (Stanley Paul, 1984)

Charlton, Bobby: *Forward For England* (Pelham, 1967)

Charlton, Cissie (with Vince Gledhill): *My Autobiography* (Bridge Studios, 1989)

Charlton, Jack (with Peter Byrne): *My World Cup Diary* (Gill & Macmillan, 1990)

Charlton, Jack: *The Autobiography* (Partridge Press, 1996)

Christian, Terry: *Reds in the Hood* (Andre Deutch, 1999)

Clayton, Ronnie: *A Slave To Soccer* (Stanley Paul, 1960)

Clough, Brian: *The Autobiography* (Partridge Press, 1994)

Crerand, Pat: *On Top With United* (Stanley Paul, 1969)

Crick, Michael and David Smith: *Manchester United – The Betrayal of a Legend* (Pelham, 1989)

Daniels, Phil: *Moore Than A Legend* (Goal, 1997)

Dawson, Jeff: *Back Home – England and the 1970 World Cup* (Orion, 2001)

Dickinson, Jason: *One Hundred Years at Hillsborough* (Hallamshire Press, 1999)

Dunphy, Eamon: *A Strange Kind of Glory* (William Heinemann, 1991)

Dykes, Garth: *The United Alphabet* (ACL & Polar, 1994)

Edworthy, Niall: *The Second Most Important Job In The Country* (Virgin, 1999)

Farmer, David & Peter Stead: *Ivor Allchurch* (Christopher Davies, 1998)

Farnsworth, Keith: *Wednesday – Every Day of the Week* (Breedon Books, 1998)

Farnsworth, Keith: *Sheffield Football – A History* (Hallamshire Press, 1995)

Ferrier, Bob: *Soccer Partnership* (William Heinemann, 1960)

Ferris, Ken: *Manchester United – Tragedy, Destiny, History* (Mainstream, 2001)

Ferguson, Alex: *My Autobiography* (Hodder & Stoughton, 1999)

Flowers, Ron: *For Wolves And England* (Stanley Paul, 1962)

Finney, Tom: *Finney on Football* (Nicholas Kaye, 1958)

Foulkes, Bill: *Back At The Top* (Pelham, 1965)

Fynn, Alex & Lynton Guest: *For Love or Money* (Andre Deutch, 1998)

Glanvill, Rick: *Sir Matt Busby – A Tribute* (Virgin, 1994)

Gowling, Alan: *Soccer Inside Out* (Souvenir Press, 1977)

Gray, Eddie: *Marching On Together – My Life with Leeds United* (Hodder & Stoughton, 2002)

Greaves, Jimmy: *This One's On Me* (Arthur Barker, 1979)

Green, Alan: *The Green Line* (Headline, 2000)

Harris, Harry: *The Ferguson Effect* (Orion, 1999)

Harris, Norman: *The Charlton Brothers* (Stanley Paul, 1971)

Harrison, Paul: *The Elland Road Encyclopedia* (Mainstream, 1994)

Haynes, Johnny: *It's All In The Game* (Arthur Barker, 1962)

Hildred, Stafford & Tim Ewbank: *Roy Keane – The Biography* (John Blake, 2000)

Hill, Jimmy: *The Jimmy Hill Story* (Hodder & Stoughton, 1998)

Hill, Dave: *1966 And All That* (Macmillan, 1996)

Holden, Jim: *Stan Cullis – The Iron Manager* (Breedon Books, 2000)

Hopcraft, Arthur: *The Football Man* (Simon & Schuster, 1988)

Hughes, Brian: *Viollet – The Life of a Legendary Goalscorer* (Empire, 2001)

Hughes, Brian: *The Tommy Taylor Story* (Empire, 1996)

Hurst, Geoff: *The World Game* (Stanley Paul, 1967)

Hurst, Geoff: *1966 And All That – My Autobiography* (Headline, 2001)

Inglis, Simon: *Soccer in the Dock* (Willow, 1985)

Kelly, Graham: *Sweet FA* (Collins Willow, 1999)

Kelly, Stephen: *Red Voices* (Headline, 1999)

Kelly, Stephen: *Bill Shankly – The Biography* (Virgin, 1996)

Kennedy, John: *The Tommy Taylor Story* (Yore, 1994)

Kirkup, Mike: *Coal Town – Growing Up in Ashington, 1934–54* (Woodhorn Press, 1995)

Kurt, Richard: *Red Devils* (Prion, 1998)

Law, Denis: *An Autobiography* (Queen Anne Press, 1979)

Law, Denis: *The Lawman* (Andre Deutch, 1999)

Law, Denis & Pat Crerand: *United – The Legendary Years* (Virgin, 1997)

Lee, Francis: *Soccer Round the World* (Arthur Barker, 1970)

Lineker, Gary & Stan Hey: *Golden Boots* (Hodder & Stoughton, 1998)

Liversedge, Stan: *Big Jack – The Life And Times of Jack Charlton* (The Publishing Corporation, 1994)

Liversedge, Stan: *This England Job* (Soccer Books, 1996)

Lovejoy, Joe: *Bestie* (Sidgwick & Jackson, 1998)

McCartney, Iain & Roy Cavanagh: *Duncan Edwards* (Temple Nostalgia, 1988)

McCartney, Iain: *Roger Byrne* (Empire Publications, 2000)

McGrath, Paul: *Ooh, Aah Paul McGrath* (Mainstream, 1994)

McIlroy, Jimmy: *Right Inside Soccer* (Nicholas Kaye, 1960)

McIlroy, Sammy: *Manchester United – My Team* (Souvenir Press, 1980)

McVay, David & Andy Smith: *The Authorised Biography of Tommy Lawton* (Sports Books, 2000)

Marquis, Max: *Sir Alf Ramsey* (Arthur Barker, 1970)

Marsh, Rodney: *Priceless* (Headline, 2001)

Matthews, Stanley: *The Way It Was* (Headline, 2000)

Meek, David & Tom Tyrrell: *Manchester United in Europe* (Hodder & Stoughton, 2001)

Miller, David: *The Boys of 66* (Pavilion, 1986)

Moore, Bobby: *My Soccer Story* (Stanley Paul, 1966)

Moore, Bobby: *England! England!* (Stanley Paul, 1970)

Moore, Brian: *The Final Score* (Hodder & Stoughton, 1999)

Mourant, Andrew: *Don Revie* (Mainstream, 1990)

Payne, Mike: *England – The Complete Post-War Record* (Breedon Books, 1993)

Pele: *My Life and the Beautiful Game* (New English Library, 1977)

Peters, Martin: *Goals From Nowhere* (Stanley Paul, 1969)

Ponting, Ivan & Steve Hale: *Sir Roger – A Liverpool Legend* (Bluecoat Press, 1996)

Powell, Jeff: *Bobby Moore – the Life and Times of a Sporting Hero* (Robson, 1993)

Roberts, John: *The Team That Would Not Die* (Arthur Barker, 1975)

Robson, Bobby: *My Autobiography* (Macmillan, 1998)

Rowan, Paul: *The Team That Jack Built* (Mainstream, 1994)

Ryan, Sean: *The Boys in Green* (Mainstream, 1997)

Stapleton, Frank: *Frankly Speaking* (Blackwater Press, 1991)

Stein, Mel: *Chris Waddle – The Authorised Biography* (Simon & Schuster, 1997)

Stein, Mel: *Gazza* (Bantam Press, 1995)

Stepney, Alex: *Alex Stepney* (Arthur Barker, 1978)

Stiles, Nobby: *Soccer My Battlefield* (Stanley Paul, 1968)

Taylor, Frank: *The Day The Team Died* (Souvenir Press, 1958)

Taylor, Rogan & Andrew Ward: *Kicking and Screaming, An Oral History of Football in England* (Robson Books, 1995)

Thomson, David: *4–2* (Bloomsbury, 1996)

Townsend, Andy (with Paul Kimmage): *Andy's Game* (Stanley Paul, 1994)

Ward, Adam: *Gifted in Green* (Hamlyn, 1999)

West, Gordon: *The Championship in my Keeping* (Souvenir Press, 1970)

Wolstenholme, Kenneth: *They Think It's All Over* (Robson, 1996)

Wright, Billy: *One Hundred Caps and All That* (Robert Hale, 1962)

Index

Dawson, Jeff 251
Dean, Dixie 203, 280–281
Dein, David 356
Denmark, Jimmy 33–34
Di Stefano, Alfredo 93, 184, 203
Dickinson, Jason 321
Dienst, Gottfried 195
Docherty, John 39
  Bobby's high spirits 69
  Bobby's tantrums 58–59
  views on Murphy 56
Docherty, Tommy 271
  appointed Manchester United manager 284
  Bobby's England debut 103
  Bobby's retirement 284–285
  criticisms of Jack 296
  Law's transfer 286
  Manchester United's relegation 268
Dougan, David 281
Dougan, Derek 204
Douglas, Bryan 103
  England's selection policy 107–108
  World Cup 1962 133, 134
Dunn, Jimmy 46
  views on Jack 111
  views on Lambton 48
Dunne, Len 400
Dunne, Tony 221, 223
Dunphy, Eamon
  after-effects of Munich on Busby 140
  Best's bad behaviour 267
  Bobby's appointment to Manchester United board 345–346
  Bobby's playing position 135–136
  Bobby's retirement 285
  Busby's backhand payments 32
  Busby's Catholicism 62
  Busby's philosophy on football 214
  Jack appointed Ireland manager 368–369
  Jack's political views 233
  match-fixing scandal 148
  Munich air disaster 86, 97–98
  players' wages 146

rift between Jack and Bobby 411–412
  support for Jack 394
  views on Armstrong 27–28
  views on Jack 394–395
  World Cup 1990 393–394, 399
Durie, Gordon 382

Eastham, George 171, 181
Edelson, Mike
  Ferguson's appointment as Manchester United manager 351–352
  involvement in Bobby's business 427
  Knighton affair 357
  support for Bobby 358
Edwards, Duncan
  army football 65
  Arsenal match 71
  Bobby's admiration for 215
  Bobby's views on 92–93
  Busby Babes 66, 97
  digs with Bobby 54
  footballing skills 52
  loss to England team 128
  Manchester United's reputation for young players 28, 31
  Manchester United youth team 60
  Munich air disaster 74, 83, 84, 92
Edwards, Gareth 427
Edwards, Louis
  death of 345
  Manchester United rights issue 344, 345
  O'Farrell's sacking 284
  World in Action programme 31–32
Edwards, Martin
  Bobby's appointment to Manchester United board 342, 344
  Bobby's influence on 349
  Ferguson's appointment as Manchester United manager 351–352
  flotation of Manchester United 357–358
  Knighton affair 356–357
  Manchester United rights issue 345

support for Ferguson 353
  World in Action programme 31
Eire see Republic of Ireland
Emmerich, Lothar 195
England
  Americas tour 1959 129–130
  Bobby's debut 102–103
  Bobby's first selection 100–101
  brothers playing for 178
  defeated by Yugoslavia 105
  defensive formation 180–181
  Greenwood appointed manager 315–316
  importance of Stiles 181
  playing formation 181–183
  refusal to appoint Jack as manager 315–316
  Revie as manager 314
  selection policy 107–108
  team spirit 185–186
  training regime 185
  World Cup 1958 105–106
  World Cup 1962 132–137
  World Cup 1966 186–196
  World Cup 1970 241–244, 249–254
English, Bob 112
Eriksson, Sven-Goran 291
Escobar, Andres 437
European Championship
  1988 380–383
  1992 405
  1996 438
European Cup
  1968 220–224
  1969 241–242
Eusebio 214, 221, 223, 270

FA Cup
  1958 98–100
  1963 148, 213
  1965 213
  1970 273–274
  1971 275
  1972 275
  1979 321
  1990 352–353
Ferguson, Charlie 30
Ferguson, Sir Alex 168. 349
  admiration for Bobby 361
  appointed Manchester